Law School Essentials:
Upper-Level Review

Constitutional Law
Corporations
Criminal Procedure
Evidence
Wills & Trusts

Welcome to the Themis Law School Essentials courses. We are excited that you have chosen Themis to help supplement your law school classes and prepare for your final exams.

As you begin reviewing these materials, we want to offer you some tips for success:

- Review the *Quick Reference Guide* on the next page so that you understand how these outlines work in conjunction with the online course components available to you.

- Go to ThemisBar.com to launch one of our free Law School Essentials courses. Courses are available for the following subjects:

  - Civil Procedure
  - Constitutional Law
  - Contracts
  - Corporations
  - Criminal Law

  - Criminal Procedure
  - Evidence
  - Property
  - Torts
  - Wills & Trusts

- For whichever subject you are studying, review the substantive outline in this book (also available online and for eReaders).

- Watch the on-demand substantive lecture, following along with the downloadable interactive handout, and answer a series of Assessment Quizzes after each video chapter to ensure that you have mastered the material.

  - Note that you do not need to watch the entire lecture at once. The subject matter is divided into chapters so that you may choose to focus on areas of law that you find difficult or for which you would like further explanation.

- Use your results on the Assessment Quizzes to identify areas of potential weakness for review.

- Finally, do the practice questions provided, and carefully read the sample answer for each question to help reinforce important points of law.

You should always feel free to reach out directly to our experienced staff attorneys via the **Message Center**, accessible online from any Themis course. Our message center is your means to submit questions about the materials. In addition, you may email us any time or call us weekdays between 9 AM and 7 PM ET.

Good luck!

Themis Bar Review
info@themisbar.com
(888) 843-6476

Law School Essentials (LSE):
Quick Reference Guide

Getting Started

To access your Themis LSE Review, follow these three easy steps:

1. Log in to your Themis account at www.Themisbar.com. There is a **Sign In** button at the top right of the home page.
2. Your LSE Course is located in the Free Programs area of the Account Summary page.
3. If your LSE Course is currently accessible, you'll see a blue **Launch** button. Click it to access the online LSE content. If it is not yet accessible, you will see the anticipated availability date.

Flex Study

Flex Study mode allows you the freedom to choose your own preparation path. On the left navigation bar, you will see a list of the types of tasks to complete in your course: Outlines, Lectures, and Practice Questions.

Outlines

The online outlines are identical to the outlines in your LSE book. They allow you to move to a particular topic or section of an outline with the Table of Contents feature. Additionally, you can use the keyword search feature to find specific concepts within an outline.

Lectures, Handouts, and Assessment Questions

Upon selecting a chapter of a lecture, click **Play** to start the video. The lecture handouts are available by clicking the **Handout** link located to the right of the video player screen. If it is the first time you are watching a chapter, there will be an **Assessments** link to the right of the video player screen. Click this link upon completion of the chapter.

Assessment questions are a series of questions designed by Themis to determine your understanding of the material and to assist in retention of the concepts. These questions must be completed for each chapter in order

Practice Questions

MULTIPLE-CHOICE QUESTIONS

You have the option to complete your practice questions sessions in Interactive or Test Mode. Interactive Mode allows you to see immediately whether your answer is right or wrong along with an explanation. Test Mode allows you to complete the session before issuing a score report and answer explanations.

Once you have completed a session, you may access (and re-access) the task to review the questions.

ESSAY QUESTIONS

Practice essays are designed to be completed in 60 minutes. After you complete a practice essay question, click the **Complete Answer** button to view the sample answer.

Constitutional Law

CONSTITUTIONAL LAW

Table of Contents

CONSTITUTIONAL LAW

PART ONE: POWERS OF THE FEDERAL GOVERNMENT

I.   JUDICIAL POWER

A.   SOURCE AND SCOPE

1.   Source—Article III

Article III, Section 1 of the United States Constitution provides that "[t]he judicial power of the United States shall be vested in one Supreme Court and in such inferior courts as the Congress may from time to time ordain and establish."

Federal courts are generally created by the United States Congress under the constitutional power described in Article III. As noted above, Article III requires the establishment of a Supreme Court and permits the Congress to create other federal courts and place limitations on their jurisdiction. Although many specialized courts are created under the authority granted in Article I, greater power is vested in Article III courts because they are independent of Congress, the President, and the political process.

2.   Scope

Article III, Section 2 delineates the jurisdiction of federal courts as limited to **cases or controversies**:

  i)   Arising under the Constitution, laws, and treaties of the United States;

  ii)   Affecting foreign countries' ambassadors, public ministers, and consuls;

  iii) Involving admiralty and maritime jurisdiction;

  iv)   When the United States is a party;

  v)   Between two or more states, or between a state and citizens of another state;

  vi)   Between citizens of different states or between citizens of the same state claiming lands under grants of different states; or

  vii) Between a state, or its citizens, and foreign states, citizens, or subjects.

a.   Judicial review of congressional and executive actions

The judiciary has the power—although it is not enumerated in the text of the Constitution—to review an act of another branch of the federal government and to declare that act unconstitutional, *Marbury v. Madison*, 5 U.S. 137 (1803), as well as the constitutionality of a decision by a state's highest court, *Martin v. Hunter's Lessee*, 1 Wheat. 304 (1816). The central ideas of *Marbury v. Madison* are that (i) the Constitution is paramount law, and (ii) the Supreme Court has the final say in interpreting the Constitution.

b.   Judicial review of state actions

The federal judiciary has the power, under the Supremacy Clause (Article VI, Section 2), to review state actions (e.g., court decisions, state statutes, executive orders) to ensure conformity with the Constitution, laws, and treaties of the United States. *Fletcher v. Peck*, 10 U.S. 87 (1810).

3. Limitations—Eleventh Amendment

The Eleventh Amendment is a jurisdictional bar that prohibits the citizens of one state from suing another state in federal court. It immunizes the state from suits in federal court for money damages or equitable relief when the state is a defendant in an action brought by a citizen of another state or a foreign country. In addition, the Eleventh Amendment bars suits in federal court against state officials for violating *state* law. *Pennhurst State School & Hospital v. Halderman*, 465 U.S.89 (1984).

The Supreme Court has expanded the amendment's reach to also preclude citizens from suing their own state in federal court. *Hans v. Louisiana*, 134 U.S. 1 (1890).

Note that the Supreme Court has also barred federal-law actions brought against a state government without the state's consent in its own courts as a violation of **sovereign immunity**. *Alden v. Maine*, 527 U.S. 706 (1999). However, neither the Eleventh Amendment nor the sovereign immunity doctrine bars a suit brought by a citizen against a state in the courts of another state. *Nevada v. Hall*, 440 U.S. 410 (1979).

a. Exceptions

There are, however, a few notable exceptions to the application of the Eleventh Amendment.

1) Consent

A state may consent to suit by waiving its Eleventh Amendment protection. *Lapides v. Board of Regents of Univ. System of Ga.*, 535 U.S. 613 (2002) (state removal of case to federal court constituted a waiver).

2) Injunctive relief

When a state official, rather than the state itself, is named as the defendant in an action brought in federal court, the state official may be enjoined from enforcing a state law that violates federal law or may be compelled to act in accord with federal law despite state law to the contrary. *Ex parte Young*, 209 U.S. 123 (1908), *Edelman v. Jordan*, 415 U.S. 651 (1974).

Note: A state also cannot invoke its sovereign immunity to prevent a lawsuit by a state agency seeking to enforce a federal right against a state official. *Virginia Office for Prot. & Advocacy v. Stewart*, 563 U.S. 247 (2011).

3) Damages to be paid by an individual

An action for damages against a state officer is not prohibited, as long as the officer himself (rather than the state treasury) will have to pay. Such is the case when an officer acts outside the law; the action is against the officer as an individual and not in his representative capacity.

4) Prospective damages

As long as the effect of a lawsuit is not to impose retroactive damages on a state officer to be paid from the state treasury, a federal court may hear an action against a state officer, even if the action will force a state to pay money to comply with a court order.

5) Congressional authorization

Congress may abrogate state immunity from liability if it is clearly acting to enforce rights created by the remedial provisions of the Thirteenth, Fourteenth, and Fifteenth Amendments (i.e., the Civil War Amendments), and does so expressly. *Fitzpatrick v. Bitzer*, 427 U.S. 445 (1976). Congress generally may not abrogate state immunity by exercising its powers under Article I (e.g., Commerce Clause powers). *Seminole Tribe of Florida v. Florida*, 517 U.S. 44 (1996).

b. Not barred by the Eleventh Amendment

1) Actions against local governments

The Eleventh Amendment applies only to states and state agencies. Local governments (e.g., counties, cities) are not immune from suit.

2) Actions by the United States government or other state governments not barred

The Eleventh Amendment has no application when the plaintiff is the United States or another state.

3) Bankruptcy proceedings

The Eleventh Amendment does not bar the actions of a Bankruptcy Court that impacts state finances. *Central Cmty. Coll. v. Katz*, 546 U.S. 356 (2006).

B. JURISDICTION OF THE SUPREME COURT

1. Original

Article III, Section 2 gives the Supreme Court "original jurisdiction" (i.e., the case may be filed first in the Supreme Court) over "all cases affecting ambassadors, other public ministers and consuls and those in which a State shall be a party." Congress may not expand or limit this jurisdiction. *Marbury v. Madison*, 5 U.S. 137 (1803). It may, however, grant concurrent original jurisdiction to lower federal courts, which it has for all cases except those between states. 28. U.S.C. § 1251.

2. Appellate

Article III, Section 2 also provides that "in all other cases before mentioned, the Supreme Court shall have appellate jurisdiction...with such exceptions, and under such regulations as the Congress shall make."

a. Means

There are two means of establishing appellate jurisdiction in the Supreme Court: certiorari (discretionary review) and direct appeal.

1) Certiorari

Almost all cases now come to the Supreme Court by way of a petition for a writ of certiorari, i.e., discretionary review. The Court takes jurisdiction only if at least four Justices vote to accept the case (the "rule of four").

2) Direct appeal

The Supreme Court **must** hear by direct appeal only a small number of cases—those that come from a decision on injunctive relief issued by a special three-judge district court panel. 28 U.S.C. § 1253. Although these panels (and appeals) were once fairly common, they are now limited to cases brought under a few specific statutes (e.g., the Voting Rights Act).

b. Limitations

Congress has some power to limit the Supreme Court's appellate jurisdiction by statute. *Ex parte McCardle*, 74 U.S. 506 (1868). There are constraints on this power, because to deny all Supreme Court jurisdiction over certain types of cases would undermine the constitutional system of checks and balances. *Boumediene v. Bush*, 553 U.S. 723 (2008) (Congress and President cannot remove Supreme Court's authority to say "what the law is" (quoting *Marbury v. Madison*, 5 U.S. 137 (1803))).

> Note that most federal cases are filed in district court and appealed, if at all, to the courts of appeals. The jurisdiction of the federal courts is set, within the framework of Article III, by statute. For example, Congress requires the amount in controversy necessary for federal jurisdiction over a case between citizens of different states to exceed $75,000. 28 U.S.C. § 1332.

c. Adequate and independent state grounds

A final state-court judgment that rests on adequate and independent state grounds may not be reviewed by the U.S. Supreme Court (or it would be an advisory opinion). The state-law grounds must fully resolve the matter (i.e., be adequate) and must not incorporate a federal standard by reference (i.e., be independent). If a state court chooses to rely on federal precedents, the court can avoid federal review by making a plain statement in its judgment or opinion that the federal cases are being used only for the purpose of guidance and did not compel the court's judgment. When it is not clear whether the state court's decision rests on state or federal law, the Supreme Court may hear the case, decide the federal issue, and remand to the state court for resolution of any question of state law. *Michigan v. Long*, 463 U.S. 1032 (1983).

C. JUDICIAL REVIEW IN OPERATION

Standing, timing (mootness or ripeness), and other issues of justiciability may dictate whether a case may be heard by a federal court.

1. Standing

Article III, Section 2 restricts federal judicial power to "cases" and "controversies." A federal court cannot decide a case unless the plaintiff has standing—a concrete interest in the outcome—to bring it. Congress cannot statutorily eliminate the constitutional standing requirement simply by allowing citizen suits, *Lujan v. Defenders of Wildlife*, 504 U.S. 555 (1992), but it can create new interests, the injury to which may establish standing, *Massachusetts v. EPA*, 549 U.S. 497 (2007).

a. General rule

To have standing, a plaintiff bears the burden of establishing three elements:

i) **Injury in fact**;

ii) **Causation** (the injury must be caused by the defendant's violation of a constitutional or other federal right); and

iii) **Redressability** (the relief requested must prevent or redress the injury).

See, e.g., Lujan v. Defenders of Wildlife, 504 U.S. 555 (1992); *Valley Forge Christian College v. Americans United for Separation of Church and State, Inc.*, 454 U.S. 464 (1982).

In addition to the Article III requirements, the federal judiciary has also established a "prudential standing" requirement, i.e., that a plaintiff is a proper party to invoke a judicial resolution of the dispute. *Bender v. Williamsport Area School District*, 475 U.S. 534 (1986). Meeting this requirement depends in large part on whether the plaintiff's grievance comes within the "zone of interests" protected or regulated by the constitutional guarantee or statute under consideration. *Bennett v. Spear*, 520 U.S. 154 (1997); *Thompson v. N.Am. Stainless, LP*, 562 U.S. 170 (2011).

> **EXAM NOTE:** When answering questions about standing, eliminate answer choices involving only the substance of the claim and focus on whether the plaintiff is legally qualified to press a claim, regardless of merit.

1) Injury in fact

The injury must be both **concrete** and **particularized.**

a) Individualized injury

When a plaintiff has been directly injured "it does not matter how many people" were also injured; when "a harm is concrete, though widely shared," there is standing. *Massachusetts v. EPA*, 549 U.S. 497 (2007). However, even though an injury may satisfy the injury-in-fact standard, the court may refuse to adjudicate a claim by the application of the principles of prudence. Under this prudential-standing principle, an injury that is shared by all or a large class of citizens (i.e., a generalized grievance) is not sufficiently individualized to give the plaintiff standing. *Warth v. Seldin*, 422 U.S. 490 (1975).

b) Type of injury

The injury need not be physical or economic. *United States v. SCRAP*, 412 U.S. 669 (1973). While a generalized harm to the environment does not confer standing, a harm that affects recreational "or even mere esthetic interests," that is sufficient. *See Summers v. Earth Island Inst.*, 555 U.S. 488 (2009).

c) Future injury

While the threat of future injury can suffice, it cannot be merely hypothetical or conjectural, but must be actual and imminent. When a future injury is alleged, damages cannot be obtained, but an injunction can be sought.

2) Causation

The plaintiff must show that the injury was fairly traceable to the challenged action—that is, that the defendant's conduct caused the injury. *Warth v. Seldin*, 422 U.S. 490 (1975).

3) Redressability

It must be likely (as opposed to speculative) that a favorable court decision will redress a discrete injury suffered by the plaintiff.

b. Taxpayer status

Usually, a taxpayer does not have standing to file a federal lawsuit simply because the taxpayer believes that the government has allocated funds in an improper way. However, a taxpayer does have standing to litigate whether, or how much, she owes on her tax bill. See *United States v.* Windsor, 570 U.S. ___, 133 S. Ct. 2675 (2013) (litigating disallowance of estate tax exemption for surviving same-sex spouse under the Defense of Marriage Act.)

1) Governmental conduct

The conduct of the federal government, or of any state government, is too far removed from individual taxpayer returns for any injury to the taxpayer to be traced to the use of tax revenues. *DaimlerChrysler Corp. v. Cuno*, 547 U.S. 332 (2006). Long-standing precedent, however, suggests that a municipal taxpayer does have standing to sue a municipal government in federal court. *Crampton v. Zabriskie*, 101 U.S. 601 (1879).

2) Exception—Establishment Clause challenge

There is an exception for a taxpayer suit challenging a **specific legislative appropriation** made under the taxing and spending powers for violation of the Establishment Clause. *Flast v. Cohen*, 392 U.S. 83 (1968) (congressional grant to religious schools). This exception does not apply to the transfer of property to a religious organization by Congress under the Property Power, *Valley Forge Christian College v. Americans United for Separation of Church and State*, 454 U.S. 464 (1982), nor to expenditures made by the President to religious organizations from monies appropriated by Congress to the President's general discretionary fund, *Hein v. Freedom From Religion Foundation*, 551 U.S. 587 (2007), nor to a tax credit for contributions to student tuition organizations that provide scholarships to students attending private schools, including religious schools. *Ariz. Christian Sch. Tuition Org. v. Winn*, 563 U.S. 125 (2011).

c. Third-party standing

A litigant generally has no standing to bring a lawsuit based on legal claims of a third party. There are a few notable exceptions to this rule, however:

i) If the third parties would experience difficulty or are **unable to assert their own rights,** such as a Caucasian defendant raising equal protection and due process objections to discrimination against African-American people in the selection of grand juries, *Campbell v. Louisiana*, 523 U.S. 392 (1998);

ii) If there is a **special relationship between the plaintiff and the third parties,** such as an employer asserting the rights of its employees, a doctor asserting the rights of his patients in challenging an abortion ruling, *Singleton v. Wulff*, 428 U.S. 106 (1976), or a private school asserting its students' rights to attend despite a statute requiring attendance at public schools, *Pierce v. Society of Sisters*, 268 U.S. 510 (1925); and

iii) If a plaintiff suffers an injury, and **the injury adversely affects the plaintiff's relationship with a third party,** the plaintiff may assert the third-party's rights. *Craig v. Boren*, 429 U.S. 190 (1976).

The rule that a litigant has no standing to bring a lawsuit on behalf of a third party is based on prudential or discretionary considerations. The federal courts may refuse to hear any case on **prudential-standing** grounds. *Elk Grove Unified School Dist. v. Newdow*, 542 U.S. 1 (2004).

1) Organizational standing

An organization may bring an action when it has suffered an injury. In addition, an organization may bring an action on behalf of its members (even if the organization has not suffered an injury itself) if:

i) Its members would have standing to sue in their own right; and

ii) The interests at stake are germane to the organization's purpose.

Hunt v. Washington State Apple Adver. Comm'n., 432 U.S. 333 (1977). When damages are sought, generally neither the claim asserted nor the relief requested can require the participation of individual members in the lawsuit. But note that the damages limitation is not constitutionally mandated and can be waived by Congress. *United Food & Commer. Workers Union Local 751 v. Brown Group*, 517 U.S. 544 (1996).

2) Parental standing

Generally, a parent has standing to bring an action on behalf of the parent's minor child. However, after a divorce, the right to bring such an action may be limited to only one of the child's parents. Moreover, when the right to bring such an action is based on family-law rights that are in dispute, the federal courts should not entertain an action if prosecution of the lawsuit may have an adverse effect on the child. *Elk Grove Unified School District v. Newdow*, 542 U.S. 1 (2004) (noncustodial parent with joint legal custody could not challenge school policy on behalf of his daughter when the custodial parent opposed the action).

d. Assignee standing

An assignee of a claim has standing to enforce the rights of an assignor, even when the assignee is contractually obligated to return any litigation proceeds to the assignor (e.g., an assignee for collection), provided the assignment was made for ordinary business purposes and in good faith. *Sprint Commc'ns Co., L.P. v. APCC Servs., Inc.*, 554 U.S. 269 (2008).

e. Citizenship standing

Citizens do not have standing to assert a claim to enforce a constitutional provision merely because they are citizens, although a citizen may bring an action against the government to compel adherence to a specific federal statute. Even in such a case, the plaintiff must have directly suffered an injury in fact.

f. Standing to assert a Tenth Amendment violation

A party has standing to challenge the constitutionality of a federal statute on the grounds that it exceeds Congress's enumerated powers and intrudes upon the powers reserved to the states by the Tenth Amendment. *Bond v. United States*, 564 U.S. 211 (2011) (defendant prosecuted for violation of federal statute).

g. Legislator's standing

Generally, a legislator who voted against a bill does not have standing to challenge the resulting statute. *Coleman v. Miller*, 307 U.S. 433 (1939) (state legislators lacked standing); *Raines v. Byrd*, 521 U.S. 811, 823 (1997) (members of Congress lacked standing).

2. Timeliness

An action that is brought too soon ("unripe") or too late ("moot") will not be heard.

a. Ripeness

"Ripeness" refers to the readiness of a case for litigation. A federal court will not consider a claim before it has fully developed; to do so would be premature, and any potential injury would be speculative.

For a case to be "ripe" for litigation, the plaintiff must have experienced a **real injury** (or imminent threat thereof). Hence, if an ambiguous law has a long history of non-enforcement, a case challenging that law may lack ripeness. *See Poe v. Ullman*, 367 U.S. 497 (1961).

b. Mootness

A case has become moot if further legal proceedings would have no effect; that is, if there is no longer a controversy. A **live controversy** must exist **at each stage of review,** not merely when the complaint is filed, in order for a case to be viable at that stage.

> **Example:** The classic example of mootness is the case of *DeFunis v. Odegaard*, 416 U.S. 312 (1974). The plaintiff was a student who had been denied admission to law school and had then been provisionally admitted while the case was pending. Because the student was scheduled to graduate within a few months at the time the decision was rendered, and there was no action that the law school could take to prevent it, the Court determined that a decision on its part would have no effect on the student's rights. Therefore, the case was dismissed as moot.

1) Exception—capable of repetition, yet evading review

A case will not be dismissed as moot if there is a reasonable expectation that the same complaining party will be subjected to the same action again ("capable of repetition") but that the action will not last long enough to work its way through the judicial system ("yet evading review"). *Turner v. Rogers*, 564 U.S. 431 (2011).

> **Example:** The most cited example of this exception is *Roe v. Wade*, 410 U.S. 113 (1973), when the state argued that the case was moot because the plaintiff, who was challenging a Texas statute forbidding abortion, was no longer pregnant by the time the case reached the Supreme Court. Because of the relatively short human gestation period (compared to a lawsuit), abortion litigation was readily capable of being repeated, but also likely to evade review, and the case was not dismissed as moot.

2) Exception—voluntary cessation

A court will not dismiss as moot a case in which the defendant voluntarily ceases its illegal or wrongful action once litigation has commenced. The court must be assured that "there is no reasonable expectation that the wrong will be repeated." *United States v. W.T. Grant Co.*, 345 U.S. 629 (1953).

3) Exception—class actions

If the named plaintiff's claim in a certified class action is resolved and becomes moot, that fact does not render the entire class action moot. *United States Parole Comm'n. v. Geraghty*, 445 U.S. 388 (1980).

3. Justiciability—Further Issues

Federal courts may invoke a variety of other reasons not to decide a case.

a. Advisory opinions

Federal courts may not render advisory opinions on the basis of an abstract or a hypothetical dispute. An actual case or controversy must exist.

> **EXAM NOTE:** Fact patterns involving a request for declaratory judgment are likely testing advisory opinion prohibition.

b. Declaratory judgments

The courts are not prohibited from issuing declaratory judgments, however, that determine the legal effect of proposed conduct without awarding damages or injunctive relief. The challenged action must pose a real and immediate danger to a party's interests for there to be an actual dispute (as opposed to a hypothetical one).

c. Political questions

A federal court will not rule on a matter in controversy if the matter is a political question to be resolved by one or both of the other two branches of government. *Baker v. Carr*, 369 U.S. 186 (1962).

A political question not subject to judicial review arises when:

i) The Constitution has assigned decision making on this subject to a different branch of the government; or

ii) The matter is inherently not one that the judiciary can decide.

> **Example:** Details of Congress's impeachment procedures (constitutionally assigned to a branch other than the judiciary) and the President's conduct of foreign affairs (not within judicial competence) are examples of political questions.
>
> **Compare:** The political question doctrine does not bar courts from adjudicating the constitutionality of a federal statute directing that an American child born in Jerusalem is entitled to have Israel listed as her place of birth in her U.S. passport. The Court held that the Constitution did not commit the issue to another branch of government and resolving the case would involve examining "textual, structural, and historical evidence" concerning statutory and constitutional provisions, something within judicial competence. *Zivotofsky ex rel. Zivotofsky v. Clinton*, 566 U.S. 189 (2012).

4. Abstention

A federal court may abstain from deciding a claim when strong state interests are at stake.

a. *Pullman* doctrine

A court may refrain from ruling on a federal constitutional claim that depends on resolving an unsettled issue of state law best left to the state courts. *Railroad Comm'n of Texas v. Pullman*, 312 U.S. 496 (1941).

b. *Younger* abstention

A court will not enjoin a pending state criminal case in the absence of bad faith, harassment, or a patently invalid state statute. *Younger v. Harris*, 401 U.S. 37 (1971). Abstention also may be appropriate with regard to a civil enforcement proceeding or a civil proceeding involving an order uniquely in furtherance of the state courts' ability to perform their judicial functions, such as a civil contempt order. *Sprint Commc'ns, Inc. v. Jacobs*, 571 U.S. ___, 134 S. Ct. 584 (2013).

II. THE POWERS OF CONGRESS

Just as the federal courts are courts of limited jurisdiction, the powers of Congress are not plenary or exclusive. As the Tenth Amendment makes clear, the federal government may exercise only those powers specifically enumerated by the Constitution; it is state governments and the people, not the national government, that retain any powers not mentioned in the federal charter. Any action by the federal government must be supported by a source of power originating in the Constitution. Article I, Section 1 vests all legislative powers of the federal government in Congress.

> **EXAM NOTE**: Congress may amend or repeal existing law and direct that the change be applied in all related *pending* actions, i.e., those in which a final judgment has not been entered. If a bar exam question involves application of new legislation, pay attention to the status of any case to which it is to be applied.

> **EXAM NOTE**: Congress has no general police power to legislate for the health, safety, welfare, or morals of citizens. The validity of a federal statute on the bar exam may not be justified based on "federal police power."

A. COMMERCE

Article I, Section 8, Clause 3 of the Constitution, known as the Commerce Clause, empowers Congress "[t]o regulate Commerce with foreign Nations, and among the several States, and with the Indian Tribes." The term "commerce" has been defined to include essentially all activity—including transportation, traffic, or transmission of gas, electricity, radio, TV, mail, and telegraph—involving or affecting two or more states.

1. Interstate Commerce

a. Power to regulate

Congress has the power to regulate (i) the **channels** (highways, waterways, airways, etc.) and (ii) the **instrumentalities** (cars, trucks, ships, airplanes, etc.) of interstate commerce, as well as (iii) any activity that **substantially affects** interstate commerce, provided that the regulation does not infringe upon any other constitutional right. *United States v. Lopez*, 514 U.S. 549 (1995).

b. Construed broadly

The Supreme Court has upheld acts of Congress seeking to prohibit or restrict the entry of persons, products, and services into the stream of interstate commerce, as well as acts regulating the interstate movement of kidnap victims, stolen vehicles, and telephone transmissions. However, the Commerce Clause does not give Congress the power to mandate that individuals not engaged in commercial activities engage in commerce. *Nat'l Fed'n of Indep. Bus. v. Sebelius (The Patient Protection and Affordable Care Cases)*, 567 U.S. 519 (2012) (requiring individuals not engaged in commercial activities to buy unwanted health insurance could not be sustained as a regulation of interstate commerce).

2. "Substantial Economic Effect"

Congress has the power to regulate any activity, intra- or interstate, that in and of itself or in combination with other activities has a "substantial economic effect upon" or "effect on movement in" interstate commerce.

a. Aggregation

With respect to an intrastate activity that does not have a direct economic impact on interstate commerce, such as growing crops for personal consumption, as long as there is a **rational basis** for concluding that the "total incidence" of the activity in the aggregate substantially affects interstate commerce, Congress may regulate even a minute amount of that total. *Gonzales v. Raich*, 545 U.S. 1 (2005) (prohibition on personal cultivation and use of medical marijuana upheld due to effect on overall interstate trade). The practical effect of this rule is that with regard to economic activity, a substantial economic effect is presumed.

> **Example:** The Supreme Court upheld congressional restriction of wheat production, even when applied to a farmer growing only 23 acres of wheat, primarily for personal use. The rationale behind the decision was that if every small farmer were allowed to grow an unrestricted amount of wheat, the combined effect could have an impact on supply and demand in the interstate market. *Wickard v. Filburn*, 317 U.S. 111 (1942).

3. Non-Economic Activity

Congress's power under the Commerce Clause to regulate **intrastate** activity that is not obviously economic (so-called "non-economic" activity) is limited to some degree by principles of federalism, at least when the regulation involves an area of traditional state concern. The non-economic activity must have a substantial economic effect on interstate commerce. *Nat'l Fed'n of Indep. Bus. v. Sebelius (The Patient Protection and Affordable Care Cases)*, 567 U.S. 519 (2012) (requiring individuals not engaged in commercial activities to buy unwanted health insurance could not be sustained as a regulation of interstate commerce); *United States v. Morrison*, 529 U.S. 598 (2000) (federal civil remedy for victims of gender-motivated violence held invalid); *United States v. Lopez*, 514 U.S. 549 (1995) (federal statute regulating possession of a firearm within 1,000 feet of a public school struck down).

B. TAXATION AND SPENDING

Article I, Section 8 provides: "Congress shall have power to lay and collect taxes, duties, imposts and excises, to pay the debts and provide for the common defense and general welfare of the United States; but all duties, imposts and excises shall be uniform throughout the United States."

> **EXAM NOTE:** If you see the terms "appropriation bill" or "authorization bill" on the exam, the power to spend is likely a consideration.

1. Taxing Power

A tax by Congress will generally be upheld if it has a **reasonable relationship to revenue production**.

> **Example:** The Affordable Health Act's individual mandate, requiring individuals to buy health insurance or pay a penalty, merely imposed a tax on those who failed to buy insurance and therefore could be sustained under the taxing power. *Nat'l Fed'n of Indep. Bus. v. Sebelius (The Patient Protection and Affordable Care Cases)*, 567 U.S. 519 (2012).

a. Any purpose

Of the three branches of the federal government, Article I, Section 8 of the Constitution gives Congress the plenary (i.e., exclusive) power to raise revenue through the imposition of taxes. The government has no burden to prove that the tax is necessary to any compelling governmental interest. Instead, the General Welfare Clause has been interpreted as permitting Congress to exercise its power to tax for any public purpose. (Note: This clause has been interpreted as having the same effect on the spending power, as discussed at § II.B.2. Spending, *infra*.)

> While the General Welfare Clause gives Congress broad power in exercising its spending and taxing powers, it does not give Congress the specific power to legislate for the public welfare in general. Such "police power" is reserved for the states.

b. Indirect tax—uniformity

The requirement that indirect federal taxes (i.e., duties, sales taxes, and import & excise taxes) must be uniform throughout the United States has been interpreted to mean **geographical** uniformity only; the product or activity at issue must be identically taxed in every state in which it is found. Differences in state law do not destroy this uniformity. *Fernandez v. Wiener*, 326 U.S. 340 (1945) (federal estate tax on "community property" valid despite variation in state laws regarding marital property).

c. Direct tax—apportionment

Article I, Section 2 provides that "[r]epresentatives and direct taxes shall be apportioned among the several states," and Article I, Section 9 provides that "no...direct tax shall be laid, unless in proportion to the Census...." A direct tax (one imposed directly on property or persons, such as an ad valorem property tax) would therefore have to be apportioned evenly among the states. The difficulty of ensuring this outcome explains Congress's reluctance to enact such taxes—or perhaps the Supreme Court's reluctance to find that federal taxes are "direct." The Sixteenth Amendment gave Congress the power to lay and collect **income tax** without apportionment among the states.

d. Export tax prohibition

Goods exported to foreign countries may not be taxed by Congress. Article I, Section 9. Under this Export Taxation Clause, a tax or duty that falls on goods during the course of exportation or on services or activities closely related to the export process is prohibited. *United States v. International Business Machines Corp.*, 517 U.S. 843 (1996) (tax on insurance premiums paid to foreign insurers of goods being exported).

e. Origination Clause

Article I, Section 7, Clause 1 provides that "All Bills for raising Revenue shall originate in the House of Representatives; but the Senate may propose or concur with Amendments as on other Bills." Known as the Origination Clause, this provision is limited to "bills that levy taxes in the strict sense of the word, and are not bills for other purposes which may incidentally create revenue." *United States v. Munoz-Flores*, 495 U.S. 385, 397 (1990), citing *Twin City Bank v. Nebeker*, 167 U.S. 196, 202 (1897).

2. Spending Power

The spending power has been interpreted very broadly. Congress has the power to **spend for the "general welfare"**—i.e., any public purpose—not just to pursue its other enumerated powers. *U.S. v. Butler*, 297 U.S. 1 (1936). For example, Congress can provide for the public funding of presidential nominating conventions as well as election campaigns. *Buckley v. Valeo*, 424 U.S. 1 (1976). Although there are areas in which Congress cannot directly regulate, it can use its spending power to accomplish such regulation indirectly by conditioning federal funding. *See South Dakota v. Dole*, 483 U.S. 203 (1987) (statute upheld withholding federal highway funds from states unless they barred the sale of alcoholic beverages to individuals under the age of 21).

Congress cannot, however, impose unconstitutional conditions that turn pressure into compulsion, such as requiring distribution of the Ten Commandments to patients as a condition of Medicaid funding. *See id.*, 210-211; *Steward Machine Co. v. Davis*, 301 U.S. 548, 590 (1937); *Nat'l Fed'n of Indep. Bus. v. Sebelius (The Patient Protection and Affordable Care Cases)*, 567 U.S. 519 (2012). Moreover, to be enforceable, conditions must be set out unambiguously. *Arlington Cent. Sch. Dist. Bd. of Educ. v. Murphy*, 548 U.S. 291 (2006) (parents who prevailed against local school board for violation of Individuals with Disabilities Education Act could not recover expert fees from local school board under a provision providing for recovery of costs).

C. WAR AND DEFENSE POWERS

Article I, Section 8 gives Congress the power to declare war, raise and support armies, provide and maintain a navy, make rules for governing and regulating the land and naval forces, and provide for the organizing of a militia.

1. Providing for the National Defense

The authority granted to Congress under the war power is very broad. Congress may take whatever action it deems necessary to provide for the national defense in both wartime and peacetime. The Court has upheld the military draft and selective service; wage, price, and rent control of the civilian economy during wartime (and even during the post-war period); and the exclusion of civilians from restricted areas.

2. Courts and Tribunals

Congress has the power to establish military courts and tribunals under Article I, Section 8, Clause 14 and the Necessary and Proper Clause. These courts may try enemy soldiers, enemy civilians, and current members of the U.S. armed forces, but they do not have jurisdiction over U.S. civilians. U.S. citizens captured and held as "enemy combatants" are entitled, as a matter of due process, to contest the factual basis of their detention before a neutral decision maker. *Hamdi v. Rumsfeld*, 542 U.S. 507 (2004). Under the Suspension Clause of Article I, Section 9, Clause 2, all persons held in a territory over which the United States has sovereign control are entitled to habeas corpus (or similar) review of the basis for their detention, unless the privilege of seeking habeas corpus has been suspended. *Boumediene v. Bush*, 553 U.S. 723, (2008).

Because military tribunals are not Article III courts, not all constitutional protections apply (such as the right to a jury trial or grand jury indictment).

3. National Guard

National Guard units are under the dual control of the federal and state governments. Under the Militia Clauses (Art. I, Sec. 8, Cl. 15, 16), Congress has the power to authorize the President to call National Guard units to execute federal laws, suppress insurrections, and repeal invasions. This constitutional authority extends to use of National Guard units in domestic situations and non-emergency circumstances, and is not subject the approval or veto of the governor of a state. *Perpich v. Dep't of Def.*, 496 U.S. 334 (1990). (Note: By statute, Congress has restricted the exercise of this constitutional authority. 10 U.S.C. §§ 331-335; 18 U.S.C. § 1385.)

D. INVESTIGATORY POWER

Congress does not have an express power to investigate, but the Necessary and Proper Clause allows Congress broad authority to conduct investigations incident to its power to legislate. *McGrain v. Daugherty*, 273 U.S. 135 (1927).

1. Scope

The investigatory power may extend to any matter within a "legitimate legislative sphere." According to the Speech and Debate Clause of Article I, Section 6, members of Congress cannot be questioned in regard to activities such as speech or debate taking place during a session in either House of Congress in relation to the business before it. This provides an absolute immunity from judicial interference. *Eastland v. Unites States Servicemen's Fund*, 421 U.S. 491 (1975).

2. Enforcement and Witness's Rights

A subpoenaed witness who fails to appear before Congress or refuses to answer questions may be cited for contempt. The witness is entitled to certain rights, including procedural due process (e.g., presence of counsel) and the privilege against self-incrimination.

E. PROPERTY POWER

The Federal Property Clause of Article IV, Section 3 gives Congress the "power to dispose of and make all needful rules and regulations respecting the territory or other property belonging to the United States." There is no express limit on Congress's power to **dispose** of property owned by the United States. Under the Fifth Amendment, however, Congress may only **take** private property for public use (eminent domain) with just compensation and in order to effectuate an enumerated power.

F. POSTAL POWER

Congress has the exclusive power "to establish post offices and post roads" under Article I, Section 8, Clause 7. Congress may impose reasonable restrictions on the use of the mail (such as prohibiting obscene or fraudulent material to be mailed), but the postal power may not be used to abridge any right guaranteed by the Constitution (e.g., the First Amendment).

G. POWER OVER ALIENS AND CITIZENSHIP

1. Aliens

Congress has plenary power over aliens. *Fiallo v. Bell*, 430 U.S. 787 (1977). Aliens have no right to enter the United States and may be refused entry for reasons such as their political beliefs. *Kleindienst v. Mandel*, 408 U.S. 753 (1972). However, this power is subject to the constraints of the Fifth Amendment Due Process Clause for an alien within the United States. *Zadvydas v. Davis*, 533 U.S. 678 (2001). An alien may generally be removed from the United States, but only after notice and a removal hearing. 8 U.S.C. §§ 1229, 1229a.

2. Naturalization

Congress has exclusive authority over naturalization. Article I, Section 8, Clause 4 allows Congress to "establish a uniform rule of naturalization."

Example: Children born abroad whose parents are U.S. citizens are not automatically entitled to U.S. citizenship. Congress can grant citizenship conditioned on the child's return to the U.S. within a specified timeframe or for a specified duration. *Rogers v. Bellei*, 401 U.S. 815 (1971).

However, the right of national citizenship in the Fourteenth Amendment prevents Congress from taking away the citizenship of any citizen without her consent, unless that citizenship was obtained by fraud or in bad faith. *Afroyim v. Rusk*, 387 U.S. 253 (1967) (federal statute that stripped citizenship for voting in a foreign election struck down); *Costello v. United States*, 365 U.S. 265 (1961) (citizen's willful failure to accurately state his occupation on a naturalization application resulted in loss of citizenship).

H. OTHER ARTICLE I POWERS

Congress has power over **bankruptcies, maritime matters, coining of money,** fixing of **weights and measures,** and **patents and copyrights.**

1. Power Over the District of Columbia

Article I, Section 8, Clause 17 provides that Congress has the power to "exercise exclusive Legislation in all Cases whatsoever, over such District (not exceeding ten Miles square) as may, by Cession of particular States, and the acceptance of Congress, become the Seat of the Government of the United States." Under this provision, which is known as the "Enclave Clause," Congress has supreme authority over Washington, D.C., and may legislate freely with regard to D.C. law.

2. Elections Clause

Article I, Section 4 of the Constitution provides: "The times, places and manner of holding elections for Senators and Representatives shall be prescribed by each state legislature, but Congress may...make or alter such regulations." The Elections Clause explicitly empowers Congress to override state laws concerning federal elections.

3. Necessary and Proper Clause

Congress is given the power to enact any legislation necessary and proper to execute any authority granted to any branch of the federal government. *McCulloch v. Maryland*, 17 U.S. 316 (1819). The Necessary and Proper Clause is not an independent source of power, but it permits Congress's otherwise designated authority to be exercised fully. This clause permits Congress to enact legislation to execute a treaty. *Missouri v. Holland*, 252 U.S. 416, 432 (1920).

> **EXAM NOTE:** Because the Necessary and Proper Clause is not an independent source of power, it is not a correct answer choice by itself unless it carries into effect other enumerated powers.

I. POWER TO ENFORCE THE THIRTEENTH, FOURTEENTH, AND FIFTEENTH AMENDMENTS (CIVIL WAR AMENDMENTS)

Each of the Thirteenth, Fourteenth, and Fifteenth Amendments contains a provision that authorizes Congress to pass "appropriate legislation" to enforce the civil rights guaranteed by those amendments.

1. Thirteenth Amendment—Ban on Slavery

Congress has the power to adopt legislation rationally related to eliminating racial discrimination, as it is among the "badges or incidents" of slavery. *Jones v. Alfred H. Mayer Co.,* 392 U.S. 409 (1968). This power has been broadly interpreted to allow Congress to regulate both private and government action, including racial discrimination by private housing sellers, private schools, and private employers. (This is the only amendment that authorizes Congress to regulate purely private conduct.) This clause also gives Congress the power to eliminate involuntary servitude.

2. Fourteenth Amendment—Equal Protection and Due Process

The Fourteenth Amendment, Section 5 Enabling Clause permits Congress to pass legislation to enforce the equal protection and due process rights guaranteed by the amendment, but not to expand those rights or create new ones. Under the separation of powers doctrine, the job of defining such rights falls to the Supreme Court. In enforcing such rights, there must be a **"congruence and proportionality"** between the injury to be prevented or remedied and the means adopted to achieve that end. *City of Boerne v. Flores,* 521 U.S. 507 (1997) (Religious Freedom Restoration Act held invalid for failure to show widespread religious discrimination and for disproportion to any purported remedial goal). Congress may override state government action that infringes upon Fourteenth Amendment rights, but it may not under this amendment regulate wholly private conduct. In the exercise of Fourteenth Amendment powers,

Congress can override the Eleventh Amendment immunity of states. *Fitzpatrick v. Bitzer*, 427 U.S. 445 (1976).

3. Fifteenth Amendment—Voting

The Fifteenth Amendment prohibits both the state and federal governments from denying any citizen the right to vote on the basis of race, color, or previous condition of servitude. The courts have interpreted the right to vote to include the right to have that vote meaningfully counted.

J. QUALIFICATIONS OF MEMBERS

The qualifications for members of Congress are set forth in Article I and cannot be altered by Congress or the states. *United States Term Limits, Inc. v. Thornton*, 514 U.S. 779 (1995) (state-mandated term limits for federal representatives invalid); *Powell v. McCormack*, 395 U.S. 486 (1969) (House of Representatives could not refuse to seat a scandal-plagued member who satisfied constitutional criteria for service).

III. THE POWERS OF THE PRESIDENT

Article II, Section 1 grants the "executive power" to the President. The extent of this power has been interpreted broadly by the Supreme Court, which has emphasized that the President has no power to make laws but does have the power to enforce them; this enforcement power includes the exercise of prosecutorial discretion. *Davis v. U.S.*, 512 U.S. 452 (1994). Generally speaking, the President's authority is broader in the area of foreign affairs than in domestic matters.

A. DOMESTIC POWER

1. Pardon Power for Federal Offenses

Article II, Section 2 provides the President with the power to "grant reprieves and pardons for offenses against the United States, except in cases of impeachment." This power applies only to federal cases; the President may not grant pardons for state crimes. The pardon or reprieve may be granted at any time after commission of the offense. *Ex parte Garland*, 71 U.S. (4 Wall.) 333, 380 (1867). The pardon or reprieve may be made subject to conditions and may take or encompass various lesser acts, such as remission of fines, penalties, and forfeitures or commutation of sentences. *Ex parte William Wells*, 59 U.S. (18 How.) 307 (1856). The power may be exercised with respect to groups of people as well as individuals. James Carter, Executive Order 11967, issued Jan. 21, 1977 (amnesty for Vietnam War draft dodgers).

2. Veto Power

Article I, Section 7 gives the President the power to veto any bill presented to him (i.e., passed) by Congress. Upon presentment, the President has 10 days to act on proposed legislation. If the President signs the bill, it becomes law. The President may also veto the bill by sending it back, with objections, to the house in which it originated. Congress may override the veto and enact the bill into law by a two-thirds vote in each house.

A third option is that the President does nothing at all. If Congress is still in session at the end of the 10-day period, the bill becomes law without the President's signature. If Congress has adjourned during that time, however, the bill does not become law, because the President could not have returned it to its originating house. The President's failure to act on a bill in this situation is known as the "pocket veto" and cannot be overridden.

The President may not exercise a "line item" veto, refusing part of a bill and approving the rest, because it violates the Presentment Clause. *Clinton v. City of New York*, 524 U.S. 417 (1998).

3. **Appointment and Removal of Officials**

   a. **Appointment**

   Article II, Section 2 authorizes the President, **with the advice and consent of the Senate,** to appoint all "officers of the United States," including ambassadors and Justices of the Supreme Court. Congress may, however, delegate the appointment of "inferior" officials to the President alone (i.e., without Senate approval), the heads of executive departments, or the courts. "Inferior" officials are those supervised by Senate-confirmed appointees. Congress may not itself appoint members of a body with administrative or enforcement powers; such persons are "officers of the United States" and must be appointed by the President. *Buckley v. Valeo*, 424 U.S. 1 (1976) (makeup of the Federal Election Commission invalidated because a majority of its members were to be appointed by the President Pro Tem of the Senate and the Speaker of the House; the FEC's tasks were executive in nature, therefore, Congress had no right to appoint such federal officers).

   b. **Removal**

   The Constitution says nothing about the President's power to remove executive officers, but it is generally accepted that the President may remove any executive appointee without cause (and without Senate approval). Congress may not shield appointees from removal by the President by imposing a multi-tiered system in which persons at each level may be removed from office only for good cause. *Free Enterprise Fund v. Public Company Accounting Oversight Bd.*, 561 U.S. 477 (2010) (holding 15 U.S.C.S. §§ 7211(e)(6) and 7217(d)(3) unconstitutional and invalid because the multilevel protection from removal of members of the Public Company Accounting Oversight Board was contrary to Article II's vesting of the executive power in the President and contravened the Constitution's separation of powers).

   Federal judges, however, are protected under Article III, Section 1, which provides that they may "hold their offices during good behavior"; they may be removed only by impeachment.

4. **Authority as Chief Executive**

   The scope of the President's power to issue executive orders and to govern domestic affairs is extensive but not clearly delineated. The best-known exposition holds that the President's authority varies with the degree of congressional authorization of the action. Thus, when the President acts:

   i) With the express or implied authorization of Congress, presidential authority is at its highest, and the action is strongly presumed to be valid;

   ii) When Congress has not spoken, presidential authority is diminished, and the action is invalid if it interferes with the operations or power of another branch of government; and

   iii) When Congress has spoken to the contrary, presidential authority is "at its lowest ebb," and the action is likely invalid. *Hamdan v. Rumsfeld*, 548 U.S. 557 (2006) (military commission had no jurisdiction to proceed because the executive order authorizing the commission exceeded congressional limitations placed on the President to convene commissions).

B. FOREIGN AFFAIRS

1. Commander in Chief

Although the President is the commander in chief of the military, only Congress may formally declare war. The President may take military action without a declaration of war in the case of actual hostilities against the United States. Congress may in turn limit the President's military activities through exercise of its military appropriation (i.e., funding) power. The questions of whether and to what extent the President may deploy troops overseas without congressional approval is unsettled; presidents routinely do so, and Congress routinely asserts its authority to approve the deployment. The courts have generally left the question to the political branches.

2. Treaties

Pursuant to the Treaty Clause (Art. II, Sec. 2. Cl. 2), the President has the exclusive power to negotiate treaties, although a treaty may only be ratified with the concurrence of two-thirds of the Senate.

a. Effect of a treaty

The Constitution is superior to a treaty, and any conflict is resolved in favor of the Constitution. *Reid v. Covert*, 354 U.S. 1 (1957). A treaty has the same authority as an act of Congress; should the two conflict, the one most recently adopted controls. A non-self-executing treaty (one that requires legislation in order to implement its provisions) does not have the same force of law as an act of Congress until legislation is passed effectuating the treaty. In the absence of implementing legislation by Congress, the President does not have the authority to make a non-self-executing treaty binding on the states. *Medellin v. Texas*, 552 U.S. 491 (2008); *Youngstown Sheet & Tube v. Sawyer*, 343 U.S. 579 (1952) (Jackson, J., conc.). A ratified treaty takes precedence over any inconsistent state law. *Missouri v. Holland*, 252 U.S. 416 (1920).

3. Executive Agreements

The President has the power to enter into executive agreements with foreign nations (e.g., reciprocal trade agreements) that do not require the approval of two-thirds of the Senate. Although not expressly provided for in the Constitution, executive agreements may be made, without congressional authorization, pursuant to the President's authority over foreign affairs.

Conflicting federal statutes and treaties take precedence over executive agreements, but executive agreements take precedence over conflicting state laws.

4. International Affairs

The President represents and acts for the United States in day-to-day international affairs. In addition to appointing and receiving ambassadors, the President has the exclusive power to recognize a foreign government. *Zivotofsky v. Kerry*, 576 U.S. ___, 135 S. Ct. 2076 (2015).

IV. FEDERAL INTERBRANCH RELATIONSHIPS

The separation of powers doctrine, which is inherent in the structure of the Constitution, ensures that the executive, legislative, and judicial branches of government remain separate and distinct in order to provide a system of checks and balances.

A. CONGRESSIONAL LIMITS ON THE EXECUTIVE

1. Impeachment

Article II, Section 4 states: "The President, Vice President and all civil officers of the United States shall be removed from office on impeachment for, and conviction of, treason, bribery, or other high crimes and misdemeanors." The House of Representatives determines what constitutes "high crimes and misdemeanors" and **may impeach (i.e., bring charges) by a majority vote.** The Senate tries the impeached official, and **a two-thirds vote is necessary for conviction.**

2. Appropriation

If Congress explicitly mandates an allocation, distribution, or expenditure of funds, the President has no power to impound those funds (e.g., refuse to spend them or delay the spending). The President is permitted to exercise discretion if the authorizing legislation so provides. *Train v. New York*, 420 U.S. 35 (1975); *Kendall v. United States*, 37 U.S. 524 (1838).

> **EXAM NOTE:** Separation of powers questions often center on the President trying to impound funds appropriated by Congress. Remember that if Congress fails to mandate that the funds are to be allocated, distributed, or spent, then impoundment is not a separation of powers violation.

3. Legislative Veto

It is unconstitutional for Congress to attempt a "legislative veto" of an executive action—that is, to retain direct control over the actions of an executive agency, rather than going through the proper channels of passing a bill.

> **Example:** In *INS v. Chadha*, 462 U.S. 919 (1983), a provision of law permitted either house of Congress to overturn a decision by the Attorney General granting an alien relief from deportation. The Supreme Court held such a one-house congressional "veto" of a matter delegated to the executive to be unconstitutional as violating the carefully wrought legislative procedures set forth in Article I, which require passage of legislation by both Houses of Congress (i.e., bicameralism) and sending to the President pursuant to the Presentment Clauses for his approval or return. Thus, the Court made clear that a two-house legislative veto would be equally unconstitutional.

B. DELEGATION OF LEGISLATIVE POWER

Because Congress is vested by Article I with "all legislative powers," it may not delegate that power to any other branch of government. This principle is known as the "nondelegation doctrine." However, delegation of some of Congress's authority to the executive branch has consistently been held constitutional, so long as Congress specifies an "intelligible principle" to guide the delegate. *Whitman v. Am. Trucking Ass'ns, Inc.*, 531 U.S. 457 (2001).

> **Example:** The IRS has been given the power to collect taxes that are assessed under the Internal Revenue Code. Although Congress has determined the amount to be taxed, it has delegated to the IRS the power to determine how such taxes are to be collected.

Almost any legislative delegation passes the "intelligible standards" requirement, so even broadly phrased standards have been upheld.

Examples: A delegation of authority to an executive agency to regulate broadcast licenses to the extent that "public interest, convenience, and necessity require" has been upheld. *Nat'l Broad. Co. v. United States*, 319 U.S. 190 (1943). Similarly, an administrative agency could set "just and reasonable" rates for natural gas sold in interstate commerce. *FPC v. Hope Natural Gas Co.*, 320 U.S. 591 (1944).

Certain powers, however, are nondelegable, such as the power of impeachment and the power to declare war.

C. JUDICIAL LIMITATION OF CONGRESSIONAL POWER

Under the doctrine of separation of powers, Congress may not reinstate the right to bring a legal action after the judgment in the action has become final.

Example: An action brought in federal court under federal question jurisdiction was dismissed with prejudice because it was not timely filed. A statute that revived the plaintiff's right to bring the action was struck down as a violation of the separation of powers doctrine. *Plaut v. Spendthrift Farm, Inc.*, 514 U.S. 211 (1995).

Similarly, Congress cannot prescribe rules of decision to the federal courts in cases pending before it. *United States v. Klein*, 80 U.S. 128 (1872). However, when Congress changes the law underlying a judgment awarding ongoing relief, that relief is no longer enforceable to the extent it is inconsistent with the new law. *Miller v. French*, 530 U.S. 327 (2000).

D. IMMUNITIES AND PRIVILEGES

1. Judicial

A judge is absolutely immune from civil liability for damages resulting from her judicial acts, including grave procedural errors and acts done maliciously or in excess of authority unless there is a clear absence of all jurisdiction. *Butz v. Economou*, 438 U.S. 478 (1987); *Stump v. Sparkman*, 435 U.S. 349 (1978). The judge is not immune, however, to lawsuits regarding nonjudicial activities, such as hiring and firing court employees. *Forrester v. White*, 484 U.S. 219 (1988).

Prosecutors are subject to similar immunity rules. *Imbler v. Pachtman*, 424 U.S. 409 (1976). Court officers who perform ministerial duties, such as court reporters, are entitled only to qualified, not absolute, immunity. *Antoine v. Byers & Anderson*, 508 U.S. 429 (1993).

Under 42 U.S.C. § 1983, a damage claim can be brought against a state official personally for violation of constitutional rights. The Supreme Court has recognized that a similar claim can be brought against federal officials. *Bivens v. Six Unknown Named Agents of Fed. Bureau of Narcotics*, 403 U.S. 388 (1971).

2. Legislative

The Speech or Debate Clause of Article I, Section 6 protects members of Congress from civil and criminal liability for statements and conduct made **in the regular course of the legislative process,** including a speech given on the floor of Congress, committee hearings, and reports. The activities of congressional aides are also protected if a legislator performing the same acts would be immune. *Gravel v. United States*, 408 U.S. 606 (1972).

State legislators: The Speech or Debate Clause does not apply to state legislators, but under the principles of federalism, state legislators are immune from liability for actions within the sphere of legitimate legislative activity (*see* § VI.B.1.b.2, State legislators, *infra*).

This protection does not foreclose prosecution for a crime, including the taking of bribes, when the crime does not require proof of legislative acts or inquiring into the motive behind those acts. *United States v. Brewster*, 408 U.S. 501 (1972). This protection also does not apply to speeches made outside Congress, or the "re-publication" (i.e., repeating) of a defamatory statement originally made in Congress. *Hutchinson v. Proxmire*, 443 U.S. 111 (1979).

3. Executive

a. Executive privilege

Executive privilege is a privilege with respect to the disclosure of confidential information by the executive branch to the judiciary or Congress. This privilege and the more narrow presidential privilege, which applies to communications made in the performance of a president's responsibilities to shape policies and make decisions, have been recognized by the Supreme Court. The presidential privilege survives an individual president's tenure, but this privilege is not absolute. *Cheney v. United States*, 542 U.S. 367 (2004); *United States v. Nixon*, 418 U.S. 683 (1974).

1) Criminal trial

Presidential communications must be made available in a criminal case if the prosecution demonstrates a need for the information. A judge may examine the communications in camera to determine whether the communications fall within the privilege. *United States v. Nixon, supra*.

2) Civil proceedings

An executive branch decision to withhold production of information in civil proceedings will be given greater deference than in a criminal trial because the need for information is "weightier" in the latter case. In a civil case, the court may be required to consider the issue of separation of powers without first requiring the executive branch to assert executive privilege. *Cheney v. United States Dist. Court, supra*.

3) Historical preservation

Congress can require the preservation of presidential papers and tape recordings. *Nixon v. Adm'r of Gen. Servs.*, 433 U.S. 425 (1977).

4) State secrets

Claims of privilege based on national security are generally accorded enhanced deference. *United States v. Reynolds*, 345 U.S. 1 (1953) (recognizing a "state secrets" privilege). *But see In re NSA Telcoms. Records Litig.*, 564 F. Supp. 2d 1109 (2008) (the "state secrets" privilege was a common-law privilege that could be limited by congressional action).

b. Executive immunity

1) Official duties

The President may not be sued for civil damages with regard to any acts performed as part of the President's **official responsibilities.** *Nixon v. Fitzgerald*, 457 U.S. 731 (1982). The President has no immunity, however, from a civil action based on conduct alleged to have occurred **before the President took office** or completely unrelated to carrying out his job. Moreover, the President may be subject to such a suit even while in office. *Clinton v. Jones*, 520 U.S. 681 (1997).

a) Presidential advisor

A senior presidential advisor (e.g., cabinet member) is not automatically entitled to enjoy derivatively the protection of absolute executive immunity. Although the Supreme Court has stated that such an advisor may be entitled to such protection when performing special functions that are vital to national security or foreign policy, the Court has also held that an Attorney General did not qualify for absolute immunity with respect to the authorization of a warrantless wiretap for national security purposes. The burden for establishing such immunity rests with the advisor. *Harlow v. Fitzgerald*, 457 U.S. 800 (1982); *Mitchell v. Forsyth*, 472 U.S. 511 (1985).

b) Federal officials

A federal official, in performing a discretionary (as opposed to ministerial) act, is entitled to qualified immunity from liability for civil damages when the official's conduct does not violate clearly established statutory and constitutional rights of which a reasonable person would have known. This is an objective standard; a plaintiff's bare allegations of malice are insufficient to overcome this immunity. *Harlow v. Fitzgerald*, 457 U.S. 800 (1982).

> **Example:** The Attorney General, in authorizing a warrantless wiretap for national security purposes, while not entitled to absolute immunity, was entitled to qualified immunity. The unconstitutionality of this authorization was not clearly established at the time of the authorization. *Mitchell v. Forsyth*, 472 U.S. 511 (1985).

PART TWO: THE FEDERAL SYSTEM

V. FEDERAL AND STATE POWERS

The federal system, under which the federal and state governments each have exclusive authority over some areas, yet share authority over other areas, is one of the Constitution's basic checks on governmental power.

A. EXCLUSIVE FEDERAL POWERS

The Constitution explicitly provides for some powers of the federal government to be exclusive, such as the powers to coin money or enter into treaties. Article I, Sec. 10. Other powers are by their nature exclusively federal, such as the power to declare war and the power over citizenship; a state's attempt to exercise authority in these areas would essentially subvert the power of the federal government.

B. EXCLUSIVE STATE POWERS

The Tenth Amendment provides that all powers not assigned by the Constitution to the federal government are reserved to the states, or to the people. In theory, this gives the states expansive, exclusive power. In practice, however, given the broad interpretation of the Commerce Clause and the spending power, the federal government has very broad authority, making state power rarely exclusive.

C. CONCURRENT FEDERAL AND STATE LAWS—SUPREMACY CLAUSE

It is possible (and common) for the federal and state governments to legislate in the same area. When this happens, the Supremacy Clause (Article VI, paragraph 2) provides that federal law supersedes conflicting state law (*see* § VIII. Federal Preemption of State Law, *infra*).

VI. INTERGOVERNMENTAL IMMUNITIES

A. FEDERAL IMMUNITY

1. Regulation by the States

The states have no power to regulate the federal government—for example, by imposing state wage-and-hour laws on local federal offices—unless Congress permits the state regulation or unless the state regulation is not inconsistent with existing federal policy.

2. Taxation by the States

The federal government and its instrumentalities (such as a national bank) are immune from taxation by the states. *McCulloch v. Maryland*, 17 U.S. 316 (1819). States may, however, impose generally applicable indirect taxes so long as they do not unreasonably burden the federal government (e.g., state income taxes on federal employees).

B. STATE IMMUNITY

1. Federal Regulation

The federal government has virtually unlimited power to regulate the states.

a. Congressional action

As long as Congress is exercising one of its enumerated powers, Congress generally may regulate the states. For example, a federal minimum wage and overtime statute enacted under the commerce power can be applied to state employees. *Garcia v. San Antonio Metropolitan Transit Authority*, 469 U.S. 528 (1985). Similarly, Congress can prohibit the disclosure by state officials of personal information obtained from driver's license applications because such information constitutes an article of commerce that is being sold in interstate commerce. *Reno v. Condon*, 528 U.S. 141 (2000).

If Congress determines that a state is violating a person's civil liberties, it can place limits on that state's activities by using the power of the Fourteenth and Fifteenth Amendments. *See Oregon v. Mitchell*, 400 U.S. 112 (1970).

1) "Commandeering" limitation

Congress cannot "commandeer" state legislatures by commanding them to enact specific legislation or administer a federal regulatory program, and it may not circumvent that restriction by conscripting a state executive officer directly. *Printz v. United States*, 521 U.S. 898 (1997); *New York v. United States*, 505 U.S. 144 (1992). There is no distinction between compelling a state to enact legislation and prohibiting a state from enacting new laws—in either case Congress is precluded from issuing direct orders to state legislatures. *Murphy v. National Collegiate Athletic Assn*, 584 U.S. ___ (2018) (act preventing states from legalizing sports betting violated anti-commandeering limitation). However, through the use of the taxing and spending powers, Congress may encourage state action that it cannot directly compel.

Example: In *South Dakota v. Dole*, 483 U.S. 203 (1987), the Court held that Congress could condition a provision of five percent of federal highway funds on the state's raising its drinking age to 21.

2) "Coercion" limitation

While, as noted, Congress, through the use of its taxing and spending powers, can encourage states to act in ways in which it cannot directly compel, Congressional encouragement may not exceed the point at which "pressure turns into compulsion." *Steward Machine Co. v. Davis*, 301 U.S. 548, 590 (1937); *Nat'l Fed'n of Indep. Bus. v. Sebelius (The Patient Protection and Affordable Care Cases)*, 567 U.S. 519 (2012).

b. Judicial action

1) Remedying constitutional violations

The federal judiciary has broad equitable powers in fashioning a remedy for a constitutional violation. For example, while a court may not directly impose a tax in order to fund a racial-discrimination remedy, it may order a local government with taxing authority to levy such a tax, and it may do so despite a state statutory limitation that would otherwise prevent such action. *Missouri v. Jenkins*, 495 U.S. 33 (1990).

2) State legislators

State legislators are absolutely immune from suit for damages and for declaratory and injunctive relief for actions within the sphere of legitimate legislative activity. *Supreme Court of Virginia v. Consumers Union of U.S., Inc.*, 446 U.S. 719 (1980); *Tenney v. Brandhove*, 341 U.S. 367 (1951).

2. Federal Taxation

Pursuant to the Supremacy Clause of Article VI, the federal government may tax a state; the Tenth Amendment does not protect a state from federal taxation. *New York v. United States*, 326 U.S. 572 (1946) (excise tax impose on sale of mineral water could be imposed on mineral water from state-owned property); *South Carolina v. United States*, 199 U.S. 437 (1905) (federal licensing tax imposed on sellers of alcohol could be imposed on sellers who were agents of the state even when the tax was paid by the state). A tax on a payment made by a state to private person that is not directly imposed on the state is constitutional, even though the tax may have a substantial adverse impact on the state. *Id.*, (federal income tax on interest received by holders of state bonds); *Helvering v. Gerhardt*, 304 U.S. 405 (1938) (federal income tax on salaries of state employees).

3. Litigation Involving the United States and Its Officers

In suits between a state and the United States, the United States must consent before the state can file suit against it; conversely, the United States does not need to obtain consent from a state to file suit against that state. As between states, no consent is needed for one state to file suit against another state.

Suits against federal officers are limited, and generally prohibited, because such suits are considered to be brought against the United States if payment of the award will be made from the public treasury. However, if the federal officer acted outside the scope of his professional capacity, then a suit may be instituted against the officer individually.

VII. STATE REGULATION AND TAXATION OF COMMERCE

The Constitution contemplates a system of regulation of commerce and taxation that includes both the federal and state governments.

A.   THE DORMANT COMMERCE CLAUSE

The Dormant Commerce Clause (sometimes referred to as the Negative Commerce Clause) is a doctrine that limits the power of states to legislate in ways that impact interstate commerce. The Commerce Clause (Article I, Section 8, Clause 3) reserves to Congress the power "[t]o regulate commerce with foreign nations, and among the several states, and with the Indian tribes"; as a corollary, individual states are limited in their ability to legislate on such matters.

1.   General Rule

If Congress has not enacted legislation in a particular area of interstate commerce, then the states are free to regulate, so long as the state or local action does not:

i)   **Discriminate** against out-of-state commerce;

ii) **Unduly burden** interstate commerce; or

iii) Regulate **extraterritorial** (wholly out-of-state) activity.

> **Note:** Unlike the Comity Clause of Article IV, Section 2, the Dormant Commerce Clause does not exclude corporations and aliens from its protection against state or local action. *See* XIV.A.1. "Prohibits State Discrimination Against Nonresidents," *infra*.

2.   Discrimination Against Out-of-State Commerce

A state or local regulation discriminates against out-of-state commerce if it protects local economic interests at the expense of out-of-state competitors. *See City of Philadelphia v. New Jersey*, 437 U.S. 617 (1978) (state statute prohibiting importation of out-of-state garbage discriminated in favor of local trash collectors); *Dean Milk Co. v. City of Madison*, 340 U.S. 349 (1959) (state law discriminated against out-of-state milk suppliers by requiring all milk sold in the city to be processed and bottled locally).

a.   Necessary to important state interest

If a state or local regulation, on its face or in practice, is discriminatory, then the regulation may be upheld if the state or local government can establish that:

i)   An important local interest is being served; and

ii) No other nondiscriminatory means are available to achieve that purpose.

Hunt v. Wash. State Apple Adver. Comm'n, 432 U.S. 333 (1977). Discriminatory regulation has rarely been upheld. In a few instances, a discriminatory state or local regulation that furthers an important, non-economic state interest, like health and safety, has not been struck down. *Maine v. Taylor*, 477 U.S. 131 (1986) (upheld a prohibition against importation into the state of out-of-state live baitfish that may pose contamination hazards to local waters).

b.   Market-participant exception

A state may behave in a discriminatory fashion if it is acting as a market participant (buyer or seller), as opposed to a market regulator. If the state is a market participant, it may favor local commerce or discriminate against nonresident commerce as could any private business. *E.g., Reeves, Inc. v. Stake*, 447 U.S. 429 (1980) (state-owned cement plant may, in times of shortage, sell only to in-state buyers).

c.   Traditional government function exception

State and local regulations may favor state and local **government** entities, though not local **private** entities, when those entities are performing a traditional governmental function, such as waste disposal. For example, an ordinance may require all trash haulers to deliver to a local **public** waste-treatment facility, but **not** to a local **private** facility. *Compare United Haulers Ass'n, Inc. v. Oneida-Herkimer Solid Waste Mgmt. Auth.*, 550 U.S. 330 (2007) (public facility), *with C & A Carbone, Inc. v. Town of Clarkstown*, 511 U.S. 383 (1994) (private facility). Similarly, a state may discriminate against out-of-state interests when raising money to fund state and local government projects. *Dep't of Revenue of Kentucky v. Davis*, 553 U.S. 328 (2008) (upholding state income tax exemption for income earned on state and local bonds, but not out-of-state bonds).

d. Subsidy exception

A state may favor its own citizens when providing for subsidy. For example, a state may offer in-state residents a lower tuition rate to attend a state college or university than out-of-state residents. *Vlandis v. Kline*, 412 U.S. 441 (1973).

e. Exception—congressionally permitted discrimination

Because Congress has exclusive authority over interstate commerce, it may explicitly permit states to act in ways that would otherwise violate the Dormant Commerce Clause. *Prudential Ins. Co. v. Benjamin*, 328 U.S. 408 (1946) (state tax only on out-of-state insurance companies upheld when Congress had enacted a law permitting states to regulate insurance in any manner consistent with federal statutes). It must be unmistakably clear that Congress intended to permit the otherwise impermissible state regulation; Congress must expressly allow or "affirmatively contemplate" such state legislation. The fact that the state policy appears to be consistent with federal policy or that the state policy furthers the goals that Congress had in mind is insufficient. *South–Central Timber Dev., Inc. v. Wunnicke*, 467 U.S. 82, 90 (1984).

3. Undue Burden on Interstate Commerce

A state regulation that is not discriminatory may still be struck down as unconstitutional if it imposes an undue burden on interstate commerce. The courts will balance, case by case, the objective and purpose of the state law against the burden on interstate commerce and evaluate whether there are less restrictive alternatives. If the benefits of the state law are grossly outweighed by the burdens on interstate commerce, then even nondiscriminatory regulation may be struck down. *Pike v. Bruce Church, Inc.*, 397 U.S. 137 (1970). This balancing test is not a cost-benefit analysis or a form of close scrutiny of state economic regulation. *United Haulers Ass'n v. Oneida-Herkimer Solid Waste Mgmt. Auth.*, 550 U.S. 330 (2007).

4. "Extraterritoriality"

States may not regulate conduct that occurs wholly beyond their borders. Thus, Connecticut could not require that beer sold in Connecticut not be priced higher than beer sold in any of the four neighboring states, because the Connecticut regime had the practical effect of regulating beer prices in those states. *Healy v. Beer Inst., Inc.*, 491 U.S. 324 (1989). There may be an exception for the regulation of the internal affairs of corporations. *CTS Corp. v. Dynamics Corp.*, 481 U.S. 69 (1987).

B. STATE TAXATION OF COMMERCE

1. Interstate Commerce

Much as with regulation, the states may tax interstate commerce only if Congress has not already acted in the particular area and if the tax does not discriminate against or unduly burden interstate commerce.

a. *Complete Auto* Test

The Supreme Court applies a four-part test to determine whether a state tax on interstate commerce comports with the Commerce Clause. *Complete Auto Transit, Inc. v. Brady*, 430 U.S. 274 (1977).

1) Substantial nexus

There must be a **substantial nexus** between the activity being taxed and the taxing state. A substantial nexus requires significant (i.e., more than minimum) contacts with, or substantial activity within, the taxing state. A physical presence within the state is not required. *South Dakota v. Wayfair, Inc.*, 585 U.S. ___ (2018).

2) Fair apportionment

The tax must be fairly apportioned according to a rational formula (e.g., taxing only the state's portion of the company's business), such that interstate commerce does not pay total taxes greater than local commerce by virtue of having to pay tax in more than one state. The burden is on the taxpaying business to prove unfair apportionment.

3) Nondiscrimination

The tax may not provide a direct commercial advantage to local businesses over their interstate competitors (unless Congress specifically authorizes such a tax). A tax that is neutral on its face still may be unconstitutional if its effect is to favor local commerce. *West Lynn Creamery Inc. v. Healy*, 512 U.S. 186 (1994) (tax affecting all milk dealers, the revenue from which went to a fund used to subsidize in-state dairy farmers, violated the Commerce Clause). In addition, the denial of tax exemption to a state entity unless the entity operates primarily for the benefit of state residents may be unconstitutional. *Camps Newfound/Owatonna v. Town of Harrison*, 520 U.S. 564 (1997).

4) Fair relationship to services provided

The tax must be fairly related to the services provided by the taxing state. *Evansville-Vanderburg Airport Auth. Dist. v. Delta Airlines, Inc.*, 405 U.S. 707 (1972) (tax on airline passengers was related to benefits the passengers received from the state airport facilities).

b. Violation of other constitutional provisions

A state tax may violate more than just the Commerce Clause.

   i)   A tax that discriminates against nonresident individuals—for example, an income tax that exempts local residents—may violate the **Comity Clause** of Article IV. *Austin v. New Hampshire*, 420 U.S. 656 (1975).

   ii) A discriminatory tax on out-of-state businesses, even if authorized by Congress and therefore allowed under the Commerce Clause, may still violate the **Equal Protection Clause** of the Fourteenth Amendment, if there is no rational basis to support it. *Metropolitan Life Ins. Co. v. Ward*, 470 U.S. 869 (1985).

   iii) An income-based tax imposed on nonresidents that taxes income earned outside the state's borders may violate the Due Process Clause of the Fourteenth Amendment. *ASARCO Inc. v. Idaho Tax Comm'n*, 458 U.S. 307 (1982).

c. Types of taxes

1) Ad valorem property tax

An ad valorem tax is based on the value of real or personal property and is often assessed at a particular time (e.g., tax day). Such taxes, which may be imposed on the full value of the property, are generally valid, but a state may **not** levy ad valorem taxes on **goods in the course of transit** (from the time the goods are delivered to an interstate carrier or begin their interstate journey until they reach their destination). *Standard Oil Co. v. Peck*, 342 U.S. 382 (1952). However, once the goods are stopped for a business purpose (i.e., obtain a "taxable situs"), they may be taxed.

A state may tax the "instrumentalities of commerce" (airplanes, railroad cars, etc.), provided that:

i) The instrumentality has a **taxable situs** within—or **sufficient contacts** with—the taxing state (i.e., it receives benefits or protection from the state); and

ii) The tax is **fairly apportioned** to the amount of time the instrumentality is in the state.

2) Sales tax

A sales tax imposed on the seller of goods is valid as long as the sale takes place within the state. Sales tax generally does not discriminate against interstate commerce as long as there is a substantial nexus between the taxpayer and the state, and the tax is properly apportioned.

It is no longer required that the seller have a physical presence in the state. States sales taxes apply to any sellers (including online retailers) who engage in a significant quantity of business within the state. *South Dakota v. Wayfair, Inc., supra.*

3) Use tax

A use tax on goods purchased out of state but used within the taxing state is valid so long as the use tax rate is not higher than the sales tax rate on the same item. Even though a use tax does, on its face, seem to discriminate against out-of-state purchases, the rationale for its validity is that such a tax equalizes the tax on in-state and out-of-state goods. *Henneford v. Silas Mason Co., Inc.*, 300 U.S. 577 (1937).

4) "Doing business" taxes

Taxes levied against companies for the privilege of doing business in a state (made up of privilege, license, franchise, or occupation taxes) are valid as long as they pass the *Complete Auto* test (see B.1.a. "*Complete Auto* Test," above). Such a tax may be measured by a flat annual fee or by a graduated rate proportional to the amount of revenue derived from the taxing state. The burden of showing that a tax is unfairly apportioned is on the taxpayer.

2. Foreign Commerce

The Import-Export Clause of Article I, Section 10 prohibits the states, without the consent of Congress, from imposing any tax on any imported or exported goods, or on any commercial activity connected with imported goods, except what is absolutely necessary for executing its inspection laws. *Brown v. Maryland*, 25 U.S. 419 (1827).

In addition, the Commerce Clause vests in Congress the power to regulate international commerce in which the United States is involved. In addition to meeting the same requirements as a tax on interstate commerce (*see* VII.B.1.a. "*Complete Auto* Test," *supra*), a state tax on foreign commerce must not (i) create a substantial risk of *international* multiple taxation or (ii) prevent the federal government from "speaking with one voice" regarding international trade or foreign affairs issues. *Barclays Bank PLC v. Franchise Tax Board*, 512 U.S. 298 (1994).

C. ALCOHOLIC BEVERAGE REGULATION

The Twenty-First Amendment repealed prohibition and specifically gave states the authority to prohibit the transportation or importation of alcoholic beverages into the state for delivery or use within the state. However, this authority is narrowly confined. State regulations concerning alcoholic beverages are subject to the restrictions of the Dormant Commerce Clause, *Granholm v. Heald*, 544 U.S. 460 (2005), as well as the protections of the First and Fourteenth Amendments. *44 Liquormart, Inc. v. Rhode Island*, 517 U.S. 484 (1996) (Free Speech Clause); *Larkin v. Grendel's Den, Inc.*, 459 U.S. 116 (1982) (Establishment Clause); *Craig v. Boren*, 429 U.S. 190 (1976) (Equal Protection Clause).

In addition, this amendment does not prevent Congress from exercising control over economic transactions that involve alcoholic beverages under the Commerce Clause or its spending power. *324 Liquor Corp. v. Duffy*, 479 U.S. 335 (1987) (Commerce Clause); *South Dakota v. Dole*, *supra* (spending power).

VIII. FEDERAL PREEMPTION OF STATE LAW

The Supremacy Clause of Article VI, Section 2 provides that the "Constitution, and the laws of the United States" are the "supreme law of the land." Any state constitutional provision or law that directly or indirectly conflicts with a federal law, including federal regulations, is void under this clause. However, the Supreme Court has frequently stated that there is a presumption against preemption, especially in areas in which states have traditionally exercised police power. *Wyeth v. Levine*, 555 U.S. 555 (2009) (health and safety).

A. EXPRESS PREEMPTION

Federal law **expressly** preempts state law in cases in which the Constitution makes the federal power exclusive (such as the powers to coin money or declare war) or when Congress has enacted legislation that explicitly prohibits state regulation in the same area (e.g., the Federal Cigarette Labeling and Advertising Act forbids state laws that regulate either cigarette labels or the "advertising or promotion" of labeled cigarettes "based on smoking and health," 15 U.S.C. § 1334).

1. Narrow Construction

An express federal preemption must be narrowly construed. *Altria Group, Inc. v. Good*, 555 U.S. 70 (2008) (Federal Cigarette Labeling and Advertising Act did not preempt a suit based on a state's general deceptive-practices statute because such a statute was not based on smoking and health).

Example: The National Bank Act prohibited states to "exercise visitorial powers with respect to national banks, such as conducting examinations, inspecting or requiring the production of books or records," but it was not clear from the Act's language whether it completely prohibited the state from exercising enforcement powers when state law is violated. The Court concluded that the Act's structure and purpose differentiate between the sovereign's "visitorial powers" and its power to enforce the law. While the state could not issue administrative subpoenas to banks, it could file suit to punish violations of state banking laws. *Cuomo v. Clearing House Ass'n*, 557 U.S. 519 (2009).

2. Savings Clause

Federal law may also contain "savings clauses" that explicitly preserve or allow state laws that regulate in the same area, e.g., 33 U.S.C. § 1365 (The Clean Water Act preserves "any right which any person (or class of persons) may have under any statute or common law.").

B. IMPLIED PREEMPTION

1. When Applicable

Federal preemption is **implied** when any of the following circumstances exist:

i) Congress intended for federal law to **occupy the field** (*e.g.*, *Hines v. Davidowitz*, 312 U.S. 52 (1941) (new federal law requiring registration of all aliens preempted preexisting state law requiring registration of aliens within the state));

> Intent to occupy a field can be inferred from a framework of regulation so pervasive that Congress left no room for states to supplement it or when there is a federal interest so dominant that the federal system will be assumed to preclude enforcement of state laws on the same subject. *Rice v. Santa Fe Elevator Corp.*, 331 U.S. 218, (1947). When Congress occupies an entire field, even complementary state regulation is impermissible. Field preemption reflects a congressional decision to foreclose any state regulation in the area, even if it is parallel to federal standards. *Arizona v. U.S.*, 567 U.S. 387 (2012) (even if state may make violation of federal law a crime in some instances, it cannot do so in a field, like alien registration, that has been occupied by federal law).

ii) The state law **directly conflicts** with the federal law by, for example, requiring conduct that is forbidden by the federal law or making it impossible (or nearly so) to comply with both, *e.g., Rose v. Arkansas State Police*, 479 U.S. 1 (1986) (federal law providing that federal death benefits for state law-enforcement officers be in addition to other state benefits preempted contrary state law requiring that other benefits be reduced by the amount of death benefits); or

> **Example 1:** Under 42 U.S.C. § 1983, all persons who violate federal rights while acting under color of state law may be sued for damages. A state law shielding state corrections officers from liability under § 1983 by excluding claims brought against them from being heard in state court violated the Supremacy Clause. *Haywood v. Drown*, 556 U.S. 729 (2009).
>
> **Example 2:** Although a federal statute provides for preemption of state tort claims with regard to medical devices approved by the Federal Drug Administration, 21 U.S.C. § 360(k), there is no express preemption with regard to prescription drugs. However, a state-imposed duty on generic drug manufacturers to warn users of dangers through labeling was preempted by an FDA rule that required the label on generic drugs to match the label of the corresponding brand name drug. The court found that it was impossible for the generic drug manufacturers to comply with both federal regulations and state law. *PLIVA, Inc. v. Mensing*, 564 U.S. 604 (2011).
>
> **Compare:** The manufacturer of a brand-name drug failed to establish preemption of a state-law duty to warn when the manufacturer was permitted under FDA regulations to change the drug label and then request FDA approval for the change. *Wyeth v. Levine, supra.*

iii) The state law **indirectly conflicts** with federal law by creating an obstacle to or frustrating the accomplishment of that law's purpose, e.g., *Perez v. Campbell*, 402 U.S. 637 (1971) (state law suspending licenses of all drivers with unpaid accident judgments frustrates the purpose of federal bankruptcy laws to provide a fresh start).

The existence of a valid purpose for a state law does not prevent federal preemption. *Id.*

2. Absence of Preemption

If federal law does not preempt state law, a state is free to enact legislation regarding the same issue. *Colorado Anti-Discrimination Comm'n. v. Continental Air Lines, Inc.*, 372 U.S. 714 (1963) (state statute prohibiting racial discrimination valid despite the existence of identical federal law). If there has not been federal preemption in a given area, a state is free to set more stringent standards than those imposed by the federal government. In addition, a state may recognize individual rights that exceed those granted by the federal constitution or federal statutes. *Pruneyard Shopping Ctr. v. Robbins*, 447 U.S. 74 (1980) (California's constitutional grant of greater free speech rights than the federal constitution confers upheld).

> **EXAM NOTE:** Under the Supremacy Clause, federal law sets a **floor** below which state law generally cannot go, but it does **not** set a **ceiling** beyond which state law cannot go.

IX. RELATIONS AMONG STATES

A. INTERSTATE COMPACTS

An interstate compact is an agreement, similar to a treaty or a contract, between two or more states. Article I, Section 10, Clause 3 (the "Interstate Compact Clause") allows states to enter into such agreements only with the consent of Congress. However, the only agreements that qualify as "compacts" requiring the consent of Congress are those that either affect a power delegated to the federal government or alter the political balance within the federal system.

B. FULL FAITH AND CREDIT

The Full Faith and Credit Clause of Article IV, Section 1 provides that "[f]ull faith and credit shall be given in each state to the public acts, records, and judicial proceedings of every other state."

1. Judgments

Full faith and credit requires that out-of-state **judgments** be given in-state effect. *Baker v. General Motors Corp.*, 522 U.S. 222 (1998). However, to be given full faith and credit, a decision must meet three requirements:

i) The court that rendered the judgment must have had **jurisdiction** over the parties and the subject matter;

ii) The judgment must have been **on the merits** rather than on a procedural issue; and

iii) The judgment must be **final**.

2. Laws (Public Acts)

The Full Faith and Credit Clause is "less demanding" with respect to choice of law (i.e., which state's law should apply in a situation when either might). *Id.*

PART THREE: INDIVIDUAL RIGHTS

X. STATE ACTION

The Constitution generally protects against wrongful conduct by the government, not private parties (with the exception of the Thirteenth Amendment's prohibition against slavery, which applies to private and government action). In other words, state action is a necessary prerequisite to triggering constitutional protections. A private person's conduct must constitute state action in order for these protections to apply. For example, state action may exist in cases of private parties carrying out traditional governmental functions or significant state involvement in the activities.

A. TRADITIONAL GOVERNMENTAL FUNCTION

State action is found when a private person carries on activities that are **traditionally performed exclusively by the state,** such as running primary elections or governing a "company town." *Terry v. Adams*, 345 U.S. 461 (1953); *Marsh v. Alabama*, 326 U.S. 501 (1946). By contrast, a shopping center that is open to the public does not thereby assume or exercise municipal functions, and therefore is not treated as a state actor. *Hudgens v. NLRB*, 424 U.S. 507 (1976) (shopping mall not required to permit picketing on its private sidewalks). Similarly, merely providing a product or service that the government **could** offer is not sufficient to make the provider a state actor. *Flagg Brothers v. Brooks*, 436 U.S. 149 (1978) (statutorily sanctioned but not compelled sale of goods by bailee not state action). However, the use of peremptory challenges, even by private litigants, constitutes state action because the selection of jurors is a traditional state function and because the judge (i.e., the government) plays a significant role in the process. *Edmonson v. Leesville Concrete*, 500 U.S. 614 (1992).

B. SIGNIFICANT STATE INVOLVEMENT

State action may exist if there are sufficient mutual contacts between the conduct of a private party and the government to find that the government is so pervasively entwined with the private entity that constitutional standards should apply to the private actor. *Brentwood Acad. v. Tenn. Secondary Sch. Ath. Ass'n*, 531 U.S. 288 (2001) (athletic association was a federal actor because the association was pervasively entwined with government policies and was managed and controlled by government officials in their government capacity). State action also exists if the actions of a private party and the government are so intertwined that a mutual benefit results, such as if the parties are involved in a joint venture. *Lugar v. Edmondson Oil Co.,* 457 U.S. 922 (1982) (state action was present when a clerk and sheriff acted together with a private citizen to obtain attachment against a property of the debtor). Similarly, when the government creates a corporation by special law for the furtherance of governmental objectives and retains permanent authority to appoint a majority of the directors of that corporation, the corporation is part of the government for the purposes of the First Amendment even if the enabling statute explicitly states that the corporation is a private entity. *Lebron v. Nat'l R.R. Passenger Corp.*, 513 U.S. 374 (1995).

The Supreme Court has not laid out a test to determine what constitutes significant state involvement, but some general guidelines exist. Mere licensing or regulation of a private party does not constitute state action; the state must **act affirmatively** to facilitate, encourage, or authorize the activity. *Moose Lodge No. 107 v. Irvis*, 407 U.S. 163 (1972). Even when the state explicitly prohibits behavior that violates a person's civil rights, state action may exist if it appears the state has sanctioned the violative act.

> States are constitutionally forbidden from facilitating or authorizing discrimination, but they are not required to make discrimination illegal.

C. INSIGNIFICANT STATE INVOLVEMENT

Businesses that the government substantially regulates or to which the government grants a monopoly, such as utility companies, do not exercise state action. Further exclusions include nursing homes that accept Medicaid, schools that receive government funds but are operated by a private corporation, and congressional grants of a corporate charter.

XI. PROCEDURAL DUE PROCESS

The Due Process Clause of the **Fifth Amendment,** which applies against the **federal government,** provides that "[n]o person shall be ... deprived of life, liberty, or property, without due process of law."

The Due Process Clause of the **Fourteenth Amendment,** which applies against the **states,** provides that "no state shall make or enforce any law which shall ... deprive any person of life, liberty, or property, without due process of the law."

A. DUE PROCESS GENERALLY

These clauses operate at a number of levels to protect the rights of individuals and other "persons"—e.g., corporations—against the government. At the most basic level, each clause ensures that the federal and state governments must follow certain procedures before depriving any person of "life, liberty, or property." These safeguards, like notice and a hearing, are the cornerstone of **procedural due process.**

At another level, the Fourteenth Amendment, through its guarantee of rights respecting life, liberty, and property, has been interpreted to make **most provisions of the Bill of Rights** (which by its terms applies to the federal government) **applicable against the states as well.** That is, the Fourteenth Amendment Due Process Clause **incorporates** the protections of the First, Second, and Fourth Amendments, as well as most of the protections of the Fifth, Sixth, and Eighth Amendments. (However, the Fifth Amendment right to grand jury indictment and the Sixth Amendment right to a unanimous jury verdict in a criminal trial are not incorporated. While the Eighth Amendment protections against cruel and unusual punishment and excessive bail are incorporated, it has not been determined whether the Eighth Amendment protection against excessive fines is incorporated.) The Seventh Amendment right to a jury in civil trials has been held not applicable to the states.

Finally, both Due Process Clauses contain a "substantive" component that guarantees certain fundamental rights to all persons. This **substantive due process** acts as something of a catchall for rights not explicitly set forth elsewhere in the Constitution.

B. PROCEDURAL DUE PROCESS APPLIED

1. General Principles

The concept of "fundamental fairness" is at the heart of the right to procedural due process. It includes an individual's right to be **notified** of charges or proceedings against him and the opportunity to be **heard** at those proceedings. When one's liberty or property interests are adversely affected by governmental action, two questions are asked:

i) Is the threatened interest a **protected** one?

ii) If so, **what process** is due?

a. Neutral decision maker

Due process entitles a person to a fair decision maker. A judge must recuse herself when she has a direct, personal, substantial, pecuniary interest in a case (i.e., actual bias) or there is a serious objective risk of actual bias. In the latter instance, proof of actual bias is not required, and subjective impartiality is not sufficient to justify a refusal to recuse. *Caperton v. A. T. Massey Coal Co.*, 556 U.S. 868 (2009).

> **Example:** An attorney running for a judgeship on the state supreme court had received a $3 million contribution that had a significant and disproportionate influence on the electoral outcome. The contribution exceeded the sum total of all other contributions the attorney had received and exceeded by 50% the combined amount spent by the attorney's and his opponent's campaigns. The contribution was made by the president of a company that had received an adverse $50 million verdict in a lower court of the state prior to the election. It was foreseeable that the judgment would be appealed to the state supreme court at the time that the contribution was made. Consequently, the Due Process Clause required the judge who had received the contribution to recuse himself. *Caperton v. A. T. Massey Coal Co., supra.*

b. Intentional conduct

Due process addresses injury that results from an intentional governmental act. Mere negligent conduct by a government employee does not trigger a due process right. *Daniels v. Williams*, 474 U.S. 327 (1986) (prisoner's injury due to correction officer's negligence was not a deprivation of liberty).

2. Protected Interests

a. Liberty

An impingement on liberty is generally construed to mean **significant** governmental restraint on one's **physical freedom,** exercise of **fundamental rights** (i.e., those guaranteed by the Constitution), or **freedom of choice or action.**

Examples of loss of liberty include commitment to a mental institution, parole revocation, and loss of parental rights. Injury to reputation alone is not a deprivation of liberty, unless the injury is so great that the individual has lost **significant employment or associational rights.**

b. Property

A cognizable property interest involves more than an abstract need or desire; there must be a "legitimate claim of entitlement" by virtue of statute, employment contract, or custom. *Board of Regents v. Roth*, 408 U.S. 564, 577 (1972) (non-tenured professor with a one-year contract had no liberty or property interest in being rehired).

The rights to government-issued licenses and continued welfare and disability benefits are legitimate property interests. For example, although a patient may have a legitimate property interest in the continued receipt of medical benefits to pay for the patient's stay in a qualified nursing home, there is no legitimate property interest in the patient's continued residence in the nursing home of the patient's choice. As a result, a patient is not entitled to a hearing before the government disqualifies a nursing home from participating in a public benefits program. *O'Bannon v. Town Court Nursing Ctr.*, 447 U.S. 773 (1980).

1) Public employment

There is a legitimate property interest in continued public employment only if there is an employment contract or a clear understanding that the employee may be fired only for cause. *Arnett v. Kennedy*, 416 U.S. 134 (1974). An "at will" governmental employee has no right to continued employment. *Bishop v. Wood*, 426 U.S. 341 (1976). If, however, the government gives the "at will" public employee assurances of continual employment or dismissal for only specified reasons, then there must be a fair procedure to protect the employee's interests if the government seeks to discharge the employee from his position. Such entitlement to procedural due process can also result from statutory law, formal contract terms, or the actions of a supervisory person with authority to establish terms of employment.

Note, though, that even those employees who lack any entitlement to continued employment cannot be discharged for reasons that in and of themselves violate the Constitution. Thus, an "at-will" governmental employee cannot be fired for having engaged in speech protected by the First Amendment. *Board of Regents v. Roth*, 408 U.S. 564 (1972). Similarly, discharge of an "at-will" governmental employee because of the employee's political views or affiliations would violate the employee's right to freedom of expression and association, unless it can be demonstrated that effective performance of the employee's job requires certain political views or affiliations. *Branti v. Finkel*, 445 U.S. 507 (1980). To be entitled to a hearing, however, the employee must make a prima facie claim that she is being discharged for reasons that violate specific constitutional guarantees. *Mt. Healthy City School Dist. Bd. of Educ. v. Doyle*, 429 U.S. 274 (1977). A dismissal will be upheld if the government can prove that the employee would have been discharged in any event for reasons unrelated to any constitutionally protected activities.

2) Public education

There is a property right to a public education. *Goss v. Lopez*, 419 U.S. 565 (1975). Although such a right is not specifically recognized by the Constitution, all states recognize the right to a public education. *See, e.g., Serrano v. Priest*, 487 P.2d 1241 (Cal. 1971); Tex. Const. art. VII. § 1. However, the Supreme Court has never determined whether a student at a public institution of higher learning has a property (or liberty) interest in her education there. *Board of Curators of University of Missouri v. Horowitz*, 435 U.S. 78 (1978) (Supreme Court assumed without deciding that a medical student had a liberty or property interest; federal appellate court had found that the student had a liberty interest); *See Regents of University of Michigan v. Ewing*, 474 U.S. 214 (1985) (Supreme Court assumed without deciding that a medical student had a liberty or property interest; federal appellate court had found that the student had a property interest).

3. Notice and Hearing

If an individual's protected interest is threatened by governmental action, the next step is to determine what type of process is due. The Court considers three factors in determining the amount of process that is due:

i)   The **private interest** affected by the governmental action;

ii) The risk of erroneous deprivation of that interest using current procedures and the probable **value of additional or substitute safeguards**; and

iii) The **burden (fiscal and administrative cost)** involved in providing the additional process.

Mathews v. Eldridge, 424 U.S. 319 (1976). The greater the importance of the threatened interest, the greater the likelihood that the Court will require extensive procedural safeguards prior to the termination of the interest.

Generally, the person whose interest is being deprived is entitled to **notice** of the government's action by an unbiased decision maker and an **opportunity to be heard,** although the hearing need not necessarily occur before the termination of the interest.

Example: While the state must give notice and hold a hearing prior to terminating **welfare benefits,** in cases of terminating **disability benefits or public employment,** the state must give prior notice, but only a post-termination evidentiary hearing is required. *Goldberg v. Kelly,* 397 U.S. 254 (1970), *Mathews v. Eldridge, supra.*

a. Enemy combatants

United States citizens held as enemy combatants are entitled to meaningful opportunity to dispute the facts of their detention by a neutral decision maker, albeit the opportunity is adapted to reduce burdens on executive authority brought on by an ongoing military conflict. *Boumediene v. Bush,* 553 U.S. 723, (2008).

b. Parental status

Different burdens of proof are applied to termination of parental rights and paternity actions. Because termination of parental rights deprives parents of a fundamental right, the state must use clear and convincing evidence to support allegations of neglect. *Santosky v. Kramer,* 455 U.S. 745 (1982).

When a mother or child is initiating a paternity suit, due process requires proof by only a preponderance of evidence. *Rivera v. Michigan,* 483 U.S. 574 (1987). In a paternity action initiated by the state, the state must pay for the necessary blood work used in determining paternity. *Little v. Streater,* 452 U.S. 1 (1981).

c. Forfeitures

Forfeiture is an involuntary relinquishment of property that the government alleges is connected to criminal activity. Generally, the government is required to provide the owner with notice and a hearing prior to seizure of real property. *United States v. James Daniel Good Real Property,* 510 U.S. 43 (1993). However, the government does not need to provide notice prior to the seizure of personal property. *Calero-Toledo v. Pearson Yacht Leasing Co.,* 416 U.S. 663 (1974).

d. Public employees

A public employee who may be discharged only for cause has a property interest in his job and therefore is entitled to **notice** of termination and a **pre-termination opportunity to respond.** A formal hearing is not required, as long as there is pre-termination notice, an opportunity to respond to the decision maker, and a **post-termination evidentiary hearing.** *Cleveland Bd. of Educ. v. Loudermill,* 470 U.S. 532 (1985). If there is a significant reason for immediately removing a "for-cause" employee from the job, a prompt post-suspension hearing with reinstatement and back pay if the employee prevails constitutes sufficient due process. *Gilbert v. Homar,* 520 U.S. 924 (1997).

e. Public education

1) Academic dismissal

A student is not entitled to a hearing with regard to dismissal from a public institution of higher learning. *Board of Curators of University of Missouri v. Horowitz, supra* (medical school student was fully informed respondent of the faculty's dissatisfaction with her clinical progress and the danger that this posed to timely graduation and continued enrollment); *See also Regents of University of Michigan v. Ewing, supra* (challenge to dismissal of medical student on substantive due process grounds rejected; court refused to override academic decision unless it is such a substantial departure from accepted academic norms as to demonstrate that the person or committee responsible did not actually exercise professional judgment).

2) Disciplinary suspension

When a student is suspended from public school for disciplinary reasons, due process requires that the student be given oral or written notice of the charges against him and, if he denies them, an explanation of the evidence the authorities have and an opportunity to present his side of the story. *Goss v. Lopez, supra*, at 581. However, a student whose presence poses a continuing danger to persons or property or an ongoing threat of disrupting the academic process may be immediately removed from school and the necessary notice and rudimentary hearing should follow as soon as practicable. *Id., at 582-3.*

3) Corporal punishment

While state-sanctioned disciplinary corporal punishment by a public-school authority that results in the restraint of the student and the infliction of appreciable physical pain implicates the student's liberty interests, the student is not entitled to notice or a hearing. If the punishment is excessive, the student could seek damages in a civil action. *Ingraham v. Wright*, 430 U.S. 651 (1977).

f. Government benefits

The state must give notice and hold a hearing *prior to* terminating **welfare benefits**. In cases of terminating **disability benefits,** the state must give prior notice, but only a *post-termination* evidentiary hearing is required. *Goldberg v. Kelly*, 397 U.S. 254 (1970), *Mathews v. Eldridge, supra*.

4. Court Access—Indigents

a. Court fees

The government cannot deny an indigent person access to the court system because of his inability to pay the required court fees, if such imposition of fees acts to deny a fundamental right to the indigent. Due process requires such fees to be waived. Conversely, if the matter does not involve a fundamental right, no waiver is required.

b. Right to counsel

While the Sixth Amendment provides that an indigent defendant has a constitutional right to have counsel appointed in any criminal case, including a non-summary criminal contempt proceeding in which the defendant is sentenced to incarceration (*United States v. Dixon*, 509 U.S. 688 (1993)), there is no similar due process right to have counsel appointed when an indigent defendant is held in contempt in a civil proceeding and incarcerated, but procedures must be in place to ensure a fundamentally fair determination of any critical incarceration-related question (e.g., defendant's ability to comply with order for which the defendant is held in contempt). *Turner v. Rogers*, 564 U.S. 431 (2011) (defendant held in contempt for violation of child support order; the plaintiff, who was the custodial parent seeking enforcement of the child support order, was also not represented by counsel).

XII. SUBSTANTIVE DUE PROCESS

The guarantee of substantive due process is based upon the idea that laws should be reasonable and not arbitrary.

A. STANDARD OF REVIEW

The standard of review in substantive due process cases is generally twofold: a governmental action that infringes upon a **fundamental right** is generally subject to **strict scrutiny.** If the interest infringed upon is not fundamental, then there need be only a **rational basis** for the regulation.

1. Strict Scrutiny

a. Test

The law must be the **least restrictive** means to achieve a **compelling** governmental interest.

1) Least restrictive means

For the law to be the least restrictive means to achieve the government's interest, there cannot be a way to achieve the same interest that is less restrictive of the right at issue. A law will not fail simply because there are other methods of achieving the goal that are equally or more restrictive.

Under strict scrutiny, the law should be neither over-inclusive (reaching more people or conduct than is necessary) nor under-inclusive (not reaching all of the people or conduct intended).

2) Compelling interest

Although there is no precise definition of what is "compelling," it is generally understood to be something that is necessary or crucial, such as national security or preserving public health or safety.

3) Strict in theory, fatal in fact

The strict scrutiny standard is very difficult to meet. The great majority of laws reviewed under strict scrutiny are struck down.

b. Burden of proof

The burden is on the government to prove that the law is necessary to achieve a compelling governmental interest.

c. Applicability

The strict scrutiny test is generally applied if a **fundamental right** is involved.

2. Rational Basis

a. Test

A law meets the rational basis standard of review if it is **rationally related** to a **legitimate** state interest. This is a test of minimal scrutiny and generally results in the law being upheld.

b. Burden of proof

Laws are presumed valid under this standard, so the burden is on the challenger to overcome this presumption by establishing that the law is **arbitrary or irrational.**

In court, the government's stated interest in enacting the law need not be one that it offered when the law was passed. Any legitimate reason will suffice.

> This factor distinguishes rational basis review from strict scrutiny, when the government must defend the interest that it stated at the outset.

c. Applicability

The rational basis standard is used in all cases to which strict scrutiny or intermediate scrutiny does not apply. *Heller v. Doe*, 509 U.S. 312 (1993). In practice, most legislation related to lifestyle, taxation, zoning, and punitive damages is reviewed under this standard.

Although punitive damages do not violate due process, excessive damages may. The court considers whether the defendant had fair notice of the possible magnitude before it will bar a punitive-damages award.

The government cannot presume facts about an individual that will deprive that individual of certain benefits or rights. By doing so, the government creates an arbitrary classification that may violate due process as well as equal protection.

1) Retroactive legislation

The retroactive application of a statute does not in and of itself violate substantive due process. Consequently, a law that is applied retroactively must merely meet the rational basis test. *United States v. Carlton*, 512 U.S. 26 (1994) (retroactive application of estate tax law that resulted in denial of a deduction upheld). Similar treatment applies to a statutory change that is remedial in nature (i.e., affects a remedy but does not create or abolish a right). *Chase Securities Corp. v. Donaldson*, 325 U.S. 304 (1945) (lengthening of statute of limitations that permitted an otherwise time-barred lawsuit to be maintained upheld). Note, however, that the extension of a criminal statute of limitations may violate the prohibition on an ex post facto law (*see* § XVI.B. Ex Post Facto Laws, *infra*).

B. FUNDAMENTAL RIGHTS

Some rights are so deeply rooted in our nation's tradition and history that they are considered fundamental. These rights include: (i) the right to travel; (ii) the right to vote; and (iii) the right to privacy (including marriage, sexual relations, abortion, child rearing, and the right of related persons to live together). Under **strict scrutiny,** a law interfering with the fundamental rights of travel and privacy will generally be upheld only if it is **necessary** to achieve a **compelling governmental interest.** With regard to the fundamental right to vote, the level of scrutiny can depend on the degree to which this right is restricted.

Government infringement upon **nonfundamental rights**—those related to social or economic interests such as business, taxation, lifestyle, or zoning—requires only a **rational relationship** between the law and a **legitimate governmental interest.**

> EXAM NOTE: If, on a question, a fundamental right is being infringed upon for all persons, the issue is likely one of substantive due process. If the right is being denied to only a particular class of persons, then equal protection is in play.

1. Travel

a. Interstate

There is a fundamental right to travel from state to state. *Shapiro v. Thompson*, 394 U.S. 618 (1969). This includes the right to enter one state and leave another, to be treated as a welcome visitor, and, for those who wish to become permanent residents, the right to be treated equally to native-born citizens with respect to state benefits. *Saenz v. Roe*, 526 U.S. 489 (1999) (state statute denying full welfare benefits to people who had not resided in the state for one year struck down; state's interests in discouraging fraud and establishing an objective residency test were not compelling). Reasonable residency restrictions may be imposed on the receipt of government benefits (i.e., in-state tuition); however, once a person qualifies as a resident, she must be treated equally. *Zobel v. Williams*, 457 U.S. 55 (1982) (division of state royalties from minerals and oil based on length of state residency unconstitutional).

b. International

Although there is a right to travel internationally, it is not a fundamental right invoking strict scrutiny. Hence, the U.S. government may limit travel to certain countries as long as it has a rational basis for doing so. *Regan v. Wald*, 468 U.S. 222 (1984).

2. Voting and Ballot Access

a. Right to vote

Under the Twenty-Sixth Amendment, the right to vote is fundamental to all U.S. citizens who are 18 years of age or older. This right applies to all federal, state, and local elections, including primary elections. Despite being a fundamental right, strict scrutiny does not apply to all laws that restrict this right. The level of scrutiny to which a governmental restriction of this right is subject depends on the degree to which the restriction affects the exercise of this right; the more significant the impact, the greater the degree of scrutiny. *Burdick v. Takushi*, 504 U.S. 428 (1992); *Crawford v. Marion County Election Bd.*, 553 U.S. 181 (2008).

1) Residency

A restriction on the right to participate in the political process of a governmental unit imposed upon those who reside within its borders is typically upheld as justified on a rational basis; nonresidents generally may be prohibited from voting. *Holt Civic Club v. City of Tuscaloosa*, 439 U.S. 60 (1978) (citizens who lived outside city boundaries could be denied the right to vote in city elections, even though they were subject to business licensing fees imposed by the city).

A person must be given the opportunity to prove residency before being denied the right to vote because of lack of residency. *Carrington v. Rash*, 380 U.S. 89 (1965).

a) Length of residency

A person may be required to be a resident of a governmental unit (e.g., state, city) for a short period prior to an election in order to vote in that election. *Marston v. Lewis*, 410 U.S. 679 (1973) (50-day period upheld); *Dunn v. Blumstein*, 405 U.S. 330 (1972) (three-month and one-year periods struck down).

b) Presidential elections

Congress can supersede state residency requirements with respect to presidential elections. *Oregon v. Mitchell*, 400 U.S. 112 (1970).

2) Property ownership

Generally, property ownership is not a valid ground upon which to restrict the right to vote. *Kramer v. Union Free School District No. 15*, 395 U.S. 621 (1969) (restriction of the right to vote on school board members to property owners or parents of school-age children struck down). A limited exception exists for elections involving special-purpose entities, such as a water-storage district. *Ball v. James*, 451 U.S. 355 (1981).

3) Poll tax

Payment of a fee in order to vote (i.e., a poll tax) in an election for federal office is prohibited by the Twenty-Fourth Amendment. More broadly, the imposition of a poll tax in order to vote in any election violates the Equal Protection Clause, as a poll tax is unrelated to voter qualifications. *Harper v. Virginia Bd. of Elections*, 383 U.S. 663 (1966).

4) Voter ID

A state may require that a citizen who votes in person present a government-issued photo ID. With regard to this neutral, nondiscriminatory requirement, the Supreme Court declined to apply a strict scrutiny standard. *Crawford v. Marion County Election Bd., supra*.

5) Felon

Pursuant to Section 2 of the Fourteenth Amendment, a state may prohibit a felon from voting, even one who has unconditionally been released from prison. *Richardson v. Ramirez*, 418 U.S. 24 (1974).

6) Write-in voting

A person's right to vote does not extend to the right to vote for any possible candidate. A state may ban all write-in candidates in both primary and general elections, at least when the state provides reasonable means by which a candidate can get on the ballot. *Burdick v. Takushi*, 504 U.S. 428 (1992) (state's legitimate interests, such as preventing unrestrained factionalism, outweighed the limited burdens placed on the right to vote by the ban).

b. Public office and ballot access

There is no fundamental right to hold office through election or appointment, but all persons do have a constitutional right to be considered for office without the burden of invidious discrimination. *Turner v. Fouche*, 396 U.S. 346 (1970).

1) Property ownership

The ownership of property cannot be made a condition of holding public office. *Turner v. Fouche, supra* (appointment to local school board).

2) Filing fee

A candidate for elected public office generally may be required to pay a reasonable filing fee, but an exorbitant filing fee, such as one that imposes the entire cost of the election on the candidates, is unconstitutional. Moreover, alternative provisions must be made for a candidate who is unable to pay the fee. *Lubin v. Parish*, 415 U.S. 709 (1974); *Bullock v. Carter*, 405 U.S. 134 (1972).

3) Public support requirements

An independent candidate for elected public office can be required to obtain the signatures of voters on a petition in order to appear on the ballot, but such a requirement cannot deny independent candidates ballot access. *Jenness v. Fortson*, 403 U.S. 431 (1971) (state requirement that an independent candidate obtain five percent of the number of registered voters at the last general election for the office in question upheld). State election laws imposing undue burdens on placing new or small parties on the state ballots must serve a compelling state interest in the regulation of a subject within the state's constitutional power. *Williams v. Rhodes*, 393 U.S. 23 (1968) (state election scheme that effectively prohibited independent candidacies in such a way as to exclude virtually all but the two major parties struck down). Unless the requirement imposes such undue burdens on minority groups, a state can deny a candidate access to the general-election ballot if the candidate failed to receive a sufficient number of votes in the primary election. *Munro v. Socialist Workers Party*, 479 U.S. 189 (1986) (minor party senatorial candidate who failed to receive one percent of the votes cast in primary election not entitled to appear on the general ballot).

4) Write-in candidates

A state may ban all write-in candidates in both primary and general elections, at least when the state provides other reasonable means by which a candidate can get on the ballot. *Burdick v. Takushi, supra*.

5) Candidate for other office

A state may prohibit a state office holder from becoming a candidate for another state office; the office holder must resign his current office in order to run for another office. *Clements v. Fashing*, 457 U.S. 957 (1982).

6) Replacement of elected official

A state may permit a political party to name a replacement for an elected public official from that party who dies or resigns while in office. *Rodriguez v. Popular Democratic Party*, 457 U.S. 1 (1982). The governor must call an election to fill a vacant congressional seat. Article I, Section 2 (House member); Seventeenth Amendment (Senator). (Note: The Seventeenth Amendment permits the state legislature to authorize the governor to appoint a temporary replacement senator.)

3. Privacy

Though it has not found that a generalized right to privacy is contained in the Constitution, the Supreme Court has recognized guaranteed "zones of privacy" under the Constitution. *See Roe v. Wade*, 410 U.S. 113 (1973). Various privacy rights have been deemed fundamental.

a. Marriage

The right to marry is fundamental. *Obergefell v. Hodges*, 576 U.S. ___, 135 S. Ct. 2584 (2015) (same-sex couples); *Loving v. Virginia*, 388 U.S. 1 (1967) (interracial couples); *Turner v. Safley*, 482 U. S. 78 (1987) (prisoners); *Zablocki v. Redhail*, 434 U.S. 374 (1978) (fathers delinquent in child-support payments).

b. Contraception

Married persons have the right to use contraceptives, *Griswold v. Connecticut*, 381 U.S. 479 (1965), as do unmarried persons, *Eisenstadt v. Baird*, 405 U.S. 438

(1972). A state may not limit the sale of contraceptives to dispensation only by pharmacists or only to individuals older than age 16. *Carey v. Population Services International*, 431 U.S. 678 (1977).

c. Intimate sexual behavior

There is no legitimate state interest in making it a crime for fully consenting adults to engage in private sexual conduct—including homosexual conduct—that is not commercial in nature. *Lawrence v. Texas*, 539 U.S. 558 (2003).

d. Abortion

The landmark case of *Roe v. Wade*, 410 U.S. 113 (1973), established the principle that a woman has a fundamental right to an abortion. The Court acknowledged that this privacy right must be considered along with the state's compelling interests in protecting both the health of the pregnant woman and the potential life of the fetus. The resulting rule allowed for varying degrees of state restriction based on the trimester of the pregnancy. The decades since *Roe* have resulted in numerous, often conflicting, judicial opinions on the subject. The current standard is the "undue burden" test, the meaning of which depends on whether the fetus is viable (likely to survive outside the womb).

1) Pre-viability

An undue burden exists when the purpose or effect of a state law places **substantial obstacles** in the way of a woman's right to seek an abortion before the fetus attains viability. *Planned Parenthood of Southeastern Pennsylvania v. Casey*, 505 U.S. 833 (1992).

The following requirements have been held **not** to impose an undue burden:

i) A requirement that only a licensed physician may perform an abortion;

ii) A requirement that the physician must provide the woman with truthful information about the nature of the abortion procedure, the associated health risks, and the probable gestational age of the fetus;

iii) A requirement that a woman must wait 24 hours after giving informed consent before the abortion is performed;

iv) A requirement that a minor obtain her parents' consent, or if consent is not required, provide the parents with notice of the abortion. However, this consent requirement has been found to be an undue burden unless, at least for mature minors, the consent requirement can be judicially bypassed. *Planned Parenthood Association of Kansas City Missouri Inc. v. Ashcroft*, 462 U.S. 476 (1983).

v) A ban on a particular uncommon abortion technique, *Gonzales v. Carhart*, 550 U.S. 124 (2007). The Court found that the State may use its regulatory power to bar certain procedures and substitute others if it has a rational basis to act and it does not impose an undue burden.

An undue burden has been found when a state requires a woman to notify her husband before having an abortion, even when the requirement provides exceptions to the rule. *Planned Parenthood v. Casey*, 505 U.S. 833, 887 (1992) (spousal notification imposed an undue burden, even when the requirement could be bypassed with the woman's signed statement certifying that a statutory exception applied).

2) Post-viability

Once the fetus reaches viability, the state may regulate, and even prohibit, abortion, as long as there is an exception to preserve the health or life of the mother. In other words, at the point of viability, the state's interest in protecting fetal life may supersede a woman's right to choose; because the state's interest in protecting fetal life cannot supersede its interest in protecting a woman's health, however, there must be an exception for the woman's health.

3) Government funding

There is no constitutional right to have the government provide indigent women with funding for an abortion or for medical care related to an abortion, even if the government does provide indigent funding for medical care at childbirth. *Maher v. Roe*, 432 U.S. 464 (1977). Furthermore, a state may prohibit all use of public facilities and public employees in performing abortions. *Webster v. Reproductive Health Services*, 492 U.S. 490 (1989).

e. Parental rights

The fundamental parental right to make decisions regarding the care, custody, and control of one's children includes the right to privately educate one's child outside the public school system subject to reasonable educational standards imposed by the state, *Pierce v. Society of Sisters*, 268 U.S. 510 (1925), *Wisconsin v. Yoder*, 406 U.S. 205 (1972), and to limit visitation of grandparents, *Troxel v. Granville*, 530 U.S. 57 (2000).

f. Family relations

Related persons, including extended family members, have a fundamental right to live together in a single household. *Moore v. City of East Cleveland*, 431 U.S. 494 (1977).

g. Obscene material

There is a fundamental right to possess obscene material in the privacy of one's home, *Stanley v. Georgia*, 394 U.S. 557 (1969), with the exception of child pornography, *Osborne v. Ohio*, 495 U.S. 103 (1990). The state, however, may severely restrict the sale, purchase, receipt, transport, and distribution of obscene material. *Paris Adult Theater v. Slaton*, 413 U.S. 49 (1973).

h. Right to refuse medical treatment

It is an established liberty interest that a person may not be forced to undergo unwanted medical procedures, including lifesaving measures, but the Court has not ruled on whether this right is "fundamental." *Cruzan v. Missouri Department of Health*, 497 U.S. 261 (1990).

There is no fundamental right to commit suicide; therefore, the state may ban the assistance of suicide. *Washington v. Glucksberg*, 521 U.S. 702 (1997). The Court distinguished this decision from *Cruzan* by stating that forced medication is a battery, and there is a long tradition of protecting the decision to refuse unwanted medical treatment.

i. Right to avoid disclosure of personal medical information

Numerous courts include personal medical information within a "zone of privacy." *See, e.g., Doe v. Attorney General of the United States*, 941 F.2d 780 (9th Cir. 1991), *United States v. Westinghouse Electric Corp.*, 638 F.2d 570 (3rd Cir. 1980).

Though the right to protect personal, confidential information is not absolute, courts weigh it against competing interests, employing a balancing test that generally includes consideration of the government's need for access to the information and the adequacy of safeguards, as well as the type and substance of the requested records and the potential for harm in non-consensual disclosure. *See C.N. v. Ridgewood Board of Education*, 430 F.3d 159, 178 (3rd Cir.2005).

4. The Second Amendment

The Second Amendment guarantees **an individual's right to possess a firearm** unconnected with service in a militia and to use that firearm for traditionally lawful purposes, such as self-defense within the home. *District of Columbia v. Heller*, 554 U.S. 570 (2008) (ban on handgun possession in the home violates Second Amendment). As mentioned previously, the Second Amendment is applicable to the states through the Fourteenth Amendment. *McDonald v. Chicago*, 561 U.S. 3025 (2010).

Like most rights, the Second Amendment right to bear arms is not unlimited. Examples of lawful regulations include imposing conditions and qualifications on the commercial sale of arms, as well as prohibitions on (i) concealed weapons, (ii) possession of firearms by felons and the mentally ill, and (iii) carrying guns in schools, government buildings, and other sensitive places are presumed to be legitimate. *District of Columbia v. Heller, supra.*

XIII. EQUAL PROTECTION

A. GENERAL CONSIDERATIONS

1. Constitutional Basis

a. State action

The Equal Protection Clause of the Fourteenth Amendment provides that "no state shall ... deny to any person within its jurisdiction the equal protection of the laws." This clause applies only to states and localities.

b. Federal action

Although there is no federal equal protection clause, the Supreme Court has held that the Fifth Amendment Due Process Clause includes the rights guaranteed by the Equal Protection Clause, thereby making discrimination by the federal government subject to review under the same standards as discrimination by the states. *Bolling v. Sharpe*, 347 U.S. 497 (1954).

2. Standards of Review

When reviewing government action under equal-protection theories, the Court applies one of three levels of review, depending on the classification of persons or the type of right concerned.

a. Strict scrutiny

1) Test

The law must be the **least restrictive** means to achieve a **compelling** governmental interest.

2) Burden of proof

The burden is on the government to prove that the law is necessary. Because the strict scrutiny test is a very difficult one to pass, the government rarely meets its burden, and most laws subjected to this standard of review are struck down.

3) Applicability

The strict scrutiny test is applied if a **fundamental right** or a **suspect classification** is involved. The suspect classifications are race, ethnicity, national origin, and, if the classification is by state law, alienage. (*See* § XIII.B., *infra,* for a complete discussion of suspect classifications.)

b. Intermediate scrutiny

1) Test

To be constitutional, the law must be **substantially related** to an **important** governmental interest.

2) Burden of proof

Although the Court has not clearly stated the rule, the burden appears generally to be on the government to prove that the law in question passes intermediate scrutiny. As with strict scrutiny (and unlike rational basis review), the government must defend the interest(s) it stated when the law was enacted, not just some conceivable legitimate interest.

3) Applicability

Intermediate scrutiny is used when a classification is based on **gender** or status as a **nonmarital child** (legitimacy). Note that in gender cases there must be an "exceedingly persuasive justification" for the classification, which may bring the standard in such cases closer to strict scrutiny. *See United States v. Virginia*, 518 U.S. 515 (1996).

c. Rational basis

1) Test

A law passes the rational basis standard of review if it is **rationally related** to a **legitimate** governmental interest. This is a test of minimal scrutiny. It is not required that there is actually a link between the means selected and a legitimate objective. However, the legislature must *reasonably believe* there is a link.

2) Burden of proof

Laws are presumed valid under this standard, so the burden is on the challenger to overcome this presumption by establishing that the law is **arbitrary or irrational.**

3) Applicability

The rational basis standard is used in all cases in which one of the higher standards (intermediate or strict scrutiny) does not apply. Thus, rational basis review applies to laws drawing distinctions based on age, wealth, weight, or most other classifications, as well as to any distinctions drawn for business or economic reasons.

The Court generally gives extreme deference to the legislature's right to define its objectives. In order to determine the legislature's purpose, the Court will look at the statute and the preamble. If the legislative purpose is not clear from the statute, the Court may consider any conceivable purpose that may have motivated the legislature. *U.S. Railroad Retirement Bd. v. Fritz*, 449 U.S. 166 (1980).

> Some classifications, although nominally subject to rational basis review, in practice receive heightened scrutiny. *See e.g., Romer v. Evans*, 517 U.S. 620 (1996) (sexual orientation); *Cleburne v. Cleburne Living Center, Inc.*, 473 U.S. 432 (1985) (developmental disability). When the government has acted out of animus toward or fear of a particular group, that action—even if not involving a suspect or a quasi-suspect classification—will be searchingly reviewed and may be struck down even under a rational basis test. *See e.g., United States v. Windsor*, 570 U.S. ___, 133 S. Ct. 2675 (2013) (Defense of Marriage Act and same-sex marriage).

3. Proving Discrimination

To trigger strict or intermediate scrutiny, there must be **discriminatory intent** on the part of the government. The fact that legislation has a disparate effect on people of different races, genders, etc., without intent, is insufficient. Discriminatory intent can be shown facially, as applied, or when there is a discriminatory motive.

a. Facial discrimination

A law that, by its very language, creates distinctions between classes of persons is discriminatory on its face.

> **Example:** An ordinance states that only males will be considered for a city's training academy for firefighters.

b. Discriminatory application

A law that appears neutral on its face may be applied in a discriminatory fashion. If the challenger can prove that a discriminatory purpose was used when applying the law, then the law will be invalidated.

> **Example:** A city's ordinance concerning the police academy says nothing about gender, but in practice only men are considered for admission.

c. Discriminatory motive

A law that is neutral on its face and in its application may still result in a disparate impact. By itself, however, a disparate impact is not sufficient to trigger strict or intermediate scrutiny; proof of discriminatory motive or intent is required to show a violation of the Equal Protection Clause. *Arlington Heights v. Metropolitan Hous. Dev. Corp.*, 429 U.S. 252 (1977).

> **Example:** A city's paramedic training school is theoretically open to both men and women, but the entrance test includes a height requirement that disproportionately excludes women.

B. SUSPECT CLASSIFICATIONS

Laws that categorize based on race, ethnicity, national origin, or (in some cases) alienage are considered suspect and therefore require closer judicial examination. Such laws are subject to strict scrutiny and are invalid unless they are **necessary** to achieve a **compelling** governmental interest.

1. Race, Ethnicity, and National Origin

Laws or regulations that intentionally disadvantage on the basis of race, ethnicity, or national origin have almost always been struck down for failing to advance a compelling state interest. One exception was *Korematsu v. United States*, 323 U.S. 214 (1944), in which the internment of Japanese-Americans during World War II was upheld in the name of national security.

a. School integration

Because discrimination must be intentional in order to violate the Constitution, only intentional (de jure) segregation in schools violates the Equal Protection Clause. *Keyes v. Sch. Dist. No. 1*, 413 U.S. 189 (1973). Moreover, a court cannot impose a remedy that involves multiple school districts unless there is evidence of intentional segregation in each district. *Milliken v. Bradley*, 418 U.S. 717 (1974); *Missouri v. Jenkins*, 515 U.S. 70 (1995) (state not compelled to create magnet schools in order to attract students from outside the district).

If a school board does not take steps to eliminate intentional racial segregation of schools, a court can order the district to implement measures, such as busing, to remedy the discrimination. Court-ordered busing is temporary, however, and must be terminated once the "vestiges of past discrimination" have been eliminated. *Bd. of Educ. v. Dowell*, 498 U.S. 237 (1991).

b. Affirmative action

Programs that favor racial or ethnic minorities are also subject to strict scrutiny. *Adarand Constructors, Inc. v. Pena*, 515 U.S. 200 (1995) (overruling application of the intermediate standard to federal discrimination).

1) Past discrimination by government

For a governmental affirmative action program based on race to survive, the relevant governmental entity must show more than a history of societal discrimination. The government—whether federal, state, or local—must itself be guilty of specific past discrimination against the group it is seeking to favor, and the remedy must be narrowly tailored to end that discrimination and eliminate its effects. In other words, the elimination of past discrimination in a particular governmental institution is a compelling state interest; attempting to remedy general societal injustice through affirmative action is not.

2) Diversity in public universities and colleges

Race may be used as a "plus factor" (i.e., one of a range of factors to consider) in determining whether a student should be admitted to a public college or university, as there is a compelling interest in obtaining the educational benefits of a diverse student body. The use of racial quotas or of race as a determinative criterion, however, violates equal protection and is unconstitutional. *Grutter v. Bollinger*, 539 U.S. 306 (2003); *Gratz v. Bollinger*, 539 U.S. 244 (2003); *Regents of University of California v. Bakke*, 438 U.S. 265 (1978). Race may not be considered unless the admissions process used to achieve a diverse student body can withstand strict scrutiny. Strict scrutiny here requires the university to clearly demonstrate that its purpose or interest is both constitutionally permissible and substantial, and that its use of the classification is **necessary** to the accomplishment of its purpose. *Fisher v. Univ. of Texas*, 570 U.S. ___, 133 S. Ct. 2411 (2013). Further, a university must regularly evaluate available data and "tailor its approach in light of changing circumstances, ensuring that race plays no greater role than is necessary to meet its compelling interest." *Fisher v. Univ. of Texas*, 579 U.S. ___, 136 S. Ct. 2198 (2016).

State laws that commit policy determinations regarding racial preferences to the voters (e.g., ballot issues) do not violate equal protection. Courts may not disempower the voters from choosing whether race-based preferences should be adopted, continued, or ended. The privilege to enact laws is a basic exercise of voters' democratic power. The constitutional validity of the choices made is a separate question. *Schuette v. Coalition to Defend Affirmative Action*, 572 U.S. ___, 134 S. Ct. 1623 (2014) (upholding amendment to Michigan's constitution prohibiting state universities from considering race as part of the admission process).

3) Diversity in public elementary and high schools

A school district may not assign students to schools on the basis of race unless it is necessary to accomplish a compelling interest—e.g., remedy past discrimination. However, a district may use facially race-neutral criteria that may have the same effect, such as strategic site selection for new schools or the redrawing of attendance zones. *Parents Involved in Community Schools v. Seattle School Dist. No. 1*, 551 U.S. 701 (2007).

The Equal Protection Clause applies only to governmental action, so private persons generally are not restricted by it (*see* X. State Action, *supra*). Discrimination by private persons in various areas, such as employment, housing, and public accommodations, is nonetheless regulated by federal statute pursuant to Congress's power under the enabling clauses of the Thirteenth and Fourteenth Amendments and the Commerce Clause, as well as in most states by statute.

c. Racial gerrymandering

Race may not be the predominant factor in determining the boundary lines of legislative districts (*see* § XIII.E.2.a., Racial discrimination, *infra*).

2. Alienage

Classifications based on status as a lawful resident of the United States (as opposed to a citizen) are subject to a variety of different standards, depending on the level of government and the nature of the classification.

a. Federal classification

Because Congress has plenary power over aliens under Article I, a federal alienage classification is likely valid unless it is **arbitrary** and **unreasonable.**

Example: Medicare regulations may require a five-year residency period for eligibility despite thereby excluding many lawful resident aliens. *Matthews v. Diaz*, 426 U.S. 67 (1976).

b. State classifications

1) Generally struck down

The Court will generally apply the strict scrutiny test and strike down state laws that discriminate against aliens, such as laws prohibiting aliens from owning land, obtaining commercial fishing licenses, or being eligible for welfare benefits or civil service jobs.

2) Exception—participation in government functions

A growing exception exists, however, for state laws that restrict or prohibit an alien's **participation in government functions.** Such laws need only have a **rational relationship** to a legitimate state interest. Laws prohibiting aliens from voting, serving on a jury, or being hired as police officers, probation officers, or public-school teachers have been upheld as preventing aliens from having a direct effect on the functioning of the government.

> **EXAM NOTE:** When determining whether a position or license from which aliens are excluded falls under the government function or political function exception, consider whether the position or license would allow the alien to "participate directly in the formulation, execution, or review of broad public policy" or would allow the alien to exercise "broad discretion."

c. Undocumented aliens

Undocumented aliens are not a suspect class, but the states may not deny primary or secondary public education benefits to undocumented aliens. *Plyler v. Doe*, 457 U.S. 202 (1982).

C. QUASI-SUSPECT CLASSIFICATIONS

1. Gender

Discrimination based on gender is "quasi-suspect" and subject to **intermediate scrutiny,** which is less stringent than strict scrutiny but tougher than the rational basis test. Just as with suspect classifications and fundamental rights, there must be **discriminatory intent** by the government to trigger intermediate scrutiny; disparate impact is not enough. Under intermediate scrutiny, the burden is on the state to show that a statute or regulation that treats the sexes differently is **substantially related** to an **important** governmental interest. This test applies whether the classification is invidious or benign, and it is now applied rather stringently, requiring the government to show that an "exceedingly persuasive justification" exists for the distinction, and that separate facilities (such as separate sports team facilities as state universities) are "substantially equivalent." *United States v. Virginia*, 518 U.S. 515 (1996).

a. Discrimination against women

Intentional discrimination through gender classification will generally be struck down under the intermediate scrutiny standard. For example, a state law giving preference to men over women to be administrators of decedents' estates was invalid. *Reed v. Reed*, 404 U.S. 71 (1971) (ease in determining who should serve as administrator is not an important interest). *See also United States v. Virginia*, 518 U.S. 515 (1996) (Virginia Military Institute could not exclude women from admission to public college based on overbroad generalizations about the physical capabilities and preferred educational methods of males and females).

b. Discrimination against men

Intentional discrimination against males is generally struck down for violating equal protection. However, there have been some instances of discrimination against men being upheld because of the important governmental interest:

   i)   Draft registration of males, but not females, *Rostker v. Goldberg*, 453 U.S. 57 (1981) (interest of preparing combat troops); and

   ii)   A statutory rape law that held only men criminally liable for such conduct, *Michael M. v. Sonoma County Superior Court*, 450 U.S. 464 (1981) (interest in preventing teenage pregnancy).

c. Affirmative action (benign discrimination)

The Court has upheld affirmative action regulations granting beneficial treatment to women over men (such as tax exemptions, increased social security benefits, and increased protection from mandatory armed forces discharge) because providing a remedy for past gender-based discrimination is an important governmental interest. *See Califano v. Webster*, 430 U.S. 313 (1977); *Schlesinger v. Ballard*, 419 U.S. 498 (1975).

2. Legitimacy

Classifications on the basis of status as a nonmarital child (i.e., those that distinguish between "legitimate" and "illegitimate" children) are subject to **intermediate scrutiny**—they must be **substantially related** to an **important** governmental interest. The Court will closely examine the purpose behind the distinction, and it will not uphold legislation designed to punish the offspring of a nonmarital relationship. To that end, states may not prohibit children of unmarried parents from receiving welfare benefits, *New Jersey Welfare Rights Org. v. Cahill*, 411 U.S. 619 (1973), workers' compensation benefits upon the death of a parent, *Weber v. Aetna Cas. and Sur. Co.*, 406 U.S. 164 (1972), or an inheritance from an intestate father, *Trimble v. Gordon*, 430 U.S. 762 (1977). In addition, a state cannot require a paternity action brought on behalf of an illegitimate child to be commenced within a limited time after birth in order to secure child support, while imposing a similar time limit on a legitimate child seeking child support from a parent. *Clark v. Jeter*, 486 U.S. 456 (1988).

D. NONSUSPECT CLASSIFICATIONS

1. Age

Age discrimination in violation of the Age Discrimination in Employment Act of 1967 does not provoke heightened scrutiny; laws and other governmental actions classifying on the basis of age are reviewed under the **rational basis** standard. *See, e.g., Massachusetts Bd. of Ret. v. Murgia*, 427 U.S. 307 (1976) (police officers may be forced to retire at age 50, even if they are as physically fit as younger officers).

2. Poverty

Most statutes and regulations that classify on the basis of wealth (i.e., discriminate against the poor) are subject only to **rational basis** scrutiny and will be upheld. There is an exception for cases in which governmental action prohibits the poor from exercising a fundamental right because of a government-imposed fee; strict scrutiny will usually apply in those situations. For example, the availability of appeal in a criminal case cannot hinge on ability to pay for a trial transcript. *Griffin v. Illinois*, 351 U.S. 12 (1956). Also, poll taxes are unconstitutional because wealth is unrelated to a citizen's ability to vote intelligently. *Harper v. Virginia Bd. of Elections*, 383 U.S. 663 (1966).

3. Sexual Orientation

There is currently a division among the federal courts as to the standard of scrutiny that is applicable to discrimination on the basis of sexual orientation. The Supreme Court has struck down bans on same-sex marriage as violations of a fundamental right on both Due Process and Equal Protection grounds, but it has not resolved the issue of whether discrimination based on sexual orientation is subject to heightened scrutiny. The government, however, cannot impose a burden upon or deny a benefit to a group of persons solely based on animosity toward the class that it affects. *Romer v. Evans*, 517 U.S. 620 (1996). Among the rights, benefits, and responsibilities of marriage to which same-sex partners must have access are birth and death certificates, which give married partners a form of legal recognition that is not available to unmarried partners. *Pavan v. Smith*, 582 U.S. ___, 137 S. Ct. 2075 (2017), citing *Obergefell v. Hodges*, 576 U.S. ___, 135 S. Ct. 2584 (2016).

E. FUNDAMENTAL RIGHTS UNIQUE TO EQUAL PROTECTION

The fundamental rights guaranteed by substantive due process are often protected by equal protection principles as well. Thus, impingement of the right to vote, to travel, or to marry may trigger an inquiry under either the Due Process Clause or the Equal Protection Clause. However, certain rights and principles are particular to equal protection.

> **EXAM NOTE:** The right to *travel* and the right to *vote* are the most frequently tested fundamental rights in the area of **equal protection**. (Often, both the Due Process Clause and the Equal Protection Clause will apply. Equal protection predominates if the question emphasizes denial of a right to a particular group, and it does not apply if the denial of the right is universal.)

1. One Person, One Vote

The principle of "one person, one vote" holds that one person's vote must be essentially equal to any other person's vote. To that end, when the government establishes voting districts for the election of representatives, the number of persons in each district must be approximately equal. *Reynolds v. Sims*, 377 U.S. 533 (1964). Voter approval of a redistricting plan will not justify a violation of the "one person, one vote" rule. *Lucas v. Colorado General Assembly*, 377 U.S. 713 (1964).

a. Congressional districts

When states establish districts for congressional elections, they must achieve nearly precise mathematical equality between the districts. This restriction is imposed on the states by Article I, Section 2, which requires members of the House to be chosen by "the People of the several States." An unexplained deviation of less than one percent may invalidate the statewide congressional district plan. Variations may be justified by the state on the basis of consistently applied, legitimate state objectives, such as respecting municipal political subdivision boundaries, creating geographic compact districts, and avoiding contests between incumbent representatives. In addition, variations based on anticipated population shifts may be acceptable when such shifts can be predicted with a high degree of accuracy, and population trends are thoroughly documented. *Kirkpatrick v. Preisler*, 394 U.S. 526 (1969) (variation in population of slightly less than six percent violated the "one person, one vote" rule); *Karcher v. Daggett*, 462 U.S. 725 (1983) (variation of slightly less than 0.7 percent violated the "one person, one vote" rule).

1) Congressional apportionment of House members

Congress, in apportioning members of the House among the states pursuant to Article I, Section 2, is not held to the "mathematical equality" standard. The method adopted by Congress is entitled to judicial deference and is assumed to be in good faith. *Dept. of Commerce v. Montana*, 503 U.S. 442 (1992) (Montana's loss of a congressional seat upheld, even though retention of the seat would have placed Montana closer to the ideal population size for a congressional district).

b. State and local districts

The size of electoral districts may vary much more in the case of state and local elections, as long as the variance is not unjustifiably large. A variation of less than 10% is rebuttably presumed to be a minor deviation that does not constitute a prima facie case for discrimination. *Cox v. Larios*, 300 F. Supp. 2d 1320 (N.D. Ga.), *aff'd*, 542 U.S. 947 (2004); *Brown v. Thompson*, 462 U.S. 835 (1983). When the maximum variation is 10% or greater, the state must show that the deviation from equality between the districts is reasonable and designed to promote a legitimate state interest. *Mahan v. Howell*, 410 U.S. 315 (1973) (maximum difference of 16% in size of population between state legislative districts permitted when the state respected the boundaries of political subdivisions).

1) Bodies performing governmental functions

The "one person, one vote" rule applies to local elections of entities that perform governmental functions, even when the functions are specialized rather than general in nature. *Hadley v. Junior College Dist.*, 397 U.S. 50 (1970) (election of trustees to junior college district).

2) Relevant population

In addition to requiring relative equality with respect to the weight of a person's vote, the Equal Protection Clause subjects the restriction of voting of a particular class of persons to strict scrutiny, which generally results in the invalidation of the law. *Kramer v. Union Free School District No. 15*, 395 U.S. 621 (1969) (state law that restricted voting in school board election to property owners and parents with school-aged children struck down). The restriction of voting to a class of persons (e.g., landowners) and the allocation of voting weight on a basis other than personhood (e.g., the amount of land owned) has been upheld only with regard to water-district elections. *Ball v. James*, 451 U.S. 355 (1981); *See Hadley v. Junior College Dist., supra* (determination of districts for junior college trustees based on school age population violated "one person, one vote" rule).

A state may draw its legislative districts on the basis of total population rather than eligible or registered voters. *Evenwel v. Abbott*, 578 U.S. ___, 136 S. Ct. 1120 (2016).

c. At-large elections

While an election in which members of a governmental unit (e.g., county council members) are elected by all voters within that unit (i.e., an at-large election) does not violate the one-person, one-vote rule, it may conflict with another constitutional provision, such as the Equal Protection Clause. *Rogers v. Lodge*, 458 U.S. 613 (1982) (use of countywide system to elect county board unconstitutionally diluted the voting power of African-American citizens).

Note: Federal law bans at-large elections for congressional representatives in states that have more than one House member (i.e., the single-member district rule). 2 U.S.C.S. § 2c.

2. Gerrymandering

a. Racial discrimination

1) Vote dilution

When a state draws election districts for the purpose of scattering a racial or ethnic minority among several districts in order to prevent the minority from exercising its voting strength, the state's action is a violation of the Equal Protection Clause. *Gomillion v. Lightfoot*, 364 U.S. 339 (1960) (redrawing city boundaries to exclude African-American voters unconstitutional); *Rogers v. Lodge, supra*.

2) Majority-minority districts

Under the Equal Protection Clause, election districts for public office may not be drawn using race as the predominant factor in determining the boundary lines, unless the district plan can survive strict scrutiny. This restriction applies even when the district is drawn to favor historically disenfranchised groups. The state can use traditional factors—such as compactness, contiguity, or honoring political subdivisions—as the bases for the district, and it may only consider race if it does not predominate over other considerations. *Miller v. Johnson*, 515 U.S. 900 (1995). To be narrowly tailored within the strict scrutiny standard, the legislature must have a "strong basis in evidence" in support of the race-based choice that it has made. Note that the legislature need not show that its action was **actually necessary** to avoid a statutory violation, only that the legislature had **good reasons to believe** its use of race was needed. *Bethune-Hill v. Virginia State Bd. Of Elections*, 580 U.S. ___, 137 S. Ct. 788 (2017), *Alabama Legislative Black Caucus, et al. v. Alabama et al.*, 575 U.S. ___, 135 S. Ct. 1257 (2015).

A district's bizarre shape can be used as evidence that race was a predominating factor, but such a shape is not necessary for a finding of racial gerrymandering. *Shaw v. Reno*, 509 U.S. 630 (1993).

a) Voting Rights Act

The Voting Rights Act (42 U.S.C. § 1973 et seq.) requires racial gerrymandering to ensure minority success in elections by creating majority-minority districts (i.e., affirmative gerrymandering). Until recently, the Act required federal pre-clearance for changes in voting rules, including redistricting, for specific southern states and a few other local governmental units. However, the formula used as a basis for subjecting jurisdictions to preclearance has been declared unconstitutional because it no longer reflects current conditions; therefore, it can no longer be used. *Shelby County v. Holder*, 570 U.S. ___, 133 S. Ct. 2612 (2013). Receiving federal pre-clearance for a redistricting plan does not ensure that plan will avoid conflicting with the Equal Protection Clause. *Miller v. Johnson*, 515 U.S. 900 (1995).

The Voting Rights Act does not require a jurisdiction to maintain a particular numerical minority percentage. Instead, it requires the jurisdiction to maintain a minority's ability to elect a preferred candidate of choice. *Alabama Legislative Black Caucus, et al. v. Alabama et al.*, 575 U.S. ___, 135 S. Ct. 1257 (2015).

b. Political discrimination

Partisan political gerrymandering may violate the Equal Protection Clause if the challenger can show "both intentional discrimination against an identifiable political group and an actual discriminatory effect on that group." *Davis v. Bandemer*, 478 U.S. 109, 127 (1986). However, lack of comprehensive and neutral principles for drawing electoral boundaries as well as the absence of rules to confine judicial intervention can prevent adjudication of political gerrymandering claims. *Vieth v. Jubelirer*, 541 U.S. 267 (2004).

XIV. PRIVILEGES AND IMMUNITIES CLAUSES

A. ARTICLE IV

Article IV, Section 2, known as the Comity Clause, provides that "the citizens of each state shall be entitled to all privileges and immunities of citizens in the several states."

1. Prohibits State Discrimination Against Nonresidents

The Comity Clause, in essence, prohibits one state from discriminating against the citizens of another state. In this context, the term "citizen" does not include corporations or aliens.

2. Rights Protected

Nonresident citizens are protected against discrimination with respect to fundamental rights or essential activities. Examples include the pursuit of employment, transfer of property, and access to state courts.

> **Example:** Discrimination against out-of-state residents in setting the fee for a ***commercial*** activity, such as a commercial shrimping license, violates the Privileges and Immunities Clause of Article IV, but similar discrimination for a ***recreational*** activity, such as a recreational hunting license, does not, if there is a rational basis for the fee differential. *Compare Toomer v. Witsell*, 334 U.S. 385 (1948) (fee for out-of-state commercial shrimper that was 100 times greater than the fee for an in-state shrimper unconstitutional), *with Baldwin v. Fish & Game Comm'n*, 436 U.S. 371 (1978) (fee for out-of-state resident to hunt elk that was 25 times greater than the fee for an in-state hunter constitutional).
>
> Note that discrimination against an out-of-state resident with regard to access to a state's natural resources may violate the Dormant Commerce Clause. *New England Power Co. v. New Hampshire*, 455 U.S. 331 (1982) (prohibition on sale of hydroelectric power outside the state unconstitutional).

3. Exception—Substantial Justification

Discrimination against out-of-state citizens may be valid if the state can show a substantial reason for the difference in treatment. A substantial reason exists if:

i) The nonresidents either cause or are a part of the problem that the state is . attempting to solve; and

ii) There are no less-restrictive means to solve the problem.

> **Example:** Discrimination against nonresidents with respect to the use of scarce water resources was upheld when the purpose was to preserve natural state-owned resources. *Sporhase v. Nebraska*, 458 U.S. 941 (1982).

> **EXAM NOTE:** Although the Privileges and Immunities Clause of Article IV and the Commerce Clause are not coextensive, they tend to mutually support each other; thus, consider both when analyzing a bar exam question.

B. FOURTEENTH AMENDMENT—NATIONAL CITIZENSHIP

The Fourteenth Amendment provides that "[n]o state shall make or enforce any law which shall abridge the privileges or immunities of citizens of the United States." This clause protects citizens (not corporations or aliens) from infringement by the states upon the privileges or immunities of **national** citizenship.

The privileges or immunities of national citizenship include the right to travel interstate, to petition Congress for redress of grievances, to vote for national offices, to enter public lands, to be protected while in the custody of U.S. marshals, and to peaceably assemble. *Twining v. New Jersey*, 211 U.S. 78 (1908). The guarantees of the Bill of Rights, however, are not privileges or immunities of national citizenship within the context of the Fourteenth Amendment. *Slaughterhouse Cases*, 83 U.S. 36 (1873). Therefore, those rights are protected from state action only by the Due Process Clause and the Equal Protection Clause.

This provision is seldom successfully invoked; under the limiting interpretation of the *Slaughterhouse Cases,* the rights that the clause provides are redundant to rights provided elsewhere in the Constitution. Although the Supreme Court has since relied on the clause to underscore the right to move freely among states, *Saenz v. Roe*, 526 U.S. 489 (1999) (invalidating a duration requirement for welfare benefits), there has been no subsequent expansion of use; the Fourteenth Amendment's Privileges or Immunities Clause applies, in practice, only to the right to travel.

XV.   TAKINGS CLAUSE

The power of the government to take private property for public purposes is known as **"eminent domain."** The Takings Clause of the Fifth Amendment acts as a check on this power; it provides that private property may not "be taken for public use, without just compensation." The Fourteenth Amendment Due Process Clause makes the Takings Clause applicable to the states.

A.   PROPERTY INTEREST

For a person to challenge a governmental action as an unconstitutional taking, the person must have a property interest. When a person does not have an interest in the property that the government takes, the Takings Clause does not apply.

Example: An organization of homeowners challenged a beach restoration project undertaken by a state agency and local governments. The homeowners objected to the creation of land beyond the mean high water line, which represented the boundary of the homeowners' property, because this infringed upon their right as owners of property along a shore to receive accretions and because they lost the right to control public access to the shoreline. However, because, under state law, the newly created land belonged to the state, and the homeowners did not enjoy property rights with respect to this land, there was no taking of their property rights. *Stop the Beach Renourishment, Inc. v. Fla. Dep't of Envtl. Prot.*, 560 U.S. 702 (2010). (Note: A plurality of the Supreme Court justices also found that the Takings Clause applies to a judicial taking.)

1.   Types of Property

Property that may be subject to the protection of the Takings Clause includes not only land and other real property, but also tangible personal property as well as intangible property, such as contract and patent rights and trade secrets. *Ruckelshaus v. Monsanto Co.*, 467 U.S. 986 (1984); *Lynch v. United States*, 292 U.S. 571 (1934); *James v. Campbell*, 104 U.S. 356 (1882).

2.   Types of Interests

In addition to the transfer of a fee simple interest in property, a taking may involve an easement, leasehold interest, or a lien. *Nollan v. California Coastal Commission*, 483 U.S. 825 (1987); *Armstrong v. United States*, 364 U.S. 40 (1960); *United States v. General Motors*, 323 U.S. 373 (1945). A taking may involve the rights of a property owner, such as the right to control access to the property. *Kaiser Aetna v. United States*, 444 U.S. 164 (1980) (federal government's imposition of public-access servitude on a waterway created on private property constituted a taking).

B. TYPES OF TAKING

1. Seizure of Property

The classic application of the Takings Clause is the seizure of private property for governmental use, such as acquiring privately held land in order to construct a courthouse or other government building. In such a case, the property owner's primary challenge to the seizure is whether he has received just compensation (*see* § XV.C., Just Compensation, *infra*).

a. Public-use challenge

A government may seize private property not only for its own direct use but also to transfer the property to another private party. Although such a seizure is subject to challenge as not being made for a public use, the taking need merely be **"rationally related** to a **conceivable public purpose."** *Hawaii Hous. Auth. v. Midkiff*, 467 U.S. 229 (1984). This is a highly deferential standard, and the burden is on the person challenging the taking to prove a lack of legitimate interest or rational basis. In addition to traditional health, safety, and welfare justifications, economic redevelopment goals constitute a sufficient public purpose to justify the seizure. *Kelo v. City of New London*, 545 U.S. 469 (2005). Moreover, a government-mandated transfer of property from one private party directly to another (e.g., from lessor to lessee) may nevertheless be for a public use. *Hawaii Housing Authority v. Midkiff*, 467 U.S. 229 (1984).

2. Damage to or Destruction of Property

A destruction of property or property rights by the federal, state, or local government can also result in a taking. The destruction need not directly benefit the government. The Takings Clause is not limited to ownership interests in property; instead, it can extend to takings of non-possessory property rights, such as easements or liens. *Armstrong v. United States*, 364 U.S. 40 (1960).

Example: A federal statute that prevented the transfer by devise or descent of fractional shares of an interest in tribal land upon the death of the owner and instead provided for such interest to escheat to the tribe constituted an unconstitutional taking when there was no provision for compensation of the owner. *Hodel v. Irving*, 481 U.S. 704 (1987).

Similarly, physical damage to property or interference with a property owner's rights by governmental action can result in a taking.

Example: County ownership of an airport that resulted in an invasion of the airspace of nearby property owners by planes taking off and landing at the airport constituted a taking. *Griggs v. Allegheny County*, 369 U.S. 84 (1962).

Note: A statute that requires an owner of property rights to take action in order to preserve an unused right does not result in a taking if the owner fails to take such action. *Texaco, Inc. v. Short*, 454 U.S. 516 (1982).

a. Exception—public peril

The governmental destruction of private property in response to a public peril does not trigger the right to compensation.

Example: The owners of infected cedar trees located near apple orchards were not entitled to compensation when the cedar trees were destroyed pursuant to a state statute in order to prevent the spread of the infection to the orchards. *Miller v. Schoene*, 276 U.S. 272 (1928).

3. Re-characterization of Property

The Takings Clause prevents a government from re-characterizing private property as public property.

> **Example:** Interest on the purchase price of an insolvent corporation placed by the buyer in an account with the court as part of an interpleader action involving the corporation's creditors was private property. A state court's interpretation of a statutory provision that the interest was public money constituted a taking. *Webb's Fabulous Pharmacies, Inc. v. Beckwith*, 449 U.S. 155 (1980).

4. Regulatory Taking

Generally, a governmental regulation that adversely affects a person's property interest is not a taking, but it is possible for a regulation to rise to the level of a taking.

In determining whether a regulation creates a taking, the following factors are considered:

i)   The economic impact of the regulation on the property owner;

ii) The extent to which the regulation interferes with the owner's reasonable, investment-backed expectations regarding use of the property; and

iii) The character of the regulation, including the degree to which it will benefit society, how the regulation distributes the burdens and benefits among property owners, and whether the regulation violates any of the owner's essential attributes of property ownership, such as the right to exclude others from the property.

Penn Central Transportation Co. v. City of New York, 438 U.S. 104 (1978).

a. Public-use challenge

In the context of a regulation, a state or local government can act under its police power for the purposes of health, safety, and welfare. In addition, a public purpose can encompass aesthetic and environmental concerns. Moreover, it is generally inappropriate for a court to examine whether a regulation substantially advances a legitimate governmental interest. (Note, however, that an arbitrary or irrational regulation may constitute a due-process violation.) *Lingle v. Chevron U.S.A. Inc.*, 544 U.S. 528 (2005).

b. Per se takings

In two instances, a regulation clearly results in a taking.

1) Physical occupation

A taking has occurred when the governmental regulation results in a **permanent physical occupation** of the property.

> **Example:** A law requiring a landlord to permit a cable company to install equipment on the landlord's property that would remain indefinitely constituted a taking, even though the installation had only a minimal economic impact on the landlord. *Loretto v. Teleprompter Manhattan CATV Corp.*, 458 U.S. 419 (1982).

2) No economically viable use

When a regulation results in a **permanent total loss of the property's economic value,** a taking has occurred. *Lucas v. South Carolina Coastal Council*, 505 U.S. 1003 (1992) (zoning ordinance precluding owner of coastal property from erecting any permanent structure on the land was a taking); *Tahoe-Sierra Preservation Council, Inc. v. Tahoe Regional Planning Agency*, 535 U.S. 302 (2002) (32-month building moratorium was not a taking).

> **Adverse economic impact:** A regulation that results in a dramatic decline in the value of the regulated property does not necessarily constitute a taking.

c. Post-adoption acquisition

A person who acquires property rights after the adoption of a regulation that affects those rights may nevertheless challenge the regulation as an unconstitutional taking. *Palazzolo v. Rhode Island.*, 533 U.S. 606 (2001).

5. Exaction as a Taking

A local government may exact promises from a developer, such as setting aside a portion of the land being developed for a park in exchange for issuing the necessary construction permits. Such exactions do not violate the Takings Clause if there is:

i) An **essential nexus** between legitimate state interests and the conditions imposed on the property owner (i.e., the conditions substantially advance legitimate state interest); and

ii) A **rough proportionality** between the burden imposed by the conditions on property owner and the impact of the proposed development.

Nollan v. California Coastal Commission, 483 U.S. 825 (1987) (state-required grant of an easement across beachfront property as a condition on the issuance of a building permit was a taking due to lack of essential nexus); *Dolan v. City of Tigard*, 512 U.S. 374 (1994) (state-required dedication of land to the city for use as a greenway and pedestrian/bicycle pathway in exchange for permit to expand a store and parking lot was a taking due to lack of rough proportionality).

In determining whether there is rough proportionality between the burden and the impact, the government must make an individualized determination that the conditions are related both in nature and extent to the impact.

The government's conditions must satisfy the requirements of *Nollan* and *Dolan* even when the government denies the permit and even when its demand is for money rather than property rights. *Koontz v. St. Johns River Water Mgmt. Dist.*, 570 U.S. ___, 133 S. Ct. 2586 (2013).

These requirements are limited to exactions; they do not apply to regulatory takings. *Lingle v. Chevron U.S.A. Inc., supra*, (rent cap was not an exaction taking, but instead was a valid regulation under the Takings Clause).

C. JUST COMPENSATION

The phrase "just compensation" has been interpreted to mean **fair market value,** which is the reasonable value of the property at the time of the taking. This value is measured in terms of the loss to the owner, not the benefit to the government.

1. Worthless Property

Property that is worthless to the owner but has value to the government may be taken without compensation.

> **Example:** Clients whose funds were held by lawyers and deposited in a trust account pursuant to state law to be paid to an entity in order to provide legal services for the poor were not entitled to compensation because each client's funds would not

2. Only Portion Taken

When only a portion of an owner's property is taken, the owner may also receive compensation for any diminution in value of the remaining portion that is attributable to the taking but must reduce any compensation by the value of any special and direct benefits (e.g., a highway access) conferred on the remaining portion.

3. Return of Property

When governmental action constitutes a taking, the government cannot escape all liability by returning the property to its owner, but instead must pay the owner compensation for the period that the government possessed the property. *First English Evangelical Church v. County of Los Angeles*, 482 U.S. 304 (1987).

D. MANNER OF TAKING

Typically, when a property owner objects to the seizure of his property by the government, the government will institute condemnation proceedings, and the property owner can raise the Takings Clause as a defense to this action. When the governmental action that allegedly constitutes a taking is a statute, regulation, or ordinance, the property owner may institute a suit seeking an injunction or a declaratory judgment; this type of legal action is sometimes referred to as an inverse condemnation.

XVI. PROHIBITED LEGISLATION

A. BILLS OF ATTAINDER

A bill of attainder is a **legislative** act that declares a person or group of persons guilty of some crime and punishes them without a trial. Article I, Sections 9 and 10 forbid the federal government and the states, respectively, from enacting such "legislative trials." It applies only to criminal or penal measures.

Barring particular individuals from government employment qualifies as punishment under the prohibition against bills of attainder. *United States v. Lovett*, 328 U.S. 303 (1946).

B. EX POST FACTO LAWS

The constitutional prohibition on an "ex post facto" law is confined to a retroactive change to a **criminal or penal** law. A law that is civil in purpose is treated as a criminal law only if its punitive effect clearly overrides its civil purpose. *Smith v. Doe*, 538 U.S. 84 (2003).

Under Article I, Sections 9 and 10, a **federal or state** statute will be struck down as being ex post facto if it:

i) **Criminalizes** an act that was not a crime when it was originally committed;

ii) Authorizes, after an act was committed, the imposition of a **more severe penalty** on that act;

iii) **Deprives the defendant of a defense** available at the time the act was committed; or

iv) **Decreases the prosecution's burden of proof** required for a conviction to a level below that which was required when the alleged offense was committed.

Collins v. Youngblood, 497 U.S. 37 (1990).

Example: A change in the relevant statute of limitations that resulted in the revival of a prosecution for an act of sexual abuse for which the statute of limitations had expired violates the prohibition on ex post facto laws; the change retroactively withdrew a complete defense to the crime after it had vested. *Stogner v. California*, 539 U.S. 607 (2003).

Compare: The retroactive application of state law that required registration of convicted sex offenders and child kidnappers, and public notification of information about the convicts, including name, current address, and place of employment did not constitute an ex post facto law. The law was a nonpunitive regulatory scheme enacted for the protection of the public. *Smith v. Doe, supra*.

C. OBLIGATION OF CONTRACTS

Article I, Section 10 prohibits the states from passing any law "impairing the obligation of contracts." This prohibition applies only to **state legislation**—not state-court decisions and not federal legislation—that **retroactively** impairs contractual rights. It does not apply to contracts not yet entered into.

1. Private Contracts

State legislation that **substantially** impairs a contract between private parties is invalid, unless the government can demonstrate that the interference was **reasonable** and **necessary** to serve an **important** governmental interest. *Allied Structural Steel Co. v. Spannaus*, 438 U.S. 234 (1978); *Energy Reserves Group, Inc. v. Kansas Power and Light Co.,* 459 U.S. 400 (1983). Substantial impairment generally requires that the state legislation destroy most or all of a party's rights under a preexisting contract. *See Home Bldg. and Loan Ass'n v. Blaisdell,* 290 U.S. 398 (1934); *Keystone Bituminous Coal Ass'n v. DeBenedictus,* 480 U.S. 470 (1987).

2. Public Contracts

Impairment by the state of a **public contract** (one to which the state or local government is a party) is subject to essentially the same "reasonable and necessary" test as private contracts, but with a somewhat stricter application. The state must show that its important interest cannot be served by a less-restrictive alternative and that the impairment it seeks is necessary because of unforeseeable circumstances. *U.S. Trust Co. v. New Jersey*, 413 U.S. 1 (1977).

Note that there is no substantial impairment if the state reserved—by statute, law, or in the contract itself—the right to revoke, alter, or amend.

XVII. FREEDOM OF RELIGION

The First Amendment provides that "Congress shall make no law respecting an establishment of religion, or prohibiting the free exercise thereof." Both the Establishment Clause and the Free Exercise Clause have been incorporated into the Due Process Clause of the Fourteenth Amendment and are therefore applicable to the states.

A. ESTABLISHMENT

When a governmental program shows preference to one religion over another, or to religion over nonreligion, strict scrutiny applies. *Bd. of Educ. v. Grumet*, 512 U.S. 687 (1994) (creation of special school district to benefit members of one religion invalid).

1. Standard of Review

Not every governmental action that impacts religion is unconstitutional. To determine whether a particular program violates the Establishment Clause, the Court has most often applied the three-part test developed in *Lemon v. Kurtzman*, 403 U.S. 602 (1971).

A governmental action that benefits religion is valid if:

i) It has a **secular purpose**;

ii) Its principal or primary effect **neither advances nor inhibits** religion; and

iii) It does not result in **excessive government entanglement** with religion.

> Though still applied, the *Lemon* test has often been modified or set aside in the Supreme Court's more recent Establishment Clause cases.

2. Financial Aid

a. Aid to religious institutions

Governmental financial assistance to religious institutions is permitted if the aid is secular in nature, used only for secular purposes, and, when the aid is distributed among secular and religious institutions, the distribution criteria must be religiously neutral. *Mitchell v. Helms*, 530 U.S. 793 (2000) (elementary and secondary school); *Tilton v. Richardson*, 403 U.S. 672 (1971) (college); *Bradfield v. Roberts*, 175 U.S. 291 (1899) (hospital). Aid in the form of secular textbooks, computers, standardized tests, bus transportation, school lunches, and sign language interpreters for deaf students has been upheld. While parochial elementary and secondary schools were at one time considered to be so pervasively sectarian that direct aid to them was not permitted, that is no longer the case. *Mitchell v. Helms, supra*. In applying the *Lemon* test, the third element (no excessive governmental entanglement) is not a separate requirement, but instead is one factor to be considered in ascertaining whether the second element (no advancement or inhibition of religion) has been met. *Agostini v. Felton* 521 U.S. 203, 233 (1997).

b. Tax exemptions for religious organizations

Property-tax exemptions for religious institutions have been held valid as being equivalent to exemptions given to other charitable organizations and therefore neither advancing nor inhibiting religion. *Walz v. Tax Comm'n*, 397 U.S. 664 (1970). Tax exemptions that are available only for religious activities or organizations, however, violate the Establishment Clause as an endorsement of religion. *Texas Monthly v. Bullock*, 489 U.S. 1 (1989).

c. Tax deductions and aid for parochial school expenses

Tax deductions given to reimburse tuition expenses only for parents of students in religious schools are invalid. If such a deduction is available to *all* parents for actual educational expenses of attending any public or private school (including parochial schools), it is valid. *Mueller v. Allen*, 463 U.S. 388 (1983).

In addition, giving parents tuition vouchers to assist them in paying religious-school tuition does not violate the Establishment Clause if the choice of whether to use the vouchers for religious or non-religious private school tuition lies with the parents. *Zelman v. Simmons-Harris*, 536 U.S. 639 (2002).

3. Public School Activities

Generally, religious activities conducted in public schools violate the Establishment Clause. The following practices have been held invalid as clearly promoting religion:

i) **Prayer** and **Bible reading,** *Engel v. Vitale*, 370 U.S. 421 (1962);

ii) A designated period of silence for **"meditation or voluntary prayer,"** *Wallace v. Jaffree*, 472 U.S. 38 (1985);

iii) **Nondenominational prayer** led by a cleric at graduation ceremonies, *Lee v. Weisman*, 505 U.S. 577 (1992); but see *Town of Greece v. Galloway*, 572 U.S.

___, 134 S. Ct. 1811 (2014) (prayer before sessions of town council did not violate Establishment Clause due to tradition of such prayers and lack of coercion with regard to participation by nonbelievers);

iv) Posting the **Ten Commandments** on public-school classroom walls, *Stone v. Graham*, 449 U.S. 39 (1980); and

v) **Prohibiting the teaching of Darwinism** (i.e., human biological evolution), or mandating that such teaching be accompanied by instruction regarding "creation science," *Edward v. Aguillard*, 482 U.S. 578 (1987); *Epperson v. Arkansas*, 393 U.S. 97 (1968).

4. Access to Public Facilities by Religious Groups

If a public school allows student groups or organizations to use its facilities when classes are not in session, allowing a religious organization to use those facilities does not violate the Establishment Clause. Furthermore, to prohibit such a group from using those facilities because religious topics would be discussed would violate the First Amendment guarantee of free speech. *Good News Club v. Milford Central School*, 533 U.S. 98 (2001); *Widmar v. Vincent*, 454 U.S. 263 (1981). The Court has often responded to public educational institutions' Establishment Clause concerns by focusing on the free speech rights of religious students. *E.g.*, *Rosenberger v. Univ. of Virginia*, 515 U.S. 819 (1995) (state university could not refuse to pay for printing of religious student newspaper on Establishment Clause grounds when it funded nonreligious papers).

5. Religious Displays

a. Ten Commandments

A display of the Ten Commandments on public property is an impermissible violation of the Establishment Clause if the display has a **"predominantly religious purpose."** *McCreary County v. ACLU*, 545 U.S. 844 (2005) (Ten Commandments posted in courthouse impermissible). If the display also communicates a secular moral message, or its context conveys a historical and social meaning, it may be upheld. *Van Orden v. Perry*, 545 U.S. 677 (2005) (Ten Commandments monument on the state capitol grounds displaying 17 monuments and 21 historical markers commemorating the state's "people, ideals, and events that compose its identity" was permitted because the "Ten Commandments have an undeniable historical meaning" in addition to their "religious significance." Because of the unique historical message, which is separate from any religious message, installing the Ten Commandments in a public park did not violate the Establishment Clause). This is a highly context-dependent, case-specific inquiry.

b. Holiday displays

Government holiday displays will generally be upheld unless a reasonable observer would conclude that the display is an **endorsement** of religion. The context of the display is key—a nativity scene in a courthouse under a banner reading "*Gloria in Excelsis Deo*" was struck down as endorsing religion, but a nearby outdoor display of a Christmas tree, Chanukah menorah, and other seasonal symbols was upheld as mere recognition that Christmas and Chanukah are both parts of a highly secularized winter holiday season. *County of Allegheny v. ACLU*, 492 U.S. 573 (1989).

B. FREE EXERCISE

The Free Exercise Clause of the First Amendment has been construed to include two freedoms: the freedom to believe and the freedom to act. The degree of protection that individuals are afforded from governmental interference in religion depends on whether religious belief or conduct is involved.

1. **Religious Belief**

The freedom to believe in any religion or none at all is absolutely protected and cannot be restricted by law. The government may not deny benefits or impose burdens based on religious belief, *Cantwell v. Connecticut*, 310 U.S. 296 (1940); it may not require affirmation of a belief, *West Virginia State Bd. of Educ. v. Barnette*, 319 U.S. 624 (1943); and it may not determine the reasonableness of a belief, although it may determine the sincerity of the person asserting that belief, *United States v. Ballard*, 322 U.S. 78 (1944). When there is a property dispute between two religious groups, a court may not decide questions of religious doctrine, but may apply religiously neutral principles of law to resolve the dispute. *Jones v. Wolf*, 443 U.S. 595 (1979).

2. **Religious Conduct**

Religious conduct, on the other hand, is not absolutely protected. Generally, only state laws that **intentionally target** religious conduct are subject to strict scrutiny. Neutral laws of general applicability that have an impact on religious conduct are subject only to the rational basis test.

a. **Targeting religious conduct**

Strict scrutiny applies when the government purposely targets conduct because it is religious or displays religious beliefs. *Church of the Lukumi Babalu Aye, Inc. v. City of Hialeah*, 508 U.S. 520 (1993) (city ordinance banning all ritual sacrifice of animals not for the purpose of food consumption struck down as targeting the Santeria religion). A state law that is designed to suppress activity because it is religiously motivated is valid only if it is necessary to achieve a compelling governmental interest.

Other laws that have been struck down as violating the Free Exercise Clause include compulsory school attendance for the Amish, *Wisconsin v. Yoder*, 406 U.S. 205 (1972), and denial of unemployment benefits to one whose faith prevented her from taking a job that required her to work on the Sabbath, *Sherbert v. Verner*, 374 U.S. 398 (1963).

Similarly, denying a church access to an otherwise available public benefit purely on account of its religious status violates the Free Exercise Clause. *Trinity Lutheran Church of Columbia, Inc. v. Comer*, No. 15-577, 2017 U.S. LEXIS 4061 (June 26, 2017).

b. **Generally applicable laws**

Neutral state laws of general applicability that have the incidental effect of interfering with one's ability to engage in religious practices are subject only to the rational basis test. *Employment Div. v. Smith*, 494 U.S. 872 (1990) (criminalization of peyote that did not contain an exception for use in Native American religious rituals upheld, as the ban was not motivated by any desire to burden religious conduct).

Example: A parent's right to pray over a child who has contracted meningitis, rather than seeking medical assistance, may be limited by state child-neglect and manslaughter laws. Parents do not have the right to endanger the lives of their children on the grounds of freedom of religion. *See Prince v. Massachusetts*, 321 U.S. 158 (1944).

c. Religious Freedom Restoration Act

Under the Religious Freedom Restoration Act, which is applicable only to the federal government, not to the states, even neutral laws of general applicability are subject to strict scrutiny if they substantially burden the free exercise of religion.

C. MINISTERIAL EXCEPTION TO DISCRIMINATION LAWS

Religious institutions can rely on a "ministerial exception" to federal and state employment discrimination laws in their decision to hire or fire a minister. The purpose of the ministerial exception, which is based on both the Establishment and Free Exercise Clauses of the First Amendment, is not merely to safeguard a church's decision to discharge a minister when it is made for a religious reason but also to ensure that the authority to select and control who will serve as a minister to the church's faithful, a strictly ecclesiastical matter, is solely the church's decision. The exception operates as an affirmative defense to an otherwise cognizable claim, but not as a jurisdictional bar. *Hosanna-Tabor Evangelical Lutheran Church and School v. E.E.O.C.*, 565 U.S. 171 (2012) (employee whose responsibilities included religious instruction was "minister" within scope of ministerial exception, and as such, church and school could not be held liable in E.E.O.C.'s discrimination enforcement action on her behalf).

XVIII. FREEDOM OF EXPRESSION AND ASSOCIATION

In addition to its religion clauses, the First Amendment provides that "Congress shall make no laws...abridging the freedom of speech, or of the press; or the right of the people to peaceably assemble, and to petition the Government for a redress of grievances." These aspects of the First Amendment are applicable to the states via the Fourteenth Amendment.

Freedom of expression is not absolute. While governmental regulation of the content of speech is severely constrained, governmental regulation of the time, place, and manner of speech is subject to less restriction.

A. REGULATION OF SPEECH

1. Expressive Conduct

Protected speech can include not only written, oral, and visual communication, but also activities such as picketing and leafleting. Expressive conduct (or symbolic speech) may also be protected as speech, but it is subject to a lesser degree of protection. Governmental regulation of expressive conduct is upheld if:

i) The regulation is **within the government's power** to enact (e.g., through a local government's police power);

ii) The regulation furthers an **important governmental interest**;

iii) The governmental interest is **unrelated to the suppression of ideas**; and

iv) The burden on speech is **no greater than necessary.**

United States v. O'Brien, 391 U.S. 367 (1968) (prohibition against burning draft cards upheld as furthering the important governmental interest in a smoothly functioning draft system).

An example of permissible regulation of expressive conduct includes upholding a ban on public nudity, such as nude dancing in adult entertainment venues, pursuant to the important governmental interest in preventing the "harmful secondary effects" of adult entertainment on neighborhoods, which is unrelated to the suppression of expression. *City of Erie v. Pap's A.M.*, 529 U.S. 277 (2000).

Examples of impermissible regulation of expressive conduct include:

    i)   A ban against students wearing black armbands to protest the war in Vietnam, because the government's only interest in banning the conduct was prohibiting communication, *Tinker v. Des Moines Indep. Cmty. Sch. Dist.*, 393 U.S. 503 (1969); and

    ii)   A federal prohibition against burning the American flag because the law was intended to suppress messages of disapproval of governmental policy, rather than any conduct-related consequences of the burning of a flag. *United States v. Eichman*, 496 U.S. 310 (1990).

    iii)   An ordinance prohibiting leafleting that results in littering on public streets, because the governmental interest in clean streets is insufficient justification, and such a ban on distribution is not narrowly tailored to protect the communication of information and opinion. *Schneider v. State of New Jersey Town of Irvington*, 308 U.S. 147 (1939).

The act of signing a petition constitutes expressive conduct. Public disclosure of the petition, and, thereby, the names of the individuals who signed the petition does not violate the First Amendment because such disclosure is substantially related to the important interest of preserving the integrity of the electoral process. *Doe v. Reed*, 561 U.S. 186 (2010).

2. Overbreadth

A law that burdens a substantial amount of speech or other conduct constitutionally protected by the First Amendment is **"overbroad"** and therefore void. A statute's overbreadth must be substantial both in an absolute sense and relative to the statute's plainly legitimate reach. The mere fact that some impermissible applications of a statute can be conceived of is not sufficient to render a statute overbroad. *United States v. Williams*, 553 U.S. 285 (2008). This doctrine does not apply to commercial speech. *Hoffman Estates v. The Flipside, Hoffman Estates, Inc.*, 455 U.S. 489 (1982).

In order to prevent a **"chilling effect"** on protected speech (i.e., frightening people .into not speaking for fear of prosecution), overbroad statutes may be challenged as **"facially invalid"** even by those who are validly regulated on behalf of those who are not. *Broadrick v. Okla.*, 413 U.S. 601 (1973). The challenger of a law bears the burden of establishing that substantial overbreadth exists. *N.Y. State Club Ass'n v. City of N.Y.*, 487 U.S. 1 (1988).

3. Vagueness

A statute is **"void for vagueness"** if it fails to provide a person of ordinary intelligence with fair notice of what is prohibited. *United States v. Williams, supra.*

As with overbreadth, vagueness is impermissible for fear that constitutionally protected speech will be "chilled." In addition, the "void for vagueness" doctrine is grounded in the due process requirement of notice. Under due process principles, laws that regulate persons or entities must give fair notice of conduct that is forbidden or required. *FCC v. Fox Television Stations, Inc.*, 567 U.S. 239 (2012), Statutes that tie criminal culpability to conduct that involves subjective judgments without providing statutory definitions, narrow context, or settled legal meanings have been struck down for vagueness. *Reno v. ACLU*, 521 U.S. 844 (1997) (indecent speech); *Coates v. Cincinnati*, 402 U.S. 611 (1971) (annoying conduct).

4. Prior Restraints

A prior restraint is a regulation of speech that occurs in advance of its expression (e.g., publication or utterance). Prior restraints are generally presumed to be unconstitutional, with limited exceptions. *Bantam Books, Inc. v. Sullivan*, 372 U.S. 58 (1963). These rare exceptions require at a minimum that:

i) There is a **particular harm** to be avoided (like publication of troop movements); and

ii) Certain **procedural safeguards** are provided to the speaker. Examples of such safeguards include:

    a) The standards must be narrowly drawn, reasonable, and definite, *Butterworth v. Smith*, 494 U.S. 624 (1990);

    b) The censoring body must promptly seek an injunction, *Teitel Films v. Cusack*, 390 U.S. 139 (1968); and

    c) There must be a prompt and final judicial determination of the validity of the restraint, *National Socialist Party v. Village of Skokie*, 432 U.S. 43 (1977).

The **burden is on the government** to prove that the material to be censored is not protected speech. *Freedman v. Maryland*, 380 U.S. 51 (1965).

Prior restraints have been rejected even when national security was at issue, *New York Times v. United States*, 403 U.S. 713 (1971) (Pentagon Papers), and even when press coverage threatened the fairness of a trial, *Nebraska Press Ass'n v. Stewart*, 427 U.S. 539 (1976) (prior restraint must be the only way to accomplish a goal).

5. Unfettered Discretion

A law or regulation that permits a governmental official to restrict speech (e.g., requires an official to issue a permit before a rally can be held) must provide definite standards as to how to apply the law in order to prevent governmental officials from having unfettered discretion over its application. Such a law or regulation must be related to an important governmental interest and contain the procedural safeguards mentioned above. A statute that gives officials unfettered discretion is void on its face; speakers need not apply for a permit and may not be punished for violating the licensing statute. *Lovell v. City of Griffin*, 303 U.S. 444 (1938).

6. Freedom Not to Speak

The First Amendment protects not only freedom of speech, but also the freedom not to speak. One such example is a child's right not to recite the Pledge of Allegiance. *West Virginia State Board of Education v. Barnette*, 319 U.S. 624 (1943). Similarly, the private organizers of a parade cannot be compelled by the government to include in the parade a group that espouses a message with which the organizers disagree. *Hurley v. Irish-American Gay, Lesbian & Bisexual Group of Boston*, 515 U.S. 557 (1995). Nor can the government mandate as a condition of federal funding that recipients explicitly agree with the government's policy to oppose prostitution and sex trafficking. *Agency for International Development v. Alliance for Open Society*, 570 U.S. ___, 133 S. Ct. 2321 (2013). However, a state can compel a private entity (e.g., a shopping mall) to permit individuals to exercise their own free-speech rights when the private entity is open to the public and the message is not likely to be attributable to the private entity. *Pruneyard Shopping Center v. Robins*, 447 U.S. 74 (1980).

a. Compelled financial support

Although one can be compelled to join or financially support a group with respect to one's employment, one cannot be forced to fund political speech by that group. *Abood v. Detroit Bd. of Educ.*, 431 U.S. 209 (1977) (teacher required to pay union dues); *Keller v. State Bar of California*, 496 U.S. 1 (1990) (lawyer required to join a bar association). A student, however, can be required to pay a university activity fee even though the fee may support groups that espouse messages with which the student disagrees, at least when the fee is allocated in accord with a viewpoint-neutral scheme. *Board of Regents v. Southworth*, 529 U.S. 217 (2000).

7. Government Speech

When the government itself speaks, it is not constrained by the Free Speech Clause of the First Amendment. Therefore, government speech (public service announcements, agricultural marketing campaigns, etc.) need not be viewpoint-neutral. *Johanns v. Livestock Mkt'ing Ass'n*, 544 U.S. 550 (2005). This Government Speech Doctrine, however, is subject to the requirements of the Establishment Clause (*See* § XVII.A., *supra*).

a. Monuments on public property

The display of a monument on public property, even if the monument has been donated by a private person, constitutes government speech. *Pleasant Grove City v. Summum*, 555 U.S. 460 (2009) (government installed a Ten Commandments monument donated by a private person in a public park; the Court held that governmental entities may exercise "selectivity" in choosing a monument being offered by a private donor).

b. Specialty license plates

Specialty license plates, even if designed by private individuals, are government speech and, as such, the state may refuse proposed designs based on the content of those designs. *Walker v. Tex. Div., Sons of Confederate Veterans*, 576 U.S. ___, 135 S. Ct. 2239 (2015) (rejection of proposed Texas license plate featuring Confederate battle flag).

c. Funding of private messages

The government may fund private messages. However, it must generally do so on a viewpoint-neutral basis. *Rosenberger v. Rector and Visitors of the University of Virginia*, 515 U.S. 819 (1995). The exception to this is when the government decides to fund artists; the decision of which artist to fund is necessarily based on the content of the artist's work. *National Endowment for the Arts v. Finley*, 524 U.S. 569 (1998).

d. Speech by government employees

When a government employee contends that her rights under the Free Speech Clause of the First Amendment have been violated by her employer, the employee must show that she was speaking as a citizen on a matter of public concern. *Borough of Duryea v. Guarnieri*, 564 U.S. 379 (2011). When a government employee is speaking pursuant to her official duties, the employee is generally not speaking as a citizen and the Free Speech Clause does not protect the employee from employer discipline. *Garcetti v. Ceballos*, 547 U.S. 410 (2006). In determining whether a government employee is speaking pursuant to her official duties, the critical question is whether the speech at issue is itself ordinarily within the scope of an employee's duties, not whether it merely concerns those duties. *Lane v. Franks*, 573 U.S. ___, 134 S. Ct. 2369 (2014).

When an employee is speaking as a citizen on a matter of public concern, the First Amendment interest of the employee must be balanced against the interest of the state, as an employer, in effective and efficient management of its internal affairs. *Pickering v. Bd. of Educ.*, 391 U.S. 563 (1968); *Connick v. Myers*, 461 U.S. 138 (1983); *Borough of Duryea v. Guarnieri, supra*. This approach also applies to a government employee who petitions the government for redress of a wrong pursuant to the Petition Clause of the First Amendment. *Id.*

8. Campaign Related Speech

a. Political campaign contributions

Statutes limiting campaign contributions are subject to intermediate scrutiny: they must be "closely drawn" to correspond with a sufficiently important interest. *McConnell v. Federal Election Commission*, 540 U.S. 93 (2003); *Randall v. Sorrell*, 548 U.S. 230 (2006). The government's failure to assist a party in exercising a fundamental right does not infringe upon that right and therefore is not subject to strict scrutiny. *Ysursa v. Pocatello Education Association*, 555 U.S. 353 (2009) (state's decision to limit public employer payroll deductions for a union's political purposes did not abridge the union's right to speech).

1) Contributions to candidates

The government may limit contributions to individual candidates because excessive contributions to candidates create a danger of corruption and the appearance of corruption. *Buckley v. Valeo*, 424 U.S. 1 (1976). However, because aggregate limits on the amount a donor may contribute to candidates for federal office, political parties, and political action committees restrict participation in the political process and do little to further the prevention of "quid pro quo" corruption or the appearance of such corruption in campaign financing, they are invalid under the First Amendment. *McCutcheon v Federal Election Commission*, 572 U.S. ___, 134 S. Ct. 1434 (2014). Limits on campaign contributions to candidates for state office ranging from $275 to $1,000 have been upheld. *Nixon v. Shrink Missouri Gov't PAC*, 528 U.S. 377 (2000). However, the government cannot set differential contribution limits that penalize a candidate who finances his own campaign. *Davis v. Federal Election Commission*, 554 U.S. 724 (2008).

2) Contributions to political parties

The government may limit contributions to a political party that are used to expressly advocate for the election or defeat of a particular candidate (also known as "hard money") as well as contributions that are used for other purposes, such as promoting the party itself (also known as "soft money"). *McConnell v. Federal Election Commission, supra*. In addition, the government may require a political party to disclose contributors and recipients unless the party can show that such disclosure would cause harm to the party. *Brown v. Socialist Workers '74 Campaign Committee*, 454 U.S. 112 (1982).

3) Contributions to political action committees (PACs)

The government may limit contributions to a political action committee (PAC). *California Medical Assn. v. FEC*, 453 U.S. 182 (1981).

b. Political campaign expenditures

In contrast to campaign contributions, restrictions on expenditures by individuals and entities (including corporations and unions) on communications during an election campaign regarding a candidate are subject to strict scrutiny. So long as the source of the funding is disclosed, there is no legal limit to the amount that corporations and unions may spend on "electioneering communications." *Citizens United v. Federal Election Comm'n*, 558 U.S. 310 (2010). In addition, expenditures by a candidate on her own behalf cannot be limited. *Buckley v. Valeo, supra*; *Davis v. Federal Election Commission, supra.*

c. Political speakers

In addition to individuals, corporations (both nonprofit and for-profit) enjoy First Amendment protection with regard to political speech. *Citizens United, supra*. Similarly, a candidate for a judgeship has a First Amendment right to express his views on disputed legal or political issues. *Republican Party of Minnesota v. White*, 536 U.S. 765 (2002). A state law banning judicial candidates from personally soliciting campaign funds, however, does not necessarily violate the First Amendment. *Williams-Yulee v. The Florida Bar*, 575 U.S. ___, 135 S. Ct. 1656 (2015).

B. REGULATION OF TIME, PLACE, AND MANNER OF EXPRESSION

The government's ability to regulate the time, place, and manner of speech varies with the forum in which the speech takes place.

1. Public Forum

A **"public forum"** may be **traditional** or **designated.** Traditional public forums are those that are historically associated with expression, such as sidewalks, streets, and parks. A designated (or limited) public forum is one that has not historically been used for speech-related activities, but which the government has opened for such use, such as civic auditoriums, publicly owned theaters, or school classrooms that the public is allowed to use afterhours. The practical difference between the two is that the government can change a designated forum to a nonpublic forum, but it cannot do the same with a traditional forum.

In either type of public forum, the government may impose reasonable restrictions on the time, place, or manner of protected speech, provided the restrictions:

i) Are **content-neutral** as to both subject matter and viewpoint (i.e., it is not necessary to hear what is said in order to apply the regulation);

ii) Are **narrowly tailored** to serve a **significant governmental interest**; and

iii) Leave open ample **alternative channels for communication** of the information.

Ward v. Rock Against Racism, 491 U.S. 781 (1989). However, additional restrictions, such as an absolute prohibition of a particular type of expression, will be upheld only if narrowly drawn to accomplish a compelling governmental interest, i.e., only if they satisfy strict scrutiny. *United States v. Grace*, 461 U.S. 171 (1983). Restrictions that are not content-neutral are also subject to **strict scrutiny** (*see* § XVIII.C., Regulation of Content, *infra*).

a. Residential areas

There is no right to focus picketing on a particular single residence. However, a person may solicit charitable funds in a residential area. Door-to-door solicitation does not require a permit, as long as the solicitation is for noncommercial or nonfundraising purposes. *Cantwell v. Conn.*, 310 U.S. 296, 306 (1940).

b. Injunctions

The test for the constitutionality of injunctions in public forums depends on whether the injunction is content-neutral or content-based. If an injunction is **content-neutral**, then the test is whether it burdens **no more speech than is necessary** to achieve an **important** governmental interest. On the other hand, if the injunction is **content-based,** it must be **necessary** for the government to achieve a **compelling** governmental interest.

c. Public schools

When a public school, as a designated (limited) public forum, permits the public to use its facilities, it cannot discriminate against organizations based on its beliefs. *Lamb's Chapel v. Center Moriches Union Free School District*, 508 U.S. 384 (1993) (religious organizations); *Widmar v. Vincent*, 454 U.S. 263 (1981); *Healy v. James*, 408 U.S. 169 (1972) (political organization). Similarly, a public school may provide funding and other benefits (e.g., free use of facilities) to student groups, but it must do so on a viewpoint-neutral basis.

> **Example 1:** A university that provided funds to various student publications could not withhold funds from a student religious publication on the grounds that the publication espoused religion. *Rosenberger v. Rector and Visitors of the University of Virginia*, 515 U.S. 819 (1995).

> **Example 2:** A public university law school could adopt an "all comers policy" with which student organizations must comply in order to receive school funding and other benefits. Under the policy, a student organization had to admit any student as a member and permit any student to hold office in the organization. Because the policy was viewpoint-neutral, its application to a religious organization was constitutional. *Christian Legal Soc'y Chapter of Univ. of California, Hastings Coll. of Law v. Martinez*, 561 U.S. 661 (2010).

2. Nonpublic Forum

A nonpublic forum is essentially all public property that is not a traditional or designated public forum. Examples include government offices, schools, jails, military bases, and polling places. Sidewalks on postal service property and airport terminals are also considered nonpublic forums. The government may regulate speech-related activities in nonpublic forums as long as the regulation is (i) **viewpoint-neutral** and (ii) **reasonably related to a legitimate governmental interest.**

> Note that a governmental fundraising campaign is a nonpublic forum for the expression of speech. The decision to exclude some charities (but not others) cannot be made because the government disagrees with a particular organization's political views; such a decision must be ideologically neutral. *Cornelius v. NAACP Legal Def. and Educ. Fund, Inc.*, 473 U.S. 788 (1985).

a. Viewpoint-neutral

The regulation need not be content-neutral, but it must be viewpoint-neutral. In other words, the government may prohibit speech on certain issues altogether, but it may not allow only one side of an issue to be presented. For example, while a restriction on all public speeches in airports related to firearms regulation would likely be upheld, a restriction only on pro-NRA speeches would not.

> **Contrast this** with restrictions on speech in a public forum, which must be both content- and viewpoint-neutral.

b. Reasonable

The restriction on speech-related activities in nonpublic forums must only be rationally related to a legitimate governmental interest. For example, a city may sell commercial advertising space inside city buses but refuse to sell such space for political advertising in order to avoid the appearance of favoritism and imposition on a captive audience. *Lehman v. City of Shaker Heights*, 418 U.S. 298 (1974).

3. Personal Property

Governmental regulation of speech on a person's own private property will rarely be upheld, particularly content-based regulations. While the government has some limited powers to regulate speech on private property, outright bans on certain types of speech, such as signs in a person's yard or window, are impermissible. *City of Ladue v. Gilleo*, 512 U.S. 43 (1994) (statute banning all residential signs in order to fight "visual clutter" was found unconstitutional).

C. REGULATION OF CONTENT

Any governmental regulation of speech that is **content-based on its face** will only be upheld if the regulation is necessary to achieve a compelling governmental interest and is narrowly tailored to meet that interest (i.e., the **strict scrutiny** test). *Reed v. Town of Gilbert*, 576 U.S. ___, 135 S. Ct. 2218 (2015). However, even regulations that are not content-based on their face may still be content-based in application or in intent, and these laws, too, will generally be subject to strict scrutiny. *Brown v. Entm't Merchs. Ass'n*, 564 U.S 786 (2011) (state law that prohibited the sale of violent video games to minors is an unconstitutional content restriction on speech); *Simon & Schuster, Inc. v. Members of the New York State Crime Victims Board*, 502 U.S. 105 (1991). The government must identify an actual problem, and the regulation of speech must be necessary to solve that problem. This standard is incredibly stringent and is not often met. *U.S. v. Playboy Entm't Group, Inc.*, 529 U.S. 803 (2000).

However, the government may restrict speech on the basis of content if the speech falls into one of the following historic and traditional categories: obscenity, subversive speech, fighting words, defamation, or commercial speech. *U.S. v. Alvarez*, 567 U.S. 709 (2012). States are not free to create new categories of content-based restrictions without persuasive evidence that such restrictions have a long-standing history of proscription. *Brown v. Entm't Merchs. Ass'n, supra.*

1. Obscenity and Child Pornography

Neither obscene speech nor child pornography is protected by the First Amendment Free Speech Clause. *Roth v. United States*, 354 U.S. 476 (1957).

a. Obscenity test

To be considered obscene, speech must meet each part of a three-prong test developed in *Miller v. California*, 413 U.S. 15 (1973). Under the *Miller* test, the **average person,** applying **contemporary community standards,** must find that the material, **taken as a whole**:

i) Appeals to the **"prurient interest"**;

ii) Depicts sexual conduct in a **patently offensive** way; and

iii) **Lacks serious literary, artistic, political, or scientific value.**

EXAM NOTE: *Standards Distinguished* – The first two prongs of this test use a contemporary **community** standard, which may be national but is generally considered to be local or statewide. A **national** standard must be applied, however, to the third prong of the test—determining the value of the work—because the work may merit constitutional protection despite local views to the contrary. *Pope v. Illinois*, 481 U.S. 497 (1987). With regard to the third prong, the judge, not the jury, determines whether this standard has been met.

Courts have recently begun to distinguish legally obscene speech from pornography. Merely establishing that speech constitutes pornography is generally insufficient to establish that the speech is obscene. Therefore, content-based restrictions on pornography are generally subject to strict scrutiny. *United States v. Playboy Entm't Grp. Inc.*, 529 U.S. 803 (2000).

Either an appellate court or a jury can assess whether the material is obscene. Evidence of similar material on newsstands is not automatically admissible, nor is expert testimony required to make such a determination.

b. Prohibited activities

The sale, distribution, and exhibition of obscene material may be prohibited. *Stanley v. Georgia*, 394 U.S. 557 (1969). However, the right to privacy generally precludes criminalization of possession of obscenity in one's own home. *Stanley v. Georgia, supra.*

c. Land-use restrictions

Narrowly drawn zoning ordinances may be used to restrict the location of certain adult entertainment businesses (e.g., adult theaters, adult bookstores, strip clubs) if the purpose of the regulation is to reduce the impact on the neighborhood of such establishments, but they may not be used to ban such establishments entirely. It does not matter that such establishments may be found in adjoining jurisdictions. *Los Angeles v. Alameda Books*, 535 U.S. 425 (2002); *City of Renton v. Playtime Theatres, Inc.*, 475 U.S. 41 (1986).

d. Minors

Material that appeals to the prurient interests of minors may be regulated as to minors, even if it would not be considered obscene to an adult audience. *Ginsberg v. New York*, 390 U.S. 629 (1968). The government may not, however, block adults' access to indecent materials in order to prevent them from reaching children. *Reno v. ACLU*, 521 U.S. 844 (1997).

e. Child pornography

The First Amendment also does not protect child pornography, which is sexually explicit visual portrayals that feature children. Because of the state's compelling interest in protecting minor children from exploitation, the sale, distribution, and even private possession of child pornography may be prohibited, even if the material would not be obscene if it involved adults. *Osborne v. Ohio*, 495 U.S. 103 (1990); *New York v. Ferber*, 458 U.S. 747 (1982).

Simulated child pornography (i.e., pornography using young-looking adults or computer-generated images) may not be banned as child pornography. *Ashcroft v. Free Speech Coalition*, 535 U.S. 234 (2002). However, offers to sell or buy simulated child pornography that contain actual depictions of children even though the sexually explicit features are simulated may be criminalized when the material is presented as actual child pornography. *United States v. Williams*, 553 U.S. 285 (2008).

f. Violence

Violence is not included in the definition of obscenity that may be constitutionally regulated. *Brown v. Entm't Merchs. Ass'n, supra; Winters v. New York,* 333 U.S. 507 (1948).

2. Incitement to Violence

A state may forbid speech that advocates the use of force or unlawful action if:

i) The speech is **directed to inciting or producing imminent lawless action**; and

ii) It is **likely to incite or produce such action** (i.e., creates a clear and present danger).

Brandenburg v. Ohio, 395 U.S. 444 (1969).

Advocacy requires the use of language reasonably and ordinarily calculated to incite persons to such action. *Yates v. United States,* 354 U.S. 298 (1957). The abstract expression of ideas, including the teaching of the moral propriety or even moral necessity for a resort to force and violence, is not the same as the actual incitement of violence. There must be substantial evidence of a strong and pervasive call to violence. *Noto v. United States,* 367 U.S. 290 (1960).

3. Fighting Words

A speaker may be criminally punished for using "fighting words," which are words that **by their very nature** are likely to incite an immediate breach of the peace. *Chaplinsky v. New Hampshire,* 315 U.S. 568 (1942). Words that are simply annoying or offensive are not fighting words; there must be a genuine likelihood of imminent violence by a hostile audience. *Cohen v. California,* 403 U.S. 15 (1971).

> **EXAM NOTE:** Attempts to forbid fighting words almost always fail as vague, overbroad, or otherwise constitutionally infirm.

Statutes designed to punish only fighting words that express certain viewpoints are unconstitutional. *R.A.V. v. City of St. Paul,* 505 U.S. 377 (1992) (the Court struck down an ordinance that applied only to fighting words that insulted or provoked on the basis of race, religion, or gender).

However, actual threats of violence are outside the protection of the First Amendment, given the need to protect individuals from (i) the fear of violence, (ii) the disruption that fear engenders, and (iii) the possibility that the threatened violence will occur. *R.A.V. v. City of St. Paul,* 505 at 388.

4. Defamation

Limits on punishment for defamatory speech may apply in cases in which the plaintiff is a public official or public figure, or when a defamatory statement involves a matter of public concern. In addition to the elements of a prima facie case of defamation, the plaintiff must in these cases prove both **fault** and the **falsity** of the statement.

a. Public figure or official

A public figure is someone who is known to the general public and includes any person who has voluntarily injected herself into the public eye. The plaintiff must prove that the defendant acted with **actual malice,** i.e., knowledge of the statement's falsity or reckless disregard for whether it was true or false. *New York Times v. Sullivan,* 376 U.S. 254 (1964). Scientists who publish in scientific journals, criminals, and spouses of wealthy persons are not considered public figures.

b. Public concern

If the plaintiff is a private figure but the defamatory statement involves a matter of public concern, then the standard is lower, but the plaintiff still must establish negligence with respect to the falsity of the statement. *Gertz v. Robert Welch, Inc.*, 418 U.S. 323 (1974).

[See the Themis Torts outline for a full discussion of defamation actions.]

5. Commercial Speech

Commercial speech—advertising and similarly economically oriented expression—is entitled to an intermediate level of First Amendment protection. Restrictions on commercial speech are reviewed under a **four-part test**:

i) The commercial speech must **concern lawful activity** and be **neither false nor misleading** (fraudulent speech or speech which proposes an illegal transaction may be prohibited);

ii) The asserted governmental interest must be **substantial**;

iii) The regulation must **directly advance** the asserted interest; and

iv) The regulation must be **narrowly tailored** to serve that interest. In this context, narrowly tailored does not mean the least restrictive means available; rather, there must be a **"reasonable fit"** between the government's ends and the means chosen to accomplish those ends. *Board of Trustees of State University of New York v. Fox*, 492 U.S. 469 (1989).

Central Hudson Gas & Elec. v. Pub. Svc. Comm'n, 447 U.S. 557 (1980). Under this test, the Court has struck down laws prohibiting truthful advertising of legal abortions, contraceptives, drug prices, alcohol prices, and attorneys' fees and regulation of billboards on the basis of aesthetic value and safety.

Example: A Massachusetts regulation that prohibited tobacco billboards within 1,000 feet of a school was struck down because the means—effectively barring most outdoor tobacco advertising in urban areas—were not narrowly tailored to the ends of protecting children. *Lorillard Tobacco Co. v. Reilly*, 533 U.S. 525 (2001).

Note that solicitation of funds, however, is recognized as a form of protected speech. *See Village of Schaumburg v. Citizens for a Better Env't*, 444 U.S. 620 (1980).

D. REGULATION OF THE MEDIA

Although the First Amendment specifically mentions freedom of the press, the media has no greater First Amendment rights than the general public.

1. General Considerations

The press has the right to publish information about matters of public concern, and the viewers have a right to receive it. This right may be restricted only by a regulation that is narrowly tailored to further a compelling governmental interest (i.e., strict scrutiny applies).

a. Gag orders

A gag order is a judicial order prohibiting the press from publishing information about court proceedings. Such orders are subject to prior-restraint analysis. Gag orders are almost always struck down because they are rarely the least restrictive means of protecting the defendant's right to a fair trial. The trial judge has other alternatives available, such as change of venue, postponement of the trial, careful voir dire, or restricting the statements of lawyers and witnesses. *Nebraska Press Ass'n v. Stuart*, 427 U.S. 539 (1972).

b. Attending trials

The public and the press both have the right to attend criminal trials, but this right is not absolute. It may be outweighed if the trial judge finds an **overriding** interest that cannot be accommodated by less restrictive means. The Supreme Court has not determined whether this right also applies to civil trials. However, the Supreme Court has held that the defendant's right to a public trial extended to voir dire, and the trial court must consider reasonable alternatives to closing the voir dire to the public in addressing the trial court's concerns. *Presley v. Georgia*, 558 U.S. 209 (2010).

c. No constitutional privilege to protect sources

A journalist has no First Amendment right to refuse to testify before a grand jury regarding the content and source of information relevant to the criminal inquiry. *Branzburg v. Hayes*, 408 U.S. 665 (1972).

d. Illegally obtained and private information

The First Amendment shields the media from liability for publishing information that was obtained illegally by a third party as long as the information involves a matter of public concern and the publisher neither obtained it unlawfully nor knows who did. *Bartnicki v. Vopper*, 532 U.S. 514 (2001).

Similarly, the First Amendment shields the media from liability for publication of a lawfully obtained private fact, e.g., the identity of a rape victim, so long as the news story involves a matter of public concern. *See Florida Star v. BJF*, 491 U.S. 524 (1989); *Cox Broadcasting v. Cohn*, 420 U.S. 469 (1975).

e. First Amendment conflict with state right of publicity

Some states recognize a right of publicity—the right of a person to control the commercial use of his or her identity. The right is an intellectual property right derived under state law, the infringement of which creates a cause of action for the tort of unfair competition. In *Zacchini v. Scripps-Howard Broad. Co.*, 433 U.S. 562 (1977), the Supreme Court considered a conflict between the First Amendment and a person's state-law right of publicity. A news program had televised a videotape of a daredevil's entire 15-second performance at a local fair when he was shot out of a cannon. The lower court held that the First Amendment protected the telecast from a tort suit regarding the right of publicity. The Supreme Court reversed, holding that the First and Fourteenth Amendments do not immunize the news media from civil liability when they broadcast a performer's entire act without his consent, and the Constitution does not prevent a state from requiring broadcasters to compensate performers. Note that a state government may pass a law shielding the press from liability for broadcasting performers' acts.

f. No immunity from laws of general applicability

As mentioned previously, the press has no greater First Amendment rights than does the general public, i.e., there is no special privilege allowing the press to invade the rights of others. As such, members of the press are not immune from the application of generally applicable laws, even if the application of such laws has a negative incidental effect on the ability to gather and report the news. *Cohen v. Cowles Media Co.*, 501 U.S. 663 (1991).

2. Broadcast

Because the broadcast spectrum is a limited resource, radio and television broadcasters are said to have a greater responsibility to the public, and they therefore can be more closely regulated than print and other media. Broadcasters may be sanctioned, therefore, for airing "patently offensive sexual and excretory speech," even if such speech does not qualify as obscene under the *Miller* test, in the interest of protecting children likely to be listening. *FCC v. Pacifica Found.*, 438 U.S. 726 (1978).

3. Cable Television

The First Amendment protection provided to cable television falls somewhere between the extensive protection given to print media and the more limited protection for broadcasting. As such, a law requiring cable operators to carry local television stations is subject to intermediate scrutiny. *Turner Broad. Sys., Inc. v. FCC*, 512 U.S. 622 (1994).

Content-based regulations of cable broadcasts are subject to **strict scrutiny,** however. *United States v. Playboy Entm't. Group, Inc.*, 529 U.S. 803 (2000).

4. Internet

Because the Internet is not composed of scarce frequencies as are the broadcast media, and because of the reduced risk of an unexpected invasion of privacy over the Internet, any regulation of Internet content is subject to strict scrutiny. *Reno v. ACLU*, 521 U.S. 844 (1997).

E. REGULATION OF ASSOCIATION

Freedom of association protects the right to form or participate in any group, gathering, club, or organization virtually without restriction, although the right is not absolute. An infringement upon this right may be justified by a compelling state interest. *See, e.g., Board of Dirs. of Rotary Int'l v. Rotary Club of Duarte*, 481 U.S. 537 (1987) (discrimination against women was not in furtherance of or necessary for any of the expressive activity undertaken by the organization); *but see Boy Scouts of America v. Dale*, 530 U.S. 640 (2000) (requiring the Boy Scouts to accept leaders who acted in a manner contrary to Boy Scout principles would unduly intrude upon the Boy Scouts' expressive associational rights).

1. Public Employment

An individual generally cannot be denied public employment based simply upon membership in a political organization. *Keyishian v. Board of Regents*, 385 U.S. 589 (1967).

a. Test

A person may only be punished or deprived of public employment based on political association if that individual:

i) Is an active member of a **subversive organization**;

ii) Has **knowledge** of the organization's illegal activity; and

iii) Has a **specific intent** to further those illegal objectives.

Scales v. United States, 367 U.S. 203 (1961) (conviction based on active, knowing, and purposive membership in an organization advocating the violent overthrow of the government upheld).

b. Loyalty oaths

Public employees may be required to take loyalty oaths promising that they will support the Constitution and oppose the forceful, violent, or otherwise illegal or unconstitutional overthrow of the government. *Connell v. Higgenbotham*, 403 U.S. 207 (1971). However, oaths that forbid or require action in terms so vague that a person of common intelligence must guess at the oath's meaning and differ as to its application are often found to be so vague or overbroad as to deprive an individual of liberty or property without due process. *E.g., Cramp v. Board of Public Instruction*, 368 U.S. 278 (1961) (striking down as vague a statute requiring public employees to swear that they have not and will not lend "aid, support, advice, counsel, or influence to the Communist Party"); *Shelton v. Tucker*, 364 U.S. 479 (1960) (striking down as overbroad a statute requiring teachers to file an affidavit listing every organization to which they have belonged or regularly contributed during the past five years).

2. Bar Membership

Although the state can inquire into the character of a candidate for bar admission, such admission cannot be denied on the basis of political association unless the candidate knowingly belongs to a subversive organization with specific intent to further its illegal ends. *Schware v. Board of Bar Exam'rs*, 353 U.S. 232 (1957). The state may, however, deny bar membership to a candidate who refuses to answer questions about political affiliations if that refusal obstructs the investigation of the candidate's qualifications. *Konigsberg v. State Bar of California*, 366 U.S. 36 (1961).

3. Elections and Political Parties

a. Voters in primary elections

A state cannot require a local political party to select presidential electors in an open primary (i.e., a primary in which any voter, including members of another party, may vote) when the national party prohibits nonparty members from voting. *Democratic Party v. LaFolette*, 450 U.S. 107 (1981). A state can require a semi-closed primary system, in which only registered party members and independents can vote in the party's primary, even if the party wants to permit anyone to vote. *Clingman v. Beaver*, 544 U.S. 581 (2005). On the other hand, a state may not prohibit a political party from allowing independents to vote in its primary. *Tashjian v. Republican Party of Connecticut*, 479 U.S. 208 (1986).

1) Blanket primary

A state may adopt a blanket primary system (i.e., a primary in which all voters regardless of party affiliation or lack thereof vote) that is nonpartisan. Under a nonpartisan primary system, the voters choose candidates for the general election without regard for their party affiliation. A nonpartisan blanket primary system in which a candidate identifies his own party preference or his status as an independent and that identification appears on the ballot has withstood a facial challenge, despite assertions that this self-designation violates the party's First Amendment rights as compelled speech and forced association. *Washington State Grange v. Washington State Republican Party*, 552 U.S. 442 (2008). By contrast, a partisan blanket primary system in which a party's nominees are chosen violates the party's First Amendment rights of free speech and association. *Cal. Democratic Party v. Jones*, 530 U.S. 567 (2000).

b. **Ballot access to general election**

A state may refuse to grant a political party's candidate access to the general-election ballot unless the party demonstrates public support through voter signatures on a petition, voter registrations, or previous electoral success. *Timmons v. Twin Cities Area New Party*, 520 U.S. 351 (1997); *Munro v. Socialist Workers Party*, 479 U.S. 189 (1986).

c. **Fusion candidate**

A state may prohibit a fusion candidate (i.e., a candidate who is nominated by more than one political party) from appearing on the general-election ballot as a candidate of multiple parties. This limitation on the associational rights of political parties is justified by the state's interests in ballot integrity and political stability. *Timmons v. Twin Cities Area New Party*, 520 U.S. 351 (1997).

d. **Replacement candidate**

When a state gives a political party the right to select an interim replacement for an elected state official who was a member of that party, the party may select the replacement through an election at which only party members may vote. *Rodriguez v. Popular Democratic Party*, 457 U.S. 1 (1982).

Corporations

CORPORATIONS

Table of Contents

CORPORATIONS

I. FORMATION OF A CORPORATION

A. PRE-INCORPORATION TRANSACTIONS

1. Promoters

Prior to the formation of a corporation, a promoter engages in activities, such as procuring capital and entering into contracts, in order to bring the corporation into existence as a business entity.

a. Liability for pre-incorporation agreements

A promoter is personally liable for **knowingly acting** on behalf of a corporation before incorporation and is jointly and severally liable for all liabilities created while so acting, even after the corporation comes into existence, unless a subsequent novation releases the promoter from liability. Revised Model Business Corporation Act (RMBCA) § 2.04. To establish liability, it is insufficient that a person should have known that the corporation was not formed; actual knowledge of the entity's pre-incorporation status is required. *See Sivers v. R & F Capital Corp.*, 858 P.2d 895, 898 (Or. Ct. App. 1993). In addition, if a party who contracts with a promoter knows that the corporation has not yet been formed and agrees to look only to the corporation for performance, then the promoter is not liable.

> **EXAM NOTE:** Promoter liability is often tested in the context of pre-incorporation agreements. Remember that promoters are liable to third parties for pre-incorporation agreements even after incorporation, unless the corporation specifically relieves the promoter of liability.

b. Fiduciary duty to the corporation

A promoter stands in a fiduciary relationship with the pre-incorporated corporation. The promoter can be liable to the corporation for violating a fiduciary duty, such as by making a secret profit (e.g., failing to disclose a commission on a pre-incorporation transaction).

c. Right to reimbursement

Although a promoter can seek compensation for pre-incorporation activities undertaken on the corporation's behalf and reimbursement for related expenses, the promoter cannot compel the corporation to make such payments, because the promoter's acts, while done to benefit the corporation, are not undertaken at the corporation's direction.

2. Corporation's Liability for Pre-Incorporation Transactions

a. General rule—no liability

A corporation is not liable for pre-incorporation transactions entered into by a promoter. The fact that the promoter entered into a transaction to benefit a future corporation is not sufficient to hold the corporation liable.

Because a corporation is not necessarily in existence during a pre-incorporation transaction, a principal-agent relationship does not exist between the corporation and the promoter.

b. Exception—liability upon contract adoption

The corporation can be liable when the corporation adopts the contract. Adoption of a contract can be express or implied. Adoption takes place when the corporation accepts the benefits of the transaction or gives an express acceptance of liability for the debt, such as through a board resolution after incorporation.

3. Incorporator Liability

An incorporator is a person who signs and files the articles of incorporation with the state. By performing such acts, an incorporator does not engender liability for a contract entered into by a promoter of the corporation.

B. INCORPORATION

1. Procedures

To form a corporation, a document, referred to as the "articles of incorporation" or "charter," must be filed with the state.

a. Articles of incorporation

The articles of incorporation must include certain basic information about the corporation, such as its **name, purpose,** the **number of shares** it is authorized to issue, **the name and address of its registered agent,** and the **name and address of each incorporator.** RMBCA § 2.02(a).

1) Corporate name

The corporation's name must contain the word "corporation," "company," "incorporated," "limited," or an abbreviation thereof.

2) Corporate purpose

The articles of incorporation must include a statement of the corporation's purposes. A broad statement of such purpose, such as "to engage in any lawful activity," is acceptable. The RMBCA presumes that each corporation has the broadest lawful purpose unless a more limited purpose is defined in the articles of incorporation. RMBCA § 3.01.

3) Corporate powers

In addition to specifying purposes, the articles of incorporation may also enumerate powers that the corporation possesses. Most states automatically grant all corporations broad powers, such as the powers to buy and sell property and to sue and be sued. RMBCA § 3.02. Some states place restrictions on various corporate actions, including corporate loans to officers and directors. For a corporation with stock listed on a national securities exchange, federal law prohibits the corporation from making personal loans to a director or executive officer of the corporation. 15 U.S.C. § 78m.

4) Corporate duration

Although a corporation can have perpetual existence, it may instead choose to limit its duration. RMBCA § 3.02.

b. Filing requirements

The articles of incorporation must be filed with a state official, usually with the secretary of state, and a filing fee paid.

Once the requirements are met, some states treat the corporation as having been formed as of the date of the filing, while other states consider the corporation a legal entity only when the state has accepted the articles of incorporation. RMBCA §§ 1.23, 2.03.

2. Ultra Vires Actions

When a corporation that has stated a narrow business purpose in its articles of incorporation subsequently engages in activities outside that stated purpose, the corporation has engaged in an ultra vires act. When a third party enters into a transaction with the corporation that constitutes an ultra vires act for the corporation, the third party generally cannot assert that the corporation has acted outside those powers in order to escape liability.

a. Challenges to ultra vires acts

An ultra vires act can be challenged in only the following three situations.

i) A shareholder can file suit to enjoin the corporation's ultra vires action;

ii) The corporation can take action against a director, officer, or employee of the corporation who engages in such action; or

iii) The state can initiate a proceeding against the corporation to enjoin its ultra vires action.

RMBCA § 3.04(b).

b. Enjoining an ultra vires act

An ultra vires act will be enjoined only if it is equitable to do so.

3. Effect of Incorporation—"De Jure" Corporation

When all of the statutory requirements for incorporation have been satisfied, a de jure corporation is created. Consequently, the corporation, rather than persons associated with the corporation (i.e., shareholders, directors, officers, and other employees), is liable for activities undertaken by the corporation.

4. Defective Incorporation

a. Lack of good-faith effort to incorporate

When a person conducts business as a corporation without attempting to comply with the statutory incorporation requirements, that person is liable for any obligations incurred in the name of the nonexistent corporation. RMBCA § 2.04.

b. Good-faith effort to incorporate

When a person makes an unsuccessful effort to comply with the incorporation requirements, that person may be able to escape personal liability under either the de facto corporation or corporation by estoppel doctrines.

1) De facto corporation

The owner must make a good-faith effort to comply with the incorporation requirements and must operate the business as a corporation without knowing that these requirements have not been met. If the owner has done so, then the business entity is treated as a de facto corporation, and the owner, as a de facto shareholder, is not personally liable for obligations incurred in the purported corporation's name. Note, however, that the RMBCA has abolished this doctrine, as have many of the jurisdictions that have adopted the RMBCA. *See, e.g., In re Estate of Woodroffe,* 742 N.W.2d 94 (Iowa 2007).

2) Corporation by estoppel

A person who deals with an entity as if it were a corporation is estopped from denying its existence and is thereby prevented from seeking the personal liability of the business owner. This doctrine is limited to contractual agreements. In addition, the business owner must have made a good-faith effort to comply with incorporation requirements and must lack knowledge that the requirements were not met.

II. GOVERNANCE

A. INSTRUMENTS

1. Articles of Incorporation

The articles of incorporation must be filed to incorporate, but they need not spell out the manner in which the corporation is to be governed. RMBCA § 2.02(b).

a. Articles of correction

If the articles of incorporation contain an inaccuracy or were defectively executed, then articles of correction may be filed with the state to correct the inaccuracy or defect. RMBCA § 1.24.

b. Amendment of articles

The corporation can amend its articles with any lawful provision. The procedure for securing approval to amend the articles of incorporation varies depending on whether the corporation has issued stock. Once the necessary approval is obtained, articles of amendment must be filed with the state.

1) No stock issued

If the corporation has not issued stock, the board of directors—or, if the board does not exist, the incorporators—may amend the articles of incorporation. RMBCA § 10.02.

2) Stock issued

If stock has been issued, then corporations generally must follow a two-step approval process:

i) The board of directors must adopt the amendment to the articles of incorporation; and

ii) The board must submit the amendment to the shareholders for their approval by majority vote.

RMBCA § 10.03(a)–(b).

2. Bylaws

The bylaws may contain any lawful provision for the management of the corporation's business or the regulation of its affairs that is not inconsistent with the articles of incorporation. When there is a conflict between the articles of incorporation and the bylaws, the articles of incorporation control. RMBCA § 2.06(b).

Generally, the board of directors adopts the initial bylaws. RMBCA § 2.06(a). However, a majority vote by either the directors or the shareholders can adopt, amend, or repeal a bylaw. RMBCA § 10.20.

B. ORGANIZATIONAL MEETING

Once the articles of incorporation are filed, an organizational meeting is held at which the appointment of officers, adoption of bylaws, and approval of contracts may take place. When the incorporators hold the meeting, election of the board of directors also takes place. RMBCA § 2.05.

C. CHARACTERISTICS OF A CORPORATION

1. Balance of Power

All corporations have the same general structure. All corporations must have (i) shareholders, (ii) officers, and (iii) a board of directors. Each part of the corporation has its own rights and responsibilities. These separate responsibilities and rights act to balance the power of the other parts of the corporation.

2. Limited Liability

One of the primary benefits of a corporation is limited liability. Parties to a corporation are only liable to the extent of their investment. As discussed below, this limited liability is occasionally overcome and certain officers and directors can be held personally liable for actions of the corporation. This is referred to as piercing the corporate veil. See § V.E.1., Piercing the Corporate Veil, *infra*.

III. BOARD OF DIRECTORS

The board of directors manages and directs the management of the corporation's business and affairs. The board also authorizes the officers and other corporate employees to exercise the powers possessed by the corporation. RMBCA § 8.01.

A. COMPOSITION REQUIREMENTS

1. Number of Directors

Traditionally, a board needed three or more directors, but today a board can have as few as one director, regardless of the number of shareholders. In its articles of incorporation or bylaws, a corporation may permit the board to vary the number of directors. RMBCA § 8.03.

2. Qualifications of Directors

A corporation cannot serve as the director of another corporation; a director must be a natural person. Unless required by the articles of incorporation or the bylaws, a director need not be a shareholder of the corporation or resident of a particular state. RMBCA §§ 8.02, 8.03.

3. Selection of Directors

Shareholders select directors at the annual shareholders' meeting and may be elected by straight or cumulative voting and by one or more classes of stock. RMBCA §§ 7.28, 8.03.

B. TERM OF DIRECTORS

1. Annual Terms

Typically, a director serves for a one-year term that expires at the first annual meeting after the director's election. RMBCA § 8.05.

2. Staggered Terms

A director may serve for longer than one year if the terms are staggered. With staggered terms, each year some directors are elected for multi-year terms. The main purpose of staggered terms is to limit the impact of cumulative voting.   RMBCA §§ 8.05, 8.06.

3.   **Holdover Director**

A director whose term has expired may continue to serve until a replacement is selected. RMBCA § 8.05(e).

4.   **Resignation of a Director**

A director may resign at any time by delivering a written notice to the board, its chair, or the corporation. RMBCA § 8.07.

5.   **Removal of a Director**

At common law, shareholders had the inherent power to remove a director. However, because directors were deemed to have an entitlement to their offices, they could only be removed for cause based on substantial grounds (such as breach of fiduciary duty, fraud, criminal conduct, etc.).

The current trend in most states and the RMBCA is to allow shareholders to remove a director with or without cause, unless the articles of incorporation provide otherwise.

a.   **Meeting requirements**

A director may be removed only at a meeting called for the purpose of removing the director, and the meeting notice must state that removal is at least one of the purposes of the meeting. RMBCA § 8.08(d).

b.   **Voting requirements**

A director who was elected by a particular voting class of stock can only be removed by that same class (or by court proceeding). RMBCA § 8.08(b).

If cumulative voting is not authorized, then a shareholder vote removes a director if the number of votes for removal exceeds the number of votes against removal. RMBCA § 8.08(c).

If cumulative voting is authorized, then a director may not be removed if the votes sufficient to elect the director are cast against the director's removal. RMBCA § 8.08.

Notwithstanding the foregoing, a director can be removed by court proceeding.

6.   **Replacement or New Director**

When there is a vacancy on the board or an increase in the number of directors, either the shareholders or the directors may fill the vacancy. When the vacancy leaves the board without a quorum, the directors remaining can elect a replacement director by a majority vote. RMBCA § 8.10(a).

C.   **COMPENSATION OF DIRECTORS**

Directors of a corporation may receive compensation for serving as directors. RMBCA § 8.11.

D.   **MEETING REQUIREMENTS**

1.   **Types of Meetings**

The board of directors may hold regular or special meetings. Unless the articles of incorporation or bylaws provide otherwise, a director is entitled to two days' notice of the date, time, and place of a **special meeting**, although the purpose is not required. A **regular meeting** may be held without notice of the date, time, place, or purpose of the meeting. A director may waive notice of a meeting at any time by a signed written waiver. In addition, a director's attendance waives notice of that meeting unless the director promptly objects to lack of notice. RMBCA §§ 8.20–.23.

2. Presence at Meetings

A director is not required to be physically present at a meeting. A meeting may be conducted through a conference call or any other means that allows each director to hear the other directors during the meeting. RMBCA § 8.20(b).

3. Action Without a Meeting

The board of directors may act without holding a meeting by unanimous written consent to the action. RMBCA § 8.21.

E. VOTING REQUIREMENTS

1. Quorum Rules

For the board of directors' acts at a meeting to be valid, a quorum of directors must be present at the meeting. RMBCA § 8.24(a).

a. Number of directors

A majority of all directors in office constitutes a quorum, unless a higher or lower number is required by the articles of incorporation or bylaws. RMBCA § 8.24.

b. Presence of directors

Unlike a shareholder, a director must be present at the time that the vote is taken to be counted for quorum purposes. RMBCA § 8.24. Presence includes appearances made using communications equipment that allows all persons participating in the meeting to hear and speak to one another.

2. Passage Level

Typically, the assent of a majority of the directors present at the time the vote takes place is necessary for board approval. However, the articles of incorporation or bylaws may specify a higher level of approval. RMBCA § 8.24(c).

3. Director Dissent

A director may incur liability for illegal or improper action taken by the board at a meeting at which the director is present, even though the director does not vote in favor of the action.

To forestall such liability, the director must:

i) Promptly object to the holding of the meeting;

ii) Ensure that his dissent or abstention from the specific action is noted in the minutes of the meeting; or

iii) Not vote in favor of the action and deliver written notice of his dissent to the presiding officer of the meeting before its adjournment or to the corporation immediately afterward.

RMBCA § 8.24(d).

4. Voting Agreements

Generally, an agreement between directors as to how to vote (i.e., a pooling agreement) is unenforceable. Each director is expected to exercise independent judgment. A director also may not vote by proxy.

F.   COMMITTEES

The board of directors may take action through one or more committees. RMBCA § 8.25.

1.   Composition of a Committee

A committee may consist of two or more directors. RMBCA § 8.25.

2.   Selection of Committee Members

Generally, a majority of the directors must vote for the creation of a committee and the appointment of a director to a committee. RMBCA § 8.25(b).

3.   Committee's Powers

A committee may generally exercise whatever powers are granted to it by the board, the articles of incorporation, or the bylaws. RMBCA § 8.25(d)–(e).

A committee may not:

   i)   Declare distributions, except within limits set by the board;

   ii) Recommend actions that require shareholder approval;

   iii) Fill vacancies on the board or its committees; or

   iv) Adopt, amend, or repeal bylaws.

4.   Type of Committees—Sarbanes-Oxley Act

Typically, the board of a publicly held corporation has an audit committee, a compensation committee, and a nominating committee. A corporation with stock listed on a national securities exchange or a national securities association must have an audit committee that has direct responsibility for selecting, compensating, and overseeing the corporation's outside auditors. The members of the audit committee must be independent directors (i.e., not otherwise employed or compensated by the corporation).

> Outside auditors cannot otherwise be employed by the corporation. Sarbanes-Oxley Act 301.

G.   DUTIES

A director owes two basic duties to the corporation: (i) a duty of care, and (ii) a duty of loyalty. In discharging these duties, a director is required to act in good faith and in a manner the director reasonably believes to be in the best interest of the corporation. RMBCA § 8.30.

1.   Duty of Care

a.   Prudent person

Directors have a duty to act with the care that a **person in a like position would reasonably believe appropriate under similar circumstances**. As an objective standard, the director is presumed to have the knowledge and skills of an ordinarily prudent person. In deciding how to act, the director is also required to use any additional knowledge or special skills that he possesses.

b.   Reliance protection

A director is entitled to rely on the performance of, as well as information, reports, and opinions supplied by the following persons if the director reasonably believes them to be reliable and competent:

   i)   Officers and other employees of the corporation;

ii) Outside attorneys, accountants, or other skilled or expert individuals retained by the corporation; and

iii) A committee of the board of which the director is not a member.

RMBCA § 8.30(e).

c. **Business judgment rule**

The business judgment rule is a rebuttable presumption that a director reasonably believed that his actions were in the best interest of the corporation. *Benihana of Tokyo, Inc. v. Benihana, Inc.* 906 A.2d 114 (2006). The exercise of managerial powers by a director is generally subject to the business judgment rule. *Smith v. Van Gorkom,* 488 F.2d 858 (Del. 985). A typical decision protected by the business judgment rule includes whether to declare a dividend and the amount of any dividend. *Kamin v. American Express Co., 282 N.Y.S. 2d 807 (1976).* Generally, a court will not interfere with the business judgment of a director or officer without a showing of fraud, illegality, or conflict of interest. *Shlensky v. Wrigley*, 237 N.E. 2d 776 (1968).

1) **Overcoming the rule**

To overcome the business judgment rule, it must be shown that:

i) The director did not act in good faith (e.g., intense hostility of the controlling faction against the minority; exclusion of the minority from employment by the corporation; high salaries or bonuses given, or corporate loans made to the officers in control; and the existence of a desire by the controlling directors to acquire the minority stock interests as cheaply as possible);

ii) The director was not informed to the extent that the director reasonably believed was necessary before making a decision;

iii) The director did not show objectivity or independence from the director's relation to or control by another having material interest in the challenged conduct;

iv) There was a sustained failure by the director to devote attention to an ongoing oversight of the business and affairs of the corporation;

v) The director failed to timely investigate a matter of significant material concern after being alerted in a manner that would have caused a reasonably attentive director to do so; or

vi) The director received a financial benefit to which he was not entitled, or any other breach of his duties to the corporation.

RMBCA § 8.31(a).

A director of a corporation may be held personally liable if the director neglects to provide the ordinary care of keeping current with corporate affairs that a director would normally do in that position, and the neglect is the proximate cause of the damages. *Francis v. United Jersey Bank,* 432 A.2d 814 (N.J. 1981).

While the primary purpose of a corporation is to earn a profit for its shareholders, directors have the authority to make charitable contributions when the activity promoted by the gift promotes goodwill of the business, However, those contributions should be less than one percent of capital and surplus and directed to an institution owning no more than ten percent of the company's stock. *A.P. Smith Mfg. Co v. Barlow*, 98 A.2d 581 (1953).

d. Exculpatory provisions in the articles of incorporation

A corporation's articles of incorporation may include an exculpatory provision shielding directors from liability for money damages for failure to exercise adequate care in the performance of their duties as directors. Typically, exculpatory provisions do not protect directors from liability for any breach of the duty of loyalty, for acts or omissions that are not in good faith, or for any transactions from which the director received an improper personal benefit. *See* Del. Gen. Corp. Law § 102(b)(7); Model Bus. Corp. Act § 2.02(b)(4).

2. Duty of Loyalty

The duty of loyalty requires a director to act in a manner that the director reasonably believes is in the best interest of the corporation. RMBCA § 8.60. Typically, a director breaches this duty by placing her own interests before those of the corporation. *Bayer v. Beran*, 49 N.Y.S. 2d 2 (N.Y. 1944).

Directors have no duty to the shareholders to monitor the personal activities of a corporation's founder. *Beam ex rel. Martha Stewart Living OmniMedia v. Stewart*, 833 A.2d 961 (2003).

a. Director's conflicting interest transaction—self-dealing

A director who engages in a conflict-of-interest transaction with his own corporation, also known as self-dealing, has violated his duty of loyalty unless the transaction is protected under the safe harbor rule. The business judgment rule does not apply when a director engages in a conflict-of-interest transaction with his corporation. In addition, a director must not profit at the corporation's expense.

Courts apply a standard of intrinsic fairness to a self-dealing transaction by a parent corporation whose majority ownership creates a fiduciary duty upon the parent corporation. Courts will find self-dealing only if the transaction is detrimental to the minority shareholders. *Sinclair Oil Corp. v. Levien*, 280 A.2d 717 (1971).

1) Type of transactions

A conflict-of-interest transaction is any transaction between a director and his corporation that would normally require approval of the board of directors and that is of such financial significance to the director that it would reasonably be expected to influence the director's vote on the transaction. RMBCA § 8.60(1)–(2). The interest involved can be direct or indirect, but it must be financial and material. The standard of determining whether the interest is material is objective and calls upon the trier of fact to determine whether a reasonable director in similar circumstances would have been influenced by the financial interest when voting on the matter. MBCA § 8.60 cmt. 4.

2) Related persons

Corporate dealings with persons who are related to the director are also subject to conflict-of-interest rules. Related individuals include the director's immediate family, parents, siblings, and grandchildren, including the spouses of these individuals, as well as a trust or estate of which any of those individuals is a substantial beneficiary or the director is a fiduciary.

In addition, the conflict-of-interest rules can apply to transactions between the corporation and another entity with which the director is associated, such as another corporation of which the director is a director, employee, or agent or a partnership of which the director is a general partner, employee, or agent. RMBCA § 8.60(1), (3).

3) Safe harbor rules

a) Standards for upholding transactions

There are three safe harbors by which a conflict-of-interest transaction may enjoy protection:

i) Disclosure of all material facts to, and approval by a majority of, the board of directors without a conflicting interest;

ii) Disclosure of all material facts to, and approval by a majority of, the votes entitled to be cast by the shareholders without a conflicting interest; and

iii) Fairness of the transaction to the corporation at the time of commencement.

RMBCA § 8.61.

b) Fairness of the transaction

The fairness test looks at the substance and procedure of the transaction. Substantively, the court determines whether the corporation received something of comparable value in exchange for what it gave to the director. Procedurally, the court determines whether the process followed by the directors in reaching their decision was appropriate. RMBCA §§ 8.60(5), 8.61(b)(3). Interested directors who were on both sides of the transactions in question have the burden of establishing the substantive and procedural fairness of the transactions. *HMG/Courtland Properties, Inc. v. Gray*, 749 A.2d 94, 115 (Del. Ch. 1999).

c) Effect of safe harbor provisions

Satisfaction of the safe harbor defenses is not necessarily a complete defense, and some states instead hold that the burden of proof shifts to the party challenging the transaction to establish that the transaction was unfair to the corporation. *Kahn v. Lynch Communication System*, 638 A.2d 1110 (Del. 1994).

4) Remedies

A conflict-of-interest transaction that is found to be in violation of the safe harbor provisions may be enjoined or rescinded. In addition, the corporation may seek damages from the director. RMBCA § 8.61.

5) Business judgment rule

Approval of a conflict-of-interest transaction by fully informed disinterested directors triggers the business judgment rule and limits judicial review to issues of gift or waste, with the burden of proof on the party attacking the transaction. *See* Del. Gen. Corp. Law § 144(a)(1); *Marciano v. Nakash*, 535 A.2d 400, 405 n.3 (Del. 1987).

b. Usurpation of a corporate opportunity

In addition to a conflict-of-interest transaction, a director may violate his duty of loyalty by usurping a corporate opportunity rather than first offering the opportunity to the corporation. RMBCA § 8.70.

1) Corporate opportunity

In determining whether the opportunity is one that must first be offered to the corporation, courts have applied the "interest or expectancy" test or the "line of business" test.

a) "Interest or expectancy" test

Under the "interest or expectancy" test, the key is whether the corporation has an existing interest (e.g., an option to buy) or an expectancy arising from an existing right (e.g., purchase of property currently leased) in the opportunity. *Broz v. Cellular Information Systems, Inc.*, 673 A.2d 148 (Del. 1996). An expectancy can also exist when the corporation is actively seeking a similar opportunity.

b) "Line of business" test

Under the broader "line of business" test, the key is whether the opportunity is within the corporation's current or prospective line of business. Whether an opportunity satisfies this test frequently turns on how expansively the corporation's line of business is characterized. *In re eBay, Inc. Shareholder Litigation,* 2004 Del. Ch. LEXIS 4 (2004).

c) Other factors

Courts look at additional factors in determining whether an opportunity belongs to the corporation. These factors include: (i) the relationship between the person offering the opportunity and the director and corporation, (ii) how and when the director acquired knowledge of the opportunity, and (iii) the relationship of the director to the corporation.

c. Competition with corporation

A director who engages in a business venture that competes with the corporation has breached her duty of loyalty to the corporation. However, a director may engage in unrelated business that does not compete with the corporation. Note that corporate officers and other employees more frequently engage in this kind of breach than directors do.

3. Good Faith Obligation

In addition to owing the shareholders the duties of care and loyalty, directors have the obligation to act in good faith when making decisions on behalf of a corporation. As long as the duties are fulfilled and the directors act in good faith, neither the corporation nor its directors will be liable to the shareholders for unfavorable transactions. For a director to breach the obligation of good faith is a "sustained and systematic failure" of the board of directors to exercise oversight. *Stone v. Ritter,* 911 A.2d 362 (2006).

Directors are not liable to the shareholders for poor hiring choices so long as they act consistent with their duty of care, duty of loyalty, and in good faith. *In re The Walt Disney Co. Derivative Litigation,* 907 A.2d 693 (2005).

Directors are not liable to the shareholders for investment and advisory fees related to investment of a corporation's funds unless the fee is so disproportionately large that it has no reasonable relationship to the services rendered and could not have been the product of arm's length bargaining. *Jones v. Harris Associates L.P.,* 130 S. Ct. 1418 (2010). The Supreme Court found that investment company fees are best regulated by the free market, not the Court. *Id.*

4. **Indemnification and Insurance**

When a director is involved in a legal action as a consequence of her role as director, she may seek indemnification for expenses incurred as well as for any judgment or award declared against her. Indemnification may be (i) mandatory, (ii) prohibited, or (iii) permissive. RMBCA §§ 8.50–8.59.

a. **Mandatory indemnification**

A corporation is **required** to indemnify a director for any reasonable expense, including court costs and attorney's fees, incurred in the **successful** defense of a proceeding against the director in his role as a director. In addition, a corporation must indemnify a director when ordered by the court. RMBCA §§ 8.52, 8.56.

b. **Prohibited indemnification**

A corporation is prohibited from indemnifying a director against liability because of the receipt of an improper personal benefit. RMBCA § 8.51(d)(2).

c. **Permissive indemnification**

A corporation **may** indemnify a director in the unsuccessful defense of a suit when:

   i)   The director acted in good faith with the reasonable belief that his conduct was in the best interests of the corporation, or that his conduct was at least not opposed to the best interests of the corporation; and

   ii) In the case of a criminal proceeding, the director did not have reasonable cause to believe that his conduct was unlawful.

> Indemnification can extend to liability as well as expenses when the action is brought by a third party, but only to expenses if the action is brought by or on behalf of the corporation. RMBCA § 8.51(a)(1), (d)(1).

The authorization for permissive indemnification requires the approval of a disinterested majority of directors or shareholders or an independent attorney chosen by disinterested directors. RMBCA § 8.55.

d. **Advance of expenses**

A corporation may, upon a petition by the director, advance litigation expenses to the director. Upon termination of the action, the director must repay such expenses if the director is not entitled to indemnification for them. RMBCA § 8.53.

e. **Liability insurance**

A corporation may acquire insurance to indemnify directors for actions arising from service as a director. The insurance can cover all awards against a director as well as expenses incurred by her, even though the corporation could not otherwise indemnify the director for such amounts. RMBCA § 8.55.

f. **Applicability to officers**

An officer of a corporation is entitled to indemnification on the same basis and subject to the same restrictions as a director. RMBCA § 8.56.

H. INSPECTION RIGHTS OF DIRECTORS

A director is entitled to inspect and copy corporate books, records, and other documents for any purpose related to the performance of his duty as a director. When the corporation refuses to grant the director access to these items, the director can seek a court order to enforce this right. RMBCA § 16.05.

IV. STOCK AND OTHER CORPORATE SECURITIES

A. TYPES

Traditionally, there are two broad types of securities by which a corporation obtains financing for its endeavors—stocks, which carry ownership and control interests in the corporation, and debt securities, which do not. Over time, many securities have been created that blur this distinction. However, every corporation is required to have stock that is entitled to vote on matters of corporate governance (e.g., the election of directors to the board) and stock that represents the basic ownership interest in a corporation. RMBCA § 6.01(b). Stocks that possess these two characteristics are referred to as "common stock." Stocks having preference over other stock to such items as distributions are referred to as "preferred stock."

In general, upon liquidation, a secured creditor of the corporation will generally take precedence over a preferred shareholder with regard to the corporation's funds, and a preferred shareholder will take precedence over a common shareholder. Preferred shareholders generally take precedence to common shareholders with regard to distributions by the corporation.

B. ISSUANCE OF STOCK

When a corporation sells or trades its stock to an investor, the transaction from the corporation's perspective requires the issuance of stock. The corporation may issue such stock, provided the articles of incorporation authorize the issuance. RMBCA § 6.03(a).

1. Authorization

In general, the issuance of stock must be authorized by the board of directors. RMBCA § 6.21(b). Many states also permit the shareholders to authorize the issuance of stock if the articles of incorporation so provide. RMBCA § 6.21(a).

2. Consideration

a. Types of consideration

The RMBCA removed restrictions on the types of consideration that can be accepted by a corporation in payment for its stock. Acceptable consideration includes money, tangible or intangible property, and services rendered to the corporation. RMBCA § 6.21(b).

b. Payment of consideration

When the corporation receives consideration for stock, the stock is deemed fully paid and non-assessable. RMBCA § 6.21(d). A shareholder who fails to pay the consideration is liable to the corporation, and any issued stock may be canceled. If stock has not been fully paid, then the corporation or a creditor of the corporation may be able to recover the unpaid amount from the shareholder. RMBCA § 6.22(a).

c. Valuation of consideration

Under the RMBCA, the board of directors must merely determine that the consideration received for the stock is adequate. Moreover, once the board makes such a determination, the adequacy of the consideration is not subject to challenge. RMBCA § 6.21(c).

1) Par value stock

A corporation may, but is not required to, issue par value stock. For such stock, the corporation is required to receive at least the value assigned to that stock (i.e., par value), which need not be its market value, and which can even be a nominal amount.

2) Watered stock

Because stock is deemed validly issued, paid in full, and non-assessable once the corporation receives adequate consideration (as determined by the board of directors), the RMBCA does not recognize or address the issue of "watered stock," i.e., stock that is issued for consideration less than par value.

3. Stock Subscriptions

Prior to incorporation, persons may subscribe to purchase stock from the corporation when it comes into existence.

a. Revocability

Unless the subscription agreement provides otherwise, a pre-incorporation subscription is irrevocable for six months from the date of the subscription, but a revocation can happen if all subscribers agree to it. RMBCA § 6.20(a).

b. Nonpayment by a subscriber

A corporation can pursue normal collection methods when a subscriber fails to pay the subscription amount. In addition, the corporation can sell the stock to someone else, provided the corporation has made a written demand for payment and given the subscriber at least 20 days to comply with the demand. RMBCA § 6.20(d).

4. Stock Rights, Options, and Warrants

In addition to stock, a corporation may issue rights, options, or warrants to buy its stock. Generally, the board of directors has the authority to issue these instruments and to dictate their terms. RMBCA § 6.24.

5. Shareholder's Preemptive Rights

When the board of directors decides to issue new shares, the rights of shareholders to purchase those shares in order to maintain their proportional ownership share in the corporation are known as "preemptive rights." Shareholders automatically had such rights at common law, but the RMBCA explicitly precludes preemptive rights unless the articles of incorporation provide otherwise. RMBCA § 6.30(a).

Example: A and B, the only shareholders of Corporation X, each own 50 shares of stock. The board of directors of Corporation X authorizes the issuance of another 20 shares. With preemptive rights, A and B would each be entitled to purchase 10 additional shares of stock and would retain a 50% ownership interest in the corporation. Without such rights, A or B could become the controlling owner of Corporation X by purchasing at least 11 additional shares of the new stock offering.

a. Waiver

If the corporation elects to have preemptive rights, then a shareholder may waive that right. A waiver evidenced by a writing is **irrevocable**, regardless of whether it is supported by consideration. RMBCA § 6.30(b)(2).

b. Exceptions

Preemptive rights do not apply to shares that are:

i) Issued as compensation to directors, officers, agents, or employees of the corporation;

ii) Authorized in the articles of incorporation and issued within six months from the effective date of incorporation; or

iii) Sold for payment other than money (e.g., property).

RMBCA § 6.30(b)(3).

6. Federal Restrictions—Registration of Securities

Under the Federal Securities Act of 1933, a corporation that issues stock or other securities may be required to register the security with the Securities and Exchange Commission (SEC). In addition to filing the required registration statement with the SEC, which involves significant disclosures about the company offering the security, the issuer is also required to provide the buyer of the security with a prospectus. The prospectus represents the main part of the registration statement and it includes information about the company, its business, and its financial performance.

a. Public offerings

In general, registration is required only for public offerings of stocks or other securities that are considered public offerings. Offerings that are considered private, called "private placements," are exempt from the registration requirements. Private placements include stock sold by a corporation to institutional investors, sophisticated investors, and companies with annual sales of less than $1 million.

b. Civil liabilities

The purchaser of a security from a corporation that has not complied with the registration requirements may sue the corporation to rescind the transaction. In addition, the purchaser can sue for compensatory damages caused by a material misrepresentation or omission in the registration statement. The purchaser need not have relied on the error or omission, but she cannot have purchased with knowledge of the error or omission. Any of the following individuals may be liable:

i) The issuer;

ii) Any other signer of the registration statement (generally senior executives of the issuer);

iii) A director of the issuer at the time the statement is filed;

iv) An expert whose opinion is used in the registration statement; or

v) The underwriter of the issue.

The issuer is strictly liable, but the other defendants may defend on the basis of the reasonableness of their actions. This is referred to as a "due diligence" defense.

C. DISTRIBUTIONS

A distribution is the transfer of cash or other property from a corporation to one or more of its shareholders. The most common form of a distribution is a dividend, which is normally a cash payment made to shareholders. Other forms of distribution include a distribution of indebtedness or a corporation's purchase of its own stock. RMBCA § 1.40(6).

1. Authorization by the Board of Directors

The power to authorize a distribution rests with the board of directors. RMBCA § 6.40. Having authorized a distribution and set sufficient parameters, the board may delegate to a board committee or corporate officer the power to fix the amount and other terms of the distribution.

In general, a shareholder cannot compel the board of directors to authorize a distribution, because that decision is usually discretionary. However, when a board acts in bad faith and abuses its discretion by refusing to declare a distribution, a court may order the board to authorize a distribution. *Dodge v. Ford Motor Co.*, 170 N.W. 668 (Mich. 1919).

2. Limitations on Distributions

A corporation may not make a distribution if it is insolvent or if the distribution would cause the corporation to be insolvent. RMBCA § 6.40(c).

a. Insolvency determination

A corporation must pass two tests to be deemed solvent and, as such, capable of making a distribution: an equity test and a balance sheet test.

1) Equity test

Under the equity test, a corporation must be able to pay off its debts as they come due in the usual course of business. RMBCA § 6.40(c)(1).

2) Balance sheet test

Under the balance sheet test, a corporation's total assets must exceed its total liabilities plus liquidation preferences of senior securities. RMBCA § 6.40(c)(1).

b. Time of measurement

In the case of a dividend, a corporation's solvency is measured on the date the dividend is declared; in the case of a stock purchase, it is the date the purchase price is paid. RMBCA § 6.40(e).

3. Director's Liability for Unlawful Distributions

A director who votes for or assents to an unlawful distribution, in violation of the director's duties of care and loyalty, is personally liable to the corporation for the amount of the distribution in excess of the lawful amount.

a. Contribution from directors

A director is entitled to contribution from any other director who also is liable for the unlawful distribution. RMBCA § 8.33(b)(1).

b. Recoupment from shareholders

If a shareholder knowingly accepts an unlawful distribution, then a director is entitled to recoupment from that shareholder's pro rata portion of the unlawful distribution. RMBCA § 8.33(b)(2).

4. Dividend Distributions

Dividends are distributed to persons who are shareholders on the record date set by the board of directors. If the board does not set a date, then the dividend is payable to persons who are shareholders on the date that the board authorized the dividend. RMBCA § 6.40(b).

5. Suit to Compel a Dividend Distribution

A shareholder can sue to enforce her individual right; this is not the same as a derivative lawsuit that the shareholders bring on behalf of the corporation. *See Doherty v. Mutual Warehouse Co.*, 245 F.2d 609 (5th Cir. 1957); *Knapp v. Bankers Securities Corp.*, 230 F.2d 717 (3d Cir. 1956) (the right to compel a dividend is a primary and personal right of the shareholder).

To prevail in a suit to compel a dividend distribution, a shareholder must prove the existence of (i) funds legally available for the payment of a dividend, and (ii) bad faith on the part of the directors in their refusal to pay. *See Gay v. Gay's Super Markets, Inc.*, 343 A.2d 577 (Me. 1975).

6. Shares Reacquired by the Corporation

Stock authorized and issued by the corporation is known as "outstanding stock." Such stock may be reacquired by the corporation through purchase or redemption (e.g., stock acquired by a forced sale). Upon repurchase or redemption, that stock constitutes authorized but unissued shares. If the articles of incorporation prohibit the reissuance of stock, then the number of authorized shares is automatically reduced by the number of shares purchased. RMBCA § 6.31.

7. Debt Distribution

Distribution of a corporation's indebtedness, such as bonds or promissory notes, is subject to the same requirements as other distributions. When indebtedness is to be repaid over time (i.e., on an installment basis), the lawfulness of the distribution is tested as of the date of distribution. RMBCA § 6.40(e). Corporate indebtedness received as a lawful distribution is on par with a corporation's general unsecured creditors. RMBCA § 6.40(f).

8. Stock Dividends—Not a Distribution

A corporation may issue its own stock to current shareholders without charge in lieu of making a distribution of cash or other property. Commonly referred to as "stock dividends" or "stock splits," these transactions do not alter the corporation's assets or liabilities, nor do they constitute a distribution. RMBCA § 6.23.

D. SALE OF SECURITIES

Generally, a shareholder is free to sell his stock to anyone at any time for any price. Such freedom is subject to two significant restrictions—limitations imposed on shareholders of closely-held corporations and penalties imposed on transactions that violate federal securities law.

1. Private Restrictions on Sale

Restrictions on the transfer of stock are generally found in closely-held corporations. Owners of closely-held corporations often seek to maintain control over their corporation's business and profits by limiting the number of shareholders. This limitation can be accomplished through restrictions on the transferability of shares.

a. Conspicuously noted

If the corporation issuing the shares imposes a restriction on transferability, the stock certificate must contain either a full and conspicuous statement of the restriction or a statement that the corporation will provide a shareholder with information about the restriction upon request and without charge. RMBCA § 6.27(b).

b. Enforceability

A restriction in the transfer of a security, even if otherwise lawful, may be ineffective against a person without knowledge of the restriction. Unless the security is certified and the restriction is conspicuously noted on the security certificate, that restriction is not enforceable against a person without knowledge of it. RMBCA § 6.27(b).

c. Forms of restrictions

Restrictions on the transfer of stocks can take various forms, including:

i) An outright prohibition on transfers;

ii) Transfers requiring consent from the corporation or its shareholders;

iii) Options to buy the stock held by the corporation or its shareholders;

iv) A right of first refusal (i.e., stock must be offered to the corporation or its shareholders before selling it to another person);

v) The corporation requires or has the right to buy back the stock; or

vi) A buy-sell agreement with either the corporation or its shareholders being obligated to buy the stock.

When a restricted transfer is permitted, the transfer itself may be required upon the occurrence of a specific event, such as retirement, death, or divorce of the shareholder. RMBCA § 6.27(d).

d. Challenge to restrictions

Stock transfer restrictions have been subject to challenge as unreasonable restraints on alienation. Of the various forms noted above, the outright prohibition on transfer and the need for prior consent are the most susceptible to attack. However, because the test is one of reasonableness, even these two forms may be justified in particular circumstances, such as when a corporation seeks to preserve its status because it is dependent on the number or identity of its shareholders. RMBCA § 6.27(c).

Because many of these restrictions are created through contractual arrangements, they may be subject to contractual defenses. In addition, the restrictions may be narrowly interpreted and subject to equitable challenges such as abandonment, waiver, or estoppel.

e. Persons bound by restrictions

Parties to an agreement that restricts stock transfers are bound by the terms of the contract. Other parties are not subject to a transfer restriction unless they are aware of it. If the restriction is noted on the face of the stock certificate, then the buyer may be treated as having constructive notice of the restriction.

A transfer restriction imposed through an amendment of the articles of incorporation or corporate bylaws raises the question of whether persons who were shareholders before the restriction was imposed are subject to it. The RMBCA does not subject such shareholders to a restriction unless the shareholders voted in favor of the restriction or were parties to the restriction agreement. RMBCA § 6.27(a).

2. Sale of Control in a Closely Held Corporation

A shareholder with a controlling interest in a corporation that sells to an outsider may have a fiduciary obligation to the other shareholders. See § V.E.2., *Controlling Shareholder's Fiduciary Obligation*, *infra*.

3. Federal Causes of Action

Violations of 17 C.F.R. § 240.10b-5 ("**Rule 10b-5**") and Section 16(b) of the Securities Exchange Act of 1934, 15 U.S.C. § 78p, ("**Section 16(b)**"), which are based on the purchase and sale of stock and other securities, are federal causes of action and must be pursued in federal court. Because each involves a federal claim, diversity of citizenship is not needed.

The SEC also may enforce these provisions through civil penalties and criminal prosecution.

a. Rule 10b-5 action

The fraudulent purchase or sale of any stock or other security (e.g., bonds, stock options, and warrants) can give rise to a Rule 10b-5 action. For a private person to pursue a Rule 10b-5 action, **each** of the following requirements must be met:

    i)   The plaintiff purchased or sold a security;

    ii)   The transaction involved the use of interstate commerce;

    iii)   The defendant engaged in fraudulent or deceptive conduct;

    iv)   The conduct related to material information;

    v)   The defendant acted with scienter (i.e., with intent or recklessness);

    vi)   The plaintiff relied on the defendant's conduct; and

    vii) The plaintiff suffered harm because of the defendant's conduct.

1) Plaintiff's purchase or sale of security

To maintain a Rule 10b-5 action, the plaintiff must have either bought or sold a security. A person who refrains from buying or selling a security because of the defendant's conduct cannot bring a Rule 10b-5 action for damages. *Blue Chip Stamps v. Manor Drug Stores*, 421 U.S. 723 (1975). (Note: Courts are split as to whether a private action for injunctive relief is possible by someone who did not buy or sell stock. However, the SEC can bring such an action).

The defendant is not required to be a participant in the transaction. Only the plaintiff must be a buyer or seller.

a) Forced sale doctrine

Under the forced sale doctrine, the forced exchange of shares in a merger or similar transaction constitutes a sale.

2) Use of interstate commerce

Interstate commerce must be used in connection with the transaction. Use of a telephone, mail, or email to make the transaction satisfies this requirement, as does the use of a national securities exchange.

An in-person transaction may not necessarily satisfy the interstate commerce requirement.

3) Fraudulent or deceptive conduct

A Rule 10b-5 action requires fraudulent or deceptive conduct by the defendant in connection with the sale or purchase of a security. The defendant can engage in such conduct by (i) making an untrue statement of a material fact, or (ii) failing to state a material fact that is necessary to prevent statements already made from being misleading.

a) Opinions and predictions

Generally, an opinion or a prediction is not false merely because it does not purport to be factual. However, such a statement may be fraudulent if the defendant made the statement without a reasonable basis or did not make the statement in good faith. *See* Securities Exchange Act Rule 3b-6.

i) "Bespeaks caution" doctrine

Under the "bespeaks caution" doctrine, a statement of opinion or prediction accompanied by adequate cautionary language does not constitute a false or misleading statement. Securities Exchange Act Rule 21E.

b) Nondisclosure and insider trading

The mere possession of material information that is not public knowledge does not give rise to Rule 10b-5 liability; a person who has such insider knowledge does not incur liability unless he also trades stock or other securities on the basis of such knowledge. This is often referred to as the **"disclose or abstain" rule**.

i) Possession as use of information

In establishing that a person has traded on the basis of nonpublic information, a person is presumed to have traded on the basis of the information that he possessed at the time of the trade. An exception exists for trades made in accordance with a pre-existing written plan. Securities Exchange Act Rule 10b-5-1.

ii) Affected traders

There are four types of traders who may be liable for failure to disclose information: (i) insiders, (ii) constructive insiders, (iii) tippees, and (iv) misappropriators.

(a) Insiders

An insider is a director, officer, or other employee of the corporation who uses nonpublic information for personal gain.

(b) Constructive insiders

A constructive insider is a person who has a relationship with the corporation that gives that person access to corporate information not available to the general public. Such individuals include lawyers, accountants, consultants, and other independent contractors.

(c) Tippees

A tippee is a person who is given information by an insider or constructive insider (the "tipper") with the expectation that the information will be used to trade the stock or other securities. The tipper must receive a personal benefit from the disclosure or intend to make a gift to the tippee.

To be liable, the tippee must have known (or should have known) that the information was provided to him in violation of the insider's duty to the corporation. *Dirks v. SEC*, 463 U.S. 646 (1983).

(d) Misappropriators

A misappropriator is a person who uses confidential information in order to trade stock or other securities in violation of the duty of confidentiality owed to the corporation. *United States v. O'Hagan*, 521 U.S. 642 (1997).

4) Materiality

A defendant's conduct must involve the misuse of material information. A fact is material if a reasonable investor would find the fact important in deciding whether to purchase or sell a security. *Basic, Inc. v. Levinson*, 485 U.S. 224 (1988).

5) Scienter

A defendant is not strictly liable for making a false or misleading statement or for negligently making such a statement. Instead, the defendant must make the statement intentionally or recklessly. This fault requirement is also known as scienter. *Ernst & Ernst v. Hochfelder*, 425 U.S. 185 (1976).

6) Plaintiff's reliance

To maintain a Rule 10b-5 action, a plaintiff must establish that she relied on the defendant's fraudulent conduct. However, when the defendant's fraudulent conduct is not aimed directly at the plaintiff, such as if the defendant issues a press release, then courts have permitted the plaintiff to establish reliance by finding that the defendant's conduct constituted a fraud on the market. *Basic Inc. v. Levinson*, 485 U.S. 224 (1988).

a) Justifiable reliance

A plaintiff must not only rely on the defendant's fraudulent conduct; the reliance must be justifiable. In ascertaining whether the plaintiff's reliance is justifiable, mere negligence by the plaintiff is not sufficient to prevent the plaintiff's recovery.

7) Harm to the plaintiff

The plaintiff must establish that he suffered harm caused by the defendant's fraudulent conduct.

a) Damages

Generally, a plaintiff is entitled to recoup his "out-of-pocket" loss, which is the difference between the stock's value at the time of the fraud and the price that the plaintiff paid or received for the stock. In determining the stock's value at the time of the fraud, the value cannot exceed the mean average market price of the stock during the 90-day period after disclosure of such fraud. Securities Exchange Act Rule 21D(e). Punitive damages are not allowed.

b) Rescission

Rescission may be permitted if the defendant was involved in the transaction as a seller or buyer.

c) The defendant's liability

When a defendant has engaged in a knowing violation, she is jointly and severally liable for the damages. If a defendant's violation results from reckless behavior, then her liability is proportionally limited to the damages for which she is responsible. Securities Exchange Act Rule 21D(f).

b. Section 16(b) action

A corporate insider can be forced to return short-swing profits to the corporation through a Section 16(b) action. An insider's reasons for trading are immaterial. Even an insider who does not possess nonpublic material information must return short-swing profits.

The following four elements are necessary for a Section 16(b) cause of action:

1) Applicable corporations

Only the following publicly traded corporations are protected by Section 16(b): (i) corporations that have securities traded on a national securities exchange, or (ii) corporations that have assets of more than $10 million and more than 500 shareholders of any class of stock or other equity security.

2) Corporate insiders

Only corporate directors, officers (e.g., president, vice-president, secretary, treasurer, or comptroller), and shareholders who hold more than 10 percent of any class of stock are subject to a Section 16(b) action. Generally, transactions made before becoming a corporate insider are not considered in determining short-swing profits. However, transactions made after ceasing to be a corporate insider are considered in determining short-swing profits.

3) Short-swing profits

During any six-month period, a corporate insider who both buys and sells his corporation's stock is liable to the corporation for any profits made. Profits are computed by matching the highest sale price with the lowest purchase price, then the next highest sale price with the next lowest purchase price, and so on, during the six-month period. Any loss is not taken into account and all shares are matched with other shares only once.

> **Example:** On January 1, President sells 200 shares of ABC Corporation's stock for $500 each that she had purchased several years before for $100 each. On May 1, President purchases 200 shares of stock for $400 each. President has a short-swing profit of $20,000 (i.e., the sale of 200 shares at $500 each, less the purchase of 200 shares at $400 each).

4) Reporting

A corporate insider is required to report a change in his stock ownership to the SEC to encourage compliance with the short-swing profits rule.

4. State Cause of Action

The primary state cause of action available to persons who have traded stock is the tort of fraud.

5. Tender Offer

A tender offer is an offer to shareholders of a publicly traded corporation to purchase their stock for a fixed price, which is usually higher than the market price. It is frequently used to affect a hostile takeover of a corporation (i.e., a takeover that is opposed by the current management of the corporation).

a. For more than five percent

A person who acquires more than five percent of any class of stock must file a statement with the SEC that reveals his ownership interest, the source of his funding, and his purpose in acquiring the stock. This notice must be filed within 10 days.

b. Persons subject to disclosure rules

A tender offer made by a person subject to the disclosure rules must also provide specific shareholder rights. Securities Exchange Act Rule 14(d)(g).

c. Tender open for 20 days

A person (or corporation) who presents a tender offer to shareholders must leave the offer open for 20 days.

d. Higher price to all if raised

If at any time the tender offer price is raised, the tenderer must pay the higher price to those who already accepted the lower tendered price.

V. SHAREHOLDERS

A. MEETING REQUIREMENTS

There are two basic types of shareholder meetings—annual and special. In addition, shareholders may express their collective will through written consent.

1. Annual Meeting

A corporation is required to hold a shareholders' meeting each year. Generally, the time and place of the meeting are specified in the corporate bylaws. The primary purpose of the annual meeting is to elect directors, but any business that is subject to shareholder control may be addressed. RMBCA § 7.01.

2. Special Meeting

A corporation may also hold a special meeting, the purpose of which must be specified in the notice of the meeting. Generally, a special meeting may be called by the board of directors or shareholders who own at least 10% of the shares entitled to vote at the meeting. RMBCA §§ 7.02, .05(c).

3. Notice of Meeting

Shareholders must be given notice of either type of meeting. To properly call a meeting, the corporation must notify all shareholders entitled to a vote at the special meeting in a timely manner. A shareholder may waive notice either in writing or by attending the meeting. Usually, notice must be given no less than 10 days and no more than 60 days before the meeting date. The notice must include the time, date, and place of the meeting. RMBCA §§ 7.05, .06.

4. Failure to Hold

The failure to hold the annual meeting does not affect the existence of the corporation or invalidate any business conducted by the corporation. RMBCA § 7.01(c). A shareholder may seek a court order compelling the corporation to hold an annual or special meeting. RMBCA § 7.03.

5. Action by Unanimous Written Consent

Instead of voting at a meeting, all shareholders may take any action by unanimous written consent that could have been undertaken at a meeting.

B. VOTING REQUIREMENTS

1. Voting Eligibility

Typically, ownership of stock entitles the shareholder to vote. There are two basic issues regarding shareholder voting: who the owner of the stock is and when such ownership is measured.

a. Ownership issues

Generally, a corporation maintains a list of shareholders who are entitled to vote (i.e., record owners). RMBCA § 7.20(a). A beneficial owner is not entitled to vote at a meeting of shareholders. A person who is not a record owner may nevertheless be entitled to vote. For example, a beneficial owner of the stock may compel the record owner to recognize the beneficial owner's right to vote. *See* RMBCA § 7.23. Similarly, a guardian for an incompetent or a personal representative of a decedent's estate may compel the corporation to allow her to vote in lieu of the record owner. Voting rights issues may also arise when stock is jointly held.

1) Unpaid stock

When stock has been subscribed to but not fully paid for, the subscriber's right to vote such stock may be limited or denied.

2) Corporation's stock

A corporation is generally not entitled to vote its stock. Stock that has been authorized but not issued by a corporation cannot be voted by the corporation. Similarly, stock that has been authorized and issued by a corporation and then reacquired by the corporation (i.e., treasury stock) cannot be voted.

3) Stock in another corporation

A corporation that owns stock in another corporation generally can vote such stock as any other shareholder can.

b. Transfer issue—record date

When stock is sold or otherwise transferred, an issue may arise as to whether the transferor or the transferee of the stock is entitled to vote at a subsequent shareholders' meeting. Typically, the record date is fixed by the board of directors, although the date can be set by reference to the articles of incorporation or the corporate bylaws and, failing corporate guidance, by statute. The record date can be no more than 70 days prior to the meeting. Only the owner of the stock at the close of business on the record date has the right to vote the stock at the upcoming meeting. A transferee of shares after the record date who wants to vote at a scheduled shareholder meeting should obtain a proxy to vote the shares from his transferor. RMBCA § 7.07.

2. Shareholder Voting

The primary issue upon which shareholders are entitled to vote is the selection of the board of directors. Shareholder approval is also required for fundamental corporate changes, such as changes to the articles of incorporation or structural changes to the corporation.

3. Voting Power

Typically, each share of stock is entitled to one vote. *Stroh v. Blackhawk Holding Corp.,* 48 Ill. 2d 471 (1971). However, a corporation, through its articles of incorporation, can create classes of stock that have greater voting power (e.g., each share is entitled to five votes) or that cannot vote (i.e., nonvoting stock). RMBCA § 7.21(a).

4. Quorum Requirements

For a decision made at a shareholders' meeting to be valid, there must be a quorum of the shares eligible to vote present at the meeting. Usually, the required quorum is a majority of votes entitled to be cast on a matter. A share that is present for any purpose at a meeting is deemed present for quorum purposes. RMBCA § 7.25.

5. Approval Requirements

While approval of the shares entitled to vote on an issue is the generally-accepted standard, when there are classes of shares, each class of stock may be required to approve the issue separately. RMBCA § 7.26.

a. Level of approval

The requisite level of shareholder approval is a majority, but approval by a plurality may be permissible, especially if the issue is the election of directors. RMBCA §§ 7.25(c), 7.28(a). A plurality vote requirement for directors means that the individuals with the largest number of votes are elected as directors up to the maximum number of directors to be chosen at the election.

b. Basis for determining level

Usually, the level of shareholder approval is based on the number of votes cast. For some issues, such as fundamental changes, the level of shareholder approval is based on the number of votes eligible to be cast.

6. Special Voting for Directors

Corporations may choose directors by cumulative voting if so provided in the articles of incorporation.

a. Cumulative voting

When more than one director is to be elected, corporations can allow shareholders to cumulate their votes and cast all those votes for only one (or more than one) of the candidates. The effect of cumulative voting is to allow minority shareholders to elect representatives to the board.

> **Example:** A owns 30 shares of X, Inc. stock. B owns the remaining 70 shares. X, Inc. has three directors. Without cumulative voting, A is unable to elect any of the three directors because B owns a majority of the shares. With cumulative voting, A can elect at least one director by casting all of her 90 votes (i.e., 30 votes per director times three directors) for one director.

b. Staggered terms

Typically, all directors of the corporation are elected annually. However, some corporations provide for the election of fewer than all of the directors, thereby staggering the terms of the directors, which provides for some continuity on the board from election to election. The main purpose for staggered terms is to limit the impact of cumulative voting.

7. Proxy Voting

A shareholder may vote in person or by proxy. A proxy vote must be executed in writing and delivered to the corporation or its agent. A proxy is valid for 11 months unless otherwise specified. A proxy is revocable unless it expressly provides that it is irrevocable and the appointment of the proxy is coupled with an interest. Any act by the shareholder that is inconsistent with a proxy, such as attending a shareholder meeting and voting the shares, revokes the proxy. RMBCA § 7.22. In the case of multiple proxies given, the last given revokes all previous proxies.

Whether a proxy is coupled with an interest depends on whether the proxy holder has (i) a property right in the shares or (ii) a security interest given to him to protect him for any obligations he incurred or money advanced. Typically, proxy holders who have a property interest in the shares or a security interest are those who have purchased the shares or otherwise have a business arrangement with the corporation (such as a creditor or employee of the corporation).

8. Voting Together With Other Shareholders

a. Voting pool—retention of legal ownership

Shareholders may enter into a binding voting agreement, also known as a voting pool, which provides for the manner in which they will vote their shares. Under such an agreement, shareholders retain ownership of their stock. Such an agreement is a contract that may be specifically enforced. It does not need to be filed with the corporation, and there is no time limit. RMBCA § 7.31.

b. Voting trust—transfer of legal ownership

A voting trust constitutes a separate legal entity to which the shareholders' stock is transferred. While the shareholders retain beneficial ownership of their shares, legal ownership is transferred to the trustee who votes the shares and distributes the dividends in accord with the terms of the trust. The trustee owes a fiduciary duty to the trust and the beneficial owners of the stock. A voting trust must be in writing, is limited to 10 years, and the trust instrument must be filed with the corporation. RMBCA § 7.30.

c. Management agreements

Generally, shareholders may agree to alter the way in which a corporation is managed even though the agreement is inconsistent with statutory provisions. Among the matters on which shareholders may agree are:

i) Elimination of the board of directors or restrictions on the discretion or powers of the board of directors;

ii) Authorization or making of distributions;

iii) Determination of who is a member of the board of directors, the manner of selection or removal of directors, and the terms of office of directors;

iv) The exercise or division of voting power by or between the shareholders and directors or by or among any of them, including director proxies;

v) A transfer to one or more shareholders or other persons all or part of the authority to exercise corporate powers or to manage the business and affairs of the corporation; and

vi) The manner or means by which the exercise of corporate powers or the management of the business and affairs of the corporation is affected.

RMBCA § 7.32(a).

1) Form of the agreement

The agreement must be set forth either (i) in the articles of incorporation or the corporate bylaws and approved by all persons who are shareholders at the time of the agreement or (ii) in a written agreement that is signed by all persons who are shareholders at the time of the agreement and is made known to the corporation. The agreement may be amended only by persons who are shareholders at the time of amendment. RMBCA § 7.32(b).

2) Length of the agreement

Unless otherwise fixed in the agreement, the agreement is valid for 10 years. RMBCA § 7.32(b).

3) Rescission of the agreement

A person who purchases stock in a corporation with a management agreement without knowledge of the agreement can rescind the purchase agreement. RMBCA § 7.32(c).

4) Limitation on the type of corporation

Such an agreement cannot be entered into with respect to a corporation the shares of which are listed on a national securities exchange, and it ceases to be effective for a corporation when its shares are listed on such an exchange. RMBCA § 7.32(d).

5) Effect on liability

If the agreement limits the discretion or powers of the board of directors, then the directors are relieved of liability for acts or omissions to the extent of the limitation, and the persons in whom such discretion or powers are vested are subject to liability. The existence of the agreement is not a ground for imposing personal liability on shareholders for corporate acts or debts, even though the shareholders, by virtue of the agreement, fail to observe the corporate formalities. RMBCA § 7.32(e)–(f).

9. **Proxy Fights**

When shareholders become unhappy with the operations of a corporation, they can use signed proxies in an attempt to pool voting power and force out members of the board of directors with whom they are unhappy.

Current directors and officers are referred to as "incumbent management," and the outside parties or shareholders that want control are referred to as "insurgents." Proxy fights are expensive to launch and to defend. There is no law against soliciting proxies by using corporate resources. *Levin v. Metro-Goldwyn-Mayer, Inc.*, 264 F. Supp. 797 (1967). The directors of a corporation may spend the corporation's money to solicit proxies in a bona fide policy contest, so long as the amount of money is **reasonable** and the directors act in **good faith**. *Rosenfeld v. Fairchild Engine & Airplane Corp.*, 309 N.Y. 168 (1955).

There are four rules that govern when and to whom a corporation can reimburse the parties in a proxy fight:

i) Corporation cannot reimburse either party unless it is a dispute over policy;

ii) Corporation can reimburse only reasonable and proper expenses;

iii) Incumbents can be reimbursed regardless of whether they win or lose; or

iv) Insurgents are reimbursed only if they win and only if ratified by shareholders.

C. **INSPECTION OF CORPORATE RECORDS RIGHTS**

A shareholder has a right to inspect and copy corporate records, books, papers, etc. upon five days' written notice stating a proper purpose. As a litigant against the corporation, the shareholder also has a right to discovery.

1. **Shareholders with Inspection Rights**

Generally, not only a shareholder of record but also a beneficial owner of the shares enjoys inspection rights. RMBCA § 16.02. Some states restrict access to corporate records to shareholders who have owned stock for at least a limited amount of time and/or own a minimum amount of stock. "Qualified shareholders" are those who own more than the minimum allowable stock or who have owned for the specified amount of time.

2. **Records Subject to Inspection**

Generally, a shareholder can inspect any corporate records, but the inspection may be limited to specified records, such as excerpts from the minutes of a board meeting. RMBCA § 16.02(b).

A qualified shareholder is allowed to inspect a corporation's stock register, in good faith, in order to notify shareholders of exchange and solicitation offers of stock. *Crane Co. v. Anaconda Co.*, 39 N.Y.2d 14 (1976). In general, a shareholder can only demand the identification information of corporate investors for a proper purpose, including when the purpose is related to investment concerns that are traditionally associated with shareholder concerns. *State ex rel. Pillsbury v. Honeywell, Inc.*, 291 Minn. 322 (1971).

3. **Time and Place Limits on Inspection**

The inspection right is usually restricted to normal business hours at the corporation's principal place of business. Five days' advance, written notice is required. RMBCA § 16.02.

4. Purpose Limitation on Inspection

A shareholder's inspection right is conditional on having a proper purpose. RMBCA § 16.02(c). A proper purpose is one that relates to the shareholder's interest in the corporation, such as determining the value of one's shares in a closely-held corporation even though the shareholder does not plan to sell the shares. Improper purposes may include harassment of corporate officials or acquiring corporate secrets.

5. Enforcement of Right

Some states enforce a shareholder's inspection right indirectly by imposing fines on the corporate official who improperly refuses a shareholder access to the corporate records. Under the RMBCA, direct enforcement of a shareholder's inspection right is recognized in an expedited court proceeding, under which the shareholder can secure access to the corporate records and reimbursement for litigation costs. RMBCA § 16.04.

6. Disclosure of Financial Statement

To enable shareholders to make an informed decision when voting, publicly held corporations that have issued securities are required to supply shareholders with an annual audited financial statement. Securities Exchange Act of 1934 Rule 14(a); Securities Acts Amendments of 1964 Rule 14(c). Likewise, the RMBCA requires all corporations to furnish shareholders with an annual financial statement. RMBCA § 16.20.

a. Formal requirements of proxy rules

The SEC proxy rules specify the scope of disclosure in proxy statements, the form of the proxy card, filing requirements, and the prohibition against proxy fraud.

Generally, a proxy statement containing certain required disclosures must accompany or precede any proxy solicitation. Rule 14a-3(a). More disclosure information is required when management solicits proxies than when non-management does. However, to comply with the prohibition against fraud, the proxy statement must not provide any false or misleading information with respect to any material fact, nor omit any material information. Rule 14a-9.

In addition, a proxy card must state who is soliciting, the matters to be acted on, and include a space for a date to be entered. Rule 14a-4. The proxy holder must vote in accordance with the boldface instructions on the proxy card.

Preliminary copies of the statement and the card must be filed with the SEC at least 10 days prior to being sent to shareholders. Rule 14a-6. Final proxy materials must be filed with the SEC at or before the time they are sent to shareholders.

b. Actions related to Rule 14(a)

Private parties have the right to bring suit against a corporation for violating Rule 14(a). *J.I. Case Co. v. Borak*, 376 U.S. 960 (1964). An omission or material misstatement in a proxy statement is enough to establish a cause of action under Section 14(a). *Mills v. Electric Auto-Lite Co.,* 396 U.S. 375 (1970).

Under Rule 14a-8, a shareholder-proposed resolution for a proxy statement can only be turned down when the proposal concerns less than five percent of total assets or earnings, and is not significantly related to the business. *Lovenheim v. Iroquois brands, Ltd.*, 618 F. Supp. 554 (1985).

A shareholder's proposal does not relate to an election under the Rule 14a-8(i)(8) for exclusion from a proxy statement if it seeks to amend the corporation's bylaws to establish a procedure by which certain shareholders are entitled to include. *AFSCME v. AIG, Inc.*, 462 F.3d 121 (2006).

The same rules for reimbursement by a corporation apply as in proxy fights. *See* § V.B.9, *infra*.

D. SUITS BY SHAREHOLDERS

A shareholder may bring a direct or a derivative action against the corporation in which the shareholder owns stock. How the action is characterized will affect the requirements for bringing suit and to whom any recovery is paid.

1. Direct Actions

A shareholder may pursue two basic types of direct actions: (i) an action to enforce shareholder rights or (ii) a non-shareholder action, the recovery from which is to the benefit of the indirect shareholder.

a. Action to enforce shareholder rights

A shareholder may sue the corporation for breach of a fiduciary duty owed to the shareholder by a director or an officer. Typical actions are based on the denial or interference with a shareholder's voting rights, the board's failure to declare a dividend, or the board's approval or failure to approve a merger.

b. Non-shareholder actions

A shareholder may sue the corporation on grounds that do not arise from the shareholder's status as a shareholder.

Example: A shareholder who is struck by a vehicle owned by the corporation and driven by a corporate employee may pursue a negligence claim against the corporation as the injured party of the corporation's tortious conduct.

2. Derivative Actions

In a derivative action, a shareholder is suing on behalf of the corporation for a harm suffered by the corporation. Although the shareholder also may have suffered harm, recovery generally goes to the corporation. For example, a shareholder may bring a derivative action to force a director to disgorge a secret profit earned by the director on a transaction with the corporation.

a. Who may bring suit—standing

In addition to being a shareholder at the time the action is filed and continuing to be a shareholder during the litigation, a plaintiff must also have been a shareholder at the time of the act or omission (or one who receives the shares through a transfer from such a shareholder) to bring a derivative action. This is known as the "**contemporaneous ownership**" rule. In addition, the shareholder must fairly and adequately represent the interests of the corporation. RMBCA § 7.41.

Excluded as a plaintiff: A creditor of a corporation cannot bring a derivative action.

b. Demand upon board

The plaintiff in a derivative action must make a written demand upon the board of directors in order to take action. A derivative action may not commence until **90 days** have passed from the date of demand.

1) Futility exception

In some states, a demand upon the board is not required if the demand would be futile. Factors for determining futility include whether the directors are disinterested and independent and whether the transaction was the product of a valid exercise of business judgment. *Marx v. Akers*, 666 N.E.2d 1034 (1996). Under the RMBCA, however, there is a universal demand requirement for all derivative actions. Therefore, the futility exception is not recognized in states that have adopted the RMBCA. RMBCA § 7.42.

2) Irreparable injury excuse

The plaintiff may be excused from waiting a reasonable time for the board to respond to the demand if the delay would result in irreparable injury to the corporation. RMBCA § 7.42(2).

3) Effect of board rejection of demand

If the board specifically rejects the demand, then the rejection is tested against the business judgment rule. If there is a business justification for the rejection, then the plaintiff must establish that the board's rejection was due to a lack of care, loyalty, or good faith to persuade the court to override the board's refusal. *Findley v. Garrett*, 240 P.2d 421 (Cal. 1952).

c. Litigation expenses

Although the plaintiff-shareholder is usually not entitled to share in a recovery, she can seek reimbursement from the corporation for reasonable litigation expenses, including attorney's fees, if the lawsuit has resulted in a substantial benefit to the corporation. If the court finds that the proceeding was commenced or maintained without a reasonable cause or for an improper purpose, then it may order the plaintiff-shareholder to pay the defendant's litigation expenses. RMBCA § 7.46.

E. LIABILITY

One reason the corporate form is favorable is that the investors in a corporation are subject to limited liability for corporate acts, and they are only at risk to the extent of their investment. This principle of limited liability is subject to challenge, primarily with respect to shareholders of closely held corporations.

1. Piercing the Corporate Veil

If a plaintiff can "pierce the corporate veil," then a corporation's existence is ignored, and the shareholders of the corporation are held personally liable.

Although courts are reluctant to hold a director or active shareholder liable for actions that are legally the responsibility of the corporation (even if the corporation has a single shareholder), they will sometimes do so if the corporation was markedly noncompliant, or if holding only the corporation liable would be singularly unfair to the plaintiff.

An individual may be held liable for the acts of a corporation through the doctrine of respondeat superior if it can be proven that the individual used his control of the corporation for personal gain. *Walkovszky v. Carlton*, 244 N.E.2d 55 (1968).

a. Totality of circumstances

In most jurisdictions, no bright-line rule exists for piercing the corporate veil, and courts look at the "totality of circumstances." Courts generally look to whether the corporation is being used as a "façade" for a dominant shareholder's personal dealings (i.e., whether the corporation is an "alter ego" of the shareholder).

Additionally, courts look to whether there is "unity of interest and ownership" between the entity and the members, that the corporation in fact did not have an existence independent of the members.

In general, a plaintiff must prove that the incorporation was merely a formality and that the corporation neglected corporate formalities and protocols, such as voting to approve major corporate actions in the context of a duly authorized corporate meeting. This is often the case when a corporation facing legal liability transfers its assets to another corporation with the same management and shareholders. It also happens most often with single-person or small, closely held corporations that are managed in a haphazard manner.

b. Factors to consider

Factors considered by the courts when piercing the corporate veil include:

i) Undercapitalization of the corporation at the time of its formation;

ii) Disregard of corporate formalities;

iii) Use of corporate assets as a shareholder's own assets;

iv) Self-dealing with the corporation;

v) Siphoning of corporate funds or stripping of corporate assets;

vi) Use of the corporate form to avoid existing statutory requirements or other legal obligations;

vii) A shareholder's impermissible control or domination over the corporation; and

viii) Wrongful, misleading, or fraudulent dealings with a corporate creditor.

Not all of the above factors need to be met for the court to pierce the corporate veil. Some courts might find that one factor is so compelling in a particular case that it will find the shareholders personally liable.

A plaintiff may pierce the corporate veil by proving (i) unity of interest between the individual and the corporation; and (ii) allowing limited liability would be unjust or fraudulent. *Sea-Land Services, Inc. v. Pepper Source,* 993 F.2d 1309 (7th Cir. 1993).

In order to pierce the corporate veil under an "alter ego" theory, a party must show that an individual controlled and dominated the organization and that failing to pierce the corporate veil would lead to inequity. *R.C. Archbishop of San Francisco v. Sheffield,* 15 Cal. App. 3d 405 (1971).

A subsidiary company of a corporation may be considered an "alter ego" under the piercing the corporate veil theory if the companies share directors, use the same legal, auditing, and other departments, file consolidated tax returns, and prepare consolidated financial reports. *In re Silicon Gel Breast Implants Litigation,* 887 F. Supp. 1447 (1995).

The failure of a shareholder to respect the corporate entity is insufficient by itself to justify piercing the corporate veil; such failure must also adversely affect the third party's ability to recover from the corporation.

2. Controlling Shareholder's Fiduciary Obligation

When one shareholder—or a group of shareholders acting in concert—holds a high enough percentage of ownership in a company to enact changes at the highest level, the shareholder or group is a "controlling shareholder." Anyone controlling 50% of a corporation's shares, plus one, is automatically a controlling shareholder. A much smaller interest, whether owned individually or by a group in combination, can be controlling if the remaining shares are widely dispersed (as in a large, publicly traded corporation) and not actively voted. Additionally, a corporation that requires a two-thirds super-majority of shares to vote in favor of a motion can effectively grant control to a minority shareholder or block of shareholders that own just more than one-third of the shares of the corporation. Thus, in some cases, a shareholder can essentially maintain control of a corporation with only 33.4% of the outstanding shares.

Generally, shareholders do not owe fiduciary duties to the corporation or to each other. *Zahn v. Transamerica Corp.*, 162 F.2d 36 (3rd Cir. 1947). However, a fiduciary duty to the minority shareholders may arise if the controlling shareholder is (i) selling that interest to an outsider, (ii) seeking to eliminate other shareholders from the corporation, or (iii) receiving a distribution denied to the other shareholders. A controlling shareholder has a duty to disclose to the minority shareholder any information that it knew or should have known if it is information that a reasonable person would consider important in deciding how to vote on a transaction. A controlling shareholder breaches its fiduciary duty to the minority shareholder if nondisclosure causes a loss to the minority shareholders. A loss includes being deprived of a state remedy that would otherwise have been available. Furthermore, when a majority shareholder purchases the interest of the minority, it has a fiduciary duty of fair dealing. The controlling shareholder bears the burden of demonstrating that the process it employed was fair and the price it selected was fair. *Weinberger v. UOP, Inc.*, 457 A.2d 701 (Del. 1983).

VI. OFFICERS AND OTHER EMPLOYEES

A. TYPES

Typically, a corporation's officers are composed of a president, secretary, and treasurer. An individual may hold more than one office, but some states prohibit a person from serving dual roles when such officers serve as a check on each other. The RMBCA does not specify which officers a corporation must have, but it simply indicates that the corporate bylaws are responsible for delineating the officers of the corporation. RMBCA § 8.40.

B. SELECTION

The primary officers of a corporation are elected by the board of directors. These officers may in turn be empowered by the board of directors or the bylaws to select other corporate officers and employees. RMBCA § 8.40(b).

C. AUTHORITY

An officer's authority can be actual, implied, or apparent. Actual authority wielded by an officer is defined by the corporate bylaws or set by the board of directors. An officer has implied authority to perform those tasks that are necessary to carry out the officer's duties by virtue of her status or position, so long as the matter is within the scope of ordinary business. However, the officer does not have the authority to bind the corporation by extraordinary acts. In determining whether a transaction is extraordinary, the court might consider the economic magnitude of the action in relation to corporate earnings and assets, the extent of the risk involved, the time span of the action's effect, and the cost of reversing the action. Finally, an officer has apparent authority if the corporation holds the officer out as having authority to bind the corporation to third parties.

D.   DUTIES—CARE AND LOYALTY

The specific duties of an officer are defined by the corporate bylaws or set by the board of directors. RMBCA § 8.41. The duties of care and loyalty that are imposed on the directors of a corporation are also owed by the officers of a corporation. Moreover, all employees, as agents of the corporation, owe the corporation these duties of care and loyalty. RMBCA § 8.42.

The chief executive officer (CEO) and chief financial officer (CFO) of a publicly traded corporation must certify the accuracy of the corporation's financial reports that are filed with the SEC. Sarbanes-Oxley Act 302. In addition to facing criminal penalties for filing a false report, a CEO and CFO must forfeit incentive-based pay and must return profits from stock sales for a year when financial reports must be restated because of such misconduct. Sarbanes-Oxley Act 304.

E.   LIABILITY

As an agent of the corporation, an officer does not incur liability to third parties merely for the performance of duties for the corporation. Of course, an officer can be liable to a third party if the officer has acted in his personal capacity (e.g., guaranteed a corporate loan) or has engaged in purposeful tortious behavior.

F.   INDEMNIFICATION AND INSURANCE

An officer is entitled to indemnification to the same extent and subject to the same restrictions as a corporate director. Similar insurance rules apply as well.

G.   REMOVAL

An officer may be removed at any time with or without cause. RMBCA § 8.43. The existence of an employment contract between an officer and the corporation does not prevent the removal of the officer, but it may give rise to contractual remedies such as damages if removal constitutes a breach of contract.

H.   OTHER EMPLOYEES

An employee who is not an officer is an agent of the corporation and is subject to the responsibilities of an agent. In turn, the employee is owed duties by the corporate principal. As an agent, the employee has the ability to act on behalf of the corporation to the extent of the employee's authority, and is usually protected as an agent from liability for actions undertaken in accordance with that authority.

VII.   MERGERS AND ACQUISITIONS

A.   MERGERS

1.   Definition

A **merger** is the combination of two or more corporations such that only one corporation survives. The surviving corporation may be created as a result of the merger, rather than existing before the merger, in which case the process is referred to as a **consolidation**. RMBCA §§ 1.40, 11.01, 11.02.

A conversion of shares to cash to complete a merger is distinct from a redemption of shares under the doctrine of independent legal significance. Therefore, redemption provisions or laws concerning redemption are inapplicable to share conversions. *Rauch v. RCA Corp.*, 861 F.2d 29 (1988).

2.   Procedure

Although the business aspects of effecting a merger can be complex, the statutory procedure is simple. To merge:

i) The board of directors for each corporation must approve of the merger;

ii) The shareholders of each corporation must usually approve of the merger; and

iii) The required documents (e.g., plan of merger, amended articles of incorporation) must be filed with the state.

RMBCA § 11.04.

a. Shareholder approval

1) Voting requirements

Shareholder approval requires a majority vote, meaning a majority of the votes cast, but the shareholders' meeting at which the vote is taken is subject to a quorum requirement, which is usually a majority of shares entitled to vote. RMBCA § 11.04.

A shareholder ratification of a merger does not automatically remove all duty of loyalty claims, but the ratification makes the business judgment rule the standard an opposing party must overcome. *In re Wheelabrator Technologies, Inc. Shareholders Litigation,* 663 A.2d 1194 (1995).

2) Voting by class

If the corporation has more than one class of stock, and the amendment would affect the rights of a particular class of stock, then the holders of that class of stock must also approve of the amendment. RMBCA § 11.04.

3) Mergers without shareholder approval

a) Parent-subsidiary merger

A merger between a parent corporation and a subsidiary corporation when the parent owns at least 90% of the voting power of each class of outstanding stock of the subsidiary may occur without the approval of the shareholders of the subsidiary. A parent corporation may also effect a merger between two 90% or more owned subsidiary corporations without the need for approval by the shareholders of either corporation. In all these mergers, approval by a subsidiary's board of directors is also not required. RMBCA § 11.05.

b) Minnow-whale merger

A merger of a small corporation (a "minnow") into a large corporation (a "whale") may not require approval of the shareholders of the surviving large corporation. Approval is not required if the merger cannot result in an increase of more than 20% in the voting power of the outstanding stock of the surviving corporation, if the articles of incorporation of the surviving corporation will not differ from the articles before the merger, and if the pre-merger shareholders of the surviving corporation are otherwise unaffected by the merger. RMBCA §§ 6.21(f), 11.04.

3. Corporate Assets and Liabilities

All assets and liabilities owned by a corporation that are merged into another corporation are then owned by the surviving corporation after the merger. RMBCA § 11.07.

B. **ASSET ACQUISITION**

The sale or other transfer of a corporation's assets does not require approval by the shareholders or board of a transferor corporation. However, asset transfers that resemble a merger may require approval by both the board of directors and the shareholders of the transferor corporation. Merger statutes and asset sale statutes are independent of one another and a corporation complying with one statute or the other is complying with the law. *Hariton v. Arco Electronics, Inc.,* 188 A.2d 123. An asset sale agreement is valid if it complies with a sale of assets statute, even if it does not comply with a merger statute. *Id.*

A reorganization by a corporation to acquire the assets of another organization is a **"de facto" merger** if the nature of the corporation is significantly changed and the shareholder's interest is significantly altered. *Farris v. Glen Alden Corp.,* 393 Pa. 427 (1958). In other words, when an asset acquisition leads to the same result as a statutory merger, shareholders are to be given the same rights as in the statutory merger. *Id.*

1. **Applicable Transfers**

A transfer involving all, or substantially all, of the corporation's assets outside the usual and regular course of business is a fundamental corporate change for the transferor corporation. Thus, the corporation must follow the fundamental change procedures.

2. **Approval Procedure**

The approval procedure for an asset transfer follows the approval procedure for a merger, except that only the transferor corporation's board of directors and shareholders are entitled to vote on the transaction. RMBCA § 12.02.

3. **Transferor's Liabilities**

a. **Transferor's continued responsibility**

Apart from an agreement with a creditor that releases the transferor corporation from liability, the transferor corporation remains liable for its debts, including the ones associated with the transferred assets. The transferor may be able to obtain indemnification from the transferee for such liability.

b. **Transferee's escape from liability**

Unlike in a merger, in a sale or other transfer, the transferee corporation is generally not responsible to the transferor's creditors for the liabilities of the transferor corporation, unless the transferee corporation assumes such liabilities.

C. **STOCK ACQUISITION**

A corporation may acquire stock in another corporation and thereby secure control of that corporation without going through the process of effecting a statutory merger. The two primary means by which a corporation can acquire stock in another corporation is by exchanging its own stock for that stock or by paying cash or other property for the stock.

1. **Stock-for-Stock Exchange**

A corporation may offer its own stock to shareholders in another corporation in exchange for their stock in that corporation (i.e., a stock swap). Generally, a shareholder in the other corporation may retain his stock and not participate in the stock swap. However, the RMBCA sets out a procedure, labeled a "share exchange," which parallels the procedure for a merger. If followed, this procedure requires all shareholders to participate in the stock swap. As with a merger, with such an exchange, dissenting shareholders are given the right of appraisal. RMBCA § 11.03.

2. Stock Purchase

A corporation may purchase stock in another corporation on the open market or make an offer to buy the stock from the current shareholders (i.e., a tender offer).

D. DISSENTING SHAREHOLDER'S RIGHT OF APPRAISAL

A shareholder who objects to a merger or acquisition may be able to force the corporation to buy his stock at a fair value as determined by an appraisal. This right is also available for shareholders whose rights are materially and adversely affected by an amendment of the corporation's articles of incorporation. RMBCA §§ 13.01-.31.

1. Qualifying Shareholders

A shareholder who is entitled to vote on a merger, acquisition, or amendment of the corporation's articles of incorporation has appraisal rights. In addition, a minority shareholder in a short form merger can exercise appraisal rights, even though such a shareholder cannot vote on the merger. RMBCA § 13.02(a).

If a shareholder can sell his stock in a market that is both liquid and reliable, such as the New York Stock Exchange or the American Stock Exchange, the shareholder does not have a right of appraisal because the market is providing him with the opportunity to sell his stock at its fair value. RMBCA § 13.02(b).

2. Procedure

a. Notice to the corporation

To exercise the right of appraisal, a shareholder must send a written notice to the corporation of her intent to do so. This notice must be delivered to the corporation **before** the shareholders vote on the proposed action. RMBCA § 13.21(a).

b. No favorable vote

When the proposed corporate action is submitted to the shareholders for their approval, the shareholder must not vote in favor of the action (i.e., she must abstain or vote "no"). RMBCA § 13.21(a).

c. Demand for payment

After the proposed corporate action has been approved, the shareholder must make a written demand upon the corporation for payment. RMBCA § 13.21.

d. Fair market value

The corporation must pay shareholders what it estimates as fair market value. If the corporation and the shareholder do not agree on a price for the shareholder's stock, then the fair value of the stock is determined through a court action.

3. Exclusivity of Remedy

A shareholder who has an appraisal right cannot challenge the corporate action except on the grounds of fraud or illegality. RMBCA § 13.02(d).

VIII. TERMINATION OF CORPORATE STATUS

A corporation may terminate its status as a corporation either voluntarily by agreement or involuntarily by court order or state action.

A. VOLUNTARY DISSOLUTION

1. Procedure Prior to the Issuance of Stock

Prior to the issuance of stock, a corporation may voluntarily dissolve by a majority vote of the incorporators or initial directors. RMBCA § 14.01.

2. Procedure After the Issuance of Stock

A corporation that has issued stock may voluntarily dissolve if (i) the board of directors adopts a proposal for the dissolution of the corporation and (ii) the majority of shareholders approve. RMBCA § 14.02.

3. Effect of Dissolution—Winding Up

A dissolved corporation may continue to exist as a corporation for the limited purpose of winding up its affairs and liquidating its business. This includes (i) collecting assets, (ii) disposing of property that will not be distributed to shareholders, (iii) discharging liabilities, and (iv) distributing property among shareholders according to their interests.

It does not include (i) transferring title to the corporation's property, (ii) preventing transfer of shares or securities, (iii) changing quorum or voting requirements, (iv) terminating the authority of the registered corporate agent, or (v) preventing commencement of a proceeding by or against the corporation. RMBCA § 14.05.

4. Dissolution Distribution

The directors of a corporation are responsible for distribution of the corporate assets and may be liable for improper distributions. Such assets must be distributed in the following order:

i) To creditors of the corporation to pay the debts and other obligations of the corporation, including bona fide obligations owed to shareholders;

ii) To shareholders of stock with preferences in liquidation; and

iii) To shareholders of other stock.

RMBCA § 14.09.

B. INVOLUNTARY DISSOLUTION

1. Petitioner

Either a shareholder or a creditor of a corporation may bring an action for involuntary dissolution of a corporation.

a. Creditor

A creditor may pursue the involuntary dissolution of a corporation only if the corporation is insolvent. RMBCA § 14.30(c).

b. Shareholder

A shareholder may pursue the involuntary dissolution of a corporation if:

i) The corporate assets are being misapplied or wasted;

ii) The directors or those in control of the corporation are acting illegally, oppressively, or fraudulently;

iii) The directors are deadlocked in the management of the corporation's affairs, the shareholders are unable to break the deadlock, and irreparable injury to the corporation is threatened or being suffered; or

iv) The shareholders are deadlocked in voting power and have failed to elect successors to the directors whose terms have expired.

RMBCA § 14.30(b).

2. Court's Power

Upon the petitioner's establishment of the necessary grounds, the court may dissolve the corporation. RMBCA § 14.30(a). The court has equitable powers to issue injunctions, appoint a receiver, and take other steps necessary to preserve the corporation's assets. RMBCA § 14.31. If the court orders the dissolution of the corporation, then the distribution of the corporation's assets generally adheres to that of a voluntary distribution unless equity requires otherwise.

C. FORFEITURE/ADMINISTRATIVE DISSOLUTION

The state may force a corporation to forfeit its right to exist or administratively dissolve the corporation if the corporation has (i) failed to pay fees or taxes, (ii) failed to file required reports or notices, or (iii) abused its powers. RMBCA §§ 14.20–14.21, 14.30(a). Continuing to operate as a corporation after forfeiture can result in the personal liability of the operators.

IX. TAKEOVERS

A. INTRODUCTION

Directors of a corporation have the burden of proof that a buyback of shares by the corporation in an attempt to remove a threat to the corporation is in the corporation's best interests. Factors the court considers are investigation by directors, receipt of professional advice, and personal observations of the company attempting a takeover. *Cheff v. Mathes*, 199 A.2d 548 (Del. 1964).

B. DEVELOPMENT

Directors of a corporation have a duty to protect the corporation from takeover threats by shareholders and other third parties, thereby granting the directors the authority under the business judgment rule to exclude certain shareholders from a stock repurchase, but only to the extent necessary. *Unocal Corp. v. Mesa Petroleum Co.,* 493 A.2d 946 (1985).

When it is inevitable that a takeover is taking place, the directors of the corporation have the duty to obtain the best price possible for the shareholders. *Revlon, Inc. v. MacAndrews & Forbes, Inc.,* 506 A.2d 173 (Del. 1986). Any duty the corporation has to note holders is outweighed by the duty to the shareholders. *Id.* Actions by the directors that show anything other than maximizing price for the shareholders is a violation of the business judgment rule. *Id.*

X. SPECIAL TYPES OF CORPORATIONS

A. CLOSELY-HELD AND CLOSE CORPORATIONS

The terms "closely held corporation" and "close corporation" are frequently used interchangeably to refer to a corporation with only a few shareholders and a more relaxed style of governance. Shareholders often serve as both directors and officers of the corporation. Stock of such a corporation is not publicly traded, and many states allow shareholders to do away with many of the corporate formalities.

1. Control

Control of a closely held corporation is similar to a traditional corporation in that the decisions are made by officers and directors, subject to shareholder approval in certain situations.

Shareholders are not authorized to form an agreement to control the decisions of a corporation that are traditionally made by the directors. *McQuade v. Stoneham,* 264 N.Y. 460 (1934). On the other hand, a shareholder agreement that controls the voting for board members and the management decisions of the members should be enforced as long as the agreement is not fraudulent of harmful. *Galler v. Galler,* 32 Ill. 2d 16 (1965).

2. Abuse of Control

Because shareholders of closely held corporations often serve as both directors and officers, there is the opportunity to abuse control. In closely held corporations, shareholders owe a duty of good faith to each other, and are in breach of that duty when terminating another shareholder in order to gain leverage. *Wilkes v. Springside Nursing Home, Inc.,* 279 Mass 842 (1976).

When a potential buyout or merger may occur in a closely held corporation, there is a duty to disclose that potential buyout or merger when attempting to buy a shareholder's shares, even if the potential deal has not materialized. *Jordan v. Duff & Phelps, Inc.,* 815 F.2d 429 (1987).

3. Transfer of Control

Shareholders of a closely held corporation often execute "buy-sell" agreements, which state how shares may be bought or sold upon the resignation or death of a shareholder. These agreements protect the corporation by allowing the owners to determine the successor owners of the corporation.

A shareholder's right of first refusal does not convey the right to control the sale of the corporation's assets or liquidation of the corporation. *Frandsen v. Jensen-Sundquist Agency, Inc.,* 802 F.2d 941 (1986).

In a closely held corporation, a person or entity is authorized to purchase a controlling share of a corporation at a premium price without extending a tender offer to all shareholders so long as good faith is maintained. *Zetlin v. Hanson Holdings, Inc.,* 48 N.Y.2d 684 (1979).

B. FOREIGN CORPORATION

A foreign corporation is a corporation that is incorporated in another state. To do business in a state other than its state of incorporation, a corporation is required to register with that state and receive a "certificate of authority." Failure to do so prevents the foreign corporation from suing, but not from being sued, in state courts until registered. However, it does not impair the validity of corporate acts or contracts or prevent the corporation from defending any proceeding within the state. Many actions, such as holding board meetings, maintaining bank accounts, and selling through independent contractors, do not constitute doing business within a state. RMBCA §§ 15.01–15.32.

C. PROFESSIONAL CORPORATION

A professional corporation is a corporation with a purpose that is statutorily limited to the rendering of a professional service. A shareholder in a professional corporation must be a member of the applicable profession. In addition, a professional corporation does not shield an employee from liability arising from her own malpractice. However, it may provide protection against vicarious liability arising from malpractice by other professionals in the corporation.

D. S CORPORATION

A corporation is usually subject to tax as a "C corporation," which is a separate taxable entity from its shareholders, causing the corporation to face double taxation. The corporation pays taxes first on profits and again as shareholders on distributions received from the corporation. However, a corporation may elect to avoid double taxation as an "S corporation," in which the income and expenses of the corporation are passed through to shareholders (who are then taxed on such items directly). 26 U.S.C. § 1361, et seq.

To become an S corporation for federal tax purposes, a corporation must file Internal Revenue Service (IRS) Form 2553, and the IRS must approve the application. Companies that file as S corporations can have no more than 100 shareholders. Only individuals, estates, certain exempt organizations, or certain trusts may be shareholders, and the shareholders must all be either U.S. citizens or resident aliens (nonresident aliens are not permitted). The S corporation may not have more than one class of stock. Each shareholder must consent to the S corporation election for a corporation to become an S corporation.

XI. LIMITED LIABILITY COMPANIES

A limited liability company ("LLC") is a legally recognized business entity that enjoys the pass-through tax advantage of a partnership but also the limited liability of a corporation. An LLC also provides flexibility in managing the entity. Many of the rules applicable to corporations and corporate governance have counterparts applicable to LLCs (e.g., the name of an LLC must include the words "limited liability company" or some abbreviation thereof). Some of these rules are detailed below.

A. CREATION

An LLC is created by filing articles of organization with the state. An LLC may adopt an operating agreement that governs any or all aspects of its affairs. This operating agreement generally takes precedence over contrary statutory provisions.

B. MEMBERSHIP

An LLC is not restricted as to the number of members it may have. However, a person cannot become a member of an LLC without the consent of all other members of an LLC.

C. MANAGEMENT

An LLC may provide for direct management of the LLC by its members. Alternatively, an LLC may provide for centralized management of the LLC by one or more managers who need not be members of the LLC.

D. LIABILITY OF MEMBERS AND MANAGERS

A member of an LLC is generally **not** liable as a member for an LLC's obligations. If a member renders professional services in an LLC, the member, as well as the LLC, may be liable for torts committed while rendering such services.

A manager or a managing member of an LLC is not personally liable for obligations incurred on behalf of the LLC. Members of a manager-managed LLC do not have the right to maintain a direct action against the manager of the LLC when the alleged misconduct caused harm only to the LLC.

Generally, members owe each other and managers (if any) a duty of loyalty and a duty of care. The operating agreement may amend those duties so long as the amendment is not "manifestly unreasonable."

The duty of loyalty of a member in a member-managed limited liability company includes the duties to account to the company for any profit or benefit derived by the member related to the company's activities or property, to refrain from dealing with the company on behalf of one having an adverse interest in the company, and to refrain from competing with the company. *See* ULLCA § 409 (b).

A member's duty of care is subject to the business judgment rule. It requires the member to act with the care that a person in a like position would reasonably exercise under similar circumstances and in a manner the member reasonably believes to be in the best interests of the company. *See* ULLCA § 409 (c).

Though managers (or members in a member-managed LLC) owe a duty of care to the LLC, they are not liable for simple negligence. The duty of care consists of refraining from engaging in grossly negligent conduct or reckless conduct, intentional misconduct, or a knowing violation of law. However, some state statutes reject the gross negligence standard and impose an ordinary negligence standard when determining breaches of a duty of care. In these states, the business judgment rule may apply to protect LLC managers from liability when decisions are made in good faith. *See* ULLCA § 409(c); Revised Uniform Limited Liability Company Act § 409(c) (2006).

E.   **ALLOCATION OF PROFITS AND LOSSES**

Typically, the operating agreement of the LLC determines the manner in which profits and losses will be allocated among the members of the LLC. In the absence of such an agreement, profits and losses are allocated and distributions are made according to each member's contributions to the LLC.

F.   **TRANSFER OF MEMBERSHIP**

The transfer of a membership interest to another person does not automatically give that person the right to participate in the management of the LLC. Instead, the transferee merely acquires the transferor's right to share in the LLC's profits and losses.

G.   **TERMINATION OF MEMBERSHIP**

Withdrawal of a member from an LLC does not automatically trigger dissolution of the LLC. The LLC may elect to liquidate the fair value of that person's interests, as of the date the person ceased to be a member, based upon the person's right to share in distributions from the LLC. The continuing members of the LLC following the withdrawal of a member will be deemed to have entered into an operating agreement in effect immediately prior to the withdrawal, and the members bound by the operating agreement shall be only those members who have not withdrawn.

H.   **MERGER AND DISSOLUTION**

As with the case for other business entities, an LLC may merge with another LLC or another business entity (e.g., partnership, corporation). An LLC may dissolve upon the occurrence of various events, such as mutual consent of the members, the lack of any members, or the existence of grounds for involuntary dissolution.

Criminal Procedure

CRIMINAL PROCEDURE

Table of Contents

CRIMINAL PROCEDURE

I. FOURTH AMENDMENT: APPLICATION TO ARREST, SEARCH AND SEIZURE

The Fourth Amendment reads: "The right of the people to be secure in their persons, houses, papers, and effects against unreasonable searches and seizures shall not be violated, and no Warrants shall issue, but on probable cause, supported by Oath or affirmation, and particularly describing the place to be searched, and the persons or things to be seized." This amendment protects persons against unreasonable arrests or other seizures as well as unreasonable searches. In addition, when a warrant is required, it must comply with these constitutional requirements.

A. GENERAL FOURTH AMENDMENT PRINCIPLES

1. Standing

Fourth Amendment rights are personal and may not be asserted vicariously. A defendant cannot successfully challenge governmental conduct as a violation of the Fourth Amendment protection against unreasonable searches and seizures unless the defendant himself has been seized or he has a reasonable expectation of privacy with regard to the place searched or the item seized. It is not enough that the introduction as evidence of an item seized may incriminate the defendant.

Example: Defendants Al and Bob are accused of burglarizing an electronics store. Police found stolen DVD players in Al's apartment after an illegal warrantless search. Only Al has standing to raise the issue of a Fourth Amendment violation; Bob may not raise it in his own defense, as his rights were not violated.

2. The Exclusionary Rule

The right to be free from unreasonable searches and seizures must be distinguished from the remedy. The primary remedy is the "exclusionary rule," which prevents the introduction at a subsequent criminal trial of evidence unlawfully seized. This remedy is judicially created, not constitutionally mandated. The remedy provided by the exclusionary rule generally applies to criminal trials; it **does not apply** in other court proceedings, including federal habeas corpus review of state convictions, grand jury proceedings, preliminary hearings, bail hearings, sentencing hearings, and proceedings to revoke parole. Evidence will also not be excluded at trial when introduced as impeachment evidence against the defendant. Finally, the exclusionary rule is not applicable to civil proceedings. *See* § I.C.6., Exclusionary Rule, *infra,* for an expanded discussion.

3. Standard of Review

The judge, not the jury, resolves suppression issues raised by a pretrial motion to suppress. A pretrial motion to suppress often involves a mixed question of fact and law. On appeal, the judge's rulings as to questions of law are reviewed de novo; factual findings are reviewed only for clear error. *Ornelas v. United States*, 517 U.S. 690 (1996).

4. Threshold of Governmental Action

The Fourth Amendment limits governmental action; it does not restrict the acts of private parties unless the private person is acting as an "instrument or agent of the government." Even if governmental action exists, there still is no constitutional violation unless the individual had a reasonable expectation of privacy and either the police did not have a valid warrant or they executed an invalid warrantless search.

> **EXAM NOTE:** Remember, the Fourth Amendment applies only to searches and seizures conducted by police or someone acting under police direction.

5. Grand Jury Subpoena

Unless a grand jury subpoena is being used for harassment or is extremely broad, requiring a person to appear before the grand jury under such subpoena does not fall under the protection of the Fourth Amendment.

6. Broader Rights Possible Under State Constitution

A state may grant broader rights under its own constitution than are granted by the federal Constitution. *See Michigan v. Long*, 463 U.S. 1032 (1983). Thus, even though the Fourth (or Fifth or Sixth) Amendment may not restrict the state government, state constitutional law may.

B. ARREST: UNREASONABLE SEIZURE OF PERSONS

1. Seizure: Objective Test—Not Free to Leave

A person is seized by the police when the officer physically touches a subject or when the subject submits to the officer's show of authority. *Terry v. Ohio*, 392 U.S. 1 (1968). When the actions of the police do not show an unambiguous intent to restrain or when the individual's submission to a show of governmental authority takes the form of passive acquiescence, a seizure occurs only if, in view of the totality of the circumstances, a **reasonable innocent person would believe he was not free to leave.** The test is whether a reasonable person would feel free to decline the officers' requests or otherwise terminate the encounter.

a. Intentional detention

The police officer must intentionally employ physical force or a show of authority in order for the officer's actions to result in a seizure.

> **Example:** During a high-speed chase, an officer forced the driver of the pursued automobile off the road. The officer's intentional use of deadly force against the driver constituted a seizure. *Scott v. Harris*, 550 U.S. 372 (2007).
>
> **Compare:** During a high-speed chase, an officer accidentally struck and killed the passenger of the pursued motorcycle when the motorcycle tipped over. The officer's accidental use of deadly force against the passenger did not constitute a seizure. *County of Sacramento v. Lewis*, 523 U.S. 833 (1998).

However, as long as the officer intentionally employs force or makes a show of authority, the officer's purpose need not be to detain the defendant in order for the defendant to be seized. Consequently, when a police officer makes a traffic stop, not only the driver but also any passengers are deemed to be seized. Therefore, the passenger as well as the driver may challenge the constitutionality of the stop. *Brendlin v. California*, 551 U.S. 249, 251 (2007).

2. Contrast Stop and Frisk

A temporary detention for the purpose of a criminal investigation is a "stop," not an arrest, but is still a seizure for Fourth Amendment purposes. The test for a stop is whether the officer, by means of physical force or show of authority (to which the subject has submitted), has in some way restrained the liberty of the citizen. Seizure includes physical restraint or an order to stop so that the officer can frisk and ask questions on the street.

3. **Arrest Warrants**

An arrest warrant is issued by a detached and neutral magistrate upon a finding of probable cause that a crime has been committed and that this person was involved in committing the particular crime. However, an arrest made pursuant to a warrant that failed to satisfy the probable cause requirement is not illegal when the officer making the arrest independently had probable cause for making the arrest.

a. **Entry into home**

A warrant to arrest an individual implicitly authorizes entry into the arrestee's home to serve the warrant if the police have reason to believe that the arrestee is present. A police officer may not arrest a person in another person's home without an arrest warrant for the subject and a search warrant for the third party's home, absent exigent circumstances or valid consent to enter the third party's home. *Steagald v. United States*, 451 U.S. 204 (1981).

4. **Warrantless Arrests**

Unlike searches, police generally do not need a warrant to make a valid arrest **in a public place,** even if they have time to get one. *U.S. v. Watson*, 423 U.S. 411 (1976). The police, however, must have a warrant to arrest an individual in his own home, absent exigent circumstances or valid consent to enter the arrestee's home. *Payton v. New York*, 445 U.S. 573 (1980).

a. **Crime committed in the presence of the arresting party**

Either a police officer or a private individual has a right to arrest without an arrest warrant if either a felony or a misdemeanor is committed in the arresting party's presence. In determining whether a crime has been committed, the question is whether an officer could conclude—considering all of the surrounding circumstances—that there was a substantial chance of criminal activity. *District of Columbia v. Wesby*, 583 U.S. ___ (2018).

b. **Crime committed outside the presence of the arresting party**

In situations in which a **felony** has been committed outside the presence of the one making the arrest, a police officer may arrest anyone whom he has probable cause to believe has committed a felony, but a private individual may make an arrest only if (i) a felony has actually been committed and (ii) the private individual reasonably believes that the person being arrested is guilty.

c. **Misdemeanor arrest**

A warrantless arrest of a person for a misdemeanor punishable only by a fine is not an unreasonable seizure under the Fourth Amendment. *Atwater v. Lago Vista*, 532 U.S. 318 (2001). Note that the misdemeanor must have been committed in the presence of the arresting party; probable cause to believe that a misdemeanor was committed, without actually witnessing the crime, is not sufficient for a valid warrantless arrest.

d. **Effect of invalid arrest**

An unlawful arrest alone has **no bearing** on a subsequent criminal prosecution, and it is not a defense to the crime charged. If the police have probable cause to detain a suspect, they may do so even if they illegally arrested him (e.g., in his home without a warrant).

An unlawful arrest has legal significance, however, when there is a seizure of evidence. Evidence seized pursuant to an unlawful arrest may be suppressed at trial. A voluntary confession made after an unlawful arrest will not automatically be suppressed. Note, however, that the unlawfulness of the arrest may be considered as a factor when determining whether a confession was truly voluntary. If the confession is too closely tied to the illegal arrest, it may be suppressed. *See Wong Sun v. U.S.,* 371 U.S. 471 (1963).

C. SEARCH AND SEIZURE

1. Governmental Action

Searches conducted by private citizens are not protected by the Fourth Amendment—there must be governmental action. However, the police may not circumvent the Fourth Amendment by intentionally enlisting private individuals to conduct a search of a suspect or areas in which the suspect has a reasonable expectation of privacy.

2. Defining "Search": The Violation of a Reasonable Expectation of Privacy

Only **unreasonable** searches and seizures are subject to Fourth Amendment protections. An unreasonable search occurs when the government (1) invades a place protected by a **reasonable expectation of privacy,** or (2) **physically intrudes** upon a constitutionally protected area (persons, houses, papers, or effects) for the purpose of gathering information. *Katz v. United States*, 389 U.S. 347 (1967); *Florida v. Jardines*, 569 U.S. 1 (2013) (using a drug-sniffing dog on a homeowner's porch for the purpose of investigating the contents of the home constituted a search); *United States v. Jones*, 565 U.S. 400 (2012) (placement of GPS device on defendant's vehicle for the purpose of monitoring the vehicle's movements constituted a search).

> **EXAM NOTE:** Be aware of fact patterns that involve an individual with no expectation of privacy, such as when incriminating evidence is seized at another individual's home. Remember that the government's action is valid unless there is a legitimate expectation of privacy or the government trespassed upon the defendant's private property.

a. Locations searched

1) Home

Although the Supreme Court has stated that "the Fourth Amendment protects people, not places," (see *id.* at 351), the Fourth Amendment, by its terms, protects against an unreasonable governmental search of a "house." This protection extends to persons who have the right to immediate possession of a dwelling, such as the renter of an apartment or a dormitory. *Chapman v. United States*, 365 U.S. 610 (1961).

a) Curtilage

In addition to the home itself, an area immediately surrounding the home known as the "curtilage" may be covered by the "umbrella" of the home's Fourth Amendment protection.

In determining whether the area is protected, the following four-factor test applies:

i) The proximity of the area to the home;

ii) Whether the area is included within an enclosure surrounding the home;

iii) The nature of the uses to which the area is put; and

iv) The steps taken by the resident to protect the area from observation by passersby.

United States v. Dunn, 480 U.S. 294 (1987).

> **Example:** A barn was 60 yards away from the main house and 50 yards away from the innermost fence surrounding the house. The barn was not being used for domestic purposes and, despite being surrounded by a fence, was fenced in a manner that did not prevent persons from observing what lay inside the fence. Consequently, the barn and the area immediately surrounding it lay outside the curtilage. Information of illegal drug activity being conducted within the barn gained by drug enforcement agents while within that area did not constitute an unreasonable search. *Id*.

b) Open fields

Private property that lies outside the curtilage of a home, such as a farmer's field, is not protected by the home's umbrella of Fourth Amendment protection. Under the "open fields" doctrine, governmental intrusion on such property is not a search. The owner does **not** have a reasonable (i.e., objective) expectation of privacy, even though the owner may have a subjective expectation of privacy based on the fact that the land is fenced, protected from public view, and "no trespassing" signs are posted. *United States v. Oliver*, 466 U.S. 170 (1984).

c) Overnight guest in a home

While an overnight guest in a home does not have an ownership interest in the home, such a guest does have a reasonable expectation of privacy, at least as to the areas of the home to which the guest has permission to enter. *Minnesota v. Olson*, 495 U.S. 91 (1990). (As to the ability of the owner or guest to consent to a search of the home, *see* § I.C.4.f, Consent searches, *infra*.)

> **Contrast short-term use of home for illegal business purpose:** Short-term use of a home (e.g., several hours) with the permission of the owner does not give rise to a reasonable expectation of privacy, at least when the home is being used for an illegal business purpose (e.g., bagging cocaine for sale on the streets). *Minnesota v. Carter*, 525 U.S. 83 (1998).

2) Motel room

As with the search of a home, the search of a motel room by a government agent may be an unreasonable search. A motel clerk's consent to a governmental search of a room during the time it is rented is insufficient to justify the search. *Stoner v. California*, 376 U.S. 483 (1964).

3) Business premises

In general, business premises are protected by the Fourth Amendment. *G.M. Leasing Corp. v. United States*, 429 U.S. 338 (1977). However, such premises may be subjected to administrative searches, *see* § I.C.4.g., Administrative searches, *infra*.

4) Prison

A prison inmate has no reasonable expectation of privacy in his cell. The limitations on Fourth Amendment rights are justified by the need to maintain institutional security and preserve internal order and discipline. *Hudson v. Palmer*, 468 U.S. 517 (1984). Unlike a convict, a pretrial detainee may have a limited expectation of privacy in his cell. However, a detainee's cell may be subject to a routine search, and the detainee's person may be subject to a strip search or a full-body search after a contact visit with someone from the outside. *Bell v. Wolfish*, 441 U.S. 520 (1979). Jail administrators may also require all arrestees committed to the general population of a jail to undergo no-touch visual strip searches, even if the arrest was for a minor offense and even in the absence of reasonable suspicion that the arrestee possesses a concealed weapon or other contraband. *Florence v. Board of Chosen Freeholders of County of Burlington*, 566 U.S. 318 (2012).

5) Trespass

While the fact that a governmental agent is on property without permission may make a warrantless search unreasonable (e.g., a search of a home), the fact that a governmental agent is illegally on property does not automatically make the search illegal (*United States v. Oliver, supra*), nor does the fact that a governmental agent is legally in a public place make the search legal (*Katz v. United States, supra*).

b. Objects sought

1) Papers and effects

The Fourth Amendment, by its terms, protects "papers and effects." For example, a person retains a reasonable expectation that items placed within his luggage will be free from a purposeful, exploratory physical manipulation of the luggage. *Bond v. United States*, 529 U.S. 334 (2000).

Compare smell emanating from object. A person does *not* have a reasonable expectation of privacy with regard to a smell emanating from his luggage, at least when the smell arises from an illegal substance. *United States v. Place*, 462 U.S. 696 (1983).

When papers and effects are transferred to a third party, such as checks and deposit slips given by a customer to a bank, a person no longer has a reasonable expectation of privacy in these items. Similarly, financial statements maintained by a bank are bank records in which the customer has no reasonable expectation of privacy. *United States v. Miller*, 425 U.S. 435 (1976).

Example: A defendant who hides drugs in a friend's purse in order to avoid their detection by police has no legitimate expectation of privacy in the purse. *Rawlings v. Kentucky*, 448 U.S. 98 (1980).

2) Automobiles

Although, under the Fourth Amendment, stopping a car constitutes a seizure of the driver and any passengers, *Brendlin v. California*, 551 U.S. 249 (2007) (passenger), *Delaware v. Prouse*, 440 U.S. 648 (1979) (driver), there is a lesser expectation of privacy with regard to the automobile and its contents than with a home. *Wyoming v. Houghton*, 526 U.S. 295 (1999). Even so, officers must have an articulable, reasonable suspicion of a violation of the law in order to stop an automobile. A call to 911 reporting erratic driving may give the police the reasonable suspicion needed to make a traffic stop if the report is reliable. *Navarette v. California*, 572 U.S. ___, 134 S. Ct. 1683 (2014). The fact that a person who is in lawful possession of a rental car is not listed on the rental agreement does not defeat his or her otherwise reasonable expectation of privacy. *Byrd v. United States*, 584 U.S. ___ (2018).

a) Checkpoints

Police may stop an automobile at a checkpoint without reasonable, individualized suspicion of a violation of the law if the stop is based on neutral, articulable standards and its purpose is closely related to an issue affecting automobiles. A roadblock to perform sobriety checks has been upheld, while a similar roadblock to perform drug checks has not. *Compare Michigan Dept. of State Police v. Sitz*, 496 U.S. 444 (1990) (sobriety check) *with Indianapolis v. Edmond*, 531 U.S. 32 (2000) (check for presence of illegal drugs).

Compare random stops: Police may generally *not* stop an automobile, even for a driving-related matter, without a reasonable, individualized suspicion of a violation of the law, unless the stop is effected on the basis of neutral, articulable standards. *Delaware v. Prouse*, 440 U.S. 648 (1979) (no random stop of a driver to verify driver's license and car registration).

i) Immigration law enforcement

When the purpose of the stop relates to the enforcement of immigration laws, any car may be stopped on a random basis at the border of the United States without a reasonable suspicion of wrongdoing. *Almeida-Sanchez v. United States*, 413 U.S. 266 (1973). When a search does not occur at the border or its functional equivalent, all cars may be stopped at a fixed checkpoint without a reasonable suspicion of violation of an immigration law, but a car may not be singled out and randomly stopped without a particularized and objective basis. *United States v. Cortez*, 449 U.S. 411 (1981) (holding the stop of one car proper when officers could reasonably surmise that the car was involved in criminal immigration activity); *United States v. Martinez-Fuerte*, 428 U.S. 543 (1976) (affirming convictions based on stops at checkpoints at which all cars were stopped).

ii) Search for witnesses

A checkpoint maintained by police for the purpose of finding witnesses to a crime (rather than suspects) is not per se unreasonable, as long as (i) the checkpoint stop's primary law enforcement purpose is to elicit evidence to help them apprehend not the vehicle's occupants but other individuals; (ii) the stop advanced a public concern to a significant degree; and (iii) the police appropriately tailored their checkpoint stops to fit important criminal investigatory needs and to minimally interfere with liberties protected by the Fourth Amendment. *Illinois v. Lidster*, 540 U.S. 419 (2004).

b) Car's VIN

The driver of a car does not have a reasonable expectation of privacy in the vehicle identification number (VIN) affixed to an automobile. *New York v. Class*, 475 U.S. 106 (1986). Consequently, a police officer's moving of papers that obstructed his view of this number did not constitute a search under the Fourth Amendment, and a gun found while doing so was admissible into evidence.

3) Abandoned property

Abandoned property is not protected by the Fourth Amendment.

Example: There is no reasonable expectation of privacy in garbage set curbside for pickup. *California v. Greenwood*, 486 U.S. 35 (1988).

c. Persons and their attributes

1) Physical characteristics

There is no expectation of privacy in one's physical characteristics; therefore, a demand for a handwriting or voice sample is not a search. *United States v. Mara*, 410 U.S. 19 (1973) (handwriting exemplar); *United States v. Dionisio*, 410 U.S. 1 (1973) (voice exemplar).

Furthermore, DNA identification of arrestees is a reasonable search that can be considered part of a routine booking procedure. When officers make an arrest supported by probable cause and they bring the suspect to the station to be detained in custody, taking and analyzing a cheek swab of the arrestee's DNA is, like fingerprinting and photographing, a legitimate police booking procedure that is reasonable under the Fourth Amendment. *Maryland v. King*, 569 U.S. 435 (2013).

2) Government informants

Some surveillance and investigation techniques have been held not to implicate any reasonable expectation of privacy because the targets of the surveillance were regarded as having assumed the risk that the people with whom they were interacting would be government agents. There is no reasonable expectation of privacy in conversations carried on with government informants or undercover officers. Similarly, if one party to a telephone call consents to wiretapping or agrees to record the call at the government's request, such monitoring will not trigger the Fourth Amendment rights of any other party to the call. *United States v. White*, 401 U.S. 745 (1971). A person also runs the risk that a third party to whom she turns over information may disclose such information to the government. *United States v. Miller*, 425 U.S. 435 (1976).

d. Methods used to search

1) Fly-over

An inspection conducted from at least 400 feet in the air, whether by an airplane or a helicopter, does not violate a reasonable expectation of privacy and therefore is not a search for the purposes of the Fourth Amendment. *Florida v. Riley*, 488 U.S. 445 (1989) (helicopter); *California v. Ciraolo*, 476 U.S. 207 (1986) (airplane).

2) Technological device

Attaching a device to a person's body without consent in order to track that person's movements is a search for Fourth Amendment purposes. *Grady v. North Carolina*, 575 U.S. ___, 135 S. Ct. 1368 (2015). Similarly, collection by law enforcement of cell-site location information records from wireless carriers in order to track a suspect's whereabouts requires a warrant. *Carpenter v. United States*, 585 U.S. ___ (2018).

With regard to automobiles, the Fourth Amendment does not prohibit the police from using technological devices to enhance their ability to search (e.g., radar detectors, computers to search license plates, surveillance equipment). *United States v. Knotts*, 460 U.S. 276 (1983) (placement of a tracking device on a car). However, physically intruding upon a suspect's property to install a technological device (e.g., a GPS tracker on a car to gather information) may constitute a search. *United States v. Jones, supra*.

> It is important to note the distinction between *Knotts* and *Jones*—in *Knotts*, the device was installed with the permission of the former owner (a person other than the suspect) before the car came into the defendant's possession; defendant Jones, on the other hand, owned the vehicle in question at the time the government installed the GPS device.

The use of a device or sense-enhancing technology (e.g., a thermal sensing device) that is not in use by the general public to explore the details of a dwelling that would previously have been unknowable without physical intrusion constitutes a search. *Kyllo v. United States*, 533 U.S. 27 (2001). Moreover, use of an electronic listening device to eavesdrop on a conversation made from a public phone booth can violate the speaker's reasonable expectation of privacy. *Katz v. United States, supra*.

> **Flashlight.** Because flashlights are ubiquitous, the use of a flashlight at night to illuminate the inside of a car does not constitute a search for Fourth Amendment purposes. *Texas v. Brown*, 460 U.S. 730 (1983).

3) Canine sniff

Use of a trained dog to sniff for the presence of drugs is a search if it involves a **physical intrusion** onto constitutionally protected property. *Florida v. Jardines*, 569 U.S. 1 (2013) (curtilage). In the absence of a physical intrusion, the use of drug-sniffing dogs does not violate a reasonable expectation of privacy. *Illinois v. Caballes*, 543 U.S. 405 (2005) (car); *United States v. Place*, 462 U.S. 696 (1983) (luggage in a public place).

> **Officer's sense of smell:** A police officer may also rely on his own sense of smell in ascertaining the presence of illegal drugs or alcohol. *United States v. Sharpe*, 470 U.S. 675 (1985) (marijuana); *United States v. Ventresca*, 380 U.S. 102, 104, 111 (1965) (alcohol).

4) Field test of substance

A field test performed on a substance to determine if the substance is contraband is not a search for Fourth Amendment purposes. *United States v. Jacobsen*, 466 U.S. 109 (1984).

3. Search Warrant Requirements

When a search occurs, a warrant serves to protect a person's privacy interests against unreasonable governmental intrusion. A valid search warrant must be issued by a neutral and detached magistrate based on probable cause, must be supported by oath or affidavit, and must describe the places to be searched and the items to be seized.

> Warrantless searches are per se unreasonable unless the search satisfies one of seven exceptions to the warrant requirement.

a. Probable cause

Facts supporting probable cause may come from any of the following sources:

i) A police officer's personal observations;

ii) Information from a reliable, known informant or from an unknown informant that can be independently verified; or

iii) Evidence seized during stops based on reasonable suspicion, evidence discovered in plain view, or evidence obtained during consensual searches.

1) Right to attack truthfulness of affidavit

Generally, a search warrant that is valid on its face may not be attacked by a defendant as lacking in probable cause. A defendant can challenge a facially valid warrant only when the defendant can establish, by a preponderance of the evidence, that:

i) The affidavit contained **false statements** that were **made** by the affiant **knowingly, intentionally, or with a reckless disregard** for their truth; and

ii) The false statements were **necessary to** the finding of **probable cause.**

Franks v. Delaware, 438 U.S. 154 (1978).

2) Informants

Courts use the **totality of the circumstances** test to determine whether information provided by a police informant is sufficient to create probable cause. The affidavit generally does not need to include any particular information about the informant, including the informant's identity, so long as a neutral magistrate can find that, based on the informant's information and all other available facts, there is probable cause to issue the warrant. *Illinois v. Gates*, 462 U.S. 213 (1983); *McCray v. Illinois*, 386 U.S. 300 (1967).

b. Particularity

A search warrant must describe with particularity the place to be searched and the objects to be seized. *United States v. Grubbs*, 547 U.S. 90 (2006). Warrants that, in addition to describing specific documents to be seized, also refer to "other fruits, instrumentalities and evidence of the crime at this [time] unknown" are not converted into illegal general warrants by the inclusion of such language. The reference to a "crime" has been interpreted as being limited to a particular crime (e.g., false pretenses), rather than any crime. *Andresen v. Maryland*, 427 U.S. 463 (1976). A warrant need not specify the manner of its execution.

c. Anticipatory warrant

Police do not have to believe that contraband is on the premises to be searched at the time the warrant is issued. The probable cause requirement is satisfied when, at the time that the warrant is issued, there is probable cause to believe that the triggering condition will occur and, if that condition does occur, there is a fair probability that contraband or evidence of a crime will be found in a particular place. *United States v. Grubbs, supra.*

d. Third-party premises

A search warrant may be issued to search the premises of a person who is not suspected of a crime. *Zurcher v. Stanford Daily*, 436 U.S. 547 (1978).

e. Execution of warrant

1) By whom

A warrant cannot be executed by a private citizen. Generally, only a police officer may execute a warrant, but administrative warrants may be executed by the appropriate governmental official (e.g., fire inspector).

2) Timing

A warrant that is not timely executed (i.e., an unreasonable delay occurs) may be subject to challenge on the grounds that probable cause ceased to exist.

3) Manner of execution—knock and announce

Most states and the federal government mandate that a police officer, when executing either a search or an arrest warrant, must generally announce his purpose before entering. The knock-and-announce rule gives individuals the opportunity to comply with the law, to avoid the destruction of property occasioned by a forcible entry, and to collect themselves with dignity before answering the door. The rule also serves to protect officers and the inhabitants of the building from physical harm, because an unannounced entry may provoke violence in supposed self-defense by the surprised resident. A state may permit an exception to the rule if the entry is made under exigent circumstances, such as when there is a reasonable belief of danger to the officer or destruction of evidence. *Ker v. California*, 374 U.S. 23, 34 (1963).

Note, however, that the interests protected by the knock-and-announce requirement do not include the shielding of potential evidence from discovery. Thus, violation of the "knock and announce" rule does not trigger the exclusionary rule (*see* § I.C.6., *infra*) with respect to evidence discovered as a result of a search conducted in violation of the "knock and announce" rule. *Hudson v. Michigan*, 547 U.S. 586 (2006).

4) Seizure of evidence not specified

A search warrant confers authority to search only the places and persons named in it. That said, any evidence of a crime, instrumentalities or fruits of a crime, or contraband found in plain view while properly executing the warrant, whether or not specified in the warrant, may be seized (*see* § I.C.4.e., "Plain view" doctrine, *infra*).

5) Treatment of persons not specified in the warrant

Independent justification is needed to search persons not named in a search warrant; mere proximity to a named person does not supply such justification. *Ybarra v. Illinois*, 444 U.S. 84 (1979). However, in conducting a search for contraband pursuant to a warrant, any occupant of the premises to be searched may be detained in a reasonable manner, which may include the use of handcuffs, for a reasonable time while the search is conducted. *Muehler v. Mena*, 544 U.S. 93 (2005); *Michigan v. Summers*, 452 U.S. 692 (1981). Such a detention is only justified for individuals within the immediate vicinity of the premises to be searched. If an individual is not in the immediate vicinity of the premises, then a detention of that individual must be justified by some other rationale. *Bailey v United States*, 568 U.S. 186 (2013) (detaining suspect one mile away from premises was unreasonable).

4.   Exceptions to the Warrant Requirement

> **EXAM NOTE:** Warrantless searches are frequently tested on the MBE. Be aware of answer choices that include concepts that apply to one type of warrantless search when another is being tested.

a.   Search incident to a lawful arrest

A warrantless search is valid if it is reasonable in scope and if it is made incident to a lawful arrest. If the arrest is invalid, any search made incident to it is likewise invalid. Therefore, if a suspect is stopped for a traffic offense and given a citation but not arrested, then there can be no search incident to lawful arrest. *Knowles v. Iowa*, 525 U.S. 113 (1999).

1)   The *Chimel* standard

A lawful arrest creates a situation that justifies a warrantless contemporaneous search of the person arrested and the immediate surrounding area (i.e., his "wingspan") from which a weapon may be concealed or evidence destroyed. *Chimel v. California*, 395 U.S. 752 (1969).

If the arrest occurs in a home, it is permissible to conduct a "protective sweep" for confederates (i.e., people who might launch an attack) in spaces immediately adjacent to the place of arrest, even without probable cause or reasonable suspicion. A "protective sweep" allows a quick and limited visual inspection of those places immediately adjacent to the place of arrest in which a person might be hiding (e.g., adjacent rooms, closets, showers). If the officers have reasonable suspicion that confederates are hiding beyond these immediately adjacent areas, they can broaden their search for people in those places too. *Maryland v. Buie*, 494 U.S. 325, 334 (1990) (finding that after police properly arrested defendant in his home after defendant came up from his basement, the police were permitted to conduct a protective sweep of the basement to ensure their safety).

2)   Time limitations (temporal unity)

A search incident to a valid arrest must take place contemporaneously with the arrest in order to be valid.

3)   Scope of search

The right to search incident to a lawful arrest includes the right to search pockets of clothing and to open containers found inside the pockets. The right also extends to containers "immediately associated" with the person (such as a shoulder bag or purse).

The search incident to lawful arrest exception does not extend to an arrestee's cell phone or laptop. Absent exigent circumstances, police must obtain a warrant before searching digital information of a person arrested. *Riley v. California*, 573 U.S. ___, 134 S. Ct. 2473 (2014).

4)   Vehicle search incident to arrest

To justify a warrantless search of an automobile incident to arrest, the Fourth Amendment requires that law enforcement demonstrate either (i) that the arrestee is within reaching distance of the passenger compartment at the time of the search and, as a result, may pose an actual and continuing threat to the officer's safety or a need to preserve evidence from being tampered with by the arrestee or (ii) that it is reasonable that evidence of the offense of arrest might be found in the vehicle. *Arizona v. Gant*, 556 U.S. 332 (2009).

5) Impounded vehicle

A legally impounded vehicle may be searched, including closed containers, such as glove box or a backpack, as part of a routine inventory search. *South Dakota v. Opperman*, 428 U.S. 364, 369–71 (1976). The warrantless search need not take place at the time that the vehicle is seized.

b. Exigent circumstances

Warrantless entry into a home or business is presumed unlawful unless the government demonstrates both probable cause and exigent circumstances. In determining the existence of exigent circumstances, courts use the "totality of circumstances" test. As a corollary to this doctrine, police may also secure the premises for a reasonable time to enable officers to obtain a warrant when the police have reason to believe that the failure to do so could result in the destruction of evidence. *Illinois v. McArthur*, 531 U.S. 326 (2001).

The exigent-circumstances rule does not apply when the police create the exigency by engaging or threatening to engage in conduct that violates the Fourth Amendment. *Kentucky v. King*, 563 U.S. 452 (2011).

1) Hot pursuit

If the police have probable cause to believe that an individual has committed a *felony* and they are pursuing him to arrest him, then they have the right to enter a private building during the pursuit, to search that building for the person or his weapons while they are present on the premises, and to seize evidence found there, even though the material found is "mere" evidence and neither fruits nor instrumentalities of a crime.

No such exigency exists in pursuing someone suspected of a nonjailable traffic offense; the hot-pursuit exception is inapplicable in that instance. *Welsh v. Wisconsin*, 466 U.S. 740 (1984).

2) Emergency situations

A search without a warrant is authorized whenever there is a reasonable apprehension that the delay required in obtaining the warrant would result in the immediate danger of evidence destruction or the threatened safety of the officer or the public, or when a suspect is likely to flee before a warrant can be obtained.

Whether a person is in need of aid is judged on the basis of a police officer's objective reasonable belief that the person needs aid. Aid includes emergency assistance to an injured occupant as well as protection of an occupant from imminent injury. Neither the officer's subjective motive for searching without a warrant nor the seriousness of the crime the officer was originally investigating are relevant in making this determination. *Brigham City v. Stuart*, 547 U.S. 398 (2006).

Except in unusual situations, blood samples require warrants, but breath samples do not. The involuntary, warrantless blood test of a drunken-driving suspect was appropriate when police could reasonably have believed that the delay necessary to obtain a search warrant would likely result in disappearance of the blood-alcohol content evidence, and the test was administered according to accepted medical practices. *Schmerber v. California*, 384 U.S.

757 (1966). However, the reasonableness of a warrantless blood test is determined case by case, based on the totality of the circumstances. The Fourth Amendment mandates that police officers obtain a warrant before a blood sample can be drawn, if they can reasonably do so without significantly undermining the efficacy of the search. *Birchfield v. North Dakota*, 579 U.S. ___, 136 S. Ct. 2160 (2016); *Missouri v. McNeely*, 569 U.S. 141 (2013).

c. Stop and frisk

1) Stop—limited seizure/detention

A "stop" (also known as a "*Terry* stop") is a limited and temporary intrusion on an individual's freedom of movement short of a full custodial arrest. Merely approaching a person, but not restricting the person's movement in any way, does not constitute a detention. A stop is justified on the **reasonable suspicion,** based upon **articulable facts,** that the detainees are or were involved in criminal activity. *Terry v. Ohio*, 392 U.S. 1 (1968). Whether reasonable suspicion exists is based on the **totality of the circumstances.** It requires more than a vague suspicion, but less than probable cause, and it need not be based on a police officer's personal knowledge.

Example: Police were justified in stopping a suspect who (i) was standing on a street corner in a high-crime area and (ii) fled upon noticing the police, even though neither factor alone would constitute reasonable suspicion to justify a stop. *Illinois v. Wardlow*, 528 U.S. 119 (2000).

Reasonable suspicion can be based on a flyer, a police bulletin, or an informant's tip, but only if the tip is accompanied by sufficient indicia of reliability. *United States v. Hensley*, 469 U.S. 221, 233–34 (1985).

In addition, a police officer's reasonable mistake of law can support reasonable suspicion to conduct a traffic stop. *Heien v. North Carolina*, 574 U.S. ___, 135 S. Ct. 530 (2014).

2) Frisk—limited search

An officer who does not have probable cause to arrest may make a limited search of a person he has lawfully stopped, such as a pat-down of the outer clothing, if he has **reasonable suspicion** that the person was or is involved in criminal activity **and** that the frisk is necessary for the preservation of his safety or the safety of others (i.e., reasonable suspicion that the person has a weapon).

Under the **"plain feel"** exception, if an officer conducting a valid frisk feels with an open hand an object that has physical characteristics that make its identity immediately obvious (i.e., he has probable cause to believe that the item is contraband), then the officer may seize the evidence. Police may also *briefly* seize items if the officers have a reasonable suspicion that the item is or contains contraband.

3) *Terry* stop and frisk of a car

Pursuant to a lawful stop of a vehicle, police may conduct a search of the passenger compartment for weapons, if:

   i) The police possess a reasonable belief that the suspect is dangerous and may gain immediate control of weapons; and

ii) The search of the passenger compartment is "limited to those areas in which a weapon may be placed or hidden."

Michigan v. Long, 463 U.S. 1032, 1048–50 (1983).

Police may order occupants out of a vehicle that they have lawfully stopped. *Maryland v. Wilson*, 519 U.S. 408 (1997).

When police make a lawful traffic stop, they are automatically detaining both the driver and the passenger. They may only frisk the driver or the passenger if they have reasonable suspicion that the person is carrying a weapon. *Arizona v. Johnson*, 555 U.S. 323 (2009).

4) Limits on time, place, and investigative method

A *Terry* stop must be temporary and last no longer than is necessary to effectuate the purpose of the stop. The investigative methods employed should be the least intrusive means reasonably available to verify or dispel the officer's suspicion in a short time.

Police may stop the person, question him for a limited period of time, and frisk him for weapons only, not evidence. Police also can require that the detained person identify himself. Failure to comply with this request can result in the arrest of the detained person.

After the conclusion of a traffic stop, absent reasonable suspicion, police extension of the stop in order to conduct a dog sniff violates the Fourth Amendment's protection against unreasonable seizures. *Rodriguez v. United States*, 575 U.S. ____, 135 S. Ct. 1609 (2015).

> When police hold a suspect beyond the amount of time necessary to effectuate the purpose of a *Terry* stop, the seizure becomes an arrest and must be supported by probable cause.

5) Development of probable cause

If the officer conducting the stop develops probable cause, the officer may then make an arrest and conduct a full search incident to that arrest. If the stop involves a vehicle, the officer may search the passenger compartment and all containers therein, whether open or closed, if the arrestee is within reaching distance of the passenger compartment of the vehicle or if it is reasonable to believe that the vehicle contains evidence of the offense of arrest. *See* § I.C.4.a.4), Vehicle search incident to arrest, *supra,* discussing the *Gant* rule.

d. Automobile exception

The Fourth Amendment does not require police to obtain a warrant to search a vehicle if they have probable cause to believe that it contains contraband or evidence of a criminal activity. The police may search anywhere in a car that they believe there to be contraband, including the trunk and locked containers, so long as they have **probable cause** to do so. *United States v. Ross*, 456 U.S. 798, 825 (1982). The search may also extend to passengers' belongings, *Wyoming v. Houghten*, 526 U.S. 295, 302 (1999), as well as to mobile homes, *California v. Carney*, 471 U.S. 386, 393–394 (1985). Any other evidence observed in plain view may also be seized.

> Note that the automobile exception does not permit the warrantless entry of a home or its curtilage in order to search a vehicle therein. *Collins v. Virginia*, 584 U.S. ___ (2018).

1) Pretextual stop

Police may use a pretextual stop to investigate whether a law has been violated, even if they have no reasonable suspicion, provided that they have probable cause to believe that the law for which the vehicle was stopped has been violated. *Whren v. United States*, 517 U.S. 806 (1996) (seizure of illegal drugs constitutional even though police stopped a car for a traffic violation as a pretext to investigate a hunch that the occupants possessed drugs).

2) Containers within a car

Probable cause to search a vehicle extends only to containers and compartments that reasonably could hold the evidence they are searching for. If the police have probable cause to search only a particular container, they may search only that container, and not the entire car. *Arkansas v. Sanders*, 442 U.S. 753 (1979); *California v. Acevedo*, 500 U.S. 565, 570 (1991). (Note, however, that what the officers find in one container may give them probable cause to believe evidence is contained elsewhere in the car.)

> **Example:** A driver left a residence holding a closed paper bag, which officers had probable cause to believe contained narcotics, based on an informant's tip. The bag was placed in the trunk, and the driver drove away. Police were authorized to stop the vehicle, open the trunk, and inspect the bag. However, the search was limited to the bag only. If they did not find the bag, they could only open and search containers big enough to store the bag. *Id.* at 579–80.

3) Trunk

If police have probable cause to search the trunk, not just a container placed in the trunk, then they can search the entire trunk and every container in the trunk, even if locked.

e. "Plain-view" doctrine

1) In public view

Items in public view may be seized without a warrant because one cannot have a reasonable expectation of privacy in things that are exposed to the public (e.g., physical characteristics, vehicle identification numbers, or items in open fields).

2) In private view

In situations in which there is a reasonable expectation of privacy, a police officer may seize an item in plain view of the officer, even if the item was not named in the search warrant, as long as (i) the officer is **lawfully on the premises**, (ii) the incriminating character of the item is **immediately apparent**, and (iii) the officer has **lawful access** to the item (e.g., viewing an object through a window is insufficient if the officer does not have lawful access to the inside of the house). The discovery of the item does not need to be inadvertent. *Horton v. California*, 496 U.S. 128 (1990); *Arizona v. Hicks*, 480 U.S. 231 (1987).

> **Example:** Officer Olivia was executing a valid warrant to search Defendant Doug's home for a gun suspected to have been used in a murder. On entering

the premises, Olivia saw bags of cocaine piled on Doug's coffee table. Under the "plain view" doctrine, Olivia could properly seize the bags, even though the warrant applied only to a gun.

f. Consent searches

Consent can serve to eliminate the need for police to have probable cause as well as to first obtain a warrant in order to conduct a search.

1) Voluntary

For permission to constitute consent, the permission must be given voluntarily. Permission given under threats of harm or compulsion does not constitute consent. In determining whether a person's response constitutes consent, courts evaluate the **totality of the circumstances** in which the response is made.

a) False assertion of authority

Permission given in acquiescence to lawful authority (e.g., a warrant) is not voluntary. Consequently, if the officer conducting the search erroneously states that he has a warrant, then permission given in reliance on that statement does not constitute consent. *Bumper v. North Carolina*, 391 U.S. 543, 549 (1968).

b) Knowledge of the right to withhold consent

The failure by police to inform the person from whom consent is sought that she has the right to withhold consent does not invalidate the consent. *Schneckloth v. Bustamonte*, 412 U.S. 218, 233 (1973).

c) Consent based on deceit

A government agent pretending to be a narcotics buyer, for example, may accept an invitation to enter the premises for the purposes contemplated by the occupant (i.e., to purchase drugs). The officer or agent may then seize things in plain view. *Lewis v. United States*, 385 U.S. 206 (1966).

2) Third-party consent

When the person from whom consent is sought is not the defendant, in addition to the voluntariness of the permission, the authority of that person to consent can be an issue.

a) Property of a third party

Generally, a third party has the authority to consent to a search of property that she owns or occupies. As such, the defendant cannot suppress evidence seized during such a search on the grounds that he (the defendant) did not consent to the search.

b) Property of the defendant

Generally, a third party does not have the authority to consent to a search of property owned or occupied by the defendant. The defendant can generally suppress evidence seized during such a search unless (i) an agency relationship exists between the third party and the defendant that gives to the third party the right to consent on behalf of the defendant, or (ii) the defendant otherwise gives the third party such rights with respect to the property that the defendant assumes the risk that the third party would allow the property to be searched (e.g., a shared duffle bag). *Frazier v. Cupp*, 394 U.S. 731, 740 (1969).

c) Jointly controlled property

When the property to be searched is under the joint control of the defendant and a third party (e.g., co-tenants of an apartment, a house jointly owned by a husband and wife), the authority of the third party to consent turns on whether the defendant is present at the time of the search.

i) Defendant not present

If the property to be searched is under the joint control of the defendant and a third party, and the defendant is not present at the time of the search, then the third party has authority to consent. The third party has actual authority when she has joint access or control for most purposes. *U.S. v. Matlock*, 415 U.S. 164, 170–171 (1974). In addition, the third party's consent may be valid even though she lacks actual authority if the police reasonably believe that she has such authority. *Illinois v. Rodriguez*, 497 U.S. 177, 184 (1990).

ii) Defendant present

When the property to be searched is under the joint control of the defendant and a third party, and the defendant is present at the time of the search, then the police may not rely on third-party consent if the defendant objects to the search. *Georgia v. Randolph*, 547 U.S. 103, 114–116 (2006). When the defendant is not present, however, a third party may consent to a search even if the defendant previously was present and objected to a search at that time. *Fernandez v. California*, 571 U.S. 292 (2014).

iii) Ownership versus current control

In some instances, ownership of the premises is not sufficient to confer authority to consent to a search. For example, a landlord may not consent to a search of the tenant's premises. *Chapman v. United States*, 365 U.S. 610, 617 (1961). Similarly, a hotel clerk cannot consent to the search of a guest's room until the guest has permanently checked out. *Stoner v. California*, 376 U.S. 483, 489 (1964). However, some circuits have held that the owner of a house can consent to a search of rooms occupied by non-paying guests.

iv) Parental consent

When a child lives with a parent, the parent has the authority to consent to a search of a child's room even if the child is an adult. However, a parent may lack authority to consent to the search of a locked container inside the child's room, depending on the age of the child. *U.S. v. Block*, 590 F.2d 535, 540 (4th Cir. 1979).

3) Scope of consent

Although a search is limited to the area to which the consent applies, the search may extend to areas that a reasonable officer would believe it extends. For example, consent by a driver to search his car for drugs extends to a closed container within the car that could contain drugs. *Florida v. Jimento*, 500 U.S. 248, 252 (1991).

4) Burden of proof

The prosecution must prove that the permission was freely given; the defendant is not required to show that the permission was coerced.

g. Administrative, special needs, and inventory searches

Administrative search warrants are generally required for nonconsensual fire, health, or safety inspections of residential or private commercial property.

1) Probable cause

The probable cause requirement for administrative searches is less stringent than that for a criminal investigation. Evidence of an existing statutory or regulatory violation or a reasonable plan supported by a valid public interest will justify the issuance of a warrant. *Camara v. Mun. Court of San Francisco*, 387 U.S. 523, 533 (1967).

2) Use of administrative searches

The government may not use administrative searches to investigate criminal activity. However, discovery of evidence during the search does not invalidate the search. The following administrative-type searches may be validly made without a warrant:

i) Searches of people entering an **airplane boarding area,** as long as the passenger can prevent the search by not boarding the plane;

ii) Searches of businesses in **highly regulated industries** such as liquor stores, gun shops, strip-mining operations, and automobile junkyards, because of urgent public interest and under the theory that the business impliedly consented to warrantless searches by entering into a highly regulated industry;

iii) Oral statements seized by **wiretaps,** when matters of national security are at issue;

iv) Searches of students by **public school officials,** so long as they are based on reasonable grounds (this standard is lower than probable cause and calls for only a "moderate chance" of finding the expected evidence, rather than a "fair probability" or "substantial chance"), and the measures adopted for the search are reasonably related to the objectives of the search and not excessively intrusive in light of the age and sex of the student and the nature of the infraction. *New Jersey v. T.L.O.*, 469 U.S. 325, 340–341 (1985); *Safford Unified Sch. Dist. #1 v. Redding*, 557 U.S. 364, 370-371 (2009).

v) **Special needs searches,** such as drug testing for railroad employees involved in an accident or student athletes during the athletic season. To be a special need, the state interest must be a real, current, and vital problem that can be effectively addressed through the proposed search. Even if the need exists, it must be balanced against the privacy interest at stake and the character of the intrusion. *Bd. of Educ. v. Earls*, 536 U.S. 822, 829 (2002);

vi) **Inventory searches** of items in official custody, such as impounded vehicles. After lawfully taking custody of property, police may conduct a warrantless search of other property to protect the owner's property while in custody, to protect police from claims of theft, and to protect officers from danger. Inventory searches must be performed according to standardized criteria and procedures. Subjective intent of the officer is irrelevant;

vii) **Routine international border** searches of border crossers and their belongings within the United States, including (i) stops, but not searches, by roving patrols who reasonably suspect that undocumented immigrants may be in an automobile, (ii) opening of international mail if authorities have reasonable cause to suspect contraband in the mail, and (iii) subsequent reopening of mail after the item had been resealed and delivered to the recipient;

viii) **Vehicle checkpoints and roadblocks** set up to stop cars on the basis of a neutral articulable standard and designed to serve a limited purpose closely related to the problem of an automobile's inherent mobility (e.g., to get drunk drivers off the road);

ix) **Factory searches** of the entire work force to determine citizenship of workers;

x) Searches of **government employees' electronically recorded documents and conduct, file cabinets, and desks** if they are justified by a reasonable suspicion of work-related misconduct or a non-investigatory, work-related need;

xi) **Detention of a traveler** whom authorities have reasonable suspicion is smuggling contraband in his stomach;

xii) Searches of **parolees and their homes,** even with no reasonable suspicion, when a parolee agrees to submit to searches by a parole officer or police officer at any time as a condition of his parole. The rationale being that because there is a greater need to search parolees since they are less likely to be law-abiding citizens, a parolee has a lower expectation of privacy;

xiii) Seizure of **contaminated or spoiled food**; and

xiv) Searches for the **cause of a fire** that occurs within a reasonable time after the fire is extinguished, but excluding searches for other evidence unrelated to the cause that would establish that the fire was attributable to arson. *Michigan v. Clifford*, 464 U.S. 287 (1984) (search of home); *Michigan v. Tyler*, 436 U.S. 499 (1978) (search of business (furniture store)).

h. Wiretapping

To obtain a warrant authorizing a wiretap, officers must satisfy the below requirements. The warrant must:

i) Be limited to a short period of time;

ii) Demonstrate probable cause that a specific crime has been or is about to be committed;

iii) Name the person or persons to be wiretapped;

iv) Describe with particularity the conversations that can be overheard; and

v) Include provisions for the termination of the wiretap.

Upon termination of the wiretap, the conversations that have been intercepted must be shown to the court. Note that a person assumes the unreliability of those to whom she speaks and has no Fourth Amendment claim if she finds out later that the listener was wired or recording the conversation. *United States v. White*, 401 U.S. 745 (1971). Furthermore, a speaker who makes no attempt to keep his conversation private has no Fourth Amendment claim. *Katz v. United States*, 389 U.S. 347 (1967).

In addition, a wiretap related to domestic security surveillance requires that a neutral and detached magistrate—not the president—make the determination that a wiretapping warrant should issue, and the wiretap must comply with the Omnibus Crime Control and Safe Streets Act. However, there is no requirement for prior authorization when a covert entry is planned to install the electronic equipment, or when a pen register is used.

5. Raising the Issue of Standing

To establish that a search violated his Fourth Amendment rights, a defendant must show a legitimate expectation of privacy with regard to the search (*see* § I.C.2., *supra*). To make such a showing, which is sometimes referred to as "standing," the defendant may have to admit facts that would incriminate him. Consequently, testimony given by the defendant to establish standing cannot be admitted as evidence against the defendant at trial.

6. Exclusionary Rule

Under the exclusionary rule, evidence obtained in violation of the accused's Fourth, Fifth, or Sixth Amendment rights may not be introduced at her trial to prove her guilt. Under the Fourth Amendment, evidence seized during an unlawful search cannot constitute proof against the victim of the search. *Weeks v. United States*, 232 U.S. 383 (1914).

a. Fruit of the poisonous tree

Subject to some exceptions, the exclusionary rule applies not only to evidence initially seized as a result of the primary government illegality, but also to secondary "derivative evidence" discovered as a result of the primary taint, also known as the "fruit of the poisonous tree."

Example: A police officer conducts an unconstitutional search of a home, finds an address book, and uses that address book to locate a witness. The witness will not be allowed to testify, because her testimony would be a "fruit" of the unconstitutional search.

b. Exceptions

Evidence, whether primary or derivative, may still be admissible if one of the following exceptions to the exclusionary rule applies.

1) Inevitable discovery rule

The prosecution can prove that the evidence would have been inevitably discovered in the same condition through lawful means.

2) Independent source doctrine

The evidence was discovered in part by an independent source unrelated to the tainted evidence.

3) Attenuation principle

The chain of causation between the primary taint and the evidence has been so attenuated as to "purge" the taint. Both the passage of time and/or intervening events may attenuate the taint.

> **Example:** An officer makes an unconstitutional investigatory stop, learns during the stop that the suspect was subject to a valid arrest warrant, arrests the suspect, and seizes incriminating evidence during a search incident to that arrest. The evidence the officer seizes as part of the search incident to the arrest is admissible. *Utah v. Strieff*, 579 U.S. ___, 136 S. Ct. 2056 (2016).

4) Good-faith exception

The good-faith exception applies to police officers who act in good faith on either a facially valid warrant later determined to be invalid or an existing law later declared unconstitutional. *Michigan v. DeFillippo*, 443 U.S. 31 (1979). Good faith is limited to the objective good faith of a reasonable police officer.

This exception does **not** apply if:

    i) No reasonable officer would rely on the affidavit underlying the warrant;

    ii) The warrant is defective on its face;

    iii) The warrant was obtained by fraud;

    iv) The magistrate has "wholly abandoned his judicial role"; or

    v) The warrant was improperly executed.

5) Isolated police negligence

Isolated negligence by law-enforcement personnel will not necessarily trigger the exclusionary rule. To trigger the rule, police conduct must be "sufficiently deliberate such that exclusion can meaningfully deter it." The exclusionary rule serves to deter deliberate, reckless, or grossly negligent conduct or, in some circumstances, recurring or systemic negligence. *Herring v. United States*, 555 U.S. 135, 144 (2009).

> **Example:** Defendant Don goes to the police station to pick up an impounded vehicle. Policeman Paul believes that there might be a warrant out from another county for Don's arrest and calls the other county's sheriff to check. The sheriff tells Paul that there is a warrant out for Don's arrest. Paul immediately arrests Don and in a search incident to the arrest finds illegal drugs and an illegal weapon on Don. Minutes later, the sheriff calls back to say that the warrant had actually been recalled and she had made a mistake. The exclusionary rule will not apply to the drugs and the weapon because Paul was relying in good faith on the erroneous information from the sheriff in conducting the arrest. The exclusionary rule should be applied only if there is substantial additional deterrence of police misconduct to be gained. *Herring v. United States*, 555 U.S. 135 (2009).

6) Knock and announce

The exclusionary rule does not apply to evidence discovered as a result of a search conducted in violation of the "knock and announce" rule, if the search was otherwise authorized by a valid warrant. *Hudson v. Michigan*, 547 U.S. 586 (2006).

7) In-court identification

A witness's in-court identification of the defendant is not fruit of an unlawful detention. Thus, the identification cannot be excluded. On the other hand, live testimony may be excluded as fruit of illegal police conduct if there is a sufficient link between the illegal police conduct and the testimony.

c. Harmless error

Even if the trial court wrongfully admitted illegally seized evidence, the appellate court can refuse to order a new trial if it finds that the error was harmless beyond a reasonable doubt, meaning that the erroneously admitted evidence did not contribute to the result.

Note: The denial of the right to counsel is never a harmless error.

d. Enforcement

When the defendant challenges a confession or the admissibility of evidence, by right, a hearing is held to determine whether the confession or evidence is fruit of the poisonous tree. This hearing is held outside the presence of the jury. The defendant has a right to testify at this hearing, and the state bears the burden of establishing admissibility by a preponderance of the evidence.

e. Obtaining evidence by questionable methods

Evidence obtained in a manner that shocks the conscience is inadmissible. Examples of such methods of gathering evidence include inducements by official actions that offend the sense of justice and serious intrusions into the body, such as with surgery to remove a bullet. Contrast that, however, with a cheek swab to obtain a DNA sample, which is a reasonable intrusion because it is quick and painless, and involves no surgical intrusion beneath the skin. *Maryland v. King*, 569 U.S. 435 (2013).

II. FIFTH AMENDMENT RIGHTS AND PRIVILEGES

A. THE PRIVILEGE AGAINST COMPULSORY SELF-INCRIMINATION

The Fifth Amendment provides that no person shall be compelled in any criminal case to be a witness against himself. It is applicable to the states through the Fourteenth Amendment.

1. Persons

A person means an individual. Artificial entities such as corporations, partnerships, and labor unions may not assert the privilege, but a sole proprietorship may. The privilege does not extend to the custodian of corporate records, even if production would incriminate the custodian individually.

2. Testimonial Evidence

The privilege protects only testimonial evidence. Nontestimonial physical evidence (such as a blood or urine sample, Breathalyzer test result, handwriting exemplar, voice sample, or other evidence of physical characteristics) is not protected.

3. Compulsory Disclosure

The privilege generally does not apply to an individual's voluntarily prepared business papers or to records required by law to be kept, such as tax returns. *Fisher v. United States*, 425 U.S. 391 (1976). However, a person can refuse to comply with a requirement to register or pay a tax where the requirement is directed at a select group "inherently suspect of criminal activities." *Marchetti v. United States*, 390 U.S.

39, 52 (1968) (occupational tax on bookies); *Leary v. United States*, 395 U.S. 6 (1969) (registration and tax based on transfer of marijuana).

a. Subpoena

A person who is served with a subpoena requiring the production of possibly incriminating documents may invoke the privilege if the act of turning over the documents constitutes self-incriminating testimony. *United States v. Hubbell*, 530 U.S. 27 (2000).

b. Warrant for seizure of documents

The Fifth Amendment does not prevent law-enforcement officials, pursuant to a valid warrant, from searching for and seizing documents that would incriminate a person. *Andresen v. Maryland*, 427 U.S. 463 (1976).

1) Diaries

Generally, the government may not compel **production** of a diary. The contents of a diary are similar to oral testimony, and as such are considered testimonial in nature. Because one cannot be compelled to testify against himself, the government may not compel production of documents that are similarly testimonial in nature. *See, e.g., Schmerber v. California*, 384 U.S. 757 (1966).

Note, however, that if the diary's production is not compelled, e.g., it is found incident to a lawful arrest, its contents likely are admissible (assuming the entries were made voluntarily).

4. Nature of Proceedings

The privilege extends to a witness in any proceeding, whether civil or criminal, formal or informal, if the answers provide some reasonable possibility of incriminating the witness in future criminal proceedings. *McCarthy v. Arndstein*, 266 U.S. 34 (1924). However, the privilege cannot be invoked when the government requires civil records to be maintained and reported on for administrative purposes, because they are public records, unless those records fulfill a registration requirement of a select group of inherently suspect criminal activities and compliance would require self-incrimination. The privilege does not extend to identification requests at *Terry* stops. A violation occurs the moment the compelled statements are used against a person.

5. Invoking the Privilege

a. Defendant's privilege

A defendant who wishes to invoke the privilege simply invokes it by not taking the stand. Included in this right is the state's inability to compel the defendant to testify. The prosecution cannot bring the defendant's failure to take the stand to the jury's attention.

b. Witness's privilege

A witness, on the other hand, may be compelled to take the stand and can invoke the privilege only in response to a specific question when there is some reasonable possibility that answering the question will incriminate the witness. However, such an invocation after testimony has already been made may violate a defendant's right to confrontation, guaranteed by the Sixth and Fourteenth Amendments, if it prevents adequate cross-examination. *Douglas v. Alabama*, 380 U.S. 415 (1965).

6. Counseling Clients to Invoke the Privilege

Attorneys may counsel their clients to invoke the privilege and will not be held in contempt of court. Otherwise, the person invoking the privilege would be denied his Fifth Amendment protection.

7. Invocation of Privilege Should Not Impose a Burden

The state cannot penalize a defendant for invoking his right against self-incrimination by not testifying or cooperating with authorities. The prosecution cannot comment to the jury on the defendant's refusal to speak in accordance with his *Miranda* rights. A violation in this regard by the state triggers the harmless-error test. However, if during trial the defendant claims that he was not allowed to explain his story, then the prosecution may comment on the defendant's failure to take the stand.

8. Waiving the Privilege

A **defendant** waives the privilege by taking the witness stand; a **witness** waives the privilege by disclosing self-incriminating information in response to a specific question. Having taken the stand, the defendant cannot assert the privilege in response to the prosecution's proper cross-examination of his testimony, including impeachment questions.

B. THE FIFTH AMENDMENT IN A POLICE INTERROGATION CONTEXT

In the seminal case of *Miranda v. Arizona,* the U.S. Supreme Court held that a suspect has a constitutional right not to be compelled to make incriminating statements in the police interrogation process. *Miranda v. Arizona*, 384 U.S. 436 (1966). *Miranda* once was considered to be necessary in nearly every encounter with police. However, the Supreme Court has been gradually narrowing the scope and limiting the use of *Miranda.*

Any incriminating statement obtained as the result of **custodial interrogation** may not be used against the suspect at a subsequent trial **unless** the police provided procedural safeguards effective to secure the privilege against self-incrimination (i.e., informed the suspect of his *Miranda* rights). An incriminating statement includes not only a confession, but other inculpatory statements, and is subject to suppression even though the defendant intended the statement to be exculpatory.

1. Custodial Interrogation

Custodial interrogation is questioning initiated by a known (as opposed to undercover) law-enforcement officer after a person is in custody.

a. "Custodial"

Custody is a substantial seizure and is defined for *Miranda* purposes as either a formal arrest or a restraint on freedom of movement to the degree associated with a formal arrest. *New York v. Quarles*, 467 U.S. 649, 655 (1984).

If there has been no formal arrest, the question is whether a reasonable person would have believed he could leave, given the **totality of the circumstances**. *Thompson v. Keohane*, 516 U.S. 99 (1995). A child's age is a relevant factor in determining whether a reasonable child would have believed he was in custody. *J.D.B. v. North Carolina*, 564 U.S. 261 (2011).

1) Police station

While police questioning an individual at a police station typically constitutes a custodial interrogation, the fact that the questioning takes place at a police station does not automatically make the encounter custodial.

> **Example:** A woman voluntarily goes to the police station to talk about a crime. As soon as she arrives, she is informed by the officer on the case that she is free to leave at any time and is not under arrest. Even though she is speaking with the police at the police station, the totality of the circumstances establishes that she is not in "custody," and therefore *Miranda* will not apply. *See California v. Beheler*, 463 U.S. 1121 (1983); *Oregon v. Mathiason*, 429 U.S. 492 (1977).

2) Crime scene

The questioning of a person at the scene of a crime or pursuant to a field investigation does not constitute custody for *Miranda* purposes as long as the person questioned is not under restraint equivalent to that of formal arrest and has the **right to leave** the presence of the questioning officer.

3) Traffic stop

Traffic stops generally are not considered custodial because they generally are brief and temporary. *Berkemer v. McCarty*, 468 U.S. 420 (1984).

4) Prison

Imprisonment alone does not necessarily create a custodial situation within the meaning of *Miranda*. The questioning of a prisoner, who is removed from the general prison population, about events that took place outside the prison is not categorically "custodial" for *Miranda* purposes. A standard, objective "totality of circumstances" analysis applies when an inmate is interviewed, including consideration of the language that is used in summoning the prisoner to the interview and the manner in which the interrogation is conducted. *Howes v. Fields*, 565 U.S. 499 (2012) (holding that defendant was not in custody for purposes of *Miranda* during seven-hour interrogation that lasted well into the night, because he was told at the outset of interrogation, and was reminded again thereafter, that he could terminate the interrogation and go back to his cell whenever he wanted).

5) Continuation of custody

The failure of a police agency to provide *Miranda* warnings to a suspect can render inadmissible a statement given to a second policy agency that continues the interrogation of the suspect in the same location immediately after the termination of the interrogation of the suspect by the first police agency, even though the second police agency gave the suspect *Miranda* warnings and questioned the suspect about an unrelated crime. *Miranda v. Arizona*, 384 U.S. 436, 494-497 (1966) (addressing *Westover v. United States*).

b. "Interrogation"

Interrogation refers not only to express questioning, but also to any words or actions that the police know or should know are **reasonably likely to elicit an incriminating response**. *Rhode Island v. Innis*, 446 U.S. 291 (1980).

1) Voluntariness of statement

Volunteered statements are not protected by *Miranda*, as they are, by definition, not the product of interrogation.

A confession is involuntary only if the police coerced the defendant into making the confession. Whether a statement is voluntary or coerced is determined based on the totality of the circumstances (including facts such as the conduct of the police, the characteristics of the defendant, and the time of the statement). A claim that a confession should be excluded because it is involuntary must be decided by the trial judge as a preliminary question of fact, and not by the jury.

a) Trickery

Trickery by the police or false promises made to the accused by the police may render a confession involuntary. However, deceit or fraud by the interrogators (i.e., lying about a co-conspirator's confession) does not itself make the confession involuntary.

b) Character of the defendant

The defendant's age, state of health, education, or intoxication are all factors in determining the coercive nature of the confession. Although a potentially significant factor, the defendant's mental condition alone cannot violate the voluntariness standard. There must be coercive police activity for the confession to be found involuntary. *Colorado v. Connelly*, 479 U.S. 157 (1986).

> **EXAM NOTE:** Remember to apply the *Miranda* warnings only when an individual is subject to a custodial interrogation. If the police have no intention of questioning the individual, or if the individual is not in police custody, then the *Miranda* warnings are not applicable.

2. Compliance

Once a custodial interrogation begins, anything the defendant says is inadmissible until the defendant is informed of the *Miranda* rights **and** the defendant waives those rights.

The failure to give a suspect the *Miranda* warnings does not require suppression of **physical fruits** of the suspect's "unwarned but voluntary statements." *United States v. Patane*, 542 U.S. 630, 640 (2004).

a. Content

The warnings, which must be given before interrogation begins, need not be a verbatim repetition of the language used in the *Miranda* decision.

Law-enforcement officials must inform defendants:

i) Of their right to remain **silent**;

ii) That any statement uttered may be **used in court**;

iii) Of their right to **consult an attorney** and to have the attorney present during an interrogation; and

iv) That an **attorney will be appointed** to represent indigent defendants.

b. Timing

The *Miranda* warning must be given before interrogation begins. If interrogation is stopped for a long duration, the warning must be given again.

c. Right to counsel invoked

The right to counsel under the Fifth Amendment is not the same as the constitutional requirement of the right to counsel under the Sixth Amendment. The right to counsel under the Fifth Amendment is not automatic. To invoke the right to counsel under the Fifth Amendment, a suspect must make a specific, unambiguous statement asserting his desire to have counsel present. If a suspect makes an ambiguous statement regarding the right to counsel, the police are not required to end the interrogation or to ask questions or clarify whether the suspect wants to invoke the right. *Davis v. United States*, 512 U.S. 452 (1994). However, once that right to counsel is invoked, **all** interrogation must stop until counsel is present. *Edwards v. Arizona*, 451 U.S. 477, 484 (1981). If the suspect voluntarily initiates communication with the police after invoking his right to counsel, a statement made by the suspect, such as a statement that the suspect spontaneously blurts out, can be admissible because it is not made in response to interrogation. In addition, police may re-open interrogation of a suspect who has asserted his Fifth Amendment right to counsel if there has been a 14-day or more break in custody (such as the release back into the general prison population of a suspect who has been incarcerated for another crime). In such circumstances, the officers must give fresh *Miranda* warnings and get a valid waiver before beginning questioning. *Maryland v. Shatzer*, 559 U.S. 98 (2010).

d. Right to silence invoked

As with the Fifth Amendment right to counsel, the defendant must make a specific, unambiguous statement asserting his desire to remain silent. Merely remaining silent in response to police questioning does not invoke the privilege. *Salinas v. Texas*, 570 U.S. 178 (2013); *Berghuis v. Thompkins*, 560 U.S. 370 (2010). If a defendant invokes his *Miranda* right to remain silent, the interrogator(s) must "scrupulously honor" that request (e.g., immediately cease interrogation, allow for a significant passage of time, give a second set of warnings). However, if after the defendant is released from custody, the defendant indicates a desire to speak to police, then a subsequent interrogation would be lawful, as long as the defendant was not coerced. The defendant must again receive fresh *Miranda* warnings.

e. Grand jury

There is no requirement to give *Miranda* warnings to a witness testifying for the grand jury. The witness may, however, consult with an attorney outside the grand jury room.

3. Exceptions to the *Miranda* Requirement

a. Public safety

When the public's safety is at risk, the police are not required to give *Miranda* warnings before questioning a suspect.

b. Routine booking

The "routine booking question" exception allows police to ask a suspected drunken driver routine biographical questions and to videotape the driver's responses without first giving the driver *Miranda* warnings.

c. Undercover police

Miranda warnings are not required if the suspect being questioned is not aware that the interrogator is a police officer. *Illinois v. Perkins*, 496 U.S. 292, 294 (1990).

Example: The police placed an undercover officer, posing as a criminal, in the defendant's jail cell, and the undercover officer engaged the defendant in a conversation designed to elicit details of the crime for which the defendant was

4. Waiver

A defendant may knowingly and voluntarily waive his *Miranda* rights. The burden is on the government to demonstrate by a preponderance of the evidence that the waiver was made knowingly and voluntarily. (Keep in mind that a defendant's mental illness does not necessarily negate the voluntariness requirement; there must be coercive police activity for a confession to be involuntary. *Colorado v. Connelly, supra.*)

There can be no effective waiver, however, until the *Miranda* warnings are properly given. Silence on the part of the suspect is not sufficient to waive his *Miranda* rights. However, a suspect who has received and understood the *Miranda* warnings, and has not invoked his *Miranda* rights, waives the right to remain silent by making an uncoerced statement to the police. *Berghuis v. Thompkins*, 560 U.S. 370 (2010). Once effectively waived, the police are not required to inform the suspect of the defense counsel's efforts to reach the defendant by telephone and need not inform counsel that the defendant is being questioned.

5. Use of Statements Taken in Violation of *Miranda*

The failure to give *Miranda* warnings is not a violation until a statement obtained without the use of warnings is used at trial. *Chavez v. Martinez*, 538 U.S. 760 (2003).

a. Impeachment purposes

Statements taken in violation of *Miranda* may be used to impeach the credibility of the criminal defendant if he takes the witness stand and gives testimony at variance with his previous admissions. *Harris v. New York*, 401 U.S. 222, 224 (1971). To be admissible for impeachment, the statement must be voluntary and trustworthy. The impeaching admissions may not be used directly in deciding ultimate issues of guilt or innocence; they may only be used in determining the defendant's veracity.

Post-arrest silence by a defendant who has received *Miranda* warnings generally may not be used by the prosecution as either impeachment or substantive evidence without violating the defendant's right to due process. *Doyle v. Ohio*, 426 U.S. 610 (1976); *United States v. Hale*, 422 U.S. 171 (1975). The Supreme Court has never applied the waiver doctrine to allow post-arrest silence to be admitted for impeachment purposes if the silence occurred after the defendant waived his right to remain silent. However, some states require a defendant to re-invoke his right to remain silent after a waiver to prevent the admission of his subsequent silence as impeachment evidence. *Compare Bass v. Nix*, 909 F.2d 297 (8th Cir. 1990), *with Schragin v. State*, 378 S.W.3d 510 (Tex. App. 2012).

b. Involuntary confessions

Involuntary confessions (e.g., those produced by coercion) cannot be used either substantively or for impeachment purposes. If a coerced confession is admitted into evidence, however, reversal is not automatic; the harmless-error test is applied, and the conviction will stand if the prosecution can show other overwhelming evidence of guilt.

C. FRUITS OF A TAINTED CONFESSION

1. Physical Evidence

Derivative **physical evidence** (e.g., a gun) obtained as a result of a non-Mirandized confession (i.e., a confession that is inadmissible due to the police's failure to give

Miranda warnings) is **admissible,** so long as that confession was not coerced. *United States v. Patane*, 542 U.S. 630 (2004).

2. Second Confession

A *Miranda* violation does not automatically require the suppression of incriminating statements made by the defendant after receiving *Miranda* warnings. *Oregon v. Elstad*, 470 U.S. 298 (1985). However, a second confession may be suppressed when the circumstances indicate that the substance of *Miranda* has been drained away. For a plurality of the court, the test is an objective one—a reasonable person in the suspect's position would not have understood the *Miranda* warnings to convey a message that the suspect retained a choice about whether to remain silent. For the justice who cast the deciding vote (Justice Kennedy), the test is a subjective one—did the police act with an intent to circumvent the purpose of the *Miranda* warnings. *Miranda; Missouri v. Seibert*, 542 U.S. 600, 611 (2004).

D. FIFTH AMENDMENT IN THE TRIAL CONTEXT

1. Scope of Privilege

A defendant may refuse to testify at a criminal trial. He may also refuse to answer questions in other proceedings (i.e., civil depositions) when the answers might incriminate him in future criminal proceedings.

The privilege does not prevent the prosecutor from using prior conflicting statements to impeach the defendant once the defendant takes the stand. This is called "opening the door" by the defendant.

2. Voluntariness

Admissions of incriminating statements made during a court-ordered psychiatric examination are generally deemed involuntary and not admissible at trial unless the defendant is given *Miranda* warnings before the interview and waives his rights.

Business papers voluntarily prepared by an individual, or required records, such as tax returns, are not protected.

3. Immunity

The prosecution may compel incriminating testimony (at trial or before a grand jury) if it grants immunity to the individual and the individual must testify. The testimony cannot be used against the individual, directly or indirectly, in a subsequent prosecution.

a. Transactional immunity

Often called "blanket" or "total" immunity, "transactional immunity" fully protects a witness from future prosecution for crimes related to her testimony.

b. Use and derivative-use immunity

"Use and derivative-use" immunity only precludes the prosecution from using the witness's own testimony, or any evidence derived from the testimony, against the witness. The Supreme Court has held that the grant of "use and derivative-use" immunity is all that is constitutionally required to compel the testimony of a witness. *Kastigar v. United States*, 406 U.S. 441, 452–453 (1972). Testimony encouraged by a promise of immunity, however, is considered coerced and involuntary.

c. Federal and state immunity

Testimony under a grant of immunity may not be used by another U.S. jurisdiction to prosecute the defendant. *See United States v. Balsys*, 524 U.S. 666 (1998); *Murphy v. Waterfront Comm'n*, 378 U.S. 52 (1964). Thus, a state grant of immunity will preclude admission of the testimony in a federal proceeding.

4. Prosecutorial Comment

The prosecutor may not comment on the defendant's exercise of the privilege against self-incrimination at trial. It is per se reversible error.

III. SIXTH AMENDMENT

The Sixth Amendment provides that the accused shall have the right to a public trial, the right to confront witnesses against him, the right to cross-examine witnesses, the right to be present at his own trial, and the right to "the assistance of counsel for his defense." The right to assistance of counsel encompasses not only the right to hire private counsel, but also the right to be provided with counsel without charge if the accused is unable to afford counsel.

A. APPLICABILITY: RIGHT TO COUNSEL

1. Types of Proceedings

The Sixth Amendment provides a constitutional right to counsel in any case in which the defendant is sentenced to incarceration, even if that sentence is suspended. *Scott v. Illinois*, 440 U.S. 367 (1979); *Alabama v. Shelton*, 535 U.S. 654 (2002).

2. Applicable Stages

The Sixth Amendment right to counsel applies at all **critical stages** of a prosecution, after formal proceedings have begun. The right automatically **attaches** when **formal judicial proceedings have begun**, whether that be at a post-arrest initial appearance before a judicial officer, or by way of formal charge, preliminary hearing, indictment, information, or arraignment. There is no right to counsel at post-conviction proceedings such as parole and probation hearings or habeas corpus hearings. For a discussion of a defendant's right to counsel on an appeal (*see* § VI.B. Appeal, *infra*).

> **EXAM NOTE:** Unlike the Fifth Amendment right to counsel, the defendant does not need to invoke the Sixth Amendment right to counsel. The failure to provide counsel results in automatic reversal of a conviction.

a. Critical stages

The Supreme Court has summarized its definition of "critical stage" as those proceedings between an individual and an agent of the state that amount to trial-like confrontations, at which counsel would help the accused in coping with legal problems or meeting his adversary. *Rothgery v. Gillespie County*, 554 U.S. 191, 212 (2008).

Generally, the Sixth Amendment right to counsel attaches at the following critical stages:

i) Post-indictment lineups and in-person identifications;

ii) Post-indictment interrogations, whether custodial or otherwise;

iii) Arraignment and preliminary hearing to determine probable cause to prosecute, bail hearings, and pre-trial motions; and

iv) Plea bargaining, guilty pleas, trials, and sentencing.

Note that direct appeals as a matter of right, while not technically covered by the Sixth Amendment, do require that the state provide counsel to the indigent on equal protection grounds. *Douglas v. California*, 372 U.S. 353 (1963).

b. Noncritical stages

The right to counsel generally does not apply to the following events:

i)   A witness viewing photos of the alleged defendant;

ii) Pre-charge (investigative) lineups;

iii) Taking of fingerprints, handwriting exemplars, voice exemplars, or blood samples;

iv) Hearings to determine probable cause to detain the defendant (*Gerstein* hearing);

v)   Discretionary appeals; and

vi) Post-conviction proceedings, such as parole or probation hearings, including habeas corpus. (The Sixth Amendment does apply, however, to probation revocation hearings that include sentencing.)

3. Indigence—Right to Appointment of Counsel

When the right to counsel exists, an indigent defendant has the right to the appointment of counsel. *Johnson v. Zerbst*, 304 U.S. 458 (1938) (federal trial); *Gideon v. Wainwright*, 372 U.S. 335 (1963) (state trial, Sixth Amendment right to counsel incorporated by Due Process Clause of the Fourteenth Amendment).

4. Right to Counsel of Choice

In general, a defendant who is able to afford a lawyer is entitled to the counsel of his own choosing, while an indigent defendant is not entitled to the appointment of counsel of his own choosing. *United States v. Gonzalez-Lopez*, 548 U.S. 140, 147–148 (2006) (defendant who retains his own counsel has the right to be represented by that attorney); *Wheat v. United States*, 486 U.S. 153, 159 (1988) (indigent defendant has right to an effective advocate, not to an attorney preferred by defendant). However, a defendant cannot compel a lawyer to represent him even if the defendant has the ability to pay the lawyer. *Id.* In addition, the court can deny a defendant his chosen counsel when the lawyer is not a member of the bar or is otherwise disqualified from representing the defendant. *Id.* (person who is not a member of the bar may not represent anyone but himself; court may disqualify a lawyer who has a serious conflict of interest).

5. Waiver

a. In general

The Sixth Amendment right to counsel can be waived so long as relinquishment of the right is voluntary, knowing and intelligent. *Patterson v. Illinois*, 487 U.S. 285 (1988); *Brewer v. Williams*, 430 U.S. 387 (1977).

Even though *Miranda* rights purportedly arise from the Fifth Amendment, an accused who receives proper *Miranda* warnings will be considered sufficiently apprised of his Sixth Amendment rights and the consequences of abandoning those rights. As long as the defendant is given *Miranda* warnings and voluntarily waives those rights, the defendant's waiver of his Sixth Amendment rights will also be considered knowing and intelligent. *Patterson v. Illinois*, 487 U.S. 285 (1988).

> **EXAM NOTE:** Remember, even if the defendant has made a valid waiver of his right to counsel, statements made during interrogation must be **voluntary** to be admissible at trial, i.e., the police still cannot use compelled statements.

b. Subsequent waivers pursuant to *Edwards* and *Montejo*

Recall that in the Fifth Amendment context, once an individual in custody asserts the Fifth Amendment right to counsel, no subsequent waiver of that right is valid in a police-initiated custodial interrogation unless counsel is present. *Edwards v. Arizona*, 451 U.S. 477 (1981). Under the *Edwards* rule, any subsequent waiver of the Fifth Amendment right to counsel under these circumstances is presumed to be involuntary. *McNeil v. Wisconsin*, 501 U.S. 171 (1991).

A similar presumption used to apply in the Sixth Amendment context, but has been overturned. *See Michigan v. Jackson*, 475 U.S. 625 (1986) (*overturned by Montejo v. Louisiana*, 556 U.S. 778 (2009)). Therefore, if an accused has not actually asserted his right to counsel (e.g., if the court automatically appoints counsel to the accused before trial), there is no presumption that any subsequent waiver of the right to counsel will be involuntary. *Montejo v. Louisiana*, 556 U.S. 778 (2009). The *Edwards* rule will still apply if the accused has actually asserted his right to counsel, but remember that the *Edwards* rule only applies in custodial interactions. *See Edwards v. Arizona*, 451 U.S. 477 (1981). Therefore, even after Sixth Amendment rights attach, the police may initiate non-custodial interactions with the accused outside the presence of his lawyer, and there will be no presumption that any knowing waiver of the right to have counsel present for the interaction is involuntary. *Montejo v. Louisiana*, 556 U.S. 778 (2009).

c. Right to proceed pro se

A defendant has the constitutional right to refuse counsel and proceed pro se at trial. The waiver of the right to counsel must be knowingly and intelligently made. To that end, the court should make the defendant aware of the dangers and disadvantages of self-representation, such as the inability to raise an "ineffective assistance of counsel" defense on appeal. *Faretta v. California*, 422 U.S. 806 (1975). In addition, the court may, even over the defendant's objection, "appoint a 'standby counsel,' to aid the accused if and when the accused requests help, and to be available to represent the accused in the event that termination of the defendant's self-representation is necessary." *Id.* at 834, fn 46. A defendant who is competent to stand trial may nevertheless be found incompetent to represent himself. *Indiana v. Edwards*, 554 U.S. 164 (2009).

6. Withholding Information

The police are under no obligation to inform a suspect that an attorney has been trying to reach him, and may even withhold that information intentionally, so long as the Sixth Amendment right to counsel has not yet attached. *Moran v. Burbine*, 475 U.S. 412 (1986). If the Sixth Amendment right has attached, this sort of interference with the attorney-client relationship might be a violation of that right.

B. OFFENSE-SPECIFIC

Once the Sixth Amendment right to counsel is properly invoked, it applies **only** to the specific offense at issue in those proceedings. *McNeil v. Wisconsin*, 501 U.S. 171, 175–176 (1991).

1. *Blockburger* Test

Two crimes committed in one criminal transaction are deemed to be the same offense for Sixth Amendment purposes unless each offense requires proof of an element that the other does not. *Texas v. Cobb*, 532 U.S. 162 (2001); *Blockburger v. United States*, 284 U.S. 299, 304 (1932).

2. **Compare to *Miranda***

Unlike under the *Miranda* standard, under the Sixth Amendment standard, the requirement for counsel to be present applies only to interrogations about the offense charged. However, like with *Miranda,* the defendant may make a knowing and voluntary waiver of the right to counsel being present.

Example: Defendant Dave has been charged with burglary and is out on bail awaiting trial. The police also suspect Dave in an unrelated arson case, and they bring him to the police station to question him about the arson. Dave is given the *Miranda* warnings and waives his right to remain silent, but he asks to see his attorney. The police do not call Dave's attorney but continue to interrogate Dave until he confesses to the arson. While the police did violate Dave's Fifth Amendment right to have an attorney present during questioning, they did not violate his Sixth Amendment right to counsel, as the arson was unrelated to the burglary, and he hadn't been charged with the arson.

C. REMEDIES FOR DENIAL OF COUNSEL

1. **Effect on Conviction**

If a right to counsel at a trial proceeding under the Sixth Amendment is denied, the defendant's conviction should be automatically reversed, even without a specific showing of unfairness. *Gideon v. Wainwright*, 372 U.S. 335, 339 (1963). Automatic reversal also applies to a conviction obtained after a court has erroneously refused to permit an attorney chosen by the defendant to represent him, when that attorney is not supplied by the state. *United States v. Gonzalez-Lopez*, 548 U.S. 140 (2006).

2. **Effect on Guilty Plea**

If the defendant has pleaded guilty at a preliminary hearing, without being given the opportunity to have counsel, then the defendant has the right to withdraw the plea, and it may not be used against the defendant as an evidentiary admission. *White v. Maryland*, 373 U.S. 59, 60 (1963).

3. **Effect on Denial of Counsel at Nontrial Proceedings**

A denial of counsel at a nontrial proceeding, such as a lineup, is subject to harmless-error analysis. *United States v. Wade*, 388 U.S. 218, 223 (1967).

4. **Admissibility of a Defendant's Statements to Informants**

Post-indictment statements that a defendant makes to a police informant are inadmissible when the police intentionally create a situation likely to induce the defendant into making incriminating statements about the crime for which he was indicted without the assistance of counsel. *United States v. Henry*, 447 U.S. 264, 274–275 (1980). There is no Sixth Amendment violation, however, if the police place an informant in the defendant's cell simply to listen and report the defendant's statements, without questioning the defendant. *Kuhlmann v. Wilson*, 477 U.S. 436, 456 (1986).

5. **Exclusionary Rule Under the Sixth Amendment**

a. **Fruits doctrine**

The fruit of the poisonous tree doctrine is applicable to violations of the Sixth Amendment right to counsel. *Nix v. Williams*, 467 U.S. 431 (1984). Both statements and physical evidence obtained as a result of a Sixth Amendment violation are inadmissible.

b. Impeachment

If the police initiate a conversation with an accused individual who has requested counsel, any incriminating statements made by the defendant may still be used for impeachment purposes, despite the fact that the improper police conduct precludes admission of the statements as part of the prosecution's case in chief. *Michigan v. Harvey*, 494 U.S. 344, 350–351 (1990).

D. INEFFECTIVE ASSISTANCE OF COUNSEL

1. Standard of Competence

The right to counsel encompasses the right to be assisted by a reasonably competent attorney and is presumed. The right to effective counsel extends to the defendant's first appeal. To reverse a conviction on the ground of ineffective counsel, the claimant has the burden to show that:

i) Counsel's representation fell below an objective standard of reasonableness; and

ii) Counsel's deficient performance prejudiced the defendant, resulting in the reasonable probability that the outcome would have been different.

Strickland v. Washington, 466 U.S. 668, 687 (1984). Counsel's mere inexperience, strategy, choice of appellate issues, or even failure to produce mitigating evidence have all been found insufficient to rise to the level of ineffective counsel. *Bell v. Cone*, 535 U.S. 685 (2002); *Jones v. Barnes*, 463 U.S. 745 (1988); *United States v. Cronic*, 466 U.S. 648 (1984). The failure of defense counsel to raise a federal constitutional issue that was law at the time of the trial, but was later overruled, does not constitute ineffective assistance of counsel. *Lockhart v. Fretwell*, 506 U.S. 364 (1993).

2. Conflict of Interest

The representation of defendants with conflicting interests may amount to ineffective assistance of counsel. In general, to overturn a conviction on the basis of a conflict of interest, a defendant must show that there was an actual conflict of interest and that such conflict adversely affected the attorney's performance.

a. Actual conflict

To find an actual conflict, a court must determine that the defense attorney is subject to an obligation or unique personal interest that, if followed, would lead her to adopt a strategy other than that most favorable to the defendant.

b. Adverse impact

Adverse impact can be established by demonstrating that some plausible alternative defense strategy or tactic might have been pursued and such strategy or tactic was inherently in conflict with, or not undertaken, due to the attorney's other loyalties or interests. The conflicting character of the strategy is not sufficient if the strategy actually was rejected because another strategy was viewed as even more favorable to the accused.

c. Knowledge of the court

If an attorney representing codefendants makes a timely motion for appointment of separate counsel based on a potential conflict of interest, then the trial judge must either grant the motion or at least conduct a hearing to determine whether appointment of separate counsel is warranted under the circumstances. Failure of the judge to do so requires automatic reversal of a subsequent conviction. *Holloway v. Arkansas*, 435 U.S. 475, 484 (1978). Actual conflict and prejudice are presumed under such circumstances.

Unless the trial court knows or reasonably should know that a conflict exists, however, the court is not required to inquire about multiple representations. *Cuyler v. Sullivan*, 446 U.S. 335, 347–348 (1980). Actual conflict (rather than potential conflict) is required to be shown on appeal if the issue of separate trials was not brought up during the trial, and the defendant must show that the conflict adversely affected counsel's performance. *Mickens v. Taylor*, 535 U.S. 162, 173 (2002).

d. Rule 44(c)

When co-defendants are represented by the same attorney, Rule 44(c) of the Federal Rules of Criminal Procedure requires the court to conduct a prompt inquiry into potential conflicts of interest and advise the defendants of the right to separate representation. Failure to comply with the Rule, though, will not constitute a per se reversible error, and an appellate court will likely ask whether the end result was representation by counsel under an actual conflict.

e. Disqualification despite waiver

A trial court has the authority to disqualify a defense attorney, even over the objection of the defendant, if the court concludes that there is serious potential of a conflict of interest. *Wheat v. United States*, 486 U.S. 153, 158–159 (1988).

3. Communication of Formal Plea Offer

The right to effective assistance of counsel extends to the plea bargaining stage. Defense counsel must accurately communicate to the defendant any formal offer from the prosecution to accept a plea on terms and conditions that may be favorable to the defendant. To show prejudice once a plea offer has lapsed or has been rejected because defense counsel failed to accurately communicate the offer, a defendant must demonstrate a reasonable probability that she would have accepted the plea offer had it been accurately communicated by defense counsel. A defendant must also demonstrate a reasonable probability that the prosecutor and trial court would have accepted the plea if they had the discretion to reject it under state law. *Missouri v. Frye*, 566 U.S. 134 (2012). Ineffective assistance of counsel at the plea bargaining stage may constitute reversible error even if the subsequent trial and conviction are fair. *Lafler v. Cooper*, 566 U.S. 156 (2012).

IV. PRETRIAL PROCEDURES

A. EYEWITNESS IDENTIFICATION PROCEDURES

1. Types

There are two types of eyewitness identification procedures: corporeal and non-corporeal. Corporeal identifications are "in-person," as in lineups or show-ups. Non-corporeal identifications are not in-person and involve police officers using photo arrays for a witness to identify the perpetrator of the crime.

2. Post-Indictment Identifications—Sixth Amendment Right to Counsel

A defendant is entitled to have counsel present at any post-indictment lineup or show-up in which the defendant is required to participate. *United States v. Wade*, 388 U.S. 218 (1967); *Gilbert v. California*, 388 U.S. 263 (1967). The prosecution bears the burden of establishing that counsel was present. The right to counsel does not apply to any pre-indictment lineup, even if it takes place after the defendant has been arrested for another unrelated crime. *Kirby v. Illinois*, 406 U.S. 682, 690–691 (1972).

a. Waiver

The defendant can waive the right to have counsel present at the lineup, provided that waiver is made knowingly and intelligently. The prosecution bears the burden of demonstrating that the waiver was valid.

b. Remedy for violation

Testimony about a post-indictment, pre-trial identification in the absence of counsel is inadmissible at trial, but the witness may still identify the defendant at trial if the prosecution can show that the identification has independent reliability. *United States v. Wade*, 388 U.S. 218 (1967).

c Non-corporeal identification procedures

There is no right to counsel during an identification through a photo array, regardless of when the photo array is conducted.

3. Impermissibly Suggestive Identification Procedures—Due Process Rights

A defendant also has a due process right pursuant to the Fifth Amendment (for federal prosecutions) and the Fourteenth Amendment (for state prosecutions) with regard to a witness's identification based on an identification procedure arranged by the police that was impermissibly suggestive. This right exists whether the identification procedure was corporeal or non-corporeal, and whether the identification took place before or after the indictment of the defendant. *Perry v. New Hampshire*, 565 U.S. 228 (2012).

a. Two-prong test

Courts use a two-prong test to determine the admissibility of a pre- or post-indictment corporeal or non-corporeal identification. To prevail, the defendant must demonstrate that the procedure was **impermissibly suggestive and** that there was a **substantial likelihood of misidentification**. In order to have the identification admitted, the prosecution can offer evidence that the identification was **nonetheless reliable**.

In making its ruling, the court is to consider the following factors:

i) The witness's **opportunity to view** the defendant at the time of the crime;

ii) The witness's **degree of attention** at the time of the crime;

iii) The **accuracy of the witness's description** of the defendant prior to the identification;

iv) The **level of certainty** at the time of the identification; and

v) The **length of time** between the crime and the identification.

Neil v. Biggers, 409 U.S. 188, 199–200 (1972). Only when the indicators of a witness's ability to make an accurate identification are outweighed by the corrupting effect of law enforcement suggestion should the identification be suppressed on due process grounds. *Perry v. New Hampshire, supra*, at 725, quoting from *Manson v. Brathwaite*, 432 U.S. 98, 114 (1977). This test applies both to an out-of-court identification and an in-court identification that is based on a prior out-of-court identification.

1) Impermissibly suggestive

Police identification procedures that are highly suggestive usually are also impermissibly suggestive. However, even when such procedures are highly suggestive, they may not be impermissibly so, if they are necessary. For example, an identification made by a witness of defendant brought in handcuffs to the witness's hospital room by uniformed police officers was not impermissible suggestive because the witness was the only person who could identify the perpetrator, the witness could not leave her hospital room, and it was uncertain whether the witness would survive. *Stovall v. Denno*, 388 U.S. 293 (1967).

In addition, a defendant's due process rights are violated only if it is the police who have arranged the identification procedure to be impermissibly suggestive. For example, when a witness, asked by a police officer to describe the perpetrator of an automobile break-in, pointed out her window to the man standing next to the police officer, the identification—although made as a consequence of suggestive circumstances—was not due to identification procedures arranged by the police. *Perry v. New Hampshire, supra.*

b. Suppression hearing

A defendant who has moved to suppress an identification is entitled to a suppression hearing. This hearing usually is held outside the presence of the jury, although exclusion of the jury is not constitutionally required.

c. Remedy for violation

A conviction as the result of a trial in which an illegal identification was admitted will be overturned **unless,** under the doctrine of harmless error, the appellate court is convinced beyond a reasonable doubt that the improperly admitted identification did not contribute to the verdict.

B. PRELIMINARY PROCEEDINGS

Subsequent to the defendant's arrest, various court proceedings may be held. These pretrial proceedings, which take various forms depending on the jurisdiction, can include a hearing to determine probable cause to detain (a *Gerstein* hearing), an initial appearance, an arraignment, a detention or bail hearing, and a preliminary hearing to determine probable cause to prosecute the defendant. Some of these proceedings may be combined, and some may not be required. In addition, the defendant may make various motions, including motions to suppress evidence obtained in violation of the defendant's constitutional rights.

1. Probable Cause to Detain (*Gerstein* Hearing)

Under the Fourth Amendment, a preliminary hearing must be held after the defendant's arrest to determine whether probable cause exists to hold the defendant, unless such determination has already been made before the defendant's arrest through a grand jury indictment or the judicial issuance of an arrest warrant. *Gerstein v. Pugh*, 420 U.S. 103 (1975). This hearing, known as a *Gerstein* hearing, need not be adversarial. There is no right to counsel at this hearing, and hearsay evidence may be introduced, but a hearing not held within 48 hours after arrest is presumptively unreasonable. *County of Riverside v. McLaughlin*, 500 U.S. 44 (1991). However, the failure to hold this hearing does not affect the prosecution of the defendant for the charged offense, other than the exclusion of any evidence discovered as a consequence of the unlawful detainment. Under the Fifth Amendment, all felony charges must be by indictment of a federal grand jury, unless waived by the defendant.

2. **Initial Appearance**

Soon after the defendant is arrested, the defendant must be brought before a judge who advises the defendant of the charges against him and of his rights and who appoints counsel if the defendant is indigent. During this initial appearance, which may be held in conjunction with a *Gerstein* hearing, the judge may also determine whether the defendant should be released prior to trial and the conditions of the release (e.g., bail), accept a plea from the defendant, and set a date for a preliminary hearing.

3. **Arraignment**

At an arraignment, the court informs the defendant of the crime with which the defendant has been charged and elicits the defendant's response (i.e., plea) to those charges. At this time, the court may appoint counsel for an indigent defendant. These events may also take place at the initial appearance.

4. **Detention Hearing**

In conjunction with the defendant's initial appearance or at a separate hearing, the court may determine whether to release the defendant and any conditions upon such release. At such time, the court may set bail (*see* § C. Right to Bail, *infra*).

5. **Preliminary Hearing to Determine Probable Cause to Prosecute**

Subsequent to the defendant's initial appearance, a preliminary hearing may be held to determine whether there is probable cause to believe that the defendant has committed a specific crime. At this hearing, which is an adversarial proceeding, the defendant has the right to counsel. *Coleman v. Alabama*, 399 U.S. 1 (1970). A defendant who has been indicted by a grand jury is not entitled to this hearing.

C. **RIGHT TO BAIL**

There is no explicit constitutional right to bail. However, any denial of bail must comply with the Due Process Clause. Therefore, the setting of excessive bail or the refusal to set bail is immediately appealable. Furthermore, bail set higher than an amount reasonably calculated to ensure the defendant's presence at trial is "excessive" under the Eighth Amendment.

1. **Statutory Bail Provisions**

The Bail Reform Act of 1984 governs release or detention determinations in federal courts in criminal proceedings. Many states have modeled similar statutory bail provisions on the Act.

2. **Presumptions Pre- and Post-Conviction**

There is a presumption in favor of pre-trial release. A detention hearing must be held at the initial appearance for there to be a release. However, there is a presumption against bail post-conviction, pending appeal. The Federal Rules of Evidence do not apply at detention hearings.

3. **Pre-Trial Detention**

Certain pretrial detention practices that are reasonably related to maintaining jail security are permissible and do not violate due process or the Fourth Amendment. These include routine inspections of inmates' cells, prohibiting receipt of outside food or personal belongings, body-cavity searches, and double bunking.

D. **COMPETENCY**

Incompetency is a bar to trial. The judge has a constitutional duty to investigate and determine the competence of the defendant to stand trial if such evidence is apparent to the judge. A separate hearing is held to assess the defendant's competency. The test for whether a defendant is competent to stand trial is the same test for determining whether the defendant is competent to plead guilty: whether the defendant comprehends the nature of the proceedings against him and has the ability to consult with a lawyer with a reasonable degree of rational understanding.

If the defendant is declared mentally incompetent to stand trial, and the charge is a serious criminal offense, then the government may administer antipsychotic drugs. Three conditions must be met before the defendant can receive these drugs:

i) The treatment should not cause serious side effects that would affect the fairness of the trial;

ii) The treatment is necessary and there is no less intrusive method to further the government's important interest; and

iii) The treatment is medically appropriate.

Sell v. United States, 539 U.S. 166 (2003).

Insanity Defense Distinguished: The insanity defense considers the defendant's mental condition at the time of the crime, whereas incompetence concerns the defendant's mental condition at the time of the trial. Detention also varies depending on whether it is based on incompetency or insanity. In a successful insanity defense, the defendant may be detained in a mental hospital for a longer term than incarceration requires. If a defendant is found to be incompetent, confinement in a mental hospital must be limited to a brief period of time for evaluation.

The conviction of a legally incompetent defendant or the failure of the trial court to provide an adequate competency determination violates due-process principles by depriving the defendant of the constitutional right to a fair trial. State courts may place the burden of proving incompetence on the defendant, but they may not require the defendant to prove it by clear and convincing evidence.

E. GRAND JURIES

1. Indictment

After hearing the prosecution's evidence, the grand jury decides whether there is probable cause to charge a particular defendant with a particular crime and, if so, returns a "true bill" of indictment. (This formal charging process is mandated by the Fifth Amendment under the federal system for felonies and is used in most eastern states, but a state is not constitutionally required to use this process, as the Fifth Amendment Grand Jury Clause has not been incorporated by the Fourteenth Amendment. In most western states, the charging process is initiated by filing an information by a prosecutor.)

2. Grand Jury Proceedings

a. Defendant's rights

The grand jury is a non-adversarial proceeding. The proceedings are conducted in secret, and the defendant has no right to present or confront witnesses or to introduce evidence. The defendant is not entitled to a dismissal due to a procedural defect in grand jury proceedings, unless the defect substantially impacted the grand jury's decision to indict. However, the defendant (or any other witness) may make a motion to seal the grand jury report if he believes that he has been defamed.

1) Double jeopardy

Because jeopardy does not attach until a trial begins, the Double Jeopardy Clause does not apply to grand jury proceedings. The refusal of a grand jury to indict a defendant with respect to a specific crime does not prevent the indictment of the defendant for the same crime by another grand jury. *United States v. Williams*, 504 U.S. 36, 49 (1992). (*See* § VI.A., Double Jeopardy, *infra*.)

b. Role of the prosecutor

The prosecutor is the advisor to the grand jury. As such, the prosecutor's role is to advise the grand jury with respect to the law and assist the grand jury in its job of issuing subpoenas for witnesses and evidence. The prosecutor has no legal obligation to present evidence exculpating the defendant to the grand jury. Thus, a grand jury indictment cannot be dismissed for the prosecutor's failure to present exculpatory evidence, unless the prosecutor violated a preexisting constitutional or legislative rule. The prosecutor is subject to the grand jury secrecy rules.

c. Witness's rights

A grand jury witness has no right to counsel in the grand jury room. The witness may request permission to consult with counsel outside of the jury room before answering a grand jury question. A prosecutor's failure to give a *Miranda* warning to a witness who then lies to a grand jury does not prevent the prosecution of the witness for perjury. *United States v. Wong*, 431 U.S. 174 (1977). Further, a witness who is a target of an investigation and may become a defendant is not entitled to a warning of his putative defendant status; the failure to receive such a warning does not protect a lying witness from a perjury conviction. *United States v. Washington*, 431 U.S. 181 (1977).

d. Grand jury's role

The grand jury has subpoena power to investigate matters before it or to initiate criminal proceedings. The subpoena can be quashed by the opposing party if he can demonstrate that the evidence sought is not relevant to the investigation. However, the witness or defendant cannot attack the subpoena based on the grand jury's lack of probable cause. The grand jury is not restricted to hearing evidence that would be admissible at trial; an indictment may generally be based on hearsay or illegally obtained evidence. *United States v. Calandra*, 414 U.S. 338, 348 (1974) (illegally seized evidence admissible in grand jury proceeding); *Costello v. United States*, 350 U.S. 359 (1956) (hearsay evidence admissible in grand jury proceeding). (Note: By federal statute, information obtained from an illegal wiretap cannot be presented to a grand jury. 18 U.S.C. 2515.) The grand jury may not exclude members of minority races, regardless of whether they are the same race as the defendant. Such exclusion will lead to a reversal of the indictment without regard to the harmlessness of the error. *Campbell v. Louisiana*, 523 U.S. 392 (1998); *Vasquez v. Hillery*, 474 U.S. 254 (1986).

F. STATE'S DUTY TO DISCLOSE

The prosecution has an affirmative duty to disclose any material evidence favorable to the defendant and relevant to the prosecution's case in chief that would negate guilt or diminish culpability or punishment. *Brady v. Maryland*, 373 U.S. 83 (1963). Failure to make such a disclosure violates the Due Process Clause and is grounds for reversal, regardless of whether the failure to disclose was intentional, if the defendant can show that (i) the evidence is favorable to the defendant (i.e., is exculpatory or impeaches) and (ii) the failure to disclose caused prejudice against the defendant (i.e., there is a reasonable probability of a different outcome had the evidence been disclosed earlier). *Strickler v. Green*, 527 U.S. 263, 281-282 (1999); *United States v. Bagley*, 473 U.S. 667, 675 (1985). This duty does not extend to disclosure of impeachment evidence prior to a plea bargain agreement, *United States v. Ruiz*, 536 U.S. 622 (2002), or to post-conviction proceedings.

V. TRIAL

A. JURY TRIAL

In the federal system, the Sixth Amendment provides the right to jury trials. States are obligated under the Fourteenth Amendment to provide jury trials in criminal cases involving only serious offenses. *Duncan v. Louisiana*, 391 U.S. 145 (1968). States have wide latitude, though, to determine the conduct and details of jury use.

Criminal defendants, with some exceptions, are entitled to be present at initial arraignments, at every trial stage (including jury empanelment and the reading of the verdict) and at sentencing. *Lewis v. United States*, 146 U.S. 370; *Diaz v. United States*, 223 U.S. 442, 455. Organizational defendants, defendants accused of misdemeanors, and defendants who persist in disruptive behavior, after being warned by the judge that such behavior could result in removal, need not be present.

1. Maximum Sentence to Exceed Six Months

There is a constitutional right to a jury trial for **non-petty offenses**—those that carry an authorized sentence of **more than six months of imprisonment,** regardless of the actual penalty imposed. *Baldwin v. New York*, 399 U.S. 66 (1970). The right to a jury trial attaches for crimes punishable by six months of imprisonment or less only if additional statutory or regulatory penalties make the offense a "non-petty offense." *United States v. Nachtigal*, 507 U.S. 1 (1993) (a misdemeanor for which the maximum punishment was six months in prison and a $5,000 fine or probation not to exceed five years was not a serious offense). There is no right to trial by jury for multiple petty offenses (those that carry a combined total maximum term exceeding six months); the prison terms imposed for such convictions are not aggregated.

a. Contempt

In a civil contempt case, there is no jury trial requirement if the witness can avoid the punishment by complying with the court order. In a criminal contempt case that has no statutorily authorized punishment, the right to a jury trial is determined by the actual penalty imposed. Thus, a sentence of over six months would trigger the right to a jury trial. However, an alleged contemnor is not entitled to a jury trial simply because a strong possibility exists that upon conviction he will face a substantial term of imprisonment regardless of the punishment actually imposed. Moreover, if a sentence is imposed for contempt and it is more than six months, an appellate court may reduce the sentence to six months or less to protect the conviction against constitutional attack for lack of a jury. There is no right to a jury trial when the sentence imposed is probation, regardless of the length of the probation, at least when imprisonment following revocation of probation does not exceed six months.

2. Waiver

A defendant may waive the right to a jury trial and opt for a trial by judge, known as a "bench trial," if the waiver is freely and intelligently made. *Adams v. United States ex rel McCann*, 317 U.S. 269 (1942). However, the defendant does not have an absolute right to a bench trial. The court or prosecutor may compel the defendant to submit to a jury trial, unless the defendant would be denied a fair trial. *Singer v. United States*, 380 U.S. 24 (1965).

3. **Compliance**

   a. **Jury size and unanimity**

   A jury of less than six members is a denial of due process, and a unanimous verdict is constitutionally required if a jury is made up of only six members. For state-court juries of seven or more, the vote need not be unanimous, but there is no strict rule as to how many votes are required for conviction. *Apodaca v. Oregon*, 406 U.S. 404 (1972).

   The Federal Rules of Criminal Procedure require a unanimous vote by a 12-member jury in federal criminal trials, unless waived in writing and approved by the court. A verdict by 11 jurors is permitted if the 12th juror is excused for good cause after deliberations begin.

   b. **Composition of the jury**

   1) **Representative cross-section of the community**

      The Equal Protection Clause bars racial discrimination in the selection of juries, including grand juries. The requirement that a jury be selected from a representative cross-section of the community also extends to gender discrimination. However, the actual jury selected need not represent a fair cross-section of the community. *Holland v. Illinois*, 493 U.S. 474, 480 (1990).

   2) **All defendants may challenge jury selection discrimination**

      The defendant has standing to challenge the jury-selection process, regardless of any showing of actual bias. *Powers v. Ohio*, 499 U.S. 400, 410–411 (1991).

   3) **Prima facie case**

      The prima facie case for absence of a representative cross-section can be established by showing that:

      i) The group allegedly excluded is a **"distinctive" group** in the community;

      ii) The group was not **fairly represented** in the venire from which the jury was chosen; and

      iii) The underrepresentation resulted from a **systematic exclusion** of the group in the jury-selection process.

      To rebut, the prosecution must show that the disproportionate exclusion manifestly and primarily advances a significant governmental interest.

   4) **State's right to use neutral principles**

      In response to a claim of intentional racial discrimination in jury selection, the state has the right to apply neutral, nonracial principles to jury selection, even though it results in a smaller percentage of minorities on juries. The state must prove "absence of discriminatory intent."

   5) **Peremptory challenges**

      Peremptory challenges are requests by both parties during the voir dire jury-selection process to disqualify potential jurors without the need to show cause.

      a) **Discriminatory use**

         The Fourteenth Amendment Equal Protection Clause prohibits both the criminal defendant and the prosecutor from exercising peremptory challenges solely based on race or gender. *J.E.B. v. Alabama*, 511 U.S. 127 (1994); *Batson v. Kentucky*, 476 U.S. 79, 84 (1986). The defendant need not be a member of the excluded group in order to have standing to contest the prosecution's use of its peremptory challenges.

If the explanation for striking a juror is deemed pretextual, then it gives rise to an inference of discriminatory intent that makes it difficult for the challenge to survive. *Snyder v. Louisiana*, 552 U.S. 472, 485 (2008).

The United States Supreme Court has set forth a three-prong test (the "*Batson*" test) to determine whether a **peremptory challenge** has been exercised on the basis of race, in violation of the Equal Protection Clause of the Fourteenth Amendment. The test requires that:

i) The moving party establishes a **prima facie case of discrimination**;

ii) The party who exercised the challenge provides a **race-neutral explanation** for the strike;

iii) The moving party carries her burden of **proving that the other party's proffered reason was pretextual** and that the strike was indeed motivated by purposeful discrimination.

Once the party who exercised the challenge offers a race-neutral explanation and the trial court has ruled on the ultimate question of intentional discrimination, the preliminary issue becomes moot. **The ultimate burden of persuasion regarding racial motivation rests with the opponent of the strike.**

b) **Not constitutionally required**

The loss of a peremptory challenge does not violate the right to an impartial jury. *Ross v. Oklahoma*, 487 U.S. 81, 88 (1988). A defendant's exercise of peremptory challenges is not denied or impaired when the defendant chooses to use such a challenge to remove a juror who should have been excused for cause. *United States v. Martinez-Salazar*, 528 U.S. 304, 307 (2000).

c) **Harmless-error doctrine**

The Constitution allows states to choose between harmless-error review and automatic reversal when a judge, acting in good faith, erroneously denies a defendant's peremptory challenge. *Rivera v. Illinois*, 556 U.S. 148 (2009). Thus, if state law permits harmless-error review of the erroneous seating of the juror, there is no constitutional requirement for automatic reversal of the defendant's conviction.

c. **Impartial jury**

The Sixth Amendment provides that an accused person is entitled to a trial by an impartial jury. Claims of juror bias and misconduct are subject to the harmless-error rule.

1) **Views on race**

A defendant is entitled to inquire on voir dire into ethnic or racial prejudice of possible jury members only when the issues to be tried involve allegations of racial or ethnic prejudice, or whenever race is "inextricably bound up in the case." *Ristiano v. Ross*, 424 U.S. 589, 597 (1976).

2) Views on capital punishment

Prospective jurors who are opposed to the death penalty may be removed for cause if their opposition to the death penalty is so strong as to prevent or substantially impair the performance of their duties at the sentencing phase of the trial. *Wainwright v. Wirr*, 469 U.S. 412, 424–425 (1985); *Adams v. Texas*, 448 U.S. 38, 44 (1980).

An improper exclusion of a juror from a jury that imposed a death sentence is subject to automatic reversal. *Gray v. Mississippi*, 481 U.S. 648, 668 (1987).

d. Sentencing

1) Enhancements

When a sentence may be increased if additional facts are established, a jury must determine the existence of such facts. Enhancement of a defendant's sentence by a judge without such a determination violates the defendant's right to a jury trial. *Apprendi v. New Jersey*, 530 U.S. 466, 476 (2000). This limitation on a judge's ability to impose an enhanced sentence also applies when the defendant has entered a guilty plea. *Blakely v. Washington*, 542 U.S. 296 (2004). However, the harmless-error test applies to determine whether a sentence enhanced in violation of a defendant's right to a jury trial must be reversed. *Washington v. Recuenco*, 548 U.S. 212 (2006).

2) Concurrent versus consecutive sentences

Judges can decide whether sentences for multiple crimes run concurrently or consecutively without violating this right. *Oregon v. Ice*, 555 U.S. 160 (2009).

e. Inconsistent verdicts

If a jury renders a verdict that a defendant is guilty of certain offenses but not guilty of other related offenses, then the verdict is not reviewable on the grounds of inconsistency, even when the jury acquits the defendant of an offense that is a predicate offense to an offense for which the same jury finds the defendant guilty. *United States v. Powell*, 469 U.S. 57 (1984). This rule, which permits inconsistent verdicts, is also applicable when a defendant is convicted of an offense for which a co-defendant, who is tried at the same time, is acquitted, even though the facts would logically dictate the same verdict for each defendant. *United States v. Dotterweich*, 320 U.S. 277 (1943). This rule extends to bench as well as jury trials. *Harris v. Rivera*, 454 U.S. 339 (1981). (Note: The defendant may challenge a jury verdict on the grounds that there was insufficient evidence to establish the defendant's commission of a crime.)

B. GUILTY PLEAS

A guilty plea is an admission of facts contained in the charging document (e.g., indictment, information).

1. Knowing and Voluntary

Because a guilty plea constitutes both a confession and a waiver of various constitutional rights, the plea must be both intelligent and voluntary. *Boykin v. Alabama*, 395 U.S. 238 (1969); *McCarthy v. United States*, 394 U.S. 459 (1969). The record must reflect that the judge has determined that the defendant knows and understands the following:

i) The nature of the charges and their essential elements;

ii) The consequences of the plea (e.g., the maximum and minimum possible sentences, possible immigration consequences); and

iii) The rights that the defendant is waiving (e.g., right to a trial).

(Note: The judge does not personally need to explain each element of the crime. It is sufficient for the defendant's counsel to explain the nature and elements of the crime to him. *Bradshaw v. Stumpf*, 545 U.S. 175 (2005).) The judge must also determine that the plea did not result from force or improper threats or from promises other than those contained in the plea agreement.

a. Factual basis for plea

The U.S. Constitution does not forbid criminal sentencing of defendants who are willing to waive their trial and accept a plea while maintaining their innocence. Therefore, because an express admission of guilt is not a constitutional requisite for the imposition of a criminal penalty, a judge may accept pleas that result in a criminal sentence without violating the Constitution, even if the defendant maintains his factual innocence. However, Rule 11(b)(3) of the Federal Rules of Criminal Procedure requires a judge to ascertain that there is factual basis for a defendant's plea in order to accept a guilty plea. Therefore, when the defendant asserts his innocence despite entering a guilty plea, the judge must determine that there is a factual basis for the plea in order to accept the plea. *North Carolina v. Alford*, 400 U.S. 25, 37 (1970).

b. Effect of violation

When the court fails to ensure that the plea was knowing and voluntary, the defendant is entitled to withdraw his plea.

2. Right to Counsel

In entering a plea, a defendant has the right to counsel. *White v. Maryland*, 373 U.S. 59 (1963).

3. Plea Bargain

A plea bargain between the prosecutor and the defendant is treated as a contract. The bargain may involve the crimes with which the defendant has been charged, such as a promise by the prosecutor to drop specific charges in exchange for the defendant's promise to plead guilty to other charges, or the defendant's sentence, such as a promise by the prosecutor to recommend a particular sentence in exchange for the defendant's guilty plea.

a. No right to bargain

A defendant cannot compel the prosecutor to bargain; the defendant does not have a constitutional right to plea bargain. *Weatherford v. Bursey*, 429 U.S. 545 (1977).

b. Pressure to bargain

A defendant's plea made in response to the prosecution's threat to bring more serious charges does not violate the protection of the Due Process Clause against prosecutorial vindictiveness, at least when the prosecution has probable cause to believe that the defendant has committed the crimes. *Bordenkircher v. Hayes*, 434 U.S. 357 (1978). Similarly, the bringing of felony charges against a defendant after the defendant asserted his right to a jury trial for misdemeanor offenses related to the same incident does not in itself constitute prosecutorial vindictiveness. *United States v. Goodwin*, 457 U.S. 368 (1982).

c. No duty to disclose impeachment information

The prosecution is not required to disclose impeachment information or information related to an affirmative defense to a defendant when the defendant enters into a plea bargain agreement prior to trial. The failure to disclose such information does not render the defendant's plea bargain involuntary. *United States v. Ruiz*, 536 U.S. 622 (2002).

d. Enforcement of the bargain

1) Court

When entering into a plea bargain, the agreement is enforceable against the defendant and the prosecutor, but not against the judge. If the judge is not satisfied with the bargain, he can reject the plea. A defendant does not have a constitutional right to have his plea accepted by the court.

2) Prosecution

Should the prosecution violate the provisions of the plea bargain, the judge decides whether specific performance of the plea is required or whether the defendant can withdraw his plea. *Santobello v. New York*, 404 U.S. 257 (1971).

3) Defense

If a defendant fails to abide by the plea agreement (e.g., fails to testify in another trial), then the prosecution can have the sentence vacated and reinstate the original charge. *Ricketts v. Adamson*, 483 U.S. 1 (1987).

4. Effect of the Plea on the Defendant's Rights

Generally, a defendant, by entering a guilty plea, waives his constitutional rights, such as the right to a trial, the privilege against self-incrimination, and the right to confront his accusers. However, a defendant may challenge a guilty plea on the due-process grounds that it was not a knowing and voluntary waiver of such rights. *Boykin v. Alabama*, 395 U.S. 238 (1969). In addition, a guilty plea does not constitute a waiver of a double jeopardy challenge unless the waiver is agreed to in the plea agreement. *Menna v. New York*, 423 U.S. 61 (1975). A defendant may also attack a guilty plea that is due to ineffective assistance of counsel. *Hill v. Lockhart*, 474 U.S. 52 (1985). (Note: A defendant may also challenge a guilty plea on the grounds that the court lacked jurisdiction. *Menna v. New York, supra*.)

C. SPEEDY TRIAL

The Due Process Clause and federal statutes protect defendants from intentional and prejudicial **pre-accusation** delay. The Sixth Amendment speedy trial guarantee, the Fourteenth Amendment, the Speedy Trial Act of 1974, and other federal and state statutes protect defendants from undue **post-accusation** delay.

1. Commencement of the Right

Statutes of limitations are the primary safeguards against pre-accusation delay. However, the Due Process Clause may be violated if the delay was used to obtain a tactical advantage for the prosecution or to harass the defendant. *United States v. Marion*, 404 U.S. 307 (1971). Delay resulting from an investigation conducted in good faith does not violate the Due Process Clause. *United States v. Lovasco*, 431 U.S. 783 (1977).

Under the Sixth and Fourteenth Amendments, the time period commences at the time of arrest or formal charge, whichever comes first. The defendant need not know about the charges against him for the right to attach.

2. Balancing Test

The factors to be considered in determining whether the defendant has been deprived of a speedy trial post-accusation are the:

i) Length of the delay;

ii) Reason for the delay;

iii) Defendant's assertion of a right to a speedy trial; and

iv) Prejudice to the defendant.

Courts weigh these factors and determine whether the state made a "diligent, good-faith effort" to bring the defendant to trial. *Barker v. Wingo*, 407 U.S. 514, 530 (1972). A delay caused by the inaction of an attorney assigned by the state to represent the defendant may be attributable to the defendant, but a delay caused by the court's failure to promptly appoint replacement counsel when an assigned attorney withdraws or by a breakdown in the public-defender system is attributable to the state. *Vermont v. Brillon*, 556 U.S. 81 (2009).

3. Remedy

If the defendant's right to a speedy trial is violated, the charges are dismissed with prejudice.

D. PUBLIC TRIAL

1. Defendant's Right

The Sixth Amendment guarantees a criminal defendant the right to a public trial. The defendant may waive the right and request a closed proceeding. However, because the request also implicates the First Amendment right of access of the press and the public, the court must consider several factors, and the likelihood of a closed proceeding is slight. The court may even allow the proceedings to be televised over the defendant's objection.

The right to a public trial extends to preliminary hearings and suppression hearings. A suppression hearing may be closed if (i) there is an overriding interest likely to be prejudiced by an open trial, (ii) the closure is not in excess of the interest, (iii) other alternatives have been considered, and (iv) the court enters adequate findings to support closure.

2. Public's Right

Regardless of the wishes of the defendant or prosecutor, a trial must be public unless there is either a *substantial likelihood* of prejudice to the defendant or a need to limit access to ensure an orderly proceeding. This right extends even to voir dire and many other preliminary matters. *Press-Enterprise Co. v. Superior Court of CA (Press-Enterprise I)*, 464 U.S. 501, 509–10 (1984).

E. FAIR TRIAL

1. Impartial Judge

Due process requires that a judge possess neither actual nor apparent bias. If actual or apparent bias exists, the judge must follow a recusal process in the federal or state jurisdiction. The impermissible bias or prejudice usually must stem from an extrajudicial source.

2. Fair Conduct by the Prosecutor

a. Examples of misconduct

A prosecutor may not:

i)   Make material misstatements of law or fact;

ii) Elicit information from the defendant outside the presence of his counsel;

iii) Express opinions about the defendant's guilt or innocence;

iv) Make unfair or improper remarks about the defendant, his counsel, or witnesses;

v)   Comment on the defendant's failure to testify at trial; or

vi) Make improper remarks to the jury to inflame their passions to convict for an improper reason.

b. No use of false testimony

A prosecutor may not knowingly use perjured or false testimony for the case in chief, for sentencing, or to impeach the credibility of a witness.

c. No suppression of favorable evidence

As discussed in IV.F., *supra,* due process requires the prosecution to disclose evidence favorable to the accused (i.e., exculpatory or impeaching) when such evidence is material to guilt or punishment. Evidence is material if there is a "reasonable probability" that disclosure would have changed the outcome of the proceeding; a reasonable probability is "a probability sufficient to undermine confidence in the outcome." *United States v. Bagley*, 473 U.S. 667, 682 (1985). The prosecution's failure to disclose evidence in its possession both favorable and material to the defense entitles the defendant to a new trial. *Brady v. Maryland,* 373 U.S. 83 (1963). Under *Bagley*, the prosecution's failure to turn over specifically requested evidence will seldom, if ever, be excused.

Similarly, police violate due process when, in bad faith, they destroy evidence that would have been useful to the defendant at trial. The defendant does not, however, have the right to require police to preserve all evidence if it is not certain that the evidence would have been exculpatory.

F. RIGHT TO CONFRONTATION

1. Trial

The accused has the right to directly encounter adverse witnesses, to cross-examine adverse witnesses, and to be present at any stage of the trial that would enable the defendant to effectively cross-examine adverse witnesses as guaranteed by the Sixth and Fourteenth Amendments. Not only does this right allow the defendant to cross-examine the adverse witness, but it also allows the defendant to observe the demeanor of the adverse witness. A witness may invoke the right against self-incrimination; however, such an invocation after testimony has already been made may violate the defendant's right to confrontation, guaranteed by the Sixth and Fourteenth Amendments, because the witness's invocation will prevent adequate cross-examination by the defendant. If the defendant was instrumental in preventing a witness from testifying, then he forfeits his right to confrontation.

2. Compliance

a. Face-to-face confrontation

Face-to-face confrontation is not an absolute right. A criminal defendant has the right to confront witnesses against him under the Sixth Amendment, unless preventing such confrontation is necessary to further an important public policy and the reliability of the testimony is otherwise assured. A defendant who voluntarily leaves the courtroom or a disruptive defendant whom the judge removes from the courtroom has not had his right to confrontation violated. This is to be determined on a case-by-case basis.

> The state's interest in protecting child witnesses from more than *de minimis* trauma as a result of testifying in the defendant's presence is considered an important public purpose under this rule. *Maryland v. Craig*, 497 U.S. 836, 855–856 (1990).

b. Cross-examination of witnesses

The right to confrontation means more than being allowed to confront the witness physically. The principal purpose of confrontation is to secure for the defendant the opportunity of cross-examination of the prosecution's witnesses.

1) Impeachment for bias

A denial of the opportunity to cross-examine a prosecution witness with regard to bias violates the Confrontation Clause. *Delaware v. Van Arsdall*, 475 U.S. 673, 679 (1986). However, such denial is subject to harmless-error analysis. Moreover, trial judges retain wide latitude to impose reasonable limits on such cross-examination based on concerns about, among other things, harassment, prejudice, confusion of the issues, the safety of the witness, or interrogation that is repetitive or only marginally relevant. *Id.*

2) Memory loss by the witness

The fact that a witness has a memory loss does not by itself violate the Confrontation Clause. *Delaware v. Fensterer*, 474 U.S. 15, 19–20 (1985). The Supreme Court has held that the Confrontation Clause does not bar testimony concerning a prior out-of-court identification when the identifying witness is unable, because of memory loss, to explain the basis for the identification. A defendant may conduct an effective cross-examination if given the opportunity to address the very fact of the poor memory of the witness. *United States v. Owens*, 484 U.S. 554, 564 (1988).

3) Confrontation Clause and the hearsay rule

The Confrontation Clause limits the use of hearsay evidence in a criminal trial. Out-of-court statements by witnesses that are "testimonial" are barred under the Confrontation Clause, unless the witnesses are unavailable and the defendant had a prior opportunity to cross-examine those witnesses, regardless of whether such statements are deemed reliable by the court. If, however, the declarant appears for cross-examination at trial, then the Confrontation Clause places no constraints at all on the use of the declarant's prior out-of-court testimonial statements. *Crawford v. Washington*, 541 U.S. 36, 59 (2004).

Out-of-court testimonial statements are not barred by the Confrontation Clause when they are used for a purpose other than establishing the truth of the matter asserted (i.e., when they are not used for a hearsay purpose). *Id. See also Tennessee v. Street*, 471 U.S. 409, 417 (1985).

The Confrontation Clause has no application to "non-testimonial" out-of-court statements. *Whorton v. Bockting*, 549 U.S. 406, 420 (2007).

a) Testimonial statements

A statement is considered "testimonial" if the declarant would reasonably expect it to be used in a prosecution. Such statements include affidavits, custodial examinations, prior testimony, and statements given in response to police interrogation. *Crawford v. Washington*, 541 U.S. 36, 40 (2004). The Supreme Court has also held that certificates of analysis, which state the results of state laboratory tests, are testimonial evidence that may not be admitted without accompanying live testimony by the analyst who conducted the tests. *Melendez-Diaz v. Massachusetts*, 557 U.S. 305, 340 (2009). It is not sufficient to substitute the testimony of another analyst who is familiar with the testing protocol but did not perform or observe the tests or sign the report. *Bullcoming v. New Mexico*, 564 U.S. 647 (2011).

b) Non-testimonial statements

The Confrontation Clause permits the admission of non-testimonial statements, even if they lack indicia of reliability. *Whorton v. Bockting,* 549 U.S. 406, 411 (2007). Statements made for the primary purpose of assisting the police in the investigation of an ongoing emergency are not testimonial. Examples of non-testimonial statements include statements made to a 911 operator during a domestic dispute, *Davis v. Washington*, 547 U.S. 813, 822 (2006), and statements made to police officers by the victim of a mortal gunshot wound as he lay in a gas-station parking lot. *Michigan v. Bryant*, 562 U.S. 344 (2011).

4) Witness unavailable

The right of confrontation is satisfied if the defense counsel had a right to cross-examine the witness at an earlier hearing, provided that the prosecution failed in a good-faith effort to produce the witness at the trial and the declarant is now unavailable. However, if the witness is unavailable because of the defendant's conduct, then testimonial hearsay is admissible. *Giles v. California*, 554 U.S. 353, 373 (2008).

5) Confession of a non-testifying co-defendant at a joint trial

a) *Bruton* rule

The admission of a confession by a non-testifying co-defendant at a joint trial against the defendant violates the Sixth Amendment, even when it merely corroborates the defendant's own confession. *Bruton v. United States*, 391 U.S. 123, 132 (1968). A limiting instruction will not cure the defect. If the co-defendant testifies, then the rule does not apply. The rule does not apply at a bench trial. *Lee v. Illinois*, 476 U.S. 530, 539 (1986). It also does not apply to the statements of an accomplice who is not tried as a co-defendant or to a co-defendant who takes the stand and denies making such a statement. *Nelson v. O'Neil*, 402 U.S. 622, 629–630 (1971); *Dutton v. Evans*, 400 U.S. 74, 88–89 (1970).

b) Harmless error

Admission of a co-defendant's statement in violation of *Bruton*, however, is subject to harmless-error analysis. *Schneble v. Florida*, 405 U.S. 427, 430 (1972).

c) Severance

The accused may assert a demand for a severance of the trial of his case from a co-defendant's case whenever the prosecution intends to introduce a confession that is hostile to one co-defendant, and the confession:

i) Implicates the confessing defendant but is not admissible against the non-confessing defendant; and

ii) Cannot be edited to exclude inculpation of the non-confessing defendant.

Bruton v. United States, 391 U.S. 123, 132 (1968). The prosecutor may avoid severance if the court denies the use of the statement or the prosecutor chooses not to use it at trial.

G. DUE PROCESS

1.   Right to Testify

A defendant has a right to testify and to present evidence on his own behalf.

2.   Burden of Proof

a. Presumptions

1) Presumption of innocence

While a defendant is not automatically entitled to a jury instruction apprising the jury of the presumption of innocence doctrine, the presumption is a basic tenet of a fair trial, and it may be required when necessary for a fair trial. *Kentucky v. Whorton*, 441 U.S. 786, 789 (1979).

2) Presumptions of facts

a) Permissive presumption

A permissive presumption (i.e., a presumption that the trier of fact is not compelled to accept and that does not shift the burden of proof) regarding an element of an offense does not violate the due-process requirement that the prosecution must prove each element of an offense unless the presumption is irrational. A presumption is not irrational if it is more likely than not to flow from the proven fact on which it depends. *County Court v. Allen*, 442 U.S. 140, 163–164 (1979) (upholding the statutory presumption that the occupants of a car in which firearms are found are in possession of the firearms).

b) Mandatory presumption

A mandatory presumption regarding an element of an offense violates the due-process requirement. *Sandstrom v. Montana*, 442 U.S. 510, 522 (1979) (jury instruction that a person intends the ordinary consequences of his voluntary acts constituted a mandatory presumption when the crime—deliberate homicide—required proof of intent). This could include either a conclusive presumption that cannot be rebutted (which would relieve the prosecution of having to prove an element of their case), or a rebuttable mandatory presumption (which shifts the burden of proof regarding the element of the offense). To the extent that these presumptions require the trier of fact to accept a fact as proving an element of the crime and disallow the trier of fact from rejecting it, or shift the burden of an element to the defense, they are unconstitutional. *County Court,* 442 U.S. at 159; *Sandstrom,* 442 U.S. at 524.

b. Elements of the prosecution's case

The Due Process Clause requires that the prosecution prove all of the elements of the case beyond a reasonable doubt. Due process does not require the court to use any particular words to advise the jury of the government's burden of proof. In some jurisdictions, the failure to instruct on reasonable doubt may result in reversible error, whereas in other jurisdictions, the lack of such an instruction is per se reversible error.

Sentencing factors need not be proved beyond a reasonable doubt unless the fact is being used to increase the penalty beyond the proscribed statutory maximum, in which case proof beyond a reasonable doubt is required. *Apprendi v. New Jersey,* 530 U.S. 466, 492 (2000).

c. Affirmative defenses

The state is not forbidden by the Due Process Clause from placing the burden of proving an affirmative defense—such as insanity, self-defense, entrapment, or duress—on the defendant. *Dixon v. United States,* 548 U.S. 1, 13 (2006).

d. Directed verdict

In a criminal case, a judge may order a directed verdict only for acquittal; the power to convict is reserved to the jury.

H. SENTENCING

1. Applicable Rights

Sentencing is considered a critical stage triggering the Sixth Amendment right to counsel. A defendant may have the right to confrontation and cross-examination at sentencing, particularly in death-penalty cases, or when a sentence is based upon a finding of new facts beyond those necessary to prove the offense charged. *Gardner v. Florida,* 430 U.S. 349, 358 (1977); *Specht v. Patterson,* 386 U.S. 605, 610 (1967).

2. Enhancement Over the Statutory Maximum

Any fact, other than a prior conviction, that can be used to increase a sentence beyond the statutorily prescribed maximum must be charged in an indictment, submitted to a jury, and established beyond a reasonable doubt. A fact is considered an element of a crime, as opposed to a sentencing enhancement, when it can increase the maximum sentence imposed. The failure to abide by the above procedure is a violation of the defendant's due-process rights under the Fifth Amendment and Sixth Amendment rights to notice and a jury trial, both of which are incorporated against the states through the Fourteenth Amendment. *Apprendi v. New Jersey,* 530 U.S. 466, 476 (2000).

It is not a Sixth Amendment violation for a judge to impose consecutive sentences based on facts that were not found by the jury, but rather by the judge. *Oregon v. Ice,* 555 U.S. 160 (2009). The rule of *Apprendi v. New Jersey, supra,* is thus limited to sentencing for single crimes, not to the arrangement for punishing multiple offenses. However, a sentencing judge, sitting without a jury, may not find the facts necessary to impose the death penalty. *Ring v. Arizona*, 536 U.S. 584 (2002). Similarly, a state law allowing a jury to issue an "advisory sentence," but allowing the judge alone to ultimately weigh the facts to decide whether to impose the death penalty, is unconstitutional. *Hurst v. Florida*, 577 U.S. ___, 135 S. Ct. 1531 (2015).

Harmless-error analysis applies in deciding whether or not to overturn a sentence for a judge's failure to submit a sentencing factor to the jury. *Washington v. Recuenco*, 548 U.S. 212, 222 (2006).

I. CRUEL AND UNUSUAL PUNISHMENT

1. Applicability

The Eighth Amendment to the U.S. Constitution prohibits the federal government from imposing cruel and unusual punishment for federal crimes, or "such punishment as would amount to torture or barbarity, any cruel and degrading punishment not known to the common law, or any fine, penalty, confinement, or treatment so disproportionate to the offense as to shock the moral sense of the community." U.S. Const. amend. VIII. The Eighth Amendment's protections are especially important when the sentences imposed are the highest form of punishment under a state's sentencing law.

2. Compliance

a. Non-death penalty

1) Physical conditions of incarceration

The physical conditions of incarceration amount to cruel and unusual punishment only if the prisoner can show that prison officials had actual knowledge of a substantial risk to the prisoners.

2) Physical force

A prisoner need not show serious injury to recover for a violation of the Eighth Amendment prohibition against cruel and unusual punishment. The inquiry is whether the physical force was applied in a good-faith effort to maintain or restore discipline, rather than applied maliciously and sadistically to cause harm.

3) Sentence proportionality

A sentence that is grossly disproportionate to the crime constitutes cruel and unusual punishment. However, a lengthy sentence does not necessarily violate the Eighth Amendment. *Compare Weems v. United States*, 217 U.S. 349 (1910) (reversing punishment of 20 years' imprisonment for falsifying a public record) *with Harmelin v. Michigan*, 501 U.S. 957 (1991) (upholding punishment of life imprisonment without the possibility of parole for drug dealing based on possession of more than 650 grams of cocaine) *and Ewing v. California*, 538 U.S. 11 (2003) (upholding punishment of an indeterminate sentence of 25 years to life for theft of merchandise valued at about $1,200 after conviction of at least two other felonies, at least one of which was serious or violent).

4) Equal protection limitations on punishment

A jail sentence is impermissible if it is imposed only because the defendant was unable to pay a fine. If a defendant has made reasonable bona fide efforts to pay the fine, then revocation of probation without consideration of alternative punishments is fundamentally unfair under the Fourteenth Amendment.

5) Repeat offenders

Some jurisdictions have statutes imposing mandatory indeterminate life sentences (e.g., 25 years to life) on defendants who commit three felonies, even if the felonies are non-violent property-related offenses. These recidivist statutes are not unconstitutional under either the Double Jeopardy Clause of the Fifth Amendment or the Cruel and Unusual Punishment Clause of the Eighth Amendment. *Ewing v. California*, 538 U.S. 11 (2003).

6) Defendant's perjured testimony

If a trial judge believes that the defendant perjured himself during the trial, then the judge may take this belief into consideration when determining the sentence.

b. Capital punishment

The death penalty may be imposed only under a statutory scheme that provides:

i)   Clear and objective standards;

ii) Specific and detailed guidance; and

iii) An opportunity for rational review of the process.

1) Homicide crimes

a) Aggravating circumstances

A defendant in a homicide case cannot be sentenced to death unless the trier of fact convicts the defendant of murder and finds at least one "aggravating circumstance" at either the guilt phase or penalty phase. *Brown v. Sanders*, 546 U.S. 212, 218–19 (2006). The aggravating circumstance must meet two requirements:

i)   It must not apply to every defendant convicted of murder; and

ii) It must not be unconstitutionally vague. (For example, "especially heinous, atrocious, or cruel" conduct definition is unconstitutionally vague.)

The trier of fact can consider both statutory and non-statutory aggravating circumstances, but the death penalty cannot be imposed without one statutorily defined aggravating factor being found.

b) Mitigating circumstances

A death sentence violates the Eighth and Fourteenth Amendments if the sentencing judge refuses to review or admit mitigating evidence. Mitigating evidence must be presented if it meets a low threshold test for relevance. *Woodson v. North Carolina*, 428 U.S. 280, 316 (1976).

> **Note:** When the death penalty is not imposed (e.g., when the defendant receives a sentence of life in prison without parole), a mandatory sentence may be imposed without the presentation of mitigating evidence. *Harmelin v. Michigan*, 501 U.S. 957, 965 (1991).

Capital-sentencing courts are not required to instruct juries that the defendant need not prove mitigating circumstances beyond a reasonable doubt. *Kansas v. Carr*, 577 U.S. ___, 136 S. Ct. 633 (2016).

c) Felony murder

In felony-murder cases, the death penalty may not be imposed if the defendant, acting as an accomplice, did not kill, attempt to kill, or intend to kill, unless the defendant significantly participated in the commission of the felony and acted with reckless indifference to human life. *Compare Enmund v. Florida*, 458 U.S. 782 (1982) (death penalty not permitted) *with Tison v. Arizona*, 481 U.S. 137 (1987) (death penalty imposed).

2) Non-homicide crimes

Punishment that is disproportionately excessive in relation to the crime committed is prohibited by the Eighth Amendment. The death penalty is considered excessive in rape cases, whether the victim was an adult woman or a child, *Coker v. Georgia*, 433 U.S. 584 (1977); *Kennedy v. Louisiana*, 554 U.S. 407 (2008).

3) Defendant insane

The Eighth Amendment prohibits states from inflicting the death penalty on a prisoner who is insane or can "demonstrate a severe mental disorder." *Panetti v. Quarterman*, 551 U.S. 930, 960 (2007).

4) Intellectual disability of the defendant

The Eighth Amendment prohibits execution of an individual with intellectual disabilities (formerly referred to as "mental retardation"). *Atkins v. Virginia*, 536 U.S. 304 (2002). In determining whether an individual has intellectual disabilities, a state cannot impose a strict cutoff that precludes a finding of intellectual disability if an individual has an IQ of more than 70 or ignore current medical guidelines in defining an intellectual disability because either approach creates "an unacceptable risk that persons with intellectual disability with be executed." *Hall v. Florida*, 572 U.S. ___, 134 S. Ct. 1986, 1990 (2014) (IQ cutoff); *Moore v. Texas*, 581 U.S. ___, 137 S. Ct. 1039, 1044 (2017) (nonmedical and out-of-date medical factors).

5) Age of the defendant

The Eighth Amendment prohibition against "cruel and unusual punishment" prohibits the execution of a defendant who was younger than 18 years of age at the time of the commission of a crime. *Roper v. Simmons*, 543 U.S. 551, 569 (2005). In addition, the Eighth Amendment prohibits the imposition of a sentence of life without the possibility of parole on a defendant who was younger than 18 years of age at the time of the commission of the crime if the crime was not a homicide. *Graham v. Florida*, 560 U.S. 48 (2010). If the crime was a homicide, the juvenile cannot be subject to a **mandatory** sentence of life imprisonment without the possibility of parole. When sentencing a juvenile, the sentencing judge must take the defendant's youth and other relevant circumstances into consideration. *Miller v. Alabama*, 567 U.S. 460 (2012).

6) Fairness of sentencing proceedings

To minimize the risk of arbitrary action, a capital sentencing process must satisfy, at a minimum, two general requirements:

i)   The process must channel or limit the sentencer's discretion in order to genuinely narrow the class of persons eligible for the death penalty and reasonably justify the imposition of a more severe sentence on the defendant compared to others found guilty of murder; and

ii) The court must allow the jury to consider any relevant mitigating evidence that might lead the sentencer to decline to impose the death penalty. The sentencer is also allowed to take into consideration victim impact statements.

If the state puts a capital defendant's future dangerousness at issue, the defendant has the right to inform the jury that the only possible sentence besides death is life imprisonment without parole. *Lynch v. Arizona*, 578 U.S. ___, 136 S. Ct. 1818 (2016).

7) Racial discrimination claims

Under *McCleskey v. Kemp*, 481 U.S. 279 (1987), the Supreme Court held that despite serious statistical evidence of racial disparity in the imposition of the death penalty (e.g., African-American defendants who kill white victims are more likely to receive the death penalty), it was not imposed as a result of unconstitutional discrimination.

8) Lethal injection

Lethal injection is not considered cruel and unusual punishment because there is only a mere possibility that the condemned may receive an improperly administered shot that would cause him unnecessary pain.

c. Adequate medical care

Although prison inmates have a right to adequate medical care, such care constitutes "cruel and unusual punishment" under the Eighth Amendment only when there is a deliberate indifference to the serious medical needs of an inmate. Mere negligence in assessing an inmate's medical condition or in providing treatment is not sufficient to trigger a constitutional violation. *Estelle v. Gamble*, 429 U.S. 97, 104–105 (1976).

VI.   POST-TRIAL CONSIDERATIONS

A.   DOUBLE JEOPARDY

The Fifth Amendment protection against double jeopardy applies to the federal government. It has been incorporated by the Due Process Clause of the Fourteenth Amendment, and consequently it also applies to the states. *Benton v. Maryland*, 395 U.S. 784 (1969).

1.   Protection Against Prosecution and Punishment

The Fifth Amendment Double Jeopardy Clause provides three protections:

i)   Protection against a second prosecution for the same offense after acquittal;

ii)   Protection against a second prosecution for the same offense after conviction; and

iii) Protection against multiple punishments for the same offense.

a. **Definition of "same offense"**

1) **Shared elements**

If a defendant's conduct may be prosecuted as two or more crimes, then the *Blockburger* test is applied to determine whether the crimes constitute the same offense for double jeopardy purposes. Under this test, each crime must require the proof of an element that the other does not in order for each to be considered as a separate offense. *Blockburger v. United States*, 284 U.S. 299, 304 (1932).

Example 1—No Jeopardy: A defendant robs a store and shoots and kills the store clerk. The state prosecutes the defendant for premeditated murder. The defendant is acquitted. The state then brings charges against the defendant for robbery. The protection against double jeopardy does not apply because robbery and murder each require the proof of an element that the other does not. Robbery requires, among other elements, the proof that the defendant took the victim's personal property; murder requires, among other elements, the death of the victim.

Example 2—Jeopardy: A defendant robs a store and shoots and kills the store clerk. The state prosecutes the defendant for felony murder based on the robbery. The defendant is acquitted. The state then brings charges against the defendant for robbery. The protection against double jeopardy applies because the state, in order to prove felony murder in the first trial, had to prove that the defendant committed a robbery. *Harris v. Oklahoma*, 433 U.S. 682, 683 (1977).

As a consequence of *Blockburger,* the Double Jeopardy Clause generally bars successive prosecutions for greater and lesser included offenses. A lesser included offense is one that does not require proof of an element beyond those required by the greater offense.

2) **Occurrence of a necessary subsequent event**

When jeopardy has attached with respect to a lesser included offense prior to the occurrence of an event necessary to establish the greater offense, the defendant may be subsequently tried for the greater offense.

Example: If a defendant who physically harms a victim is tried for a crime such as battery, and the victim subsequently dies as a consequence of the defendant's conduct, then the defendant may be tried for murder without running afoul of the Double Jeopardy Clause. *Diaz v. United States*, 223 U.S. 442, 449 (1912). However, if he had been acquitted of the lesser offense, the lesser offense cannot serve as grounds for a subsequent felony murder charge.

3) **Statutory offenses**

At a single trial, a defendant may be convicted of two offenses, one of which is a lesser included offense of the other, if both offenses are statutory and the legislature has specifically authorized cumulative punishment. *Missouri v. Hunter*, 459 U.S. 359, 368–369 (1983) (first-degree robbery and armed criminal action).

4) **Conspiracy**

An offense and the conspiracy to commit that offense are not the same offense for double-jeopardy purposes because each requires proof of different elements. *United States v. Felix*, 503 U.S. 378, 389 (1992).

5) Sentence enhancement use

The use of a defendant's prior conviction to enhance the sentence imposed on a defendant for a current conviction does not violate the Double Jeopardy Clause. *Witte v. United States*, 515 U.S. 389, 400 (1995).

b. Acquittal

A defendant who has been acquitted of a crime generally may not be retried for the same crime. A grant of a demurrer or motion to dismiss in favor of the accused at the close of the state's case is the equivalent of an acquittal. *Smalis v. Pennsylvania*, 476 U.S. 140 (1986) (court, having dismissed charge, could not permit prosecution to reinstate charge later in the same trial based on defendant's testimony). There must be a final verdict of acquittal, however, for the Double Jeopardy Clause to apply. *See Blueford v. Arkansas*, 566 U.S. 599 (2012) (holding that defendant could be retried for murder even though jury in first trial had announced in open court that they had unanimously voted against murder charges, because declaration in open court was not equivalent to verdict of acquittal since jury was sent back to deliberate on lesser-included charges of manslaughter and negligent homicide and might have revisited decision on murder charges). An acquittal based on an error of law is nonetheless an acquittal for Double Jeopardy purposes. *Evans v. Michigan*, 568 U.S. 313 (2013) (retrial following court-decreed acquittal barred even though the court misconstrued the statute under which defendant was charged).

2. Attachment of Jeopardy

The protection against double jeopardy is not triggered until jeopardy attaches. In a jury trial, jeopardy attaches when the jury is empaneled and sworn in. In a bench trial, jeopardy attaches when the first witness is sworn in.

3. Different Jurisdictions

Under the dual-sovereignty doctrine, the protection against double jeopardy does not preclude prosecution of a crime by both federal and state governments. Consequently, a defendant may be charged and convicted for the same type of crime in a federal court and a state court. Similarly, a defendant may be prosecuted by two different states for the same conduct. However, a state and state-created entity, such as a municipality, cannot both prosecute a defendant for the same conduct. *Waller v. Florida*, 397 U.S. 387, 394 (1970) (municipality's conviction of defendant for violation of city ordinance for destruction of city property precluded state prosecution for grand larceny).

4. Civil Actions

The Double Jeopardy Clause does not preclude a criminal punishment and civil penalty for the same conduct. Therefore, even if a defendant has been found guilty in a criminal action, the state may still bring a civil action against the defendant that arises out of the same conduct. The protection does not apply to administrative proceedings such as a disciplinary hearing stemming from criminal conduct, nor does it apply to a parole, probation, or bond-revocation hearing related to a criminal charge or punishment.

A civil penalty may be treated as a criminal punishment when the penalty amount is grossly disproportionate to governmental loss and it serves only a deterrent or retributive purpose. *Dep't of Revenue of Montana v. Kurth Ranch*, 511 U.S. 767, 783 (1994) (tax imposed on possession of illegal drugs after satisfaction of state and federal fines and forfeitures). However, a civil forfeiture proceeding is typically not punitive in nature. *United States v. Ursery*, 518 U.S. 267, 275 (1996) (forfeiture of property used in the commission of drug crimes).

> **Note:** Juvenile adjudicatory proceedings are criminal, not civil, actions for purposes of the Double Jeopardy Clause. A minor who is subject to an adjudicatory hearing regarding conduct that would constitute a crime if committed by an adult cannot subsequently be tried as an adult for a crime based on such conduct. *Breed v. Jones*, 421 U.S. 519, 541 (1975).

5. **Guilty Plea**

A defendant does not automatically waive her double-jeopardy rights by entering a guilty plea, but the plea agreement may include a provision that the charges against the defendant may be reinstated if the defendant breaches the agreement. *Ricketts v. Adamson*, 483 U.S. 1, 11 (1987). A guilty plea to a lesser included offense does not preclude prosecution for a greater offense if the greater offense has been charged before the plea is entered. *Ohio v. Johnson*, 467 U.S. 493, 501 (1984).

6. **Mistrial**

The Double Jeopardy Clause does not prohibit a retrial following a mistrial if "taking all the circumstances into consideration, there is a manifest necessity for [declaring a mistrial]." Although the decision to declare a mistrial is left to the sound discretion of the judge, the power should be used with "the greatest caution, under urgent circumstances, and for very plain and obvious causes." *United States v. Perez*, 22 U.S. 579, 580 (1824). If the trial judge fails to exercise sound discretion or "acts for reasons completely unrelated to the trial problem which purports to be the basis for the mistrial ruling," the trial court's decision is not entitled to absolute deference, and close appellate scrutiny is appropriate. *Renico v. Lett*, 559 U.S. 766 (2010). A mistrial for the death or illness of a judge or juror, or because of a hung jury, generally constitutes manifest necessity and permits a retrial.

If the judge grants an acquittal instead of declaring a mistrial after there has been a hung jury, then a retrial is not permitted. Moreover, if the prosecution asks for a mistrial because of its inability to locate a witness, then double jeopardy prevents a retrial.

If the defendant asks for or consents to a mistrial, then she generally can be retried, unless the request is based on bad-faith conduct by the prosecutor or judge directed toward goading the defendant into seeking a mistrial. The manifest necessity standard does not apply when the defendant requests a mistrial. *United States v. Dinitz*, 424 U.S. 600, 606–607 (1976).

7. **Appeal**

   a. **By the prosecution**

   The government may appeal an adverse ruling in a criminal case only when authorized by statute. If the trial judge grants an acquittal on an issue that does not relate to the defendant's guilt or innocence, such as the failure to give the defendant a speedy trial, then the prosecution may appeal and, if the appeal is successful, the defendant may be retried. In addition, a prosecutor may appeal an order dismissing an indictment or suppressing evidence, a bail determination, the sentence imposed on a defendant, and a post-verdict new-trial order.

   b. **By the defendant**

   The Double Jeopardy Clause generally does not prevent the retrial of a defendant after an appeal on the basis of an error made at trial, such as the admission of improper hearsay evidence or improper jury instructions. *Lockhart v. Nelson*, 488 U.S. 33, 38 (1988). This is true even when a conviction is overturned due to the weight of the evidence. *Tibbs v. Florida*, 457 U.S. 31, 42 (1982). However, a retrial after reversal of a conviction due to **insufficiency** of the evidence is barred by the Double Jeopardy Clause. A conviction is based upon insufficient evidence if the evidence presented, when viewed in the light most favorable to the prosecution, is such that **no rational fact-finder** could have found the defendant guilty beyond a reasonable doubt. *Burks v. United States*, 437 U.S. 1, 18 (1978).

8. **Retrial Offenses**

    A defendant who was tried for a crime but convicted only of a lesser included offense may not be retried on the originally charged crime even if the conviction is reversed. *Price v. Georgia*, 398 U.S. 323, 329 (1970).

    > **Example:** A defendant on trial for murder is found guilty of voluntary manslaughter. The conviction is overturned on appeal due to trial error. The defendant's retrial for murder violates the Double Jeopardy Clause, even if on retrial the defendant again is convicted only of voluntary manslaughter.

9. **Retrial Punishment**

    The Double Jeopardy Clause generally does not preclude a greater sentence from being imposed on a defendant upon reconviction after a successful appeal. However, the Due Process Clause does prevent the imposition of a greater sentence upon reconviction if the greater sentence is imposed as a penalty for the exercise of a statutory right to appeal or to seek a collateral remedy. Consequently, when imposing a greater sentence upon reconviction, the judge must articulate reasons for the greater sentence that are based on objective information concerning identifiable conduct by the defendant that occurred after the original sentencing proceeding. *Alabama v. Smith*, 490 U.S. 794 (1989). In a jurisdiction where a jury rather than the judge determines the sentence, the jury in the retrial may impose a greater sentence unless it has been told of the defendant's original sentence. *Chaffin v. Stynchcombe*, 412 U.S. 17, 24 (1973).

    a. **Capital sentencing procedures**

        The Double Jeopardy Clause is applicable to capital sentencing proceedings when there is a determination that the government failed to establish an aggravating factor that would justify the death penalty. Consequently, if a jury imposes a life sentence rather than the death penalty, then the defendant, upon retrial, may not be sentenced to death. *Bullington v. Missouri*, 451 U.S. 430, 445 (1981).

10. **Collateral Estoppel**

    The Double Jeopardy Clause recognizes the doctrine of collateral estoppel. For collateral estoppel to apply, the earlier decision must have necessarily determined the issue on which collateral estoppel is sought by the defendant.

    > **Example 1:** Several victims were robbed at the same time. The defendant is initially tried for the crime with respect to only one of the victims. The sole contested issue at the trial is whether the defendant was a perpetrator of the crime. The defendant is acquitted of the crime. The acquittal prevents the defendant's prosecution for the robbery with respect to any other victim. The fact that the jury determined that the defendant was not a perpetrator of a robbery estops the government from trying the defendant for robbery of any of the other victims. *Ashe v. Swenson*, 397 U.S. 436 (1970).

If a jury acquits a defendant on one crime but deadlocks on another crime that contains the same element, then the jury's verdict may serve to prevent retrial on the crime over which the jury was deadlocked. In such a case, issue preclusion applies to the issue(s) that the jury did determine.

Example 2: A defendant was charged with both insider trading and fraud. An element of both crimes is the possession of insider information. The jury acquitted the defendant of fraud but deadlocked over insider trading. By acquitting the defendant, the jury determined that the defendant did not possess insider information. Consequently, under the doctrine of collateral estoppel, the government could not retry the defendant for insider trading. *Yeager v. United States*, 557 U.S. 110 (2009).

The burden is on the defendant to prove that the jury's verdict **necessarily** determined the issue that the defendant seeks to foreclose. Because a jury usually renders a general verdict in a criminal trial, it is rare that a defendant will be able to meet this burden.

B.   APPEAL

The Constitution neither provides for nor guarantees an individual the right to appeal. Nevertheless, appeals are commonplace in the U.S. justice system. When a defendant is entitled to a first appeal as of right, the defendant is guaranteed certain rights, among them equal protection and the right to counsel pursuant to the Fifth and Fourteenth Amendments. *Douglas v. California*, 372 U.S. 353 (1963) (indigent entitled to appoint of counsel). However, despite this latter right, if an attorney believes that the appeal is frivolous, she may withdraw so long as the appellant's right to appeal is protected. *Anders v. California*, 386 U.S. 738 (1967). There is also no right of self-representation during an appeal. *Martinez v. Court of Appeal*, 528 U.S. 152 (2000). When an appeal is discretionary, an indigent defendant does not have the right to the appointment of counsel unless the conviction was based on a plea of guilty or *nolo contendere*. *Ross v. Moffitt*, 417 U.S. 600, 610, 612 (1974); *Halbert v. Michigan*, 545 U.S. 605, 616-17 (2005).

Errors generally must be preserved by a timely objection to be considered on appeal, and even if properly preserved, any error, defect, irregularity, or variance that does not affect substantial rights (i.e., a "harmless" error) will not serve as grounds for reversal. However, under the plain-error doctrine, a defendant who has failed to preserve a claim of error in district court is still entitled to appellate relief when (1) the district court committed error under the law in effect at the time the appeal is heard, (2) the error is obvious under that law, and (3) the error affected the defendant's substantial rights. Fed. R. Crim. P. 52(b). A constitutional error is harmless only when it appears beyond a reasonable doubt that the error did not contribute to the verdict obtained. *Mitchell v. Esparza*, 540 U.S. 12 (2003).

C.   CONVICTIONS

1.   Writ of Habeas Corpus

Convicts may attack their convictions, even if their appeal was unsuccessful or not available, by challenging the lawfulness of the detention under a writ of habeas corpus. The convict does not have to be in custody; she may be out on probation or parole. However, if the defendant's sentence has expired and her prior conviction is being used to enhance a later one, then the defendant does not satisfy the in-custody requirement to petition for the habeas writ.

A writ of habeas corpus proceeding is civil in nature. Therefore, the "beyond a reasonable doubt" standard is not applicable. The petitioner must demonstrate only the unlawfulness of the detention by a preponderance of the evidence. If the petitioner is granted the writ, then the state may appeal, and double jeopardy does not apply to either the appeal or the retrial after the granting of the writ. An indigent person does not have a right to have counsel appointed to assist in perfecting her habeas petition.

2. Parole and Probation

If a new sentence can be imposed upon the revocation of parole, then the right to counsel is activated, and the parolee is entitled to representation to the same extent as a trial. On the other hand, if an already-imposed sentence is triggered by parole revocation, then the right to counsel is limited. The right to counsel applies only if it is necessary for a fair hearing.

3. Access to Courts

Reasonable access to courts, with no unreasonable limitations on presenting arguments, is a right of prison inmates. In addition, inmates cannot be prohibited from consulting with other inmates if there is no reasonable alternative in the prison, such as a law library.

4. Disenfranchisement

Some states disenfranchise a convicted felon. This prohibition on voting does not violate the Fourteenth Amendment, even when it applies to felons who have been released from incarceration. *Richardson v. Ramirez*, 418 U.S. 24, 54 (1974).

EVIDENCE

Table of Contents

EVIDENCE

Editor's Note

This outline discusses the Federal Rules of Evidence ("Federal Rules"), which apply in all civil and criminal proceedings (except grand jury proceedings) in United States district courts, courts of appeal, Bankruptcy Court, and Claims Court, and in proceedings before United States magistrates. The outline also covers important evidentiary issues that the Federal Rules do not specifically address, such as common-law or statutory testimonial privileges and constitutional limitations on the admissibility of evidence.

I. PRESENTATION OF EVIDENCE

With some exceptions, the Federal Rules apply to all civil and criminal proceedings before United States district courts, courts of appeal, Bankruptcy Court, and Claims Court, and in proceedings before United States magistrates. Fed. R. Evid. 1101(a).

The Federal Rules do not apply to:

i) The court's determination of a preliminary question of fact governing admissibility (*see* § I.A.1.a. Judge, *infra*);

ii) Grand jury proceedings; and

iii) Criminal proceedings for the following purposes:

   a) The issuance of a search or arrest warrant or a criminal summons;

   b) A preliminary examination in a criminal case;

   c) Extradition or rendition;

   d) Consideration of bail or other release;

   e) Sentencing; and

   f) Granting or revoking probation or supervised release.

Fed. R. Evid. 1101(c), (d).

A. INTRODUCTION OF EVIDENCE

1. Role of Judge and Jury

In a jury trial, the jury is traditionally the trier of fact and the judge the trier of law.

a. Judge

The trial judge generally decides **preliminary questions** regarding the competency of evidence, including the admissibility of evidence, whether privilege exists, and whether a person is qualified to be a witness. The court is not bound by the Federal Rules in deciding these questions, except with respect to privileges, and it may consider otherwise inadmissible evidence. Fed. R. Evid. 104(a). With respect to preliminary questions, the party offering the evidence ordinarily bears the burden to persuade the trial judge by a preponderance of the evidence. *Bourjaily v. United States*, 483 U.S. 171 (1987) (confession of co-conspirator as admission of party opponent); *Daubert v. Merrell Dow Pharm.*, 509 U.S. 579 (1993) (expert opinion); Rule 702, Notes of Advisory Committee (2000).

Hearings on preliminary matters must be conducted outside the presence of the jury when the hearing involves the admissibility of confessions, when a defendant in a criminal case is a witness and so requests, or when justice requires it. Fed. R. Evid. 104(c).

b. Jury

A party has the right to present evidence (e.g., bias) that is relevant to the weight and credibility of other evidence (e.g., the testimony of a witness). Once evidence has been admitted, it is the role of the jury to determine the **weight and credibility** of the evidence. Fed. R. Evid. 104(e).

2. Challenge to Evidence Ruling

A party may challenge an evidentiary ruling as erroneous only if the ruling affects a substantial right of a party, and the party notifies the judge of the error. There are two ways to call the court's attention to the error—objection and offer of proof. Fed. R. Evid. 103(a). (Note: While the judge in a jury trial must permit a party to challenge the court's ruling, the judge must also conduct the trial to the extent practicable so that inadmissible evidence is not suggested to the jury. Fed. R. Evid. 103(d).)

a. Objection to admission of evidence

If the ruling **admits** evidence, a party must make a timely **objection** or motion to strike and must usually state the specific ground for the objection or motion in order to preserve the admissibility issue for appeal. A party is not required to state the ground if it is apparent from the context. Fed. R. Evid. 103(a)(1).

b. Offer of proof for exclusion of evidence

If the ruling **excludes** evidence, a party must make an **offer of proof** in order to preserve the evidence for appellate review of the ruling. An offer of proof is an oral or written explanation of the relevance and admissibility of the evidence made on the record. The court may direct that an offer of proof be made in question-and-answer form. An offer of proof is not necessary if the substance of the evidence is apparent from the context. Fed. R. Evid. 103(a)(2),(c).

c. Consequence of a definitive ruling

Once a judge has made a definitive ruling on the admissibility of evidence, a party need not renew an objection or offer of proof, even if the ruling was made before the trial began. Fed. R. Evid. 103(b).

d. Plain error rule

A plain error is one that is obvious to a reviewing court. A plain error that affects a substantial right is grounds for reversal, even if no objection or offer of proof was made. Fed. R. Evid. 103(e). A court may take notice of a plain error to prevent a miscarriage of justice or to preserve the integrity and the reputation of the judicial process.

3. Limited Admissibility

Evidence may be admissible for one purpose but not for another (e.g., for impeachment but not substantive purposes), or against one party but not against another. In these cases, if a party makes a timely request, the court must restrict the evidence to its proper scope and instruct the jury accordingly. Fed. R. Evid. 105.

4. Completeness Rule

Under the rule of completeness, when a party introduces part of a writing or recorded statement, an adverse party may compel the introduction of an omitted portion of the writing or statement if, in fairness, it should be considered at the same time, such as when the omitted portion explains or clarifies the admitted portion. This rule also applies to a separate writing or recorded statement that relates to the introduced writing or recorded statement, such as the original letter when the reply letter has been introduced. Fed. R. Evid. 106. The rule of completeness does not require the admission of irrelevant portions of a statement. *United States v. Kopp*, 562 F.3d 141 (2d Cir. 2009).

> **Timing of introduction of omitted evidence:** While the rule of completeness permits an adverse party to compel the immediate introduction of evidence during the presentation of related evidence, the rule does not *require* the adverse party to do so. The adverse party may instead choose to present the omitted evidence subsequently, such as during cross-examination.

5. Judicial Notice

Judicial notice is the court's acceptance of a fact as true without requiring formal proof. The Federal Rules only address judicial notice of adjudicative facts, which are the facts of the case at hand—those that relate to the parties and their activities, and that typically are decided by the jury. The Federal Rules do not apply to judicial notice of legislative facts, which are policy facts related to legal reasoning and the lawmaking process. Fed. R. Evid. 201.

> **Example (adjudicative fact):** A witness testifies that an accident happened on a Saturday. The accident report indicates that the accident happened on July 21, 2007. Whether July 21, 2007, was indeed a Saturday is an adjudicative fact.
>
> **Example (legislative fact):** A judge must decide whether to recognize an exception to the common-law marital privilege. The fact that allowing the exception would undermine the sanctity of marriage is a legislative fact.

a. Facts subject to judicial notice

Not all adjudicative facts are subject to judicial notice. Judicial notice may be taken of an adjudicative fact only if it is **not subject to reasonable dispute** because (i) it is **generally known** within the territorial jurisdiction of the trial court, or (ii) it can be **accurately and readily determined** from sources whose accuracy cannot reasonably be questioned. Fed. R. Evid. 201(b).

1) Generally known facts within jurisdiction

A fact does not need to be known by everyone to be "generally known"; it must only be well known within the community. Fed. R. Evid. 201(b).

> **Example:** A judge could take judicial notice that a bank provides a checking account customer with a monthly account statement. *Kaggen v. IRS*, 71 F.3d 1018 (2d Cir. 1995).
>
> Despite being termed "judicial notice," a judge may not take notice of a fact based solely on his own personal knowledge.
>
> Example: A judge could not take judicial notice of informal judicial procedures for the issuance of court orders within a jurisdiction. *Switzer v. Coan*, 261 F.3d 985 (10th Cir. 2001).

2) Accurately and readily determined facts

A fact that can be accurately and readily determined need not be generally known as long as it can be determined from a source whose accuracy cannot be reasonably questioned, such as a geographic and historical fact obtained from a respected reference source.

> **Example:** A judge could take judicial notice of the state's statutory rate for post-judgment interest in determining the appropriate interest rate for pre-judgment interest. *Fox v. Kane-Miller Corp.*, 398 F. Supp. 609 (D. Md. 1975).
>
> **Contrast:** A judge could not take judicial notice of information about a company found on the company's website, because such information is often self-serving and subject to puffery. *Victaulic Co. v. Tieman*, 499 F.3d 227 (3d Cir. 2007).

b. Procedure

A court may take judicial notice at any time during a proceeding, including on appeal, whether upon request of a party or by the court's own initiative. Note, however, that a court may not take judicial notice against a criminal defendant for the first time on appeal. *U.S. v. Jones*, 580 F.2d 219 (6th Cir. 1978). If a party makes a request and the court is supplied with the necessary information, then the court must take notice of the fact. Fed. R. Evid. 201(c), (d).

1) Party's opportunity to be heard

When a party makes a timely request, the judge must give the party an opportunity to be heard on the propriety of taking judicial notice and the nature of the fact to be noticed. This right to be heard exists even if the court has taken judicial notice of a fact before notifying the party. Fed. R. Evid. 201(e).

2) Instructing the jury

a) Civil case

In a civil case, the jury must be instructed to accept the noticed fact as **conclusive**. Fed. R. Evid. 201(f).

b) Criminal case

In a criminal case, the jury must be instructed that it **may or may not accept** any judicially noticed fact as conclusive. Fed. R. Evid. 201(f).

B. MODE AND ORDER OF PRESENTATION OF EVIDENCE

1. Trial Process

A trial traditionally begins with the plaintiff's case-in-chief, followed by the defendant's case, followed by the plaintiff's rebuttal.

a. Judicial control of process

Subject to the evidentiary rules, a party is generally free to present evidence in the manner and order that the party feels is most effective. The order of the witnesses and presentation of the case, however, are within the discretion of the court, in order to effectively determine the truth, avoid wasting time, and protect witnesses from harassment. Fed. R. Evid. 611(a).

b. Judicial presentation of evidence

A judge may question, or even call, a witness. If the judge calls a witness, all parties may cross-examine that witness. A party objecting to the judge's calling or interrogation of a witness may wait to object until the next opportunity when the jury is not present. Fed. R. Evid. 614.

2. Examination of Witness

A party who calls a witness may examine the witness subject to the evidentiary rules. Another party may then cross-examine that witness.

a. Scope of cross-examination

The scope of cross-examination generally is limited to the subject matter of the direct examination and the credibility of the witness; however, the court may allow inquiry into additional matters. Fed. R. Evid. 611(b).

b. Additional examination

After cross-examination, the party who called the witness may engage in redirect examination, ordinarily to reply to any significant new matter raised on cross-examination. Recross-examination is also generally permissible with respect to significant new matters brought up during redirect examination. For both redirect and recross, the court has discretion to permit inquiry into other matters.

c. Examination of a defendant

The Fifth Amendment privilege against self-incrimination protects a defendant in a criminal case from being compelled to testify. A defendant in a criminal case who testifies as to a preliminary question, such as the voluntariness of the defendant's confession, has not opened himself up to cross-examination on other issues in the case. Fed. R. Evid. 104(d).

d. Motions to strike

During trial testimony, objections should be made after an improper question is asked but before the witness responds. If it is the witness's answer that makes the testimony improper (i.e., unresponsive to the question, hearsay, etc.), counsel should move to strike the answer as inadmissible.

> **EXAM NOTE:** Unresponsive answers are only subject to motions to strike by the examining counsel.

3. Form of Questions

a. Leading questions

1) Direct examination

On direct examination of a witness, a leading question—that is, a question that suggests the answer within the question—generally is not permitted. Fed. R. Evid. 611(c).

> **Example:** The question "Didn't you start the fire at 10:00?" suggests when the person being questioned started the fire. In contrast, the question "When did you start the fire?" does not suggest the answer.

a) Exceptions

A leading question is permitted on direct examination when it is necessary to develop the witness's testimony. For example, a leading question is usually permitted to elicit preliminary background information that is not in dispute. In addition, a leading question is typically permitted on direct examination of a witness who has difficulty communicating due to age or a physical or mental condition. Finally, when a party calls a witness who is likely to be antagonistic, such as an adverse party or a person associated with an adverse party, or a witness who presents adverse testimony (i.e., a hostile witness), even if such testimony is unanticipated, then the party ordinarily is permitted to use leading questions.

2) Cross-examination

There is generally no restriction on the use of leading questions during cross-examination. Fed. R. Evid. 611(c). If questions concerning matters beyond the subject matter of the direct examination are permitted, however, those inquiries must be made as if on direct examination. Fed. R. Evid. 611(b).

b. Improper questions

1) Compound question

A question that requires answers to multiple questions is compound and is not permitted.

Example: "Didn't you leave the house at 7:00, lock the door behind you, get in your car, and drive away?" (A "no" answer could mean that the witness did not leave at all, left at a time other than 7:00, did not lock the door, etc.)

2) Assumes facts not in evidence

A question that assumes as true facts that have not been established is not permitted.

Example: "When did you stop beating your wife?" (The question assumes that the witness is married and used to beat his wife. If neither fact has been established, this question is objectionable.)

3) Argumentative

A question that is intended to provoke an argument, rather than elicit a factual response, is not permitted.

Example: "You don't really expect the jury to believe you, do you?"

4) Calls for a conclusion or opinion

A question that requires the witness to draw a conclusion or state an opinion that he is not qualified to make is not permitted.

Example: "How did your mother feel after you told her the news?" (The witness cannot know how her mother felt and would have to give an opinion to answer the question.)

5) Repetitive

A question that has been asked and answered is not permitted, although judges may allow some repetition, particularly on cross-examination.

4. Exclusion of Witnesses

At a party's request or upon the court's own initiative, the court must exclude witnesses from the courtroom so that they do not hear the testimony of other witnesses.

Some witnesses, however, may not be excluded under this rule, including:

i) A party who is a natural person;

ii) An officer or employee of a party that is not a natural person, after the individual has been designated as the party's representative by its attorney;

iii) A person whose presence is essential to a party's presentation of its case, such as a police officer in charge of the investigation in a criminal case; or

iv) A person, such as a victim, whose presence is permitted by statute.

Fed. R. Evid. 615. Note that a victim may be excluded if the court determines, by clear and convincing evidence, that the victim's testimony would be materially altered by the victim hearing other testimony. 18 U.S.C. § 3771.

C. BURDENS AND PRESUMPTIONS

1. Burden of Proof

The burden of proof comprises two distinct burdens: the burden of production and the burden of persuasion.

a. Burden of production

The party with the burden of production (or burden of going forward) must produce legally sufficient evidence as to each element of a claim or defense, so that a reasonable trier of fact could infer that the alleged fact has been proved. In meeting this burden, a plaintiff or prosecutor has made a **prima facie** case. Failure to meet this burden can result in a directed verdict against the party bearing the burden. The determination of whether it has been met rests with the court. The burden of production may shift during trial.

> **Example:** In a negligence action in which the plaintiff produces uncontroverted evidence of the defendant's negligence, the defendant who does not have an affirmative defense bears the burden of producing evidence that challenges the case made by the plaintiff.

b. Burden of persuasion

The burden of persuasion (or standard of proof) is the degree to which legally sufficient evidence must be presented to the trier of fact. For example, in a civil case, this burden usually lies with the plaintiff to prove the allegations in the complaint and with the defendant to prove any affirmative defenses. This burden does not shift. Typically, determination of whether it has been met rests with the trier of fact.

1) Civil standards

The standard in most civil cases is a **preponderance of the evidence.** A fact is proven by a preponderance of the evidence if it is more likely to exist than not.

A higher standard used in some civil cases (such as fraud) is **clear and convincing evidence.** Under this standard, the existence of a fact must be highly probable or reasonably certain.

2) Criminal standard

In criminal cases, the prosecution must prove each element of a crime **beyond a reasonable doubt** to overcome the defendant's presumption of innocence. *In re Winship*, 397 U.S. 358 (1970).

2. Presumptions

A presumption is a conclusion that the trier of fact is required to draw upon a party's proof of an underlying fact or set of facts (i.e., basic facts). A rebuttable presumption may be overcome by evidence to the contrary; a conclusive presumption may not.

a. Rebuttable

A rebuttable presumption shifts the burden of production, but not the burden of persuasion, to the opposing party. Under the "bursting bubble" approach followed by the Federal Rules in a civil case, a presumption "bursts" (i.e., no longer has a preclusive effect) after the introduction of sufficient evidence by the opposing party to sustain a contrary finding. If no contrary evidence is introduced, the judge must instruct the jury to accept the presumption. If contrary evidence is introduced, the burden of persuasion remains on the party who had it originally. While the presumption no longer has preclusive effect after the introduction of contrary evidence, a judge may instruct the jury that it may, but is not required to, draw the conclusion (e.g., a person is dead) from the basic facts (e.g., the person has been missing for seven years). Fed. R. Evid. 301.

Limitation: The "bursting bubble" approach does not apply when a federal statute or another Federal Rule of Evidence, such as Federal Rule 302 (*see* § c. Diversity cases, *below*), provides otherwise.

b. Conclusive

Conclusive (or irrebuttable) presumptions are treated as rules of substantive law and may not be challenged by contrary evidence, no matter how strong the proof. One example is the presumption in some states that a child under the age of four lacks the ability to form the intent necessary to commit an intentional tort; no evidence to the contrary is permitted to disprove this assumption.

c. Diversity cases

In a federal diversity action, the federal court generally applies the Federal Rules to determine the resolution of evidentiary issues. However, when state substantive law is determinative of the existence of claim or defense under the *Erie* doctrine, then state law, rather than the Federal Rules, also governs the effect of a presumption related to the claim or defense. Fed. R. Evid. 302.

3. Destruction of Evidence

In general, the intentional destruction of evidence relevant to a case raises a presumption or inference that such evidence would have been unfavorable to the party that destroyed the evidence. To be entitled to such an inference, the alleged victim of the destruction of the evidence must establish that (i) the destruction was intentional, (ii) the destroyed evidence was relevant to the issue about which the party seeks such inference, and (iii) the alleged victim acted with due diligence as to the destroyed evidence. The presumption that arises from the destruction of evidence is rebuttable.

II. RELEVANCE

A. GENERAL CONSIDERATIONS

As a rule, evidence must be relevant to be admissible, and all relevant evidence is admissible unless excluded by a specific rule, law, or constitutional provision. Fed. R. Evid. 402. Evidence is relevant if:

i) It has any tendency to make a fact more or less probable than it would be without the evidence (i.e., **probative**); and

ii) The fact is of consequence in determining the action (i.e., **material**).

Fed. R. Evid. 401.

Sufficiency Distinguished: To be relevant, evidence need not, by itself, establish an element that a party must prove (e.g., the death of an individual in a homicide prosecution) or serve to refute such an element (e.g., a defendant's lack of a duty in a negligence action). The test of sufficiency of a party's evidence focuses on all evidence submitted by a party and admitted by the court. By contrast, under the test of relevancy, evidence is admissible even if it is only a single brick that is part of a wall of evidence establishing a party's position. Fed. R. Evid. 401, Notes of Advisory Committee, referring to Professor McCormick's famous statement, "A brick is not a wall."

1. **Direct and Circumstantial Evidence**

   a. **Direct evidence**

   Direct evidence is identical to the factual proposition that it is offered to prove. An eyewitness who testifies that she saw the defendant shoot the victim dead is an example of direct evidence that the defendant committed a homicide.

   Conviction without direct evidence: There is no rule that requires the presentation of direct evidence in order to convict a defendant. In other words, a defendant can be convicted solely upon circumstantial evidence.

   b. **Circumstantial evidence**

   Evidence that tends to indirectly prove a factual proposition through inference from collateral facts is circumstantial. An eyewitness who testifies that, moments before entering a room, she heard a shot, and upon entering the room saw the defendant standing over the body of the victim holding a smoking gun is circumstantial evidence that the defendant committed a homicide.

   Compare direct evidence: While it is sometimes said that direct evidence is better than circumstantial evidence, circumstantial evidence may have greater probative value. For example, testimony as to the identity of a thief based on a fleeting glimpse by an eyewitness with poor vision may not be as persuasive as testimony that the stolen item was found in the defendant's home.

2. **Exclusion of Relevant Evidence**

   Relevant evidence may be excluded if its probative value is **substantially outweighed** by the danger of unfair prejudice, confusing the issues, misleading the jury, undue delay, wasting time, or needlessly presenting cumulative evidence. This exclusion is often denominated by the applicable rule; that is, it is referred to as a "Rule 403" exclusion. Fed. R. Evid. 403.

   Matter of degree: Evidence may be admissible even if the danger of prejudice or other factors outweigh the probative value, so long as the danger does not do so **substantially.**

3. **Relevance Dependent on Existence of Fact**

   When the relevance of evidence depends upon whether a fact exists, proof must be introduced sufficient to support a finding that the fact does exist. The court may admit the proposed evidence on the condition that the proof is introduced later. Fed. R. Evid. 104(b). In making its determination that sufficient evidence has been introduced, the court must examine all of the evidence and decide whether the jury could reasonably find the conditional fact by a preponderance of the evidence; the court itself is not required to find that the conditional fact exists by a preponderance of the evidence. *Huddleston v. United States*, 485 U.S. 681 (1988).

4. Admission of Irrelevant Evidence—Curative Admission

Generally, irrelevant evidence is inadmissible. However, when a court admits evidence that is not relevant, the court may permit the introduction of additional irrelevant evidence to rebut the previously admitted evidence. Known as a curative admission, such evidence is admitted when necessary to remove unfair prejudice. The failure of a party to object to the admission of the initial irrelevant evidence is a factor to be considered in determining whether the party was unfairly prejudiced by it. *United States v. Hall*, 653 F.2d 1002 (5th Cir. 1981); *Crawford v. United States*, 198 F.2d 976 (D.C. Cir. 1952).

5. Laying a Foundation

Various types of evidence are admissible subject to the existence of a necessary predicate (i.e., a foundation), such as the authentication of tangible evidence. The failure of the proponent of the evidence to establish that foundation may be challenged by an objection for lack of proper foundation.

B. CHARACTER EVIDENCE

Character evidence, which is generalized information about a person's behavior—such as information that the defendant is a criminal, a bad parent, or an inattentive driver—is generally inadmissible.

1. Civil Cases

a. Inadmissible to prove conforming conduct

In a civil case, evidence of a person's character (or character trait) generally is inadmissible to prove that the person acted in accordance with that character (or character trait) on a particular occasion. Fed. R. Evid. 404(a)(1).

Example: A plaintiff cannot introduce evidence that the defendant is a reckless driver to prove that the defendant drove recklessly on the day in question.

Evidence concerning past sexual assault or child molestation by a *defendant* in a case in which the claim for relief is based on the defendant's sexual misconduct is admissible. Evidence concerning the past sexual behavior of a victim of sexual misconduct (e.g., rape) is admissible in limited circumstances (*see* § V.B.6. Sexual Conduct, *infra*).

b. Character at issue

Character evidence is admissible, however, when character is an **essential element** of a claim or defense, rather than a means of proving a person's conduct. Character is most commonly an essential element in defamation (character of the plaintiff), negligent hiring or negligent entrustment (character of the person hired or entrusted), and child-custody cases (character of the parent or guardian). Fed. R. Evid. 404(b); 405.

2. Criminal Cases

a. Defendant's character

1) By prosecution—defendant's bad character

In general, the same rule that applies in a civil action applies to the prosecution in a criminal case. The prosecution is not permitted to introduce evidence of a defendant's **bad character** to prove that the defendant has a **propensity** to commit crimes and therefore is likely to have committed the crime in question. Fed. R. Evid. 404(a)(1).

Example: A defendant is charged with brutally murdering his wife. The prosecution may not present evidence of the defendant's violent nature.

2) By defendant—defendant's good character

A defendant is **permitted** to introduce evidence of his **good character** as being inconsistent with the type of crime charged.

Example 1: A defendant is charged with brutally murdering his wife. The defendant may present evidence of his peaceable nature.

The defendant's character evidence must be pertinent to the crime charged.

Example 2: A defendant is charged with embezzling money from her employer. The defendant may not present evidence of her peaceable nature.

Proof of good character offered by the defendant must be in the form of **reputation** testimony or **opinion** testimony. Reputation evidence is defined as a defendant's reputation in the community. "Community" includes people with whom the defendant engages on a regular basis.

3) Defendant "opens the door"

Although the prosecution cannot introduce evidence of the defendant's bad character, the defendant makes his character an issue in the case if he offers evidence of his good character. When the defendant **"opens the door,"** the prosecution is free to rebut the defendant's claims by attacking the defendant's character. Fed. R. Evid. 404(a)(2)(A).

Defendant as witness: The defendant does not "open the door" to character evidence merely by taking the stand, but as a witness, the defendant is subject to impeachment.

In addition, the defendant "opens the door" for the prosecution to introduce evidence of his bad character by introducing evidence of the victim's bad character. The prosecution's evidence regarding the defendant must relate to the same character trait (e.g., violence) that the defendant's evidence about the victim did. Fed. R. Evid. 404(a)(2)(A).

b. Victim's character

1) By defendant—victim's bad character

A criminal defendant may introduce reputation or opinion evidence of the alleged victim's character when it is relevant to the defense asserted. Fed. R. Evid. 404(a)(2)(B). (Note: The introduction of evidence of the character of an alleged victim of sexual misconduct in a criminal case, however, is subject to significant limitations (*see* § V.B.6. Sexual Conduct, *infra*).)

> **Example:** A defendant is charged with assault. The defendant may offer evidence of the alleged victim's character trait of violence to support a claim of self-defense by showing that the alleged victim was the aggressor.

2) By prosecution—victim's good character

Generally, the prosecution may offer rebuttal evidence of the alleged victim's good character only after the defendant has introduced evidence of the alleged victim's bad character. Fed. R. Evid. 404(a)(2)(B).

> **Example:** A defendant is charged with assault. The defendant presents evidence of the alleged victim's character trait of violence to support a claim of self-defense. The prosecution may then rebut the defendant's evidence with evidence of the alleged victim's character trait of peacefulness. Note: The prosecution may also offer evidence of the defendant's character trait of violence.

In a homicide case, the prosecution may also offer evidence of the alleged victim's trait for peacefulness to rebut evidence that the alleged victim was the first aggressor. Fed. R. Evid. 404(a)(2)(C).

3. Methods of Proving Character

When character evidence is admissible, it may always be proved by testimony about the person's reputation or in the form of the witness's opinion. Fed. R. Evid. 405(a). For use of specific instances of conduct, *see* § II.C.2. Introduction of Specific Acts as Character Evidence, *infra*.

4. Impeachment

Character evidence is admissible for impeachment purposes. Character evidence about the witness may be introduced to show that the witness is not a person whose testimony should be believed. In such instances, the witness's character for untruthfulness is relevant. When permitted, the witness's testimony may be supported by testimony as to the witness's character for truthfulness. Fed. R. Evid. 404(a)(3). *See* § III.B. Impeachment, *infra*.

C. BAD ACTS

In addition to general evidence of a person's character (or character trait), evidence of a bad act is not admissible to prove a person's character in order to show that the person acted in accordance with that character on a particular occasion. Fed. R. Evid. 404(b)(1).

> **Example 1:** A driver is sued to recover for injuries inflicted on the plaintiff allegedly due to the driver's negligent failure to stop at a stop sign. The plaintiff cannot introduce testimony by a witness that the driver failed to stop at the same stop sign the day before the accident in question for the purpose of proving that the plaintiff failed to stop at the stop sign on the day of the accident.

Although a defendant's crimes or other wrongful acts are not admissible to show his criminal propensity in order to prove that he committed the crime for which he is charged, such bad acts are admissible for another purpose, such as proving motive, opportunity, intent, preparation, plan, knowledge, identity, absence of mistake, or lack of accident. Fed. R. Evid. 404(b)(2).

> **Example 2:** A defendant is charged with murder. Evidence that the defendant was previously convicted of robbery is likely admissible if the murder victim was the prosecutor on the robbery case against the defendant. Such evidence establishes the defendant's motive for killing the victim.

MIMIC evidence: This type of evidence is sometimes referred to as "MIMIC" evidence (**M**otive, **I**ntent, absence of **M**istake, **I**dentity, or **C**ommon plan), but it is important not to treat this list as all-inclusive. Subject to the other restrictions on the admissibility of evidence (e.g., relevancy, Rule 403 exclusion), a defendant's bad act may be introduced for any purpose so long as that purpose is not to prove that, because the defendant had a propensity to commit crimes, the defendant committed the charged crime.

1. **Advance Notice**

    When a criminal defendant requests, the prosecution must provide reasonable notice of the general nature of such evidence that the prosecution intends to offer at trial. Such notice must generally be given before trial, but it can be given during trial when the court, for good cause, excuses the lack of pretrial notice. Fed. R. Evid. 404(b)(2).

2. **Introduction of Specific Acts as Character Evidence**

    a. **Civil cases**

        When character evidence is admissible as evidence in a civil case (i.e., evidence that is an essential element of a claim or defense), it may be proved by specific instances of a person's conduct as well as either by testimony about the person's reputation or by testimony in the form of an opinion. Fed. R. Evid. 405(b).

    b. **Criminal cases**

        Generally, when character evidence is admissible as evidence in a criminal case (e.g., evidence of good character introduced by the defendant), specific instances of a person's conduct are not admissible. Character must be proved by either reputation or opinion testimony. Fed. R. Evid. 405(a).

        Non-propensity use: When a defendant's bad act is not used to show the defendant's criminal propensity but for another purpose (e.g., motive, identity), such instance of conduct may be admissible for that purpose.

        Essential element of the crime charged: When character or a character trait is an essential element of the crime charged, the defendant may introduce relevant specific acts inconsistent with the crime. Fed. R. Evid. 405(b).

    c. **Cross-examination of character witness**

        When a character witness is cross-examined, the court may allow a party to inquire into specific acts committed by the person about whom the witness is testifying. Fed. R. Evid. 405(a).

        Rule 403: Keep in mind that evidence of a bad act that is otherwise admissible is especially subject to challenge under Federal Rule 403, which permits the court to exclude evidence when its probative value is substantially outweighed by the danger of unfair prejudice (*see* § II.A.2. Exclusion of Relevant Evidence, *supra*).

D. **HABIT EVIDENCE**

    Evidence of a **person's habit** or an **organization's routine** is admissible to prove that the person or organization acted in accordance with the habit or routine on a particular occasion. A habit is a person's particular routine reaction to a specific set of circumstances.

    Example: A person drives the same route to work and parks in the same spot every day.

    Habit evidence may be admitted without corroboration and without an eyewitness. Fed. R. Evid. 406.

> **EXAM NOTE:** Habit is more specific than character evidence. In exam questions, words like "always" or "every time" generally refer to habit, whereas "often" or "frequently" are more likely to imply character evidence.

III. WITNESSES

A. COMPETENCE

Generally, every person is presumed to be competent to be a witness. Common-law prohibitions on a witness's ability to testify because of a lack of religious belief or conviction of a crime are inapplicable in proceedings governed by the Federal Rules. Questions of mental competence go to the weight rather than the admissibility of the testimony. However, in cases that turn on state law, such as diversity cases, a witness's competency is determined by state law. Fed. R. Evid. 601.

1. Personal Knowledge

A non-expert witness must have personal knowledge of a matter in order to testify about that matter. Personal knowledge may be established by the witness's own testimony as well as through other means. Fed. R. Evid. 602.

2. Oath or Affirmation

A witness must give an oath or affirmation to testify truthfully. The oath or affirmation must be in a form designed to impress that duty on the witness's conscience. Fed. R. Evid. 603. An interpreter must give an oath or affirmation to make a true translation. Fed. R. Evid. 604.

3. Judge as Witness

The presiding judge is absolutely barred from testifying as a witness in the trial. A party is not required to object in order to preserve the issue. Fed. R. Evid. 605.

4. Juror as Witness

a. At trial

A juror may not testify as a witness at trial in front of the members of the jury. If a juror is called to testify, the opposing party must be given the opportunity to object outside the presence of the jury. A juror may be called to testify outside the presence of the other jurors as to matters that occur during the trial, such as the bribery of a juror or a juror's failure to follow the court's instruction (e.g., discussing the case with family members). Fed. R. Evid. 606(a).

b. After trial

During an inquiry into the validity of a verdict, a juror generally may not testify about:

i) Any statement made or incident that occurred during the course of the jury's deliberations (e.g., refusal to apply the court's instructions);

ii) The effect of anything upon that juror's, or any other juror's, vote; or

iii) Any juror's mental processes concerning the verdict.

Fed. R. Evid. 606(b).

1) Exceptions

A juror may testify about whether:

i) Extraneous prejudicial information was brought to the jury's attention (e.g., the circulation of a newspaper article not introduced into evidence about the trial and the defendant's guilt);

ii) An outside influence was improperly brought to bear on a juror (e.g., a threat on the life of a juror's spouse); or

iii) A mistake was made in entering the verdict onto the verdict form.

The mistake exception, item iii above, does not extend to mistakes about the consequences of the agreed-upon verdict. Fed. R. Evid. 606(b).

> **Grand jury:** The same rule applies with regard to a challenge to the validity of an indictment by a grand jury.

5. Child as Witness

The competence of a child depends on his intelligence, his ability to differentiate between truth and falsehood, and his understanding of the importance of telling the truth. *Wheeler v. United States*, 159 U.S. 523, 524, 526 (1895) (finding a five-year-old child competent to testify at a capital murder trial). A witness who is so young that he is unable to understand the requirement to tell the truth would be disqualified. There is, however, no specific age at which a person becomes competent. The decision with regard to competency is one for the court.

6. Dead Man's Statutes

At common law, a party with a financial interest in the outcome could not testify in a civil case about a communication or transaction with a person whose estate was party to the case and the testimony was adverse to the estate, unless there was a waiver. Dead Man's Statutes do not apply in criminal cases.

> The Federal Rules do not include such a restriction, but most jurisdictions have adopted such "Dead Man's Statutes," which may be applicable in federal cases when state law applies (i.e., diversity cases).

a. Protected parties

The rationale of a Dead Man's Statute is to protect a decedent's estate from parties with a financial interest in the estate. Therefore, protected parties generally include an heir, a legatee, a devisee, an executor, or an administrator of an estate.

b. Disqualified witnesses

Any person directly affected financially by the outcome of the case may be disqualified as a witness under a Dead Man's Statute. A predecessor in interest to the party may be disqualified in order to prevent circumvention of the statute by transference of property to a relative or friend.

c. Interested person

A personal representative of the decedent or a successor in interest may also be protected under a Dead Man's Statute as an interested person.

d. Waiver

An interested person or protected party may waive the protection afforded by a Dead Man's Statute in several ways, including (i) failing to object to the introduction of testimony by a disqualified witness or (ii) introducing evidence of a conversation or transaction to which the statute applies.

B. IMPEACHMENT

A witness may be impeached by calling into question her credibility. Typically, a witness's testimony is challenged based on her character for untruthfulness, bias, ability to perceive or testify accurately, or prior statement that contradicts the witness's testimony at trial. In addition, a witness may be impeached by another witness or by other extrinsic evidence that contradicts the witness's testimony.

1. Who May Impeach a Witness

Any party, including the party that called the witness to testify, may attack the credibility of a witness. Fed. R. Evid. 607.

2. Witness's Character for Truthfulness

a. Reputation and opinion testimony

A witness's credibility may be attacked by testimony regarding the witness's character for untruthfulness. Generally, this testimony must be about the witness's **reputation** for having a character for untruthfulness or in the form of an **opinion** of the witness's character for untruthfulness. Fed. R. Evid. 608(a).

b. Truthful character evidence

The credibility of a witness may not be bolstered. Evidence of the truthful character of the witness is admissible only after the witness's character for truthfulness has been attacked. Evidence that impeaches the witness but does not specifically attack the witness's character for truthfulness, such as testimony that the witness is biased, does not constitute an attack. As with evidence regarding a witness's character for untruthfulness, evidence as to a witness's character for truthfulness is generally admissible only in the form of reputation or opinion testimony. Fed. R. Evid. 608(a).

c. Specific instances of conduct

Generally, a specific instance of conduct (e.g., lying on a job application) is not admissible to attack or support the witness's character for truthfulness. However, on cross-examination, a witness may be asked about specific instances of conduct if it is probative of the truthfulness or untruthfulness of (i) the witness or (ii) another witness about whose character the witness being cross-examined has testified. Fed. R. Evid. 608(b).

1) Limitations

The judge may refuse to allow such questioning of a witness under either Federal Rule 403 (the probative value is substantially outweighed by the danger of unfair prejudice) or Federal Rule 611 (protection of the witness from harassment or undue embarrassment). In addition, the lawyer who examines the witness must have a good-faith basis for believing that the misconduct occurred before asking the witness about it. *United States v. Davenport*, 753 F.2d 1460 (9th Cir. 1985).

2) Arrest

Because an arrest for misconduct is not itself misconduct, a witness may not be cross-examined about having been arrested solely for the purpose of impeaching the witness's character for truthfulness; however, the witness may be cross-examined about the underlying conduct that lead to the arrest. *See Michelson v. United States*, 335 U.S. 469 (1948).

3) Use of extrinsic evidence

When, on cross-examination, the witness denies a specific instance of conduct, extrinsic evidence is not admissible to prove that instance in order to attack or support the witness's character for truthfulness. This prohibition also bars references to any consequences that a witness may have suffered because of the conduct (e.g., suspension from a governmental job for improper personal use of governmental property). (An exception exists for criminal convictions, *see* § 3. Criminal Conviction, *below*.)

Note, however, that extrinsic evidence of specific conduct can be admissible to impeach the witness on other grounds, such as bias. Fed. R. Evid. 608(b), Notes of Advisory Committee (2003).

While a document is generally considered to be extrinsic evidence, *United States v. Elliott*, 89 F.3d 1360, 1368 (8th Cir. 1996), when the foundation for the document is established through the witness being impeached, it is possible that the document might be admissible to impeach the witness's character for truthfulness. Kevin C. McMunigal & Calvin W. Sharpe, *Reforming Extrinsic Impeachment*, 33 Conn. L. Rev. 363, 372–73 (2001).

4) Privilege against self-incrimination

By testifying on another matter, a witness does not waive the privilege against self-incrimination for testimony that relates only to the witness's character for truthfulness. Fed. R. Evid. 608(b).

3. Criminal Conviction

A witness's character for truthfulness may be impeached with evidence that the witness has been convicted of a crime, subject to the limitations discussed below. It does not matter whether the conviction is for a state or federal crime. Fed. R. Evid. 609.

a. Crimes involving dishonesty or false statement

Subject to the 10-year restriction (*see below*), **any witness** may be impeached with evidence that he has been convicted of **any crime**—felony or misdemeanor—**involving dishonesty or false statement,** regardless of the punishment imposed or the prejudicial effect of the evidence. A crime involves dishonesty or false statement if establishing the elements of the crime requires proof (or admission) of an act of dishonesty or false statement, such as perjury, fraud, embezzlement, or false pretense. Crimes of violence, such as murder, assault, and rape, are not crimes involving dishonesty or false statement, even though the perpetrator acted deceitfully in committing the crime of violence. Fed. R. Evid. 609(a)(2).

b. Crimes not involving dishonesty or false statement

Subject to the 10-year restriction (*see below*), a conviction for a crime not involving fraud or dishonesty is admissible to impeach a witness only if the crime is **punishable by death or imprisonment for more than one year** (typically, a felony). Fed. R. Evid. 609(a)(1).

1) Criminal defendant

When the witness is a criminal defendant, evidence of a felony conviction for a crime not involving dishonesty or false statement is admissible **only if** its probative value outweighs the prejudicial effect to that defendant. This stricter-than-usual balancing test gives extra protection to a criminal defendant who takes the stand in his own defense.

2) Other witnesses

For witnesses other than a criminal defendant, such evidence generally must be admitted. The court does have the discretion, however, to exclude the evidence when the party objecting to the impeachment shows that its probative value is **substantially outweighed** by its prejudicial effect (i.e., the Rule 403 standard).

c. Convictions more than 10 years old

If more than 10 years have elapsed since the conviction (or release from confinement, whichever is later), then evidence of the conviction is admissible only if:

i)   The probative value of the conviction, supported by specific facts and circumstances, **substantially outweighs** its prejudicial effect; and

ii)   The proponent gives an adverse party reasonable written notice of the intent to use such evidence so that the adverse party has a fair opportunity to contest the use of such evidence.

Fed. R. Evid. 609(b).

d. Effect of pardon

Evidence of a witness's conviction is not admissible if the conviction has been the subject of a pardon, annulment, or other action based on a finding of innocence. This rule also applies to an action based on a finding that the witness has been rehabilitated, provided that the witness has not been convicted of a later crime punishable by death or imprisonment in excess of one year (typically, a felony). Fed. R. Evid. 609(c).

e. Juvenile adjudications

Evidence of a juvenile adjudication is not admissible to impeach a defendant. When the witness is not the defendant, evidence of a juvenile adjudication can be used to impeach the witness's character for truthfulness only if:

i)   It is offered in a criminal case;

ii)   An adult's conviction for that offense would be admissible to attack the adult's credibility; and

iii)   Admitting the evidence is necessary to fairly determine guilt or innocence.

Fed. R. Evid. 609(d).

> **Used to show bias:** Under the Sixth Amendment Confrontation Clause, evidence of a witness's juvenile adjudication can also be used by a criminal defendant to impeach a witness's credibility by showing bias, such as when the witness's juvenile adjudication could provide a motive for the witness to lie. *Davis v. Alaska*, 415 U.S. 308 (1974).

f. Manner of proof

Evidence of a prior conviction may be produced by way of an admission by the witness, whether during direct testimony or on cross-examination, as well as by extrinsic evidence (e.g., a record of the conviction). Fed. R. Evid. 609, Notes of Advisory Committee (1990).

g. Pendency of appeal

A witness's conviction may be used for impeachment purposes even if an appeal is pending. Evidence of the pendency is also admissible. Fed. R. Evid. 609(e).

4. Prior Inconsistent Statements

A witness's prior statement that is inconsistent with a material part of the witness's testimony may be used to impeach the witness.

a. Disclosing the statement to the witness

A party who is examining a witness about the witness's prior statement is not required to show it or disclose its contents to the witness, but the statement must be shown, or its contents disclosed, to an adverse party's attorney upon request. Fed. R. Evid. 613(a).

b. Extrinsic evidence

Extrinsic evidence (i.e., evidence other than the witness's own testimony) of a witness's prior inconsistent statement may be introduced only if the witness is given the opportunity to **explain or deny** the statement, and the opposing party is given the opportunity to **examine the witness** about it. The witness's opportunity to explain or deny the statement need not take place before the statement is admitted into evidence.

1) Exceptions to the opportunity to explain

The opportunity to explain or deny a prior inconsistent statement does not apply when the statement (i) impeaches a hearsay declarant (*see* § 7. Impeachment of a Hearsay Declarant, *below*) or (ii) qualifies as an opposing party's statement under Rule 801(d)(2) (*see* § VI.B.2., Opposing Party's Statement, *infra*). Fed. R. Evid. 806, 613(b).

2) Collateral matter

Extrinsic evidence of a prior inconsistent statement cannot be used to impeach a witness regarding a collateral (i.e., irrelevant) matter; the questioning party is bound by the witness's answer.

5. Bias or Interest

Because a witness may be influenced by his relationship to a party (e.g., employment), his interest in testifying (e.g., avoidance of prosecution), or his interest in the outcome of the case (e.g., receipt of an inheritance), a witness's bias or interest is always relevant to the credibility of his testimony, and consequently, a witness may be impeached on that ground.

Although the Federal Rules do not expressly require that a party ask the witness about an alleged bias before introducing extrinsic evidence of that bias, many courts require that such a foundation be laid before extrinsic evidence of bias can be introduced.

> **EXAM NOTE:** Bias is often tested in the context of witnesses who are employed by one of the parties, or witnesses for the prosecution who testify in exchange for reduced or dropped charges.

6. Sensory Competence

A witness may be impeached by showing a deficiency in her testimonial capacities to perceive, recall, or relate information. This can be achieved by demonstrating that the witness is physically or mentally impaired, or through evidence of outside interference with the witness's abilities, such as thunder impeding the ability to hear or darkness impeding the ability to see.

7. Impeachment of a Hearsay Declarant

When a hearsay statement is admitted into evidence, the credibility of the declarant may be attacked (and, if attacked, supported) by any evidence that would be admissible if the declarant had testified as a witness. The declarant need not be given the opportunity to explain or deny any inconsistent statement or conduct, whether such statement or conduct occurred before or after the hearsay statement. If the party against whom a hearsay statement has been admitted calls the declarant as a witness, then the party is entitled to examine the declarant on the statement as if under cross-examination. Fed. R. Evid. 806.

Similar impeachment treatment is accorded a nonhearsay statement made by a co-conspirator, agent, or authorized spokesperson for an opposing party that has been admitted into evidence.

8. Rehabilitation of a Witness

A witness who has been impeached may be "rehabilitated" by the introduction of rebuttal evidence by either party to support the witness's credibility. Rehabilitation may be accomplished by:

i) **Explanation** or clarification on redirect examination;

ii) Reputation or opinion evidence of his **character for truthfulness,** if the witness's character was attacked on that ground under Fed. R. Evid. 608(a); or

iii) A **prior consistent statement** offered to rebut an express or implied charge that the witness lied due to improper motive or influence.

Fed. R. Evid. 801(d)(1)(B).

9. Religious Opinions and Beliefs

Evidence of a witness's religious opinions or beliefs is not admissible to attack or support a witness's credibility. Fed. R. Evid. 610. However, such evidence may be admissible to show bias or interest, such as when the witness is affiliated with a church that is a party to a lawsuit.

10. Impeachment by Contradictory Evidence

A witness may be impeached by evidence that contradicts the witness's testimony. Impeachment may be by extrinsic evidence as well as by cross-examination.

Example: The plaintiff in a negligence action based on a car accident testifies that, due to the defendant's reckless driving, the plaintiff's car was damaged. The defense may introduce a record of an insurance claim filed by the plaintiff prior to the accident for such damage due to another incident. Alternatively, the defense attorney may cross-examine the plaintiff about that claim.

11. Collateral Issues

While the Federal Rules do not explicitly prohibit impeachment on collateral issues, a court may refuse to admit evidence related to a collateral issue under the Rule 403 balancing test. Generally, a party may not impeach the credibility of a witness by introducing extrinsic evidence of a collateral matter. Instead, the party must accept the witness's testimony.

Example: A defendant is charged with assault. A prosecution witness testifies that the defendant assaulted the victim, who was wearing a plaid shirt. The defense may not call another witness to testify that the victim was wearing a striped shirt in order to establish the type of shirt that the victim was wearing.

C. RECOLLECTION REFRESHED

1. Present Recollection Refreshed

A witness may examine any item (e.g., writing, photograph) to "refresh" the witness's present recollection. The witness's testimony must be based on the witness's refreshed recollection, not on the item itself (e.g., the witness cannot read from the refreshing document).

a. Adverse party's options

When the item used to refresh a witness's recollection is a writing, the adverse party is entitled to have the document produced, to inspect the document, to cross-examine the witness about it, and to introduce any relevant portion into evidence. If the producing party claims that the document contains unrelated matter, the court may examine the document in camera and delete any unrelated portion before ordering that the rest be delivered to the adverse party. The adverse party may object to the deletion, in which case the deleted portion must be preserved in the record. Fed. R. Evid. 612(b).

Evidentiary purpose: When an adverse party seeks to introduce a writing used to refresh a witness's memory, the writing typically will be admissible for only the purpose of impeaching the witness's credibility. It will be admissible for substantive purposes only if it satisfies the other restrictions on admissibility, such as the hearsay rule.

When the refreshing of a witness's memory with a writing takes place before the witness testifies, the court may permit an adverse party to utilize these options, if justice so requires. Fed. R. Evid. 612(a).

b. Failure to produce or deliver the writing

In a criminal case, if the prosecution refuses to comply with a court order to produce or deliver a writing, the court must strike the witness's testimony, or may, when justice requires, declare a mistrial. In other circumstances, the court is free to issue any appropriate order. Fed. R. Evid. 612(c).

2. Past Recollection Recorded

A memorandum or record about a matter that a witness once had knowledge of but now has insufficient recollection of to testify to it may be admissible under a hearsay exception (*see* § VII.B.5. Recorded Recollection, *infra*). Although the record may be read into evidence, it is received as an exhibit only if offered by an adverse party.

> **Refreshed and recorded recollections distinguished:** The item used to refresh a witness's present recollection is generally not admitted into evidence, but a document introduced under the recorded recollection hearsay exception may be.

D. OPINION TESTIMONY

1. Lay Witness

A lay (non-expert) witness is generally not permitted to testify as to his opinion. However, lay opinions are admissible with respect to common-sense impressions such as appearance, intoxication, speed of a vehicle, or another's emotions. To be admissible, the opinion must be:

  i) Rationally **based on the perception** of the witness; and

  ii) Helpful to a **clear understanding** of the witness's testimony or the determination of a fact in issue.

Additionally, the opinion must **not** be based on scientific, technical, or specialized knowledge. Fed. R. Evid. 701.

2. Expert Witness

a. Subject matter of testimony

Before an expert witness may testify, the court must first determine that the subject matter of the witness's testimony:

  i) **Is scientific, technical, or other specialized knowledge,** which focuses on the *reliability* of the testimony; and

  ii) Will **help the trier of fact** understand the evidence or determine a fact in issue, which focuses on the *relevance* of the testimony.

b. Qualified expert

Once the testimony is determined to be reliable and relevant, an expert witness may testify as to her opinion, provided:

  i) The witness is **qualified as an expert** by knowledge, skill, experience, training, or education;

  ii) The testimony is based on **sufficient facts or data**;

  iii) The testimony is the product of **reliable principles and methods** (i.e., the factual data, principles, and methods used as a basis for the testimony are of the type reasonably relied on by experts in the field, although the data need not be admissible itself); and

  iv) The witness **applied the principles and methods reliably to the facts** of the case.

Fed. R. Evid. 702. The expert must also possess a reasonable degree of certainty in her opinion, which may be expressed using language such as "probably." *United States v. Mornan*, 413 F.3d 372 (3d Cir. 2005); *see also, Kumho Tire Co. v. Carmichael*, 526 U.S. 137 (1999); *Daubert v. Merrell Dow Pharm.*, 509 U.S. 579 (1993).

c. Ultimate issue

Generally, an expert's opinion may be admissible even though the opinion embraces an ultimate issue in the case (including the defendant's state of mind). However, an expert **may not** state an opinion about whether a criminal defendant had the **requisite mental state** of any element of the crime charged or of a defense. That determination lies in the province of the trier of fact. Fed. R. Evid. 704.

d. Basis of opinion

The expert's opinion may be based on facts and data that the expert has personally observed or about which the expert has been made aware. When such facts and data are not admissible, the opinion itself may nevertheless be admissible if experts in the particular field would reasonably rely on those kinds of facts and data in forming an opinion on the subject. If such facts are inadmissible, the proponent nevertheless may disclose them to the jury if their probative value in helping the jury evaluate the opinion substantially outweighs their prejudicial effect. Fed. R. Evid. 703.

1) Disclosure of underlying facts and data

An expert may state an opinion and give the reasons for it without first testifying as to the underlying facts or data, unless the court orders otherwise. Another party, when cross-examining the expert, may, of course, require the expert to disclose those facts or data. Fed. R. Evid. 705.

2) Use of hypothetical

In making facts known to the expert at trial, use of a hypothetical question is not required.

3) Lack of knowledge

A party can challenge the credibility of an expert witness on cross-examination by attacking the adequacy of the expert's knowledge, both their general knowledge in their field of expertise and their specific knowledge of the facts underlying their testimony.

e. Court-appointed expert

The court may appoint an expert witness and must inform the expert, either orally or in writing, of the expert's duties. Such a witness must advise each party of any findings. Each party may depose the witness, call the witness to testify, and cross-examine the witness. The court may authorize disclosure to the jury that the court appointed the expert. In a criminal case, the expert is paid by funds provided by law; in most civil cases, the expert's compensation is paid by the parties. Fed. R. Evid. 706.

f. Interpreter

An interpreter is subject to the rules for expert witnesses. Fed. R. Evid. 604.

IV. TANGIBLE EVIDENCE

Tangible evidence is evidence that is not presented in the form of testimony by a witness; it includes both documentary evidence (e.g., a written contract, a letter) and physical objects (e.g., a gun, torn clothing, an injured foot, a sound recording).

A. AUTHENTICATION

All tangible evidence must be authenticated. To authenticate an item, the proponent must produce sufficient evidence to support a finding that the thing is what its proponent claims it is. This is a lesser standard than a preponderance of the evidence. Fed. R. Evid. 901(a).

1. **Physical Objects**

   a. **Personal knowledge**

   A physical object may be authenticated by testimony of **personal knowledge** of the object. Fed. R. Evid. 901(b)(1).

   > **Example:** The owner of a stolen pocket watch may authenticate the watch by simply identifying it, "Yes, that is my pocket watch that was stolen."

   b. **Distinctive characteristics**

   A physical object may be authenticated by testimony of its **distinctive** characteristics. Fed. R. Evid. 901(b)(4).

   > **Example:** An electronically stored document may be authenticated by its metadata (e.g., filename, file type, creation date, permissions).

   c. **Chain of custody**

   Authentication by chain of custody must be used with respect to a physical object that could easily be tampered with or confused with a similar item, such as a blood sample. The witness testifying must account for the whereabouts of the item from the time it was obtained up until its introduction at the trial.

   d. **Reproductions and explanatory evidence**

   When reproductions (e.g., photographs, diagrams, maps, movies) are introduced into evidence, they may be authenticated by the testimony of a witness with personal knowledge that the object accurately depicts what its proponent claims it does. It is generally not necessary to call the person who created the reproduction to authenticate it. However, the creator may be called to authenticate the reproduction and may do so by testifying that the reproduction method produces an accurate result. Fed. R. Evid. 901(b)(9).

   e. **X-ray images and electrocardiograms**

   X-ray images, electrocardiograms, and similar items are physical representations of things that cannot otherwise be seen (i.e., the inner workings and functionality of a human body), and, as such, unlike other reproductions, they cannot be authenticated merely by the testimony of a witness that they are accurate reproductions of the facts. To authenticate such an item, it must be shown that an accurate process was used, that the machine used was working properly, and that the operator of the machine was qualified to operate it. The chain of custody must also be established.

2. **Documentary Evidence**

   Documentary evidence is commonly authenticated by stipulation, testimony of an eyewitness, or handwriting verification.

   a. **Ancient documents and data compilations**

   A document or data compilation, including data stored electronically, is considered authentic if it is (i) at least **20 years old,** (ii) in a **condition unlikely to create suspicion** as to its authenticity, and (iii) **found in a place where it would likely be** if it were authentic. Fed. R. Evid. 901(b)(8).

b. Public records

A public record may be authenticated by evidence that the document was recorded or filed in a public office as authorized by law or that the document is from the office where items of that kind are kept. Fed. R. Evid. 901(b)(7).

c. Reply letter doctrine

A document may be authenticated by evidence that it was written in response to a communication, so long as it is unlikely, based on the contents, that it was written by someone other than the recipient of the first communication.

d. Handwriting verification

There are two methods by which handwriting verification may be used to authenticate a writing.

1) Comparison

An expert witness or the trier of fact may compare the writing in question with another writing that has been proven to be genuine in order to determine the authenticity of the writing in question. Fed. R. Evid. 901(b)(3). This method may also be used for authenticating other items, such as fingerprints, cloth fibers, and hair.

2) Non-expert opinion

A lay witness with personal knowledge of the claimed author's handwriting may testify as to whether the document is in that person's handwriting. The lay witness must not have become familiar with the handwriting for the purposes of litigation. Fed. R. Evid. 901(b)(2).

e. Self-authenticating documents

The following items of evidence are self-authenticating—they do not require extrinsic evidence (i.e., evidence outside the document) of authenticity in order to be admitted:

i) Public documents bearing a governmental seal and a signature of an authorized governmental official or that are not sealed but are signed by an authorized governmental official and certified by another authorized governmental official;

ii) Certified copies of public records;

iii) Official publications issued by a public authority;

iv) Newspapers and periodicals;

v) Trade inscriptions (e.g., labels affixed in the course of business that indicate ownership);

vi) Notarized (acknowledged) documents;

vii) Commercial paper (including the signature thereon, and related documents);

viii) Any document, signature, or other item declared by federal statute to be authentic; and

ix) Records of a regularly conducted activity (e.g., a business) certified by a custodian of the records.

Although a proponent of a self-authenticating document generally is not required to give an adverse party advance notice of the intent to introduce the document, the proponent of business records (item ix, *above*) must give an adverse party reasonable written notice prior to the trial or hearing of the intent to offer the record and must make the record available for inspection so that the party has a fair opportunity to challenge them. Fed. R. Evid. 902.

f. Attesting witness

The testimony of a witness who attests or subscribes to a document generally is not required to authenticate a document. However, such testimony may be required by state law, such as to authenticate a will. Fed. R. Evid. 903.

3. Oral Statements

Oral statements may need to be authenticated as to the identity of the speaker in cases in which that identity is important (e.g., an opposing party's statement).

a. Voice identification

A voice can be identified by **any person** who has heard the voice **at any time** (including one made familiar solely for the purposes of litigation, in contrast to the rule for handwriting verification). It makes no difference whether the voice was heard firsthand or through mechanical or electronic transmission or recording. Fed. R. Evid. 901(b)(5).

b. Telephone conversations

A party to a telephone conversation may authenticate statements made during that conversation as having been made by a particular individual by testifying that:

i) The caller recognized the speaker's voice;

ii) The speaker knew facts that only a particular person would know;

iii) The caller dialed a number believed to be the speaker's, and the speaker identified himself upon answering; or

iv) The caller dialed a business and spoke to the person who answered about business regularly conducted over the phone.

Fed. R. Evid. 901(b)(4)–(6).

B. BEST EVIDENCE RULE

The best evidence rule (also known as the original document rule) requires that the original document (or a reliable duplicate) be produced in order to prove the contents of a writing, recording, or photograph, including electronic documents, x-rays, and videos. A "writing" is defined as "letters, words, numbers or their equivalent set down in any form." A "recording" and "photograph" are similarly broadly defined. Fed. R. Evid. 1001(a)–(c).

This rule applies only when the **contents of the document are at issue** or a witness is **relying on the contents of the document** when testifying. Fed. R. Evid. 1001–08.

Caution: Despite its name, the best evidence rule does not require a party to present the most persuasive evidence, nor does it require the presentation of documentary evidence instead of a witness's testimony simply because a document is available.

Example: A witness writes down her observations of an accident immediately after it happens. The best evidence rule does not prevent the witness from testifying about the event simply because a writing of her observations exists.

1. **Contents at Issue**

   The contents of a document are at issue when:

   i) The document is used as proof of the happening of an event, such as with a photograph of a bank robbery;

   ii) The document has a legal effect, such as with a contract or a will; or

   iii) The witness is testifying based on facts learned from the writing (as opposed to personal knowledge), such as with an x-ray image.

   Fed. R. Evid. 1002, Notes of Advisory Committee.

2. **"Original"**

   An original of a writing or recording includes any counterpart intended to have the same effect as the original by the person who executed or issued it. If the information is stored electronically, any legible printout (or other output readable by sight) that reflects the information accurately is an original. An original of a photograph includes the negative and any print made from it. Fed. R. Evid. 1001(d).

3. **Exceptions**

   a. **Duplicates**

      A duplicate is a counterpart produced by any process or technique that accurately reproduces the original. Fed. R. Evid. 1001(e). A duplicate is admissible to the same extent as an original unless:

      i) There is a genuine question as to the authenticity of the original; or

      ii) The circumstances make it unfair to admit the duplicate, such as may be the case when only part of the original is duplicated.

      Fed. R. Evid. 1003.

      > **Handwritten copies:** Handwritten copies of an original are not duplicates and are admissible only when the original or duplicate is lost, destroyed, or in the possession of an adversary who fails to produce it.

   b. **Original unavailable**

      The original is not required, and other evidence of its contents is admissible if:

      i) All of the originals are lost or destroyed, and not by the proponent acting in bad faith;

      ii) The original cannot be obtained by any available judicial process;

      iii) The party against whom the original would be offered (a) had control of the original, (b) was at that time put on notice that the original would be the subject of proof at the trial or hearing, and (c) failed to produce it at the trial or hearing; or

      iv) The writing, recording, or photograph is not closely related to a controlling issue (i.e., it is a collateral matter).

      In such cases, once the party has accounted for the absence of an original, the party may prove the contents of the writing, recording, or photograph by other means. Fed. R. Evid. 1004.

c. Public records

The contents of a public record (i.e., an official record or a document recorded or filed in a public office as authorized by law) may be, and generally are, proved by a certified copy rather than by the original record. Alternatively, a public record may be proved by a copy of the record plus the testimony of a person who has compared the copy with the original. If a certified or compared copy cannot be obtained by reasonable diligence, the contents may be proved by other evidence. Fed. R. Evid. 1005.

d. Summaries

The contents of voluminous writings, recordings, or photographs may be presented in the form of a chart, summary, or calculation, if such contents cannot be conveniently examined in court. The proponent must make the originals or duplicates available for examination and copying by other parties at a reasonable time and place. The court may order the proponent to produce the originals or duplicates in court. Fed. R. Evid. 1006.

e. Admission by party

The proponent may prove the contents of a writing, recording, or photograph by the testimony, deposition, or written statement of the party against whom the evidence is offered. In such a case, the proponent does not need to account for the original. Fed. R. Evid. 1007.

> **Oral out-of-court statement:** If a party against whom a document is offered admits to the contents of the document in an oral statement made out of court (other than during a deposition), the best evidence rule applies. The proponent must account for the original before using the adverse party's oral statement to prove the contents of the document.

4. Role of Court and Jury

Ordinarily, the court determines whether the proponent has fulfilled the conditions for admitting other evidence of the content of a document. In a jury trial, however, the jury determines any issue as to whether:

i) An asserted writing, recording, or photograph ever existed;

ii) Another writing, recording, or photograph produced at trial is the original; or

iii) Other evidence of content correctly reflects the content.

Fed. R. Evid. 1008.

C. PAROL EVIDENCE RULE

1. General Rule

The parol evidence rule operates to exclude evidence that, if introduced, would change the terms of a written agreement. The rule is based on the assumption that a written contract represents the complete agreement between the parties.

a. Complete integration

If a written agreement is a complete integration (i.e., contains all of the terms to which the parties agreed), then the parol evidence rule is in effect, and no extrinsic evidence may be introduced.

b. Partial integration

A contract that contains some, but not all, of the terms to which the parties agreed is a partial integration. In this case, extrinsic evidence that **adds to** the writing may be admitted. Evidence that **contradicts** the writing may not be admitted.

2. Exceptions

Extrinsic evidence can always be admitted for the following purposes:

i) To clarify an ambiguity in the terms of the writing;

ii) To prove trade custom or course of dealings;

iii) To show fraud, duress, mistake, or illegal purpose on the part of one or both parties; or

iv) To show that consideration has (or has not) been paid.

3. Applicable Evidence

Only evidence of **prior or contemporaneous negotiations** is subject to the parol evidence rule. In other words, evidence of negotiations conducted **after** the execution of the written contract is not prohibited by the parol evidence rule and may be offered to prove subsequent modifications of the agreement.

D. DEMONSTRATIVE AND EXPERIMENTAL EVIDENCE

A court may allow demonstrations and experiments to be performed in the courtroom. This may include exhibition of injuries in a personal injury or criminal case. A court has discretion to exclude evidence of personal injuries if the demonstration of such severe injuries would result in unfair prejudice. A court may also exclude a demonstration that cannot be effectively cross-examined. Science experiments are permitted but may be excluded if they will result in undue waste of time or confusion of the issues.

V. PRIVILEGES AND OTHER POLICY EXCLUSIONS

A. PRIVILEGES

The Federal Rules have no specific privilege provisions but instead defer to common-law privileges, except in diversity cases, when state rules generally apply. Fed. R. Evid. 501. A claim of privilege applies at all stages of a case or proceedings. Fed. R. Evid. 1101(c).

1. Confidential Communication

For a privilege to apply, there must be a confidential communication.

a. Presence of third party

Generally, if the communication is overheard by a third party, the privilege is destroyed. However, the presence of the third party does not destroy the privilege if:

i) The first two parties do not know that the third party is present (e.g., an unknown eavesdropper); or

ii) The third party is necessary to assist in the communication (e.g., a translator).

b. Waiver

A privilege may be waived if the person who holds the privilege:

i) Fails to assert the privilege in a timely manner (i.e., when the testimony is offered);

ii) Voluntarily discloses, or allows another to disclose, a substantial portion of the communication to a third party, unless the disclosure is privileged; or

iii) Contractually waives the privilege in advance.

A wrongful disclosure without the privilege holder's consent does not constitute a waiver. For limitations on waiver of the attorney-client privilege due to inadvertent disclosure, *see* § 3.c. Effect of disclosure on waiver, *below*.

2. Spousal Privilege

"Spousal privilege" comprises two distinct privileges: spousal immunity and confidential marital communications.

a. Spousal immunity

The general rule is that the spouse of a **criminal defendant** may not be called as a witness by the prosecution. Nor may a married person be **compelled** to testify against his spouse in any criminal proceeding, including a grand jury proceeding, regardless of who is the defendant.

1) Holder of the privilege

a) Federal courts

In federal courts (and a majority of states), the **witness spouse** holds the privilege and may choose to testify but cannot be compelled to do so.

b) State courts

In a minority of jurisdictions, the **party spouse** (as opposed to the witness spouse) holds the privilege and may prevent the witness spouse from testifying, even if the witness spouse wants to testify.

2) Period to which the privilege applies

The spousal immunity privilege applies to testimony about events that occurred **before and during the marriage.**

3) Time limit on assertion of the privilege

The spousal immunity privilege can be asserted **only during a valid marriage.** The right to assert the privilege expires upon divorce or annulment.

b. Confidential marital communications

Communication made between spouses **while they were married** is privileged if the communication was made **in reliance on the sanctity of marriage.**

1) Holder of the privilege

The majority view is that the privilege is held by **both spouses.** Some courts, however, have taken the position that only the communicating spouse can assert the privilege. *See* 1 Kenneth S. Broun et al., McCormick on Evidence § 83 (6th ed. 2006).

2) Scope of the privilege

This privilege applies only to communications made **during marriage.** This privilege applies to both **civil and criminal cases.**

3) Lack of time limit on assertion of the privilege

The time for asserting this privilege extends **beyond the termination of the marriage.** Thus, either party may assert the privilege—by refusing to testify or by preventing the other party from doing so—at any time, even after divorce or the death of one spouse.

> **Comparison of timing:** Spousal immunity applies to events occurring before marriage but ends when the marriage does, whereas the confidential communication privilege begins with marriage but continues beyond the length of the marriage.

c. Exceptions

Spousal privileges are subject to limitations in cases in which one spouse is suing the other, or when one spouse is charged with a crime against the other spouse or the children of either. For example, a defendant-spouse accused of battery of a witness-spouse would not be able to prevent the witness-spouse from testifying as to confidential marital communications.

3. Attorney-Client Privilege

A confidential communication between a client and an attorney for the purpose of seeking legal advice or representation is privileged.

a. Elements

1) Confidential

The communication must be intended to be confidential in order to be privileged. A communication made in the presence of a third party generally is not privileged, but the presence of, or communication by or through, a representative of the client or the attorney does not destroy the attorney-client privilege.

2) Communication

The communication must be **for the purpose of seeking legal advice or representation,** but the attorney does not need to give advice or agree to the representation for the privilege to exist.

a) Non-privileged statements

A statement made to an attorney that is not about legal advice or services sought by the client is not privileged. This includes statements regarding the fact of employment, the identity of the client, and the fee arrangements for the representation. If providing such information would divulge a confidential communication or incriminate the client, then it may be protected.

Furthermore, the attorney-client privilege does not protect disclosure of the underlying facts. A client cannot be compelled to answer the question "What did you say to your attorney?" but cannot refuse to reveal a fact within her knowledge merely because she told that fact to her attorney. *Upjohn Co. v. United States*, 449 U.S. 383 (1981) (quoting *Philadelphia v. Westinghouse Electric Corp.*, 205 F.Supp. 830, 831 (E.D. Pa. 1962)).

Finally, communications are not privileged when they are made to an attorney who is acting in a capacity other than as an attorney, such as a tax preparer, business partner, or witness to a will.

b) Corporate client

When an attorney represents a corporation, some states limit the privilege to communications received by the attorney from a member of the "control group" of the corporation (employees in a position to control or take a substantial part in a decision). *See, e.g., Consolidation Coal Co. v. Bucyrus-Erie Co.*, 432 N.E.2d 250 (Ill. 1982). However, in cases in which federal law controls, the privilege extends to communications by a non-control-group employee about matters within the employee's corporate duties made for the purpose of securing legal advice for the corporation. *Upjohn Co. v. United States*, 449 U.S. 383 (1981) (protecting communications by lower-level employees who were directed by their superiors to communicate with the corporation's attorney).

3) Client holds the privilege

The client holds the privilege and is the only one who may waive it. The attorney, however, must assert the privilege on the client's behalf to protect the client's interests. The privilege exists until it is waived, and it can survive the client's death.

b. Exceptions

The attorney-client privilege does not protect these confidential communications:

i) Communications made to enable or aid the commission of what the client **knew or should have known** was a crime or fraud;

ii) Communications relevant to a dispute between attorney and client (e.g., a malpractice allegation);

iii) Communications relevant to a dispute between parties who claim through the same deceased client; and

iv) Communications between former co-clients who are now adverse to each other.

> **Work product documents:** Documents prepared by an attorney for his own use in connection with the client's case are not covered by the attorney-client privilege because **they are not communications.** However, such documents are protected under the "work product" doctrine and are not subject to discovery unless the party seeking disclosure (i) demonstrates a substantial need for the information, and (ii) cannot obtain the information by any other means without undue hardship. The mental impressions, conclusions, and trial tactics of an attorney are always protected from discovery. Fed. R. Civ. P. 26(b)(3).

c. Effect of disclosure on waiver

Although the Federal Rules generally do not address the existence or scope of common-law privileges, there is one exception. Federal Rule 502 addresses the effect that a litigation-related disclosure of protected information has on the waiver of the attorney-client privilege, drawing a distinction between an intentional disclosure and an unintentional disclosure. The rule applies to confidential communications as well as material protected by the work-product doctrine. Fed. R. Evid. 502.

1) Inadvertent disclosure—no waiver

When made during a federal proceeding, the inadvertent disclosure of privileged communication or information does not waive the privilege if the holder of the privilege:

i)   Took reasonable steps to prevent disclosure; and

ii) Promptly took reasonable steps to rectify the error.

Fed. R. Evid. 502(b). In determining whether the holder took reasonable steps to prevent disclosure, factors such as the number of documents to be reviewed, the time constraints for production, or the existence of an efficient records-management system may be relevant.

2) Intentional disclosure—limitation on the scope of waiver

When made during a federal proceeding, the intentional disclosure of privileged material operates as a waiver of the attorney-client privilege. The waiver extends to undisclosed information only in those unusual situations in which (i) the disclosed and undisclosed material concern the same subject matter and (ii) fairness requires the disclosure of related information because a party has disclosed information in a selective, misleading, and unfair manner. Fed. R. Evid. 502(a).

3) Effect of disclosure made in a state proceeding

When privileged material is disclosed in a state proceeding and the state and federal laws are in conflict as to the effect of the disclosure, the disclosure does not operate as a waiver in a subsequent federal proceeding if the disclosure (i) would not be a waiver had it been made in a federal proceeding or (ii) is not a disclosure under the law of the state where it was made. In other words, the federal court must apply the law that is most protective of the privilege. This rule does not apply if the state court has issued an order concerning the effect of the disclosure; in such a case, the state-court order would be controlling. Fed. R. Evid. 502(c).

4) Controlling effect of a federal confidentiality order

A federal court may order that the privilege or protection is not waived by disclosure connected with the pending litigation (i.e., a confidentiality order). In such a case, the disclosure does not constitute a waiver in any other federal or state proceeding. Fed. R. Evid. 502(d).

5) Parties' agreement

An agreement between the parties regarding the effect of a disclosure binds only the parties unless the agreement is incorporated into a court order. Fed. R. Evid. 502(e).

4. Physician-Patient Privilege

Although there is no common-law privilege covering statements made by a patient to a doctor, many states protect such communications by statute, so long as the communications were made for the purpose of obtaining medical treatment. The patient holds the privilege; thus, only the patient may decide whether to waive it.

The privilege does not exist if:

i)   The information was acquired for **reasons other than treatment**;

ii) The patient's **physical condition is at issue**;

iii) The communication was made as part of the **commission of a crime or tort**;

iv) A **dispute exists** between the physician and the patient;

v) The patient contractually **agreed to waive** the privilege; or

vi) A **case is brought in federal court** and state law does not apply (e.g., most cases that involve a federal question).

> If an attorney requests that a physician consult with his client, then the physician-patient privilege applies only if treatment is contemplated during the consult.

5. **Psychotherapist-Patient Privilege**

The federal courts and most states recognize a privilege for confidential communications between a psychiatrist, psychologist, or licensed social worker and a patient in the course of diagnosis or treatment. The patient holds the privilege, but the psychotherapist must assert the privilege in the patient's absence.

The privilege does not exist if (i) the patient's mental condition is at issue, (ii) the communication was a result of a court-ordered exam, or (iii) the case is a commitment proceeding against the patient.

> The psychotherapist-patient privilege is more widely recognized than the traditional physician-patient privilege.

6. **Self-Incrimination**

   a. **In general**

   The Fifth Amendment protection against self-incrimination allows a witness in any proceeding to refuse to give testimony that may tend to incriminate the witness. The protection covers only current (not prior) statements and the fruits derived therefrom, and it does not apply to physical characteristics or mannerisms. The privilege belongs only to human beings. A corporation or other organization is not able to assert the privilege. *Bellis v. United States*, 417 U.S. 85 (1974). The Fifth Amendment only protects against domestic prosecutions; it cannot be invoked out of a fear of foreign prosecution. *United States v. Balsys*, 524 U.S. 666 (1998).

   b. **Comment and inference**

   In a criminal case, a prosecutor may not comment on the defendant's failure to take the stand and may not argue that the jury should draw a negative inference from the assertion of the privilege. *Griffin v. California*, 380 U.S. 609 (1965).

   In a civil case, however, it is proper for the opposing party to ask the jury to draw an adverse inference from a witness's claim of privilege.

   c. **Immunity**

   A witness may be compelled to provide incriminating testimony if the government grants him immunity from prosecution. The witness is not entitled to "transactional" immunity, i.e., protection against prosecution for the entire transaction about which he was testifying; instead, the government is constitutionally required to offer mere "use" immunity, which prohibits only the use of the compelled testimony against the witness. *Kastigar v. United States*, 406 U.S. 441 (1972). If the government does prosecute the witness in such a case, the government has the burden to show that the compelled testimony did not provide an investigatory lead that was helpful to the prosecution.

A witness may lose the right to invoke the privilege if the danger of incrimination has been removed through acquittal or conviction of the underlying charge. If the questioning about the adjudicated crime can lead to prosecution for other crimes, however, the privilege can be invoked.

7. Other Privileges

a. Clergy-penitent

In some jurisdictions, a confidential communication made by a penitent to a member of the clergy is privileged. The penitent holds the privilege, but the clergy member must assert the privilege on the penitent's behalf.

b. Accountant-client

Although not available at common law, many jurisdictions recognize a privilege for confidential communications made by a client to his accountant. The privilege operates similarly to the attorney-client privilege.

c. Professional journalist

There is no federal privilege protecting a journalist's source of information, but some states have enacted statutes extending some protection to journalists.

d. Governmental privileges

The government, at all levels, is privileged against disclosing:

i) The identity of an informant in a criminal case; and

ii) The communication of **official information** (i.e., information that relates to the internal affairs of the government and is not open to the public) by or to public officials.

B. PUBLIC POLICY EXCLUSIONS

1. Subsequent Remedial Measures

When measures are taken that would have made an earlier injury or harm less likely to occur (e.g., repairing an area where a customer slipped), evidence of the subsequent measures is **not admissible to prove negligence, culpable conduct, a defective product or design, or the need for a warning or instruction.** However, evidence of subsequent remedial measures may be admissible for other purposes, such as impeachment or—if disputed—ownership or control of the cause of the harm (e.g., a car) or the feasibility of precautionary measures. Fed. R. Evid. 407.

Product liability: The exclusion of evidence of a subsequent remedial measure applies to product liability actions based on negligence and those based on strict liability. To be excluded, the remedial measure must be undertaken **after** the plaintiff is injured; a remedial measure made after a product was manufactured but **before** the plaintiff was injured is not subject to exclusion under this rule. Fed. R. Evid. 407, Notes of Advisory Committee (1997).

2. Compromise Offers and Negotiations

Compromise offers made by any party, as well as any conduct or statements made during compromise negotiations, are not admissible to prove or disprove the **validity or amount of a disputed claim,** nor may they be admitted for impeachment by prior inconsistent statement or contradiction. Fed. R. Evid. 408.

a. Exceptions

1) Negotiation with a governmental agency

A person's conduct or statements made during compromise negotiations with a governmental agency (e.g., the IRS) during the exercise of its regulatory, investigative, or enforcement authority may be introduced in a subsequent criminal case against the person.

2) Admissibility for other reasons

Evidence of settlement offers and negotiations is admissible to prove bias or prejudice of a witness, to negate a claim of undue delay, or to prove obstruction of a criminal investigation or prosecution.

b. No immunization of evidence

Evidence may be admissible through means other than as an admission made during compromise negotiations. A party does not immunize (i.e., protect from admission) evidence simply by discussing it during compromise negotiations. Fed. R. Evid. 408, Notes of Advisory Committee (2006).

c. Prohibition on all parties

Compromise evidence is not admissible on behalf of **any party** who participated in the compromise negotiations, even the party who made the settlement offer or statement. The protection of this rule cannot be waived unilaterally. Moreover, when there are more than two parties, a settlement agreement entered into by a party with an adverse party cannot be used by a remaining adverse party to prove or disprove the validity or amount of an unsettled claim. Fed. R. Evid. 408, Notes of Advisory Committee (2006); *Branch v. Fid. & Cas. Co.*, 783 F.2d 1289 (5th Cir. 1986).

3. Offers to Pay Medical Expenses

Evidence of the payment, offer to pay, or promise to pay medical, hospital, or similar expenses resulting from an injury is **not admissible to prove liability for the injury.** Fed. R. Evid. 409.

4. Plea Negotiation

In a civil or criminal case, evidence of the following is generally not admissible against the defendant who made the plea or participated in the plea discussions:

i) Withdrawn guilty pleas;

ii) Pleas of no contest (i.e., a *nolo contendere* plea);

iii) Statements made while negotiating a plea with a prosecutor (e.g., an offer to plead guilty); and

iv) Statements made during a plea proceeding (e.g., a Rule 11 proceeding under the Federal Rules of Criminal Procedure).

Fed. R. Evid. 410(a).

a. Exceptions

Statements made during pleas or negotiations are admissible, however, if another statement made during the same plea or negotiation has already been admitted, and fairness requires that the statement in question also be admitted. Such statements also are admissible in a subsequent perjury prosecution if they were false statements made under oath, on the record, and with counsel present. Fed. R. Evid. 410(b).

b. Waiver

A defendant may waive the protection of Rule 410 if the waiver is knowing and voluntary. *United States v. Mezzanatto*, 513 U.S. 196 (1995).

5. Liability Insurance

Evidence that a person was or was not insured against liability is not admissible to prove whether the person acted negligently or otherwise wrongfully. However, such evidence may be admissible for another purpose, such as to prove agency, ownership, or control, or to prove a witness's bias or prejudice. Fed. R. Evid. 411.

6. Sexual Conduct

a. Victim's conduct

Under the "rape shield" rule, evidence offered to prove the sexual behavior or sexual predisposition of a victim (or alleged victim) generally is not admissible in any civil or criminal proceeding involving sexual misconduct. The exclusion applies to the use of such evidence for impeachment as well as substantive purposes.

Sexual behavior includes not only sexual intercourse or contact but also activities that imply such sexual intercourse or contact, such as the use of contraceptives or the existence of a sexually transmitted disease. Sexual predisposition can include the victim's mode of dress, speech, or lifestyle. Fed. R. Evid. 412(a), Notes of Advisory Committee (1994).

1) Exceptions

a) Criminal cases

In a criminal case involving sexual misconduct, evidence of specific instances of a victim's sexual behavior is admissible to prove that someone other than the defendant was the source of semen, injury, or other physical evidence. In addition, evidence of sexual behavior with the person accused of sexual misconduct is admissible if offered by the defendant to prove consent or if offered by the prosecution. Fed. R. Evid. 412(b)(1).

Note that, in contrast with the general preference under the Federal Rules for reputation or opinion testimony over evidence of specific acts, in criminal cases involving sexual misconduct, reputation or opinion evidence of a victim's sexual behavior or predisposition is not admissible.

Finally, any evidence whose exclusion would violate the defendant's constitutional rights is admissible under Rule 412. For example, under the Sixth Amendment Confrontation Clause, a defendant in a rape case may be able to cross-examine an alleged victim who testified that she lived with her mother about her cohabitation with another man in order to show that the alleged victim denied having consensual sex with the defendant in order to protect her relationship with the other man. *Olden v. Kentucky*, 488 U.S. 227 (1988).

b) Civil cases

In a civil case, evidence offered to prove a victim's sexual behavior or predisposition is admissible if its probative value **substantially outweighs** the danger of harm to any victim and of unfair prejudice to any party. Evidence of a victim's reputation is admissible only when it has been placed in controversy by the victim. Fed. R. Evid. 412(b)(2).

> The restriction on evidence of a victim's sexual behavior or predisposition applies only when the party against whom the evidence is offered can be characterized as a victim of sexual misconduct. For example, a plaintiff in a defamation action based on a statement about the plaintiff's sexual behavior is not a victim of sexual misconduct. By contrast, a plaintiff who brings a Title VII sexual harassment action can be characterized as a victim of sexual misconduct. Fed. R. Evid. 412, Notes of Advisory Committee (1994).

c) Procedure for admission

In a criminal or civil case, the party intending to offer evidence of the victim's sexual behavior or predisposition must file a motion describing the evidence and stating the purpose for its introduction. The motion must be filed at least 14 days before trial unless the court sets a different time. The motion must be served on all parties, and the victim (or the victim's guardian or representative) must be notified. The court must conduct an *in camera* hearing and give the victim and the parties the right to attend and to be heard. Unless the court orders otherwise, the record of the hearing is sealed. Fed. R. Evid. 412(c).

b. Defendant's conduct

In a criminal case in which a defendant is accused of sexual assault, attempted sexual assault, or conspiracy to commit sexual assault, evidence that the defendant committed any other sexual assault is admissible to prove any relevant matter. Similarly, in a criminal case in which a defendant is accused of child molestation, evidence that the defendant committed any other child molestation is admissible to prove any relevant matter. A similar rule applies in civil cases alleging sexual assault or child molestation. Fed. R. Evid. 413–15.

> **Propensity evidence:** Unlike Federal Rule 404(b), which applies to other crimes or bad acts committed by a defendant, these rules permit the use of a defendant's previous commission of a sexual assault or child molestation as evidence of the defendant's propensity to commit the charged sexual assault or child molestation. Consequently, for example, a defendant's prior conviction for rape can be used as evidence of the defendant's propensity to commit the charged rape, but a defendant's prior conviction for robbery cannot be used as evidence of the defendant's propensity to commit the charged robbery.

The court does have discretion to exclude such evidence under Rule 403 when the probative value is substantially outweighed by the danger of unfair prejudice. *United States v. Kelly*, 510 F.3d 433 (4th Cir. 2007); *Johnson v. Elk Lake Sch. Dist.*, 283 F.3d 138 (3d Cir. 2002).

1) Not limited to convictions

An arrest or even testimony of an incident that was unreported to the authorities may be admitted as evidence that a defendant has committed sexual assault or child molestation. Moreover, unlike Rule 609 regarding the use of a conviction to impeach a witness, there is no specific time restriction on the use of such evidence. *See, e.g., United States v. Horn*, 523 F.3d 882 (2008).

2) Pretrial disclosure

The prosecutor or plaintiff who intends to introduce such evidence must disclose it to the defendant at least 15 days before trial unless the court, for good cause, allows a later disclosure. Fed. R. Evid. 413(b), 414(b), 415(b).

VI.   HEARSAY

A.   WHAT IS HEARSAY

Hearsay is a statement that the declarant makes at a time other than while testifying at the current trial or hearing (i.e., an out-of-court statement) that is offered to prove the truth of the matter asserted. Fed. R. Evid. 801(c). Hearsay evidence generally is inadmissible unless it falls within an exception or exclusion set out in the Federal Rules, a federal statute, or a Supreme Court rule. Fed. R. Evid. 802.

1.   Declarant—Person

The declarant (i.e., the maker of the statement) must be a person. Evidence generated by a machine or an animal is not hearsay. Fed. R. Evid. 801(b). Examples of such nonhearsay evidence include:

i)   A dog's bark;

ii) An automatically generated time stamp on a fax;

iii) A printout of results of computerized telephone tracing equipment; and

iv) Raw data (such as blood-alcohol level) generated by a forensic lab's diagnostic machine.

Witness as declarant: A witness's own prior statement may be hearsay, and if hearsay, the witness may be prohibited from testifying as to her own statement unless an exception or exclusion applies.

2.   Statement—Assertion

A statement is a person's oral or written assertion, or it may be nonverbal conduct intended as an assertion. Fed. R. Evid. 801(a). An example of assertive conduct is a defendant nodding his head up and down to indicate a "yes" answer to a question.

Contrast nonassertive conduct: Nonassertive conduct is not hearsay. An example of nonassertive conduct is a pilot's act of flying an airplane, when such evidence is offered as evidence of the plane's safety.

3.   Offered to Prove the Truth of the Matter Asserted

Statements offered to prove something other than the truth of the matter asserted are not hearsay.

EXAM NOTE: A statement that is not hearsay is not automatically admissible. For exam purposes, it is important to keep in mind that the statement must be admissible under the other rules restricting admission, such as the rules on privileges.

a. Legally operative facts

A statement offered to prove that the statement was made, regardless of its truth, is not hearsay.

Example: In a slander action, the defendant's statement that the plaintiff is a murderer may be admissible to prove that the defendant made the statement but not to prove that the plaintiff is a murderer.

b. Effect on recipient

A statement offered to show the effect on the person who heard it is not hearsay.

Example: In a negligence action, the defendant's statement to the plaintiff that the sidewalk in front of the defendant's house was icy may be admissible to show that the plaintiff had notice of the danger but not to show that the sidewalk was actually icy.

c. State of mind

A statement offered as circumstantial evidence of the declarant's mental state is not hearsay.

Example: A testator's statement, "I am the queen of England," is not admissible to show its truth, but it is admissible to prove that the testator is not of sound mind.

d. Impeachment

A statement offered solely to impeach a witness is not being introduced for its truth and therefore is not hearsay (*see* III.B.4. Prior Inconsistent Statement, *supra*).

4. Multiple Hearsay

A statement that contains hearsay within hearsay may be admissible as long as each part of the combined statement conforms to a hearsay exception. Fed. R. Evid. 805.

Example: A plaintiff sues a defendant for battery, claiming that the defendant struck the plaintiff's kneecaps with a baseball bat. At trial, the plaintiff seeks to introduce as evidence a hospital record, which consists of a note from a physician that the plaintiff told the physician that the plaintiff's injury was caused by being struck with a baseball bat. Both the plaintiff's statement to the physician and the note are hearsay; they are out-of-court statements being offered to prove the truth of the matter asserted—the cause of the plaintiff's injury. However, because each part of the statement falls within a hearsay exception (the plaintiff's statement is a statement made for the purpose of obtaining medical treatment, and the doctor's note is a business record), the hospital record may be admissible.

B. WHAT IS NOT HEARSAY

The following types of statements, which otherwise would qualify as hearsay, are expressly defined as nonhearsay. Fed. R. Evid. 801(d).

1. Declarant-Witness's Prior Statements

The Federal Rules identify three types of prior statements that are not hearsay. In all three cases, the witness who made the statement (declarant witness) must testify at the present trial or hearing and be subject to cross-examination concerning the statement in order for it to be admissible. Fed. R. Evid. 801(d)(1).

a. Prior inconsistent statements

A prior inconsistent statement **made under penalty of perjury** at a trial, hearing, or other proceeding, or in a deposition may be admissible to **impeach** the declarant's credibility and as **substantive evidence.** Statements made in a prior legal action that is unrelated to the current action may be admitted under this rule. Fed. R. Evid. 801(d)(1)(A).

Statement not made at a former proceeding: An inconsistent statement that was not made under penalty of perjury may be admissible to impeach a witness but is not admissible under this provision as substantive evidence.

b. Prior consistent statements

A prior consistent statement, whether made under oath or not, may be admissible (i) to rebut an express or implied charge that the declarant recently fabricated it or acted from a recent improper influence or motive in testifying, only if it was made **before the declarant had reason to fabricate or the improper influence or motive arose;** or (ii) to rehabilitate the declarant's credibility as a witness when attacked on another ground. Fed. R. Evid. 801(d)(1)(B).

c. Prior statement of identification

A previous out-of-court identification of a person after perceiving that person (e.g., lineup) is not hearsay and may be admissible as substantive evidence. Fed. R. Evid. 801(d)(1)(C). Even if the witness has no memory of the prior identification, it will be admissible because the witness is subject to cross-examination about the prior identification. *United States v. Owens*, 484 U.S. 554 (1988).

EXAM NOTE: Beware of fact patterns involving prior out-of-court identifications by a witness who is not testifying at the current trial and therefore is not subject to cross-examination. This rule cannot apply, for instance, if the witness is dead or otherwise unavailable to testify.

2. Opposing Party's Statement

A statement made by a **party to the current litigation** is not hearsay if it is offered by an opposing party. The statement may have been made by the party in his individual or representative capacity (e.g., trustee). Fed. R. Evid. 801(d)(2)(A). This type of statement traditionally was known as an admission of a party-opponent.

Contrast statement against interest exception: Unlike with the statement against interest hearsay exception (*see* § VII.A.4. Statement Against Interest, *infra*), an opposing party's statement need not have been against the party's interest at the time that it was made.

Unlike most testimony by a lay witness, an opposing party's statement may be admitted even if it is not based on personal knowledge. In addition, an opposing party's statement in the form of an opinion may be admitted, even if the statement is about a matter that normally would be beyond the scope of lay witness opinion testimony. Fed. R. Evid. 801(d)(2), Notes of Advisory Committee.

a. Judicial admission

An admission made during the discovery process or a stipulation otherwise made during a proceeding is conclusive evidence, as is a statement made in a pleading, unless amended. Otherwise, although a statement in a pleading or an admission or stipulation made in another proceeding is usually admissible, it may generally be rebutted.

Note: A *withdrawn* guilty plea is generally not admissible in a subsequent civil or criminal proceeding (*see* § V.B.4. Plea Negotiation, *supra.*)

b. Adoptive admission

An adoptive admission is a statement of another person that a party expressly or impliedly adopts as his own. Fed. R. Evid. 801(d)(2)(B). Silence in response to a statement is considered an adoptive admission if:

    i)   The person was present and heard and understood the statement;

    ii)   The person had the ability and opportunity to deny the statement; and

    iii)   A reasonable person similarly situated would have denied the statement.

Post-arrest silence by a defendant who has received *Miranda* warnings may not be used as an adoptive admission of a statement made by another person (e.g., a police officer). *Doyle v. Ohio*, 426 U.S. 610 (1976).

c. Vicarious statements

A statement made by one person may be imputed to another based on the relationship between them. In determining whether a statement constitutes an opposing party's statement, the statement is considered, but the statement itself cannot establish the necessary relationship between the parties.

1) Employee or agent

A statement made by a party's agent or employee constitutes an opposing party's statement if it was made concerning a matter **within the scope of and during the course of the relationship.** Fed. R. Evid. 801(d)(2)(D).

2) Authorized speaker

A statement about a subject that is made by a person who is **authorized** by a party to make a statement on the subject constitutes an opposing party's statement. Fed. R. Evid. 801(d)(2)(C).

3) Co-conspirators

Although a statement made by one co-party is not admissible against another co-party based solely on their status as co-parties, a statement made by a co-conspirator **during and in furtherance of** the conspiracy is admissible as an opposing party's statement against other co-conspirators. Fed. R. Evid. 801(d)(2)(E). A statement made by a co-conspirator after being arrested generally is not admissible, since it was not made during the conspiracy.

VII. HEARSAY EXCEPTIONS

Although hearsay generally is inadmissible, the Federal Rules identify some situations in which hearsay is allowed, either because of necessity (i.e., the declarant is unavailable) or because the statements are inherently trustworthy, in which case the declarant's availability is immaterial.

A. DECLARANT UNAVAILABLE AS A WITNESS

There are five exceptions to the hearsay rule that apply only if the declarant is unavailable as a witness: former testimony, dying declaration, statement against interest, statement of personal or family history, and statement offered against a party that wrongfully caused the declarant's unavailability.

1. Unavailable Declarant

An unavailable declarant is a person who:

    i)   Is exempt on the grounds of privilege;

    ii)   Refuses to testify despite a court order to do so;

    iii) Lacks memory of the subject matter of the statement;

    iv) Is unable to testify due to death, infirmity, or physical or mental disability; or

    v)   Is absent and cannot be subpoenaed or otherwise made to be present.

A declarant is not deemed unavailable if the unavailability is due to the procurement or wrongdoing of the proponent of the statement in order to prevent the declarant from testifying at or attending the trial. Fed. R. Evid. 804(a).

2. Former Testimony

Testimony that was given **as a witness** at a trial, hearing, or lawful deposition is not excluded as hearsay if the party against whom the testimony is being offered (or, in a civil case, a party's predecessor-in-interest) had an **opportunity and similar motive** to develop the testimony by direct examination, redirect examination, or cross-examination. This exception applies whether the testimony was given during the current proceeding or during a different one, but the witness who gave the testimony must now be unavailable. Fed. R. Evid. 804(b)(1).

Grand jury testimony generally does not fall within the former testimony exception, but it may be admissible nonhearsay evidence as a prior inconsistent statement.

3. Dying Declaration

A statement qualifies as a "dying declaration" if:

    i)   The declarant **believes that her death is imminent**; and

    ii) The statement pertains to the **cause or circumstances** of the death she believes to be imminent.

Under this exception to the hearsay rule, although the declarant must be unavailable, the declarant need not have actually died in order for the statement to avoid exclusion as hearsay. The dying-declaration exception applies **only in homicide prosecutions and civil cases.** Fed. R. Evid. 804(b)(2).

4. Statement Against Interest

A statement made by a declarant who is unavailable to testify is not excluded as hearsay if the statement:

    i)   Was against the declarant's interest at the time it was made; and

    ii) Would not have been made by a reasonable person unless he believed it to be true.

Under this exception to the hearsay rule, the statement must have been against the declarant's proprietary or pecuniary interest, have invalidated the declarant's claim against someone, or have exposed the declarant to civil or criminal liability. A statement that would subject the declarant to criminal liability is not admissible unless corroborating circumstances clearly indicate the trustworthiness of the statement. Fed. R. Evid. 804(b)(3).

5. Statement of Personal or Family History

A statement concerning the unavailable declarant's own birth, adoption, marriage, divorce, legitimacy, familial relationship, or other similar fact of personal or family history is not excluded as hearsay. Fed. R. Evid. 804(b)(4).

6. Statement Against Party That Caused Declarant's Unavailability

Formerly known as the "forfeiture against wrongdoing" exception, a statement offered against a party that wrongfully caused the declarant's unavailability is not excluded as hearsay. Under this exception, the wrongful party forfeits the right to object to the admission of the declarant's statement as hearsay. The wrongdoing, which need not be criminal, may be accomplished by a deliberate act or by acquiescing to another's act, but must be done with the intent of preventing the witness from testifying. This exception applies to all parties, including the government. Fed. R. Evid. 804(b)(6).

Note: For the effect of the Confrontation Clause on this exception, *see* § VIII.A.1.b. Unavailability of the declarant, *infra*.

B. DECLARANT'S AVAILABILITY AS A WITNESS IMMATERIAL

The following hearsay exceptions do not require that the declarant be unavailable because the circumstances under which the statements were made suggest that the statements are inherently trustworthy. Fed. R. Evid. 803.

1. Present Sense Impression

A statement describing or explaining an event or condition that is made **while or immediately after the declarant perceived it** is not excluded as hearsay. Fed. R. Evid. 803(1).

a. Res gestae

A common-law hearsay exception labeled "res gestae" (meaning "things done") existed for a statement that was precipitated by an event or was about a contemporaneous condition. The Federal Rules do not contain a general res gestae exception but instead recognize several distinct, related exceptions, including exceptions for a present sense impression; an excited utterance; a dying declaration; a statement of mental, emotional, and physical condition; and a statement made for purposes of medical treatment or diagnosis.

2. Excited Utterance

A statement made about a startling event or condition **while the declarant is under the stress of excitement that it caused** is not excluded as hearsay. Under this exception to the hearsay rule, the event must shock or excite the declarant, and the statement must relate to the event, but the declarant need not be a participant in the event (i.e., the declarant can be a bystander). Fed. R. Evid. 803(2).

Example 1: Adele looks out the window and states, "It sure is raining hard tonight." She has made a statement of present sense impression, which is admissible to prove that it rained on the night in question.

Example 2: Bob discovers that he has a winning lottery ticket and shouts, "I just won a million dollars!" He has made an excited utterance, which is admissible to prove that he won the money.

Note: There is some overlap between these exceptions, and a statement, such as one describing a murder made immediately after the murder took place, could fall into both categories.

3. Statement of Mental, Emotional, or Physical Condition

A statement of the declarant's **then-existing** state of mind or emotional, sensory, or physical condition is not excluded as hearsay. Fed. R. Evid. 803(3).

a. State of mind

A statement of **present intent, motive, or plan** can be used to prove **conduct in conformity** with that state of mind. A statement of a memory or past belief is inadmissible hearsay when used to prove the fact remembered or believed, unless the statement relates to the validity or terms of the declarant's will.

> **EXAM NOTE:** Do not confuse this "state of mind" hearsay exception with circumstantial evidence of the declarant's state of mind, which is not hearsay. (*See* § VI.A.3.c. State of mind, *supra*.) To fall under the hearsay exception, the statement must be offered to prove that the declarant acted in accordance with his stated intent.

b. Physical condition

When a declarant's physical condition at a particular time is in question, a statement of the declarant's mental feeling, pain, or bodily health made **at that time** can be used to prove the **existence** of that condition but not its cause.

In most states, a statement made by a patient to a doctor relating to a **past** condition is not admissible under this exception. Under the Federal Rules, such a statement is admissible under the hearsay exception for statements for purposes of medical diagnosis or treatment (*see* 4. Statement Made for Medical Diagnosis or Treatment, *below*).

4. Statement Made for Medical Diagnosis or Treatment

A statement describing medical history or past or present symptoms is not hearsay if it is made for medical **diagnosis or treatment.** A statement of the cause or source of the condition is admissible as an exception to the rule against hearsay if it is reasonably pertinent to diagnosis or treatment. Fed. R. Evid. 803(4).

Effect of physician-patient privilege: A statement that falls within this hearsay exception still may be inadmissible if it is protected by the physician-patient privilege.

a. Statement made to a person other than a physician

The statement need not be made to a physician to fall under this exception. Statements to other medical personnel, including hospital attendants and ambulance drivers, or even to family members, may be included. Fed. R. Evid. 803(4), Notes of Advisory Committee.

b. Statement made to nontreating physician

Statements made to a physician consulted only for the purpose of enabling the physician to testify at trial are admissible. Fed. R. Evid. 803(4), Notes of Advisory Committee on Proposed Rules, Exception (4); Fed. R. Evid. 703.

c. Statement made by a person other than the patient

Under this hearsay exception, the statement need not necessarily be made by the patient, so long as it is made for the purpose of medical diagnosis or treatment. The relationship between the declarant and the patient usually determines admissibility—the closer the relationship, the stronger the motive to tell the truth, and, as such, the more presumably reliable the statement. The court must assess the probative value of the statement pursuant to Rule 403, weighing that value against the risk of prejudice, confusion, or waste of time. *See Weinstein's Evidence,* Vol. 4 (1993), p. 803-145.

5. Recorded Recollection

If a witness is unable to testify about a matter for which a record exists, that record is not excluded as hearsay if the following foundation is established:

i)   The record is on a matter that the witness once knew about;

ii) The record was made or adopted by the witness when the matter was fresh in the witness's memory;

iii) The record accurately reflects the witness's knowledge; and

iv) The witness states that she cannot recall the event well enough to testify fully and accurately, even after consulting the record on the stand.

Under this exception, the record, if admitted, may be read into evidence, but it may be received as an exhibit only if offered by an adverse party. Fed. R. Evid. 803(5).

Present recollection refreshed distinguished: An item—which need not be a writing—used to refresh a witness's recollection is not admitted into evidence (*see* § III.C.1. Present Recollection Refreshed, *supra*), so there is no hearsay problem.

6. Records of Regularly Conducted Activity (Business Records)

A record (e.g., memorandum, report, data compilation) of an act, event, condition, opinion, or diagnosis is not excluded as hearsay if:

i)   The record was kept in the course of a regularly conducted activity of a business, organization, occupation, or calling;

ii) The making of the record was a regular practice of that activity; and

iii) The record was made at or near the time by (or from information transmitted by) someone with knowledge.

Although this exception is commonly referred to as the "business records" exception, it extends to any regularly conducted activity of an organization, including a nonprofit organization. Fed. R. Evid. 101(b)(4); 803(6)(A)–(C).

Recorded recollection exception distinguished: Unlike the recorded recollection exception, the business records exception does not require the inability to remember, but it does require that the record be kept in the course of a regularly conducted activity.

a. Authentication

For the record to be admissible under the business records hearsay exception, the custodian of the record or other qualified witness may testify that the above requirements have been met. Alternatively, a record may be self-authenticated if properly certified (*see* § IV.A.2.e. Self-authenticating documents, *supra*). Fed. R. Evid. 803(6)(D).

b. Lack of trustworthiness

A business record that otherwise qualifies under this hearsay exception is nevertheless inadmissible if the opponent shows that the source of information for the record or the method or circumstances of its preparation indicate a lack of trustworthiness. Fed. R. Evid. 803(6)(E).

Anticipation of litigation: Records prepared in anticipation of litigation, such as an employee's accident report, may not qualify under this exception due to a lack of trustworthiness. *Palmer v. Hoffman*, 318 U.S. 109 (1943).

c. Medical records

Medical records are considered business records to the extent that the entries relate to diagnosis or treatment. Statements related to fault associated with the cause of injury generally do not qualify under the business records exception.

d. Police reports

A police report can qualify under the business records exception, but a statement made by a witness that is contained in the report does not generally qualify because the witness is not acting on behalf of the police in making the statement. The statement may, however, qualify under another hearsay exception, such as an opposing party's statement.

e. Absence of a record

Evidence that a **matter is not included in a record** of a regularly conducted activity may be admissible to prove that the matter did not occur or exist, provided that a record was regularly kept for a matter of that kind. The opponent may prevent admission by showing circumstances, including the possible source of the information, that indicate a lack of trustworthiness. Fed. R. Evid. 803(7).

7. Public Records

A hearsay exception applies to a record or statement of a public office or agency that sets out:

i) The **activities** of the office or agency;

ii) An **observation** of a person under a duty to report the observation (except for an observation of a law enforcement officer offered in a criminal case); or

iii) **Factual findings of a legal investigation,** when offered in a civil case or against the government in a criminal case.

Fed. R. Evid. 803(8).

Investigative reports: In addition to factual findings, opinions, evaluations, and conclusions contained in an investigative report that are based on factual findings are included in the public records exception. *Beech Craft Corp. v. Rainey*, 488 U.S. 153 (1988).

a. Lack of trustworthiness

As with the business records exception, the court may exclude any evidence offered under this exception if the opponent shows that the source of the information or other circumstances indicate a lack of trustworthiness. Fed. R. Evid. 803(8)(B).

b. Absence of a record

Similarly, testimony that a diligent search failed to disclose a public record or statement may be admitted to prove that the record or statement does not exist, or that a matter did not occur or exist, if a public office regularly kept a record of statements for a matter of that kind. In a criminal case, a prosecutor must provide the defense with written notice of the intent to offer such evidence at least 14 days before trial, and the defendant has seven days from receipt of notice to object in writing. Fed. R. Evid. 803(10), *Melendez-Diaz v. Massachusetts*, 557 U.S. 305 (2009).

c. Public records of vital statistics

A record of a birth, death, or marriage is not excluded as hearsay if the event is reported to a public office in accordance with a legal duty. Fed. R. Evid. 803(9).

8. Learned Treatises

A statement contained in a treatise, periodical, or pamphlet is not excluded as hearsay if:

i)   An expert witness **relied on the statement during direct examination** or it was **called to the expert's attention on cross-examination**; and

ii) The publication is established as a **reliable authority** by admission or testimony of the expert witness, by another expert's testimony, or by judicial notice.

If admitted, the statement is read into evidence, but the publication itself may not be received as an exhibit. Fed. R. Evid. 803(18).

9. Judgment of Previous Conviction

Evidence of a final judgment of conviction is not excluded as hearsay if:

i)   The judgment was entered after a trial or guilty plea, but not a plea of no contest (i.e., *nolo contendere*);

ii) The conviction was for a crime punishable by death or imprisonment for more than one year; and

iii) The evidence is offered to prove any fact essential to sustain the judgment.

If the prosecutor in a criminal case offers evidence of a final judgment of conviction for a purpose other than impeachment, the judgment must have been against the defendant. The pendency of an appeal may be shown but does not affect admissibility. Fed. R. Evid. 803(22).

Traffic offense: A driver's guilty plea to a traffic offense that is punishable by a fine or imprisonment for one year or less cannot be used as evidence of the driver's negligence under this hearsay exception.

10. Other Exceptions

Other hearsay exceptions for which the declarant's availability is immaterial include:

i) A statement concerning personal or family history, such as a birth, death, marriage, or divorce contained in a regularly kept record of a religious organization (Fed. R. Evid. 803(11));

ii) A statement of fact in a marriage or baptismal certificate (Fed. R. Evid. 803(12));

iii) A statement of fact about personal or family history contained in a family record, such as a Bible or an engraving on a ring (Fed. R. Evid. 803(13));

iv) Records of, and statements in, documents affecting an interest in property (Fed. R. Evid. 803(14), (15));

v) Statements in ancient documents (i.e., authenticated documents in existence at least 20 years) (Fed. R. Evid. 803(16));

vi) Market reports and similar commercial publications generally relied upon by the public (Fed. R. Evid. 803(17));

vii) Reputation concerning personal or family history, boundaries or general history, or character (Fed. R. Evid. 803(19)–(21)); and

viii) A judgment admitted to prove a matter of personal, family, or general history or a boundary, if the matter was essential to the judgment and could be proved by evidence of reputation. Fed. R. Evid. 803(23).

C. RESIDUAL EXCEPTION

There is a "catch-all" exception for a statement that is not otherwise covered by the Federal Rules. A hearsay statement may be admissible under this exception if:

i) The statement has equivalent circumstantial guarantees of trustworthiness;

ii) It is offered as evidence of a material fact;

iii) It is more probative on the point for which it is offered than any other evidence that the proponent can reasonably obtain; and

iv) Admission will best serve the purposes of the Federal Rules and the interests of justice.

The proponent must give an adverse party reasonable notice before the trial or hearing of the intent to offer the statement as well as its particulars, including the declarant's name and address. Fed. R. Evid. 807.

VIII. CONSTITUTIONAL LIMITATIONS

A. HEARSAY EVIDENCE RESTRICTIONS

Hearsay evidence has successfully been challenged on two constitutional grounds.

1. Sixth Amendment—Confrontation Clause and Hearsay Evidence

In a criminal trial, the Confrontation Clause of the Sixth Amendment requires that, in order to admit an out-of-court testimonial statement of a declarant (i.e., hearsay) against a defendant:

i) The declarant must be unavailable; and

ii) The defendant must have had a prior opportunity to cross-examine the declarant.

Crawford v. Washington, 541 U.S. 36 (2004).

Note: The Supreme Court suggested in dicta in *Crawford* that the Confrontation Clause does not preclude the admission of a dying declaration as hearsay, even if the statement is testimonial, since this common-law exception predates the Confrontation Clause. *Crawford v. Washington*, 541 U.S. 36, 56, n.6 (2004).

a. Testimonial statements

In determining whether a statement is testimonial, an objective analysis of the circumstances, rather than the subjective purpose of the participants, is key. A statement made during a police interrogation that had the primary purpose of ascertaining past criminal conduct is testimonial, as is a certificate of a governmental laboratory analyst that a substance was an illegal drug. *Melendez-Diaz v. Massachusetts*, 557 U.S. 305 (2009).

By contrast, a statement made to police during the course of questioning with the primary purpose of enabling police to provide assistance to meet an ongoing emergency (e.g., a 911 call) is not testimonial, *Davis v. Washington*, 547 U.S. 813 (2006), nor is a statement made by a fatally wounded victim as to the identity of his assailant in response to police questioning, because the statement was made to assist the police in addressing an on-going emergency, *Michigan v. Bryant*, 562 U.S. 344 (2011).

b. Unavailability of the declarant

The Confrontation Clause mandates that the use of hearsay evidence based on the forfeiture-by-wrongdoing exception requires the defendant to have acted with the particular purpose of making the witness unavailable. The mere fact that the declarant is unavailable due to the defendant's act (e.g., murder of the witness) is not sufficient to establish such a purpose when the defendant is on trial for the act that made the witness unavailable. *Giles v. California*, 554 U.S. 353 (2008).

2. Fourteenth Amendment—Due Process Clause

The Due Process Clause of the Fourteenth Amendment may prevent application of a hearsay rule when such rule unduly restricts a defendant's ability to mount a defense.

Example: Application of a state evidentiary rule that prevents a defendant from using a witness's hearsay statements to impeach the witness's in-court testimony operated to deny the defendant the ability to present witnesses in the defendant's own defense. *Chamber v. Mississippi*, 410 U.S. 284 (1973).

B. FACE-TO-FACE CONFRONTATION

The Confrontation Clause reflects a preference for face-to-face confrontation of a defendant and a witness in court.

Example: A defendant who is charged with committing a sex crime against a child can force the child victim to testify in open court rather than from behind a screen that blocks the witness's view of the defendant. *Coy v. Iowa*, 487 U.S. 1012 (1988).

This type of confrontation may be denied, however, if there is an important public interest at stake, such as protecting a child.

Example: A child victim of a sex crime could testify via a one-way closed circuit television when there was a specific finding that the child witness would suffer serious emotional distress if the witness was required to testify in open court. *Maryland v. Craig*, 497 U.S. 836 (1990). The Court in *Coy*, above, refused to recognize a *presumption* of trauma to witnesses who were victims of sexual abuse.

Wills and Trusts

WILLS AND TRUSTS

Table of Contents

WILLS AND TRUSTS

I. THE "RIGHT" TO INHERIT AND CONVEY

A. GENERALLY

While a decedent generally has the right to dispose of her property upon her death, states have broad authority to regulate that process. The complete abolition of the rights of an owner to dispose of her property rights, however, is a taking without just compensation, violating the owner's rights under the Fifth Amendment to the U.S. Constitution. *Hodel v. Irving*, 481 U.S. 784 (1987) (escheat provision of Indian Land Consolidation Act of 1983 constituted unconstitutional taking of decedent's property without just compensation).

B. PROBLEM OF THE "DEAD HAND"

Testators sometimes condition gifts to beneficiaries on the beneficiary doing something or behaving in a certain way after the testator has died. These attempts to control behavior from beyond the grave have generally been held **valid**, unless they violate public policy or the enforcement of the testator's condition would constitute state action that violates a fundamental constitutional right of the beneficiary.

1. Restraints on Marriage

a. Absolute restrictions are prohibited

Provisions in a will imposing a forfeiture of a gift if the beneficiary should ever marry are **void** as against public policy. Similarly, requirements that a beneficiary may marry only with the consent of executors or trustees who would profit under the terms of the will by withholding consent have been held invalid.

b. Partial restraints are generally valid

Most provisions, however, that might initially be viewed as absolute restraints on marriage have been construed as mere statements of the testator's motives or attempts by the testator to provide for a person until marriage, and as such, have been upheld. Conditions in partial restraint of marriage are not against public policy if they merely impose reasonable restrictions on marriage or attempt to prevent an ill-advised marriage (e.g., to a specific individual). A provision conditioning a gift upon the beneficiary's not marrying a person outside his own religious group has been held to be valid. *Shapira v. Union National Bank*, 39 Ohio Misc. 28 (1974) (upholding testator's testamentary gifts to sons requiring each to be married within seven years of testator's death to Jewish girl, both of whose parents were Jewish).

2. Other Conditions Violating Public Policy

a. Gift requiring practice of religion

Testamentary gifts that require a beneficiary to practice a particular religion have generally been held to be invalid as violative of the freedom of religion.

b. Gift requiring separation or divorce

Testamentary gifts that are conditioned on a beneficiary divorcing or separating from his spouse are void as against public policy. A gift that provides for a beneficiary's support in the event of divorce or separation, however, would be valid. Courts look to the intent of the testator to decide validity. If the testator intended to encourage the divorce or separation through the gift, it will be invalid.

3. Remedy

In the event a conditional gift is found to violate public policy, to decide what happens to the gift, courts look to whether the instrument providing for the gift contains a "gift-over" clause that specifies what is to happen in the event a condition is not satisfied. If there is a gift-over clause, a court will strike the gift as violating public policy, but the court will not generally allow the beneficiary subject to the condition to take. Instead, the alternative beneficiary under the gift-over clause will receive the gift. If there is no gift-over clause in the instrument, most courts strike the condition and allow the beneficiary subject to the condition to take the gift despite the condition.

> **EXAM NOTE:** On an exam, remember that conditional gifts are generally valid, so long as they do not fall within one of the exceptions discussed above.

II. INTRODUCTION TO PROBATE

Each state has a set of statutes (i.e., a Probate Code), which governs the intestate distribution scheme, the requirements for a valid will, and rules of construction and interpretation, etc. Probate performs three key functions: (1) **provides evidence** of transfers of title; (2) **protects creditors** by requiring payment of debts; and (3) **directs distribution** of the decedent's property after creditors are paid.

A. TERMINOLOGY

1. Personal Representative

When a person dies and probate is necessary, the first step is the appointment of a personal representative to oversee the winding up of the decedent's affairs. A personal representative is either named in the will (generally called an "executor") or appointed by the court (generally called an "administrator"). Any person with the capacity to contract may serve as a personal representative.

2. Probate Court

The court that supervises the administration of the probate estate is generally referred to as the probate court. One court in each county has jurisdiction over administration of decedent's estates. Sometimes this court is called a "surrogate's court," an "orphan's court," or the probate division of the district court. To "go through probate" means to have an estate administered by a probate court.

3. Probate Versus Non-Probate Property

A decedent's assets as of the date of his death are divided between probate and non-probate property.

a. Probate property

Probate property is property that passes under intestacy or under the decedent's will. Distribution of probate property generally requires a court proceeding involving the probate of a will or a finding of intestacy followed by appointment of a personal representative to settle the probate estate.

b. Non-probate property

Non-probate property passes under an instrument other than a will. Distribution of non-probate property does not involve a court proceeding, but is made in accordance with the terms of the controlling contract or trust or deed.

1) Joint tenancy property

Both real and personal property that is held under a joint tenancy will pass outside of probate. The decedent's interest vanishes at death and the survivor has the whole property, with no need for probate.

2) Life insurance

Life insurance proceeds from a policy on the decedent's life are paid by the insurance company directly to the beneficiary named in the insurance contract upon receipt of the insured's death certificate. No probate is needed.

3) Contracts with payable-on-death provisions

When a decedent has a contract with a bank, an employer, or some other entity to distribute property upon the decedent's death to a named beneficiary, all the beneficiary need do is provide a death certificate to the custodian of the property. Pension plans, for example, often provide survivor benefits.

4) Trust interests

Property held in a testamentary trust created under the decedent's will, will pass through probate. Property put into an inter vivos trust during the decedent's lifetime, however, does not pass through probate.

> **EXAM NOTE:** When analyzing how to distribute property, first pass any **non-probate property** to those identified in the non-probate instrument. Any remaining property is **probate property**, and the takers of probate property depend on whether there is a valid will. If the decedent did not have a valid will (or if there is property not properly disposed of in the will), the property is distributed **intestate**, pursuant to the jurisdiction's statute on distribution.

B. PROCEDURE

1. Jurisdiction

The administration of the decedent's probate estate is governed by state statute. The Uniform Probate Code (UPC), originally promulgated in 1969 and substantially revised in 1990, 2006, and 2008, is representative of statutes regulating probate procedure in the states.

Note that because only a small minority of states has adopted the 2008 amendments, references to the UPC in this outline are to the 2006 version.

a. Primary jurisdiction

The county in which the decedent was domiciled at the time of his death has jurisdiction over the decedent's personal property and over any real property within that jurisdiction.

b. Notice

Most jurisdictions require that notice be given to interested parties before the administrator is appointed.

c. Ancillary jurisdiction

Ancillary jurisdiction applies to real property located in another jurisdiction for the purpose of protecting local creditors and ensuring adherence to the jurisdiction's recording system.

2. **Personal Representative**

Each state has a detailed statutory procedure for authorizing an executor or administrator to act on behalf of the estate. If an executor is not named in a will, then the court will appoint an administrator. In either case, the authority of the personal representative to act on behalf of the estate comes from the court. Generally, the personal representative must also file a bond, unless the will states otherwise.

a. **Principal duties**

The principal duties of the personal representative are to:

i) **Provide notice** to legatees, heirs, and claimants;

ii) **Inventory** and collect the assets of the decedent;

iii) **Manage** the assets during administration;

iv) **Receive** and pay claims of creditors and tax collectors; and

v) **Distribute** the remaining assets to those entitled thereto.

The scope of power to administer the estate varies among jurisdictions. Some jurisdictions permit unsupervised administration absent special circumstances with a final accounting to the court, while others require constant supervision and authorization.

b. **Fiduciary duty**

The personal representative of an estate is a fiduciary, and owes the highest duty of loyalty and care to those whose interests he represents, which means that he cannot profit from the trust instilled in him. The personal representative is not discharged from his fiduciary duties until the court grants such discharge. Common law permits a personal representative to be held personally liable for the actions of the estate. Under the UPC, personal representatives can be sued in their representative capacity only for a breach of the fiduciary duty. Unif. Probate Code §§ 3-712; 7-306.

c. **Administration**

After the court issues its "letters testamentary" or "letters of administration," the personal representative is authorized to begin performing his duties on behalf of the estate.

Bona fide purchasers from personal representatives or heirs are protected after the granting of letters of administration, even if the will presented at the time the letters were granted is subsequently invalidated.

3. **Ex Parte Versus Notice Probate**

Under common law, a will could be probated at any time, even decades after the testator's death. The UPC provides that probate proceedings must be brought within **three years of death**, after which there is a presumption of intestacy. The party requesting probate can choose to have it occur through either ex parte probate or notice probate. Unif. Probate Code § 3-102.

a. **Ex parte probate (informal or no notice)**

Ex parte probate under the UPC is informal and requires no notice for the representative to petition for appointment. The original will must accompany the petition and the executor must swear that, to the best of his knowledge, the will was validly executed.

Within 30 days of appointment, the personal representative must give notice to all interested persons, including heirs apparently disinherited by the will.

b. Notice probate (formal)

Notice probate under the UPC is a formal judicial determination made after notice is given to interested parties. Any interested party can demand formal probate. A formal proceeding may be used to probate a will, to block an informal proceeding, or to secure a declaratory judgment of intestacy. Formal proceedings are final if not appealed.

4. Creditors' Claims

a. Period of limitations

Each state has **non-claim statutes** that bar creditors from filing claims after a specified time period has elapsed. If a claim is not made within that specified period after probate is opened, then the claims are barred.

b. Notice

The personal representative must provide notice to creditors of the estate, advising them of when and where to file claims. Failure to give the proper notice to creditors extends the time period they have to file a claim against the estate.

c. Priority of claims

All jurisdictions have statutes that provide the order in which expenses and debts are to be paid:

i) Administrative expenses;

ii) Last medical expenses and funeral expenses;

iii) Family allowance;

iv) Tax claims;

v) Secured claims;

vi) Judgments against the decedent; and

vii) All other claims.

5. Closing the Estate

The personal representative is expected to complete the administration and distribute the assets promptly, including paying creditors and tax collectors. Judicial approval of the personal representative's actions is required to release the personal representative from potential liability. The personal representative may receive compensation for his services. The compensation is determined by statute based on the estate's value, or by the court. However, the court may deny compensation if the personal representative has breached his fiduciary duties.

C. AVOIDING PROBATE

The probate process can cost a lot of money. To avoid probate, theoretically, a person could put all of her property into non-probate arrangements. This can often be difficult to do. All states have a small estate probate process that allows for expedited probate with very limited court supervision to minimize the cost and time required. In Louisiana, "universal succession" applies to automatically pass the property to the appropriate heirs by operation of law, with no need for probate. The heirs are then required to pay the decedent's creditors from the property they receive.

III. PROFESSIONAL RESPONSIBILITY

A. MALPRACTICE CLAIMS IN ESTATE PLANNING

There is a split between the common law approach and the majority modern approach as to whether an attorney representing a client in wills and trusts work owes a professional duty to both the client who hired her and the intended beneficiaries of the client's estate planning.

1. Common Law Approach

At common law, courts construed the attorney-client relationship narrowly to protect attorneys from malpractice claims by persons who thought they would take under the decedent's will or other estate planning mechanisms but did not. For tort claims of malpractice, the common law held that the attorney owed a duty of reasonable care only to the testator client and not to any of the intended beneficiaries. Only a testator, while alive, or the personal representative of the estate after the testator's death, could sue for malpractice based on tort. For contract claims of malpractice, the common law required privity of contract and an attorney is only in privity of contract with her client, the testator. Thus, only the testator, while alive, or the personal representative of the estate after the testator's death, could sue the attorney for breach of contract.

2. Majority Modern Approach

The majority approach today extends the attorney-client relationship for both tort and contract purposes to intended beneficiaries, allowing them to also sue the drafting attorney for malpractice with regard to the testator's estate planning. For tort malpractice, courts look to whether the injury to the intended beneficiaries was "reasonably foreseeable." See *Simpson v. Calivas*, 650 A.2d 318 (N.H. 1994) (attorney drafting will owes duty of reasonable care to intended beneficiaries of will). For breach of contract, courts adopting the modern approach hold that a non-party may sue if she qualifies as a third-party beneficiary of the contract between the attorney and the testator.

> **EXAM NOTE:** If the fact pattern on an essay exam does not tell you which approach the jurisdiction follows with regard to malpractice claims, be prepared to provide an analysis under both the common law and modern approaches.

B. DUTY TO DISCLOSE

An estate planning attorney may have a duty to disclose what would otherwise be considered the confidential information of the testator to another client of the attorney. In *A v. B*, 158 N.J. 51 (N.J. 1999), a law firm represented a husband and wife for purposes of planning their estates. Both the husband and wife signed a waiver of conflict of interest form, which permitted the law firm to disclose confidential information obtained from one party to the other, but said nothing about information obtained from outside sources. As the result of a clerical error, another attorney in the firm agreed to represent a woman who wanted to bring a paternity action against the husband for fathering her child. On realizing the conflict, the law firm withdrew from representing the woman in the paternity action. The estate planning lawyers believed, however, that they had an ethical duty to disclose to the wife the possible existence of an illegitimate child and the potential estate planning consequences of such a situation. Invoking the ethical duty of confidentiality, the husband sought to restrain the firm from revealing this information. The court concluded that under Rule 1.6(c) of the New Jersey Rules of Professional Conduct, the law firm was permitted (but not required) to disclose the confidential information to rectify the consequences of a client's criminal, illegal, or fraudulent act in furtherance of which the lawyer's services had been used. Concluding that the husband's decision not to disclose to the wife the information would have constituted a fraud on the wife, the court found disclosure proper. Note that New Jersey's Rules of

Professional Conduct are broader than the ABA Model Rules, which permit disclosure only when failure to do so would likely result in imminent death or substantial bodily harm. ABA Model Rule 1.6.

IV.   INTESTATE SUCCESSION

Intestacy is the default statutory distribution scheme that applies when an individual dies without having effectively disposed of all of his property through non-probate instruments or a valid will. Intestacy statutes vary from state to state, but they generally favor the decedent's **surviving spouse** and **issue (descendants)**, followed by the decedent's other relations, and they direct that property escheat to the state only if none of the statutory takers survive the decedent. The actual intent of the decedent is irrelevant with regard to any property that passes by intestacy.

The individuals who are entitled to a decedent's property if she dies intestate are the decedent's **"heirs."**

> **EXAM NOTE:** On an exam, if a will fails to dispose of all of the decedent's property, analyze the problem using the rules of intestacy for any property not included in the will.

A.   GENERALLY

The primary policy involved in framing an intestacy statute is to carry out the probable intent of the average intestate decedent. The most common statutory scheme assumes that the decedent would wish for her surviving spouse to succeed to all of her property if she had no surviving issue, and otherwise to share her property with her surviving issue.

1.   UPC Intestacy Scheme

The UPC is considerably more generous to the surviving spouse than are the provisions of most state intestacy laws. Under the UPC:

i)   If all of the decedent's descendants are also descendants of the surviving spouse, and the surviving spouse has no other descendants, then the surviving spouse takes the entire estate to the exclusion of the decedent's descendants.

ii)   If the decedent's descendants are not also the descendants of the surviving spouse, the surviving spouse takes $300,000 and 75% of the remainder of the estate if there are no issue, but there is a surviving parent of the decedent.

iii)   The surviving spouse receives $225,000 and 50% of the remainder of the estate if all of the decedent's issue are also issue of the surviving spouse and the surviving spouse has other issue.

iv)   If the decedent has issue not related to the surviving spouse, then the surviving spouse receives $150,000 and 50% of the remainder of the estate.

v)   If the decedent has a spouse but no descendants or parents, then the surviving spouse takes the entire estate.

Unif. Probate Code §§ 2-102, 2-103, 2-105.

In addition to favoring the surviving spouse, the UPC also favors the state. The decedent's property escheats to the state much sooner than under most state statutes, as it does not consider the issue of parents. Unif. Probate Code § 2-102(1)(i).

> **Example:** Wife dies with an estate worth $550,000 and is survived by her husband and a child from a prior marriage. Since there is a child from a prior marriage, the husband will take $150,000 plus 50% of the remainder of the estate ($200,000), or $350,000. If, however, Wife dies with $550,000, survived by her husband, her parents, her cousin Rhonda, and her best friend Jane, but not by any children, the

husband takes the entire estate under the UPC. The husband, as the surviving spouse, will take everything over all other people except children or issue.

2. Community Property

The general intestate distribution scheme presumes that the jurisdiction does not recognize community property. Community property considers all property acquired during a marriage as jointly owned by the parties unless it is a gift, inheritance, or devise given to only one spouse. In a community property jurisdiction, the community property of the decedent is divided equally and 50% of the community property is given to the surviving spouse. If the decedent was intestate, then the surviving spouse generally receives the decedent's remaining 50% share of the community property. The decedent's separate property is then distributed pursuant to the general intestate scheme.

B. INTESTATE SHARE OF SURVIVING SPOUSE

1. Marriage Requirement

To be entitled to take under an intestacy statute, the surviving spouse must have been legally married to the decedent. Several states, including Connecticut, Iowa, Maine, Massachusetts, New Hampshire, New York and Vermont, recognize same-sex marriage and spouses in such marriages would be entitled to intestate succession rights.

a. Cohabitation insufficient

Generally, unmarried couples who simply live together do not qualify as spouses.

1) Common law marriage

Some states recognize common law marriage, which exists when the parties: (i) agree they are married; (ii) cohabitate as husband and wife; and (iii) hold themselves out in public as married, even though no marriage ceremony has taken place and no license has been issued by the state.

2) Domestic partners and civil unions

A minority of jurisdictions afford couples who have registered as domestic partners or entered civil unions similar treatment to spouses for inheritance purposes.

b. Putative spouses

Even if a marriage is not valid, as long as one party believes in good faith in its validity, the spouses are termed putative and qualify as spouses for inheritance purposes.

c. Abandonment

In many states, if one spouse abandons the other for a prescribed period, then the marital relationship is terminated and the two are no longer considered spouses. The abandonment must be voluntary, permanent, and non-consensual on the part of the spouse who has been abandoned.

d. Separation

Spouses who are separated, or are in the process of obtaining a divorce, remain spouses until the issuance of a final decree of dissolution of the marriage. Decrees of separation that do not terminate the status of husband and wife do not constitute a divorce. Unif. Probate Code § 2-208(a).

2. Survival Requirements

If an heir of a decedent fails to meet the survival requirement, then the heir is considered to have predeceased the decedent and does not take under the laws of intestacy.

a. Common law

The common-law requirement was that an heir must be proved to have survived the decedent by a **preponderance of the evidence**.

b. Uniform Simultaneous Death Act (USDA)

The USDA has been enacted in most states in an attempt to alleviate the problem of simultaneous death in determining inheritance. Originally, as enacted in 1940, the USDA essentially codified the common law rule, providing that when there was no sufficient evidence as to which person survived the other, the party claiming a right to take was to be treated is having predeceased the decedent. *See e.g., Janus v. Tarasewicz*, 135 Ill. App. 3d 936 (Ill. App. Ct. 1st Dist. 1985) (holding that there was sufficient evidence to find that wife placed on respirator survived husband).

The common law (original USDA) standard came under criticism because it was difficult to determine what constituted "sufficient evidence" of the order of deaths. The USDA standard was then changed in 1991 to require that an heir be proven **by clear and convincing evidence** to have survived the decedent by **120 hours** (five days) in order to take under his will or by intestacy, unless the testator has provided otherwise in his will. The 120-hour rule does not apply if its application would result in an escheat to the state.

The USDA is applicable to all types of transfers of property, whether through will, joint tenancy, contract, or intestacy. However, the USDA is applied only when there is no instrument to state otherwise.

c. UPC

The UPC has the same requirements with respect to survival as the USDA. The UPC also requires clear and convincing evidence that an individual in gestation at the decedent's death lived for 120 hours after the death. Unif. Probate Code § 2-104.

d. Determination of death

At common law, in most instances, death can be determined based upon the irreversible cessation of circulatory and respiratory functions. The modern standard redefines death as brain death. There are no established criteria for brain death, but a court will require that the determination of death under either the modern or the common-law standard adhere to the usual and customary standards of medical practice. *See Janus v. Tarasewicz*, 135 Ill. App. 3d 936 (Ill. App. Ct. 1st Dist. 1985) (determination of legal death must be made in accordance with usual and customary standards of medical practice).

e. Burden of proof

Survivorship is a question of fact that must be proven by the **party whose claim depends on survivorship** (i.e., the person attempting to take under the laws of intestacy has the burden of proof). At common law, a preponderance of the evidence standard applied. Some jurisdictions, including the UPC and USDA, have applied the higher "clear and convincing evidence" standard as a litigation deterrent.

Example 1: Husband and Wife are in a car accident together. Husband is pronounced dead at the scene. Wife is in a coma and does not die for another two days. Husband is survived by his son, A. Wife is survived by her daughter, B. They are both children from prior marriages. Wife has a $500,000 estate. Husband has a $1 million estate. Since Husband and Wife are treated under the USDA as having died simultaneously because they died within 120 hours of each other, each is treated as having predeceased the other for purposes of disposing of each person's estate. In which case, under the UPC intestacy statute (*see* § IV.A.1, *supra*), Husband's estate ($1 million) goes to his son A. Wife's estate ($500,000) goes to her daughter B. Simultaneous death means that in dividing Husband's estate, we assume that the wife had predeceased him, so that he did not have a surviving spouse. But in dividing up the wife's estate, we assume that her husband predeceased her and so she does not have a surviving spouse.

Example 2: Contrast example 1 with what happens when death is not simultaneous. Thus, Husband dies at scene of car accident, but Wife is rushed to the hospital and put on life support and does not actually die for more than 120 hours. After that 120 hour point, Wife is treated as having survived Husband. Thus, Wife will take her intestate share from Husband's estate. He had a $1 million estate. Under the UPC intestacy statute (*see* § IV.A.1, *supra*), she therefore takes $150,000 plus 50% of the rest of the estate ($850,000), which equals $575,000. Wife dies a few days later. Her daughter, B, then will take all of Wife's estate -- the $500,000 she had, and the money that Wife inherited from Husband who died first. Thus, B gets $1,075,000. A, Husband's son, only gets $425,000 (50% of $850,000) under this scenario.

C. ISSUE

1. Qualifications

A decedent's issue includes all lineal descendants, including children, grandchildren, great-grandchildren, and the like, but excluding the descendants of living lineal descendants. A parent-child relationship must be established for an individual to be classified as issue of another.

a. Married parents

1) Presumption

A child of a marriage is presumed to be the natural child of the parties to the marriage.

2) Posthumously-born children

A child conceived before but born after the death of his mother's husband is a posthumously-born child. In most jurisdictions, a rebuttable presumption exists that the child is the natural child of the deceased husband if the child is born within 280 days (ten lunar months) of the husband's death. A posthumously-born child born more than 280 days after the husband's death has the burden of proving that he is the deceased husband's natural child.

Note: The Uniform Parentage Act, Article 2, § 4 increases the number of days in which the rebuttable presumption applies to 300.

b. Adoption

References in a will to "children" are deemed to include adopted children unless the will otherwise indicates. An adopted child is treated as a biological child for purposes of inheritance.

1) Inheritance from and through parents

Adoption generally curtails all inheritance rights between the natural parents and the child. Unif. Probate Code § 2-119(a).

Historically, many courts held that an adopted child had the right to inherit from, but not through, her adoptive parents. The majority rule today, however, is to permit an adopted child to inherit both from and through her adoptive parents, unless the will expresses a contrary intent.

2) Stepparent exception

The majority of jurisdictions, including the UPC, modify the general rule curtailing an adoptee's inheritance rights from her natural parents when the adoption is by a stepparent. The adoption does sever the parent-child relationship with either natural parent, essentially replacing the child's family with a "fresh start." The adoption does not curtail the parent-child relationship or the inheritance rights of a natural parent who is married to the stepparent. Rather, the adoption establishes a parent-child relationship between the stepparent and child, including full inheritance rights in both directions.

However, a parent-child relationship still does exist with the other genetic parent, but only for the purpose of the right of the adoptee or a descendant of the adoptee to inherit from or through that other genetic parent. Unif. Probate Code § 2-119(b).

A minority of jurisdictions hold that the parent-child relationship with the natural parent is entirely severed. *See, e.g., Hall v. Vallandingham*, 75 Md. App. 187 (Md. Ct. Spec. App. 1988) (holding that an adopted child is no longer considered a child of either natural parent and loses all rights of inheritance from the natural parents).

Example: H and W are married and have a child, A. H dies, and W then marries Z, who subsequently adopts A. H's brother dies without any children of his own, without any issue, and without a surviving spouse. Can A take through his natural father, H, who would have taken part of his brother's estate, even though A has been adopted by Z? Under the majority rule, yes. The decedent was a descendent of the adopted child's grandparent. He is taking from his uncle. His uncle was the son of his grandparent. The adoptive parent, Z, was married to the child's other biological parent. The same thing happens if instead of H dying, H and W had divorced and W and Z had married and Z adopted A. Even then, the adoption will not prevent A from inheriting from or through his natural father.

3) Adoption after death of both parents

The UPC provides that when a child is adopted after the death of both natural parents, the child retains the right to inherit through both natural parents. Unif. Probate Code § 2-119(d).

4) Adult adoption

Most state intestacy schemes make no distinction between the adoption of a minor and the adoption of an adult. In some states, adoption of a person with whom one has had a sexual relationship is not permitted.

The majority rule today is to permit an adoptee, whether child or adult, to inherit both from and through her adoptive parents, unless the will expresses a contrary intent. Some courts, though, have been reluctant to apply this rule when the adoptee is an adult. In *Minary v. Citizens Fidelity Bank & Trust Co.*, 419 S.W.2d 340 (Ky. Ct. App. 1967), a testatrix's will devised her estate in trust with income to her husband and three children for life and, on the death of the last beneficiary, the principal to be distributed to her "then surviving heirs" under the then existing Kentucky intestacy rules. After the testatrix's death, the husband and two of the three children died. The remaining child adopted his adult wife. Following the last child's death, his wife demanded that the bank distribute the principal of the trust to her, as an heir of the testatrix. The court held that the adoption statutes should not be interpreted to allow adoption of an adult for the purpose of bringing that person under the provisions of a pre-existing testamentary instrument when the person was not intended to be so covered by the instrument.

5) Inheritance from and through an adopted child

If an adopted child dies intestate, his property is distributed among those individuals who would have been his heirs had he actually been born to his adoptive parents. Unif. Probate Code § 2-119(b).

c. Equitable adoption

1) In general

Equitable adoption involves a situation in which the natural parents transfer their child to a person who agrees to adopt the child and treats the child as her own but then fails to legally adopt the child. Under the principles of equity, the child will be treated as the child of the person who promised to adopt with regard to the distribution of that person's intestate estate.

Thus, for example, a foster child who was never legally adopted may be treated as the child of a foster parent who dies intestate if the foster parent made an agreement with the natural parents of the child to adopt him and proceeded to treat the child as his own.

2) Agreement

The agreement may be oral or in writing and may be express or implied.

3) Limitations

Generally, under equitable adoption, a child can inherit from, but not through, the equitable adoptive parent. Additionally, the equitable adoptive parents cannot inherit from or through the child. Unlike a true adoption, the parent-child relationship and the inheritance rights between the child and the natural parents are not affected.

4) Cases

In *O'Neal v. Wilkes*, 263 Ga. 850 (Ga. 1994), a woman who had been raised by the testator, but never formally adopted, petitioned for a declaration of equitable adoption. The court denied the claim, finding that the woman's aunt, who had transferred physical custody of the woman when she was twelve to the testator, never had legal authority to consent to an adoption by the testator. The court held that a contract to adopt may not be enforced in equity unless it was entered into by a person with legal authority to consent to the adoption. The dissent argued that the doctrine of equitable adoption should apply whenever a child is led to believe that she was adopted.

Other courts have been less strict in requiring a contract. In *Welch v. Wilson*, 516 S.E.2d (W.Va. 1999), for example, the court did not require a contract and primarily relied on the evidence of a close, loving parent-child relationship to allow a woman who was raised by her grandmother and step-grandfather to be treated as having been equitably adopted and to inherit the step grandfather's estate.

d. Half-bloods

At common law, relatives who shared only one common parent were not entitled to inherit from or through one another. The UPC and the majority of jurisdictions have abolished the distinction between whole- and half-blooded relatives. Unif. Probate Code § 2-107.

e. Children born out of wedlock

1) Common-law and modern trend

The common-law rule was that if a child was born out of wedlock, then he could not inherit from his natural father. The modern trend adopted by most jurisdictions is that an out-of-wedlock child cannot inherit from his natural father unless:

    i)   The father **subsequently married** the natural mother;

    ii) The father **held the child out** as his own and either received the child into his home or provided support;

    iii) **Paternity was proven** by clear and convincing evidence after the father's death; or

    iv) **Paternity was adjudicated** during the lifetime of the father by a preponderance of the evidence. It is unconstitutional to deny inheritance rights to a nonmarital child when the father's paternity was adjudicated during his lifetime. *See Trimble v. Gordon*, 430 U.S. 762 (1977); *Reed v. Campbell*, 476 U.S. 852 (1986).

The current trend is to allow more ways for out-of-wedlock children to prove parentage after the alleged parent is deceased.

2) Uniform Parentage Act (UPA)

The UPA requires proof of paternity before a child can inherit from or through her natural father.

a) Presumption of paternity

The child can bring an action to establish paternity for inheritance purposes at any time if a presumption of paternity exists.

b) No presumption of paternity

A child must bring an action to establish paternity for inheritance purposes within three years of reaching the age of majority when there is no presumption of paternity, or the action is barred.

c) Acknowledgment of child

A presumption of paternity arises if the father acknowledges the child as his own, either by holding the child out as his own or by stating so in writing and filing the writing with the appropriate court.

f. New forms of parentage

1) Posthumously-conceived children

As science has developed reproductive technology allowing eggs and sperm to be frozen and used at any time, children can now be conceived after the death of a parent.

a) Intestacy

Jurisdictions are only beginning to confront the issue of whether a posthumously-conceived child can inherit under an intestacy act. Some, like New Jersey and Massachusetts allow inheritance under certain circumstances. In *Woodward v. Commissioner of Social Security*, 435 Mass. 536 (Mass. 2002), the Massachusetts Supreme Court held that a child posthumously conceived through reproduction technology may constitute "issue" under the state intestacy statute if there is a genetic relationship between the child and the decedent and the decedent consented to the posthumous conception and to the support of any resulting child. Other jurisdictions, such as Virginia, have adopted the Uniform Status of Children of Assisted Conception Act (USCACA), which does not recognize posthumously-conceived children as natural children of a parent who dies before conception.

b) Wills and trusts

A person can specifically provide in a will or other written instrument (e.g., an inter vivos trust) that a posthumously-conceived child is to be treated as her child under the instrument. If the instrument fails to specifically indicate the decedent's intent, the trend is to consider the child to be the child of the decedent. *See e.g., In re Martin B.*, 841 N.Y.S.2d 207 (Sur. Ct. 2008) (holding that when instrument is silent, posthumously-conceived child should be granted same rights as children conceived prior to parent's death).

c) UPC

The UPC provides that a posthumously-conceived child can inherit from a deceased parent if the parent authorized the posthumous conception in a signed writing, or there is clear and convincing evidence of consent, and the child is living in utero within 36 months of, or born within 45 months of the parent's death. Unif. Probate Code §§ 2-120; 2-705(b)(g).

2) Surrogate motherhood

A surrogate mother contracts to bear a child for another person or couple, agreeing that the child will belong to that other person or couple. The child may or may not be genetically related to the surrogate mother. If the agreement breaks down, courts must determine who should have custody of the child and who constitutes the child's legal parents. Under the UPC, a "gestational carrier" does not constitute a parent unless she is the child's genetic mother and no one else has a parent-child relationship with the child. A person who entered into an agreement with the surrogate to be the parent would constitute the legal parent if the person functioned as a parent of the child within two years of the child's birth. Unif. Probate Code § 2-121.

2.   **Calculating Share**

The UPC adopts the **per capita at each generation** approach, although most jurisdictions are split between the **per stirpes** and the **per capita with representation** schemes.

a.   **Per capita with representation**

The per capita with representation approach divides the property equally among the first generation when at least one member survives the decedent, with the shares of each member of that generation who does not survive the decedent passing to the then-living issue of the non-living member. If the non-living member has no then-living issue, then the non-living member does not receive a share.

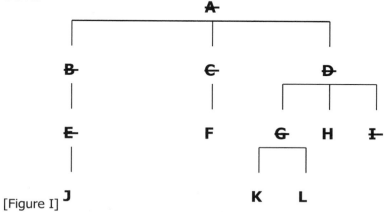

[Figure I]

> **Example:** In Figure I, above, A dies and is predeceased by her children B, C, and D, all of whom have surviving issue. Application of a per capita by representation scheme causes A's estate to be first divided at E's generation (because there are no surviving members of B's generation) and then to be distributed among all living members and all non-living members who are survived by issue. Because I is deceased without issue, I does not receive a share, and E, F, G, and H each take one-fourth. At J's generation, J takes E's one-fourth share in its entirety, and K and L share G's one-fourth share.

b.   **Per stirpes**

A distribution occurs per stirpes when the issue take in equal portions the share that their deceased ancestor would have taken, if living. The estate is first divided into the total number of children of the ancestor who survive or leave issue who survive.

> **Example:** Applying a per stirpes distribution scheme to Figure I, above, A's estate is divided equally at B's generation even though there are no survivors. J takes B's share (because E predeceased A), F takes C's share, and G and H share equally in D's share. Because G has predeceased A, K and L will equally split G's share. I, who predeceased A and left no issue, gets nothing.

c.   **Per capita at each generation**

The per capita at each generation approach, followed by the UPC, divides the property into as many equal shares as there are members of the nearest generation of issue who survive the decedent and deceased members of that generation with issue who survive the decedent. Unif. Probate Code § 2-106(b).

> **EXAM NOTE:** When analyzing fact patterns using the per capita at each generation approach, begin as per capita with representation, but then divide the remaining shares equally among the members of the next generation.

> **Example:** Applying a per capita at each generation scheme to Figure I., above, A's estate is divided into four shares: one each for F and H, who survived, and one each for E and G, who left living descendants. E and G's shares are pooled and divided among J, K, and L equally. In other words, F and H each get one-fourth, and J, K, and L divide the remaining one-half equally.

d. Negative inheritance

Under common law, the only way for an individual to disinherit an heir was to execute a will disposing of all of his property, because any property not so disposed of could potentially pass to that heir through intestacy.

The UPC allows an individual to disinherit an heir by properly executing a will expressing such intent, even if not all property is disposed of within the will. The barred heir is then treated as having predeceased the decedent. Unif. Probate Code § 2-101(b).

D. ANCESTORS AND REMOTE COLLATERALS

If no surviving spouse or issue exist to succeed to the decedent's estate, then the property may be distributed to the decedent's ancestors (e.g., parents, grandparents, great-grandparents) and more remote collateral relatives (i.e., those related to the decedent through a common ancestor, such as siblings, cousins, aunts, and uncles).

1. Parentelic Approach

The parentelic approach follows collateral lines until a live taker is found, at which point the decedent's property is distributed within that taker's parentelic line. A decedent's estate would first pass to the decedent's parents and their issue (the decedent's siblings); if there are none, then to the decedent's grandparents and their issue (aunts, uncles, and cousins), and so on.

2. Degree-of-Relationship Approach

The degree-of-relationship approach results in those with closer degrees of relationship to the decedent taking to the exclusion of more remote relatives. The degree of relationship is calculated by counting the number of relatives between the living taker and the decedent using the closest common ancestor.

3. Combined Approach

The parentelic approach is used as a tiebreaker in the event that the degree-of-relationship approach results in a tie between multiple living takers sharing the same lowest degree of relationship. Those in the closer collateral line take to the exclusion of those in the more remote collateral line.

4. UPC Approach

If there is no surviving spouse or descendant, then the estate passes in the following order to the individuals designated below who survive the decedent:

   i) To the decedent's parents equally if both survive, or to the surviving parent;

   ii) If there is no surviving descendant or parent, then to the descendants of the decedent's parents;

iii) If there is no surviving descendant, parent, or descendant of a parent, then the estate passes to the decedent's maternal and paternal grandparent, one-half to each, or to the descendants of the decedent's maternal and paternal grandparents if the grandparents are deceased;

vi) If there is no surviving grandparent or descendant of a grandparent on either the paternal or the maternal side, then the entire estate passes to the decedent's nearest maternal and paternal relative;

v) If there are no surviving relatives, then the entire estate passes to the descendants of any predeceased spouse; and

v) If there are no descendants of any predeceased spouse, the estate escheats to the state.

A parent cannot inherit through a child if her parental rights have been terminated, or if the child dies before the age of 18 and there is clear and convincing evidence that the parental rights of the parent **could** have been terminated under state law. Unif. Probate Code § 2-114.

V. TRANSFERS TO CHILDREN

A. ADVANCEMENTS

If a child wants to share in the intestate distribution of a deceased parent's estate, the child must permit the administrator of the estate to include in the determination of the distributive shares the value of property that the decedent, while alive, gave to child. Such gifts are known as "advancements." If the child can show that the transfer was intended as an absolute gift, not to be counted against her share of the estate, the doctrine would not apply. The doctrine of advancements usually applies only to intestate succession. However, there is some authority for the proposition that the doctrine of advancements would apply if a will leaves property to the testator's "heirs."

1. Common Law

At common law, any lifetime gift to a child was presumed to be an advancement of that child's intestate share and was binding on those who would have succeeded to the child's estate had the child predeceased the decedent.

a. Burden

The child had the burden of demonstrating that the lifetime transfer was intended to be an absolute gift that was not to be counted against the child's share of the estate.

b. Hotchpot

If a gift is treated as an advancement, the donee must allow its value to be brought into the **hotchpot**. The advancement is added back into the estate, and the resulting total estate is divided by the number of children taking. The advancement is then deducted from the total share of the child to whom it was given.

> **Example:** D died intestate with a probate estate worth $150,000. D is survived by children A, B, and C, each of whom had received from D an inter vivos gift ($25,000 to A, $50,000 to B, and $75,000 to C). Under the advancement doctrine, the inter vivos gifts (totaling $150,000) are added back into the estate (for a total of $300,000) and then divided evenly among the three children (so each is entitled to $100,000) minus their individual gifts. As a result, A would take $75,000 (her $100,000 share less the $25,000 already received), B would take $50,000 (his

$100,000 share less the $50,000 already received), and C would take $25,000 (his $100,000 share less the $75,000 already received).

If a child receives an inter vivos share that exceeds the hotchpot share to which each child is entitled, then that child does not take, but is not required to pay back into the estate.

2. Modern Trend

The UPC approach, which is the modern trend, provides that a gift is an advancement only if:

i) The decedent declared in a **contemporaneous writing** (or the heir acknowledged in a writing) that the gift was an advancement; or

ii) The decedent's contemporaneous writing or the heir's written acknowledgment **otherwise indicates** that the gift was to be taken into account in computing the division and distribution of the decedent's intestate estate.

Unif. Probate Code § 2-109.

The value of an inter vivos gift is determined at the time the recipient takes possession or enjoys it, whichever is first. Unlike the common-law approach, the UPC applies to all heirs, not just the decedent's children.

3. Satisfaction of Legacies

Lifetime gifts to beneficiaries who take under a will are examined in a similar manner and follow the same rules as advancement of intestate shares. An inter vivos transfer occurring between the testator and beneficiary will satisfy the legacy under the will if (i) the testator intends that the transfer satisfy a testamentary gift and (ii) there is a written acknowledgment of such satisfaction by the testator or beneficiary. Inclusively, situations in which the testator's intent is not apparent and cannot be proven will satisfy the legacy and give rise to the doctrine of ademption, if the testator makes an inter vivos transfer to the beneficiary of the specifically-bequeathed item. *See* XII.C, *infra*.

B. TRANSFERS TO MINORS

As minors lack the legal capacity to hold property, the law provides various ways in which others might manage property for minors. The three property management options are: (i) guardianship, (ii) custodianship, and (iii) trusteeship. Custodianship and trusteeship are available only through the creation of a will.

1. Guardianship

A guardian has minimal power over property and must go through a difficult process to obtain the necessary court approval to act on behalf of a minor. The modern trend is to transform this function into a conservatorship, wherein the conservator acts as a trustee for the minor, with annual accounting to the court.

2. Uniform Transfers to Minors Act (UTMA)

The Uniform Transfers to Minors Act, enacted in all states, appoints a custodian to use the property of a minor at the custodian's discretion on the minor's behalf without court approval and with no accounting requirement. The custodian must turn any remaining property over to the minor upon the minor's attainment of age 21.

If the beneficiary was a minor at the time the will was executed, but attains age 21 prior to the testator's death, then the property passes directly to the minor absent an instruction otherwise contained in the will.

3. Trust

The third alternative is to establish a trust for a minor, which is the most flexible of the property arrangements. A testator can tailor a trust specifically to the family circumstances and to his particular desires.

Whereas under a guardianship or conservatorship the child must receive the property at age 18 or 21, a trust can postpone possession until a time when the donor thinks the child will be competent to manage the property.

VI. BARS TO SUCCESSION

A. HOMICIDE

In most states, by statute, a party cannot take property from a decedent when the party was responsible for the decedent's death. This includes an intestate share, an elective share, an omitted spouse's share, exempt property, a homestead allowance, and a family allowance. Additionally, a joint tenant loses the right of survivorship benefits. The UPC and the majority of jurisdictions treat the killer as if she had predeceased the decedent. Unif. Probate Code § 2-803(b). In the absence of a statute, courts are split on how to address the question. Some allow the killer to take the decedent's property. Other courts have taken the view that equity prevents the killer from taking the property because otherwise the killer would be profiting from her own wrongdoing. Still other courts impose a constructive trust in favor of the next persons in line to take the property. *See e.g., In re Estate of Mahoney*, 220 A.2d 475 (Vt. 1966) (with no statute on point, court imposed constructive trust to prevent wife convicted of manslaughter of husband from obtaining intestate share of his estate).

1. Intentional and Felonious

In general, for both statutory and judicial bars to succession based on homicide, the killing must have been intentional and felonious. For example, involuntary manslaughter and self-defense killings do not fall within the homicide doctrine, although assisted suicide killings do. If a conviction fails, the court nonetheless may make a determination as to the lawfulness of the killing, using a preponderance of the evidence standard.

2. Killer's Issue

Jurisdictions are split as to whether the killer's issue should also be barred from taking. The UPC treats the killer as if she disclaimed the property, which allows the killer's issue potentially to take under the anti-lapse, per stirpes, and per capita doctrines, if the issue qualify. Unif. Probate Code § 2-803(b).

3. Scope

Under the UPC, the homicide doctrine applies to all property, whether probate or non-probate. Purchasers of such property for value and without notice are protected, but the killer is liable for the proceeds. If a statute only covers probate property, a court might impose a constructive trust or apply principles of equity to prevent succession to non-probate property, such as joint tenancy property, life insurance, and pensions.

B. DISCLAIMER

Since acceptance of a testamentary gift is presumed, a party must actively disclaim if she wishes not to accept it. The disclaiming party is treated as if she had predeceased the decedent, and the property is distributed to the next eligible taker.

1. Requirements

Most disclaimer statutes have specific requirements that must be followed for the disclaimer to be effective. For example, an interest cannot be disclaimed once an heir or beneficiary has accepted the property or any of its benefits. Most jurisdictions require that the disclaimer be in writing, signed, and filed within nine months of the decedent's death. The nine-month period begins to run at the later of the death of the decedent or the date the interest becomes vested. However, under federal law, and for the disclaimer to be valid for tax purposes, the disclaimer must be filed nine months from the later of the decedent's date of death or the heir's or beneficiary's attainment of age 21.

When disclaiming an interest acquired through joint tenancy, the surviving joint tenant has nine months from the date of the other joint tenant's death to disclaim the interest. With future interests, while certain jurisdictions allow an heir or beneficiary up to nine months from the date the interest vests in possession to disclaim an interest, to avoid federal taxation, the interest must be disclaimed within nine months of its creation. When the future interest being disclaimed is a life estate, the testator's remaindermen are determined at the testator's death rather than the life tenant's death as would generally be the case. The remainder is accelerated because the interest passes as though the disclaimant, in this case the life tenant, predeceased the decedent.

Jurisdictions vary as to whether the disclaimer statute applies to probate property (the traditional approach) or whether it also includes non-probate property (the modern approach) and must identify the decedent, describe the interest being disclaimed, and state the extent of the disclaimer.

2. Who May Disclaim

A disclaimer can be made by a third party, such as a guardian, custodian, trustee, or personal representative, on behalf of a minor, incompetent, or decedent. A spendthrift clause in a will does not preclude a disclaimer.

C. ABANDONMENT

Some states bar an individual from taking if she is guilty of abandonment. The individual is generally treated as having predeceased the decedent.

D. ELDER ABUSE

Some states bar an individual from taking if she is guilty of elder abuse. Jurisdictions vary on the requirements, with some barring a taker when the conduct is only short of homicide and others barring a taker after a showing of abandonment. Most jurisdictions treat the abuser as if they have predeceased the decedent.

E. ALIENS

A few states restrict the inheritance rights of nonresident aliens.

VII. WILL CONTESTS

A will contest is an objection raised against the validity of a will, based on the contention that the will does not reflect the actual intent of the testator. The basis of a will contest is the assertion that the testator: (i) lacked testamentary capacity; (ii) was operating under an insane delusion; or (iii) was subject to undue influence or fraud.

A. PERIOD OF LIMITATIONS

Jurisdictions vary, but in general, a will contest must be filed very soon (typically within six months) after the will is admitted to probate. Proper notice should also be given to all heirs and legatees under the will, as well as to creditors of the estate. Will contests must be made within the specified period after probate is opened, or the claims are barred.

B. STANDING TO CONTEST

Only directly interested parties who stand to benefit financially may contest a will, such as beneficiaries under the current or prior will. Creditors of beneficiaries, spouses of beneficiaries under prior wills, and pretermitted heirs cannot contest.

1. Decedent's Creditors

Because the decedent's creditors have the same rights regardless of whether the will is contested, general creditors cannot contest, though a judgment creditor of a beneficiary under a will may be able to contest.

2. Spouse of a Beneficiary Under a Prior Will

Neither a spouse nor any other prospective heir of a beneficiary under a prior will may contest.

3. Omitted Heir

Because the omitted heir's share is the same regardless of whether the will is contested, no omitted heir can contest a will.

C. TESTAMENTARY CAPACITY

1. Requirements

To execute or revoke a will, the testator must be at least **18 years old** and possess a **sound mind** at the time of execution or revocation.

The testator lacks the requisite mental capacity if he, **at the time of execution**, did not have the ability to know the:

i) Nature of the act;

ii) Nature and character of his property;

iii) Natural objects of his bounty; and

iv) Plan of the attempted disposition.

Note: The testator need only have the **ability** to know; actual knowledge is not required.

Old age alone is insufficient to constitute lack of capacity. Courts will uphold wills of elderly testators who at least grasp the big picture about their financial affairs. *See e.g., Wilson v. Lane*, 279 Ga. 492 (Ga. 2005) (holding that evidence that testator was eccentric, feeble, and elderly at time will was signed not sufficient, by itself, to establish lack of testamentary capacity). Adjudication of incompetence is not dispositive on the issue of testamentary capacity; the above-listed factors must also be applied. Also, just because a conservator was appointed, it does not automatically mean that the testator lacks capacity.

Some states also require a deficiency in one of the following areas to prove lack of capacity: alertness and attention, information processing, thought processing, or mood modulation. Such deficiencies are also considered only if they significantly interfere with the individual's ability to understand and appreciate the consequences of his actions.

2. Burden of Proof

In general, once the proponent of a will adduces prima facie evidence of due execution of the will, the party contesting the will for lack of capacity will have the evidentiary burden of persuasion. See Unif. Probate Code § 3-407. Only those parties that would financially benefit, if successful, have standing to contest a will.

3.   Drafting Attorney's Ethical Responsibility

Under the Model Rules of Professional Conduct, a lawyer is not permitted to draft a will for a person the lawyer believes to be incompetent, but the lawyer may rely on his own judgment to determine if the client is competent. A lawyer should take steps to preserve evidence regarding the client's testamentary capacity.

D.   INSANE DELUSION

An insane delusion is a belief for which there is no factual or reasonable basis, but to which the testator adheres despite all reason and evidence to the contrary. Courts will generally not apply the doctrine to religious or spiritual beliefs. An insane delusion is not capable of correction. Even if you tell the testator the truth, it will make no difference. A mistake, on the other hand, can be corrected by telling the testator the truth. While the traditional rule is that a mistake in a will cannot be reformed or invalidated, an insane delusion can invalidate all or part of the will. *See e.g., In re Striimater*, 140 N.J. Eq. 94 (N.J. Ct. Err & App. 1947) (holding that will that is product of insane delusion cannot be probated).

1.   Rational-Person Test

The majority rule is that a belief is an insane delusion if a rational person in the testator's situation could not have reached the same conclusion. A minority of jurisdictions hold that if there is any factual basis to support the testator's belief, it does not constitute an insane delusion.

2.   "But For" Causation

Once it is determined that the testator suffered from an insane delusion, it must be shown that this was the sole cause of the testamentary disposition. The majority view requires "but for" causation, such that the testator would not have disposed of the property in the same manner but for the insane delusion. If an insane delusion is shown, but the delusion did not affect any dispositions, the will remains valid. *See e.g., Breeden v. Stone*, 992 P.2d 1167 (Co. 2000) (finding that testator suffered from insane delusion that everyone he knew was spying on him, but that there was insufficient evidence delusion materially affected the provisions of his will). The minority rule asks only if the insane delusion might have caused or affected the disposition. *See e.g., In re Honigman*, 168 N.E.2d 676 (N.Y. App. 1960) (denying probate to a will on grounds that the testator's failure to provide for his wife might have been caused or affected by his insane delusion that his wife was promiscuous).

> **EXAM NOTE:** Remember to discuss **causation** when analyzing whether an insane delusion exists. Under the majority rule, unless the insane delusion was the cause of the strange disposition, there is no defect in capacity.

E.   UNDUE INFLUENCE

1.   In General

Undue influence is mental or physical coercion, exerted by a third party on the testator with the intent to influence the testator, such that he loses control of his own judgment. Simply having an opportunity to exert influence or demonstrating the testator's susceptibility to being influenced (e.g., due to old age, poor health, or memory problems) does not establish that the testator's mind was overpowered.

Several factors are considered in determining the extent of a beneficiary's involvement in procuring the will. Among them are the beneficiary's recommendation of an attorney and providing the attorney with instructions, the beneficiary's presence during the writing and execution of the will, and the beneficiary's securing of witnesses. Once a will is determined to have been the product of undue influence, it may be invalidated in whole or in part, as long as the overall testamentary scheme is not altered thereby. Most courts will invalidate only those portions that are infected by undue influence.

2. Traditional Doctrine

Under the majority view, the undue influence doctrine has the following elements, all four of which must be shown:

i) **Susceptibility** (the testator was susceptible to being influenced);

ii) **Motive** or predisposition (the influencer had reason to benefit);

iii) **Opportunity** (the influencer had the opportunity to influence); and

iv) **Causation** (the influencer caused an unnatural result).

> **EXAM NOTE:** As with insane delusions, undue influence is extremely fact-sensitive. Remember to discuss causation and the specific facts of the particular case when analyzing whether the will was a product of undue influence. Unless the undue influence is the cause of the strange disposition, there is no defect in capacity.

3. Burden of Proof

The burden of proof rests on the contestant to show (i) the existence and exertion of influence and (ii) that the effect of the influence was to overpower the mind and will of the testator. The result must be a will that **would not have been executed but for the influence.**

4. Presumption

a. Confidential relationship

Because the defendant is in the best position to provide evidence, the majority of jurisdictions require a burden-shifting approach. If the elements of the jurisdiction's statute are satisfied, then a presumption of undue influence arises that shifts the burden to the defendant. A presumption of undue influence arises when the principal beneficiary under a will stands in a **confidential relationship** to the testator (such as the testator's attorney or physician), when he participated in executing the will, and when the gift to the beneficiary is unnatural or consists of the majority of the estate. Some jurisdictions also include whether the testator was of a weakened intellect.

> **Note:** To have a confidential relationship, the testator must confide, trust, or rely upon on the other party as a result of his weakened or dependent state.

b. Burden of proof shifts

When a presumption of undue influence arises, the burden shifts to the beneficiary to show by a preponderance of the evidence that such influence was not exercised. Some courts have held that a higher standard applies, especially in cases involving alleged physician or attorney misconduct.

c. Treatment of a beneficiary

A beneficiary who is shown to have exerted undue influence is treated as having predeceased the testator to the extent that the gift to her exceeds her intestate share of the testator's estate.

5. Gifts to Attorneys

a. Special presumption

Most jurisdictions hold that a presumption of undue influence arises any time an attorney who drafts an instrument for a client receives a substantial gift under that instrument unless the attorney is married to or related to the client. To overcome the presumption, most jurisdictions require clear and convincing evidence that the testator intended to make the gift. A few jurisdictions make the presumption of undue influence irrebuttable.

One jurisdiction has extended the presumption of undue influence to an attorney with whom the testator had a continuing fiduciary relationship, even though the attorney did not actually draw up the will. *See, In re Will of Moses*, 227 So.2d 829 (Miss. 1969) (holding that a presumption of undue influence arises wherever an attorney with whom the testator had a continuing fiduciary relationship is a beneficiary under the will and that the presumption is not necessarily overcome merely by the fact that the will was actually drawn up by an independent attorney).

b. Ethical responsibility

Under Rule 1.8(c) of the Model Rules of Professional Conduct, a lawyer is not permitted to prepare on behalf of a client an instrument giving the lawyer or a person related to the lawyer any substantial gift unless the lawyer or other recipient of the gift is related to the client. Even if the lawyer is related to the client, the lawyer should exercise special care if the gift would be disproportionately large in comparison to gifts to others who are equally related. If a client wishes to make a gift to the lawyer, the lawyer should refer the client to a disinterested lawyer for preparation of the instrument. Model Rule 1.8 also requires that when an attorney is engaged to draft a will or trust that would name the attorney as executor or trustee, the attorney obtain the client's informed consent, advising the client of the nature and extent of the attorney's financial interest in the appointment, as well as the availability of alternative persons for the position.

F. DURESS

Duress is threatening or coercive behavior by one person that causes another person to do something that she would not otherwise do. It is undue influence that becomes overly coercive. A transfer that was procured by duress is invalid. *See e.g., Latham v. Father Divine*, 85 N.E.2d 168 (1949) (testator was prevented from executing new will in favor of intended beneficiary by duress, physical force, and fraud and court imposed constructive trust in favor of intended beneficiary). The duress must have been present when the instrument was executed.

G. FRAUD

Fraud, like undue influence and duress, must have been present when the will was executed. The burden of proving fraud is on the contestant.

1. Elements

The misrepresentation must be made **by the beneficiary** with both:

i)   The **intent** to deceive the testator; and

ii) The **purpose** of influencing the testamentary disposition.

The result must be a will that would not have been executed but for the fraud.

2. Fraud in the Inducement

Fraud in the inducement is a knowingly false representation that causes the testator to make a different will than he would have otherwise made. A fraudulently procured inheritance or bequest is invalid *only if* the testator would not have left the inheritance or made the bequest had he known the facts.

3. Fraud in the Execution

Fraud in the execution (or "fraud in the factum") is fraud as to the very nature of the instrument or its contents.

4. Constructive Trust

A constructive trust can be imposed upon the defendant to rectify any alleged fraud or undue influence perpetrated upon the testator. A constructive trust is sometimes said to be a fraud-rectifying trust. However, a constructive trust may also be imposed when no fraud is involved but the court believes that unjust enrichment would result if the defendant retained the property.

5. Probate Must be Contested

A person who objects to a will based on fraud or undue influence must contest its probate; the will may be partially probated if the fraud or undue influence goes only to certain provisions.

Note: If fraud, duress, or undue influence prevented the execution of a will in favor of the plaintiff, then she may request the imposition of a constructive trust, although some courts impose intestate succession laws.

H. NO-CONTEST CLAUSES

A no-contest clause (also called an "in terrorem" clause) is an express clause within a will designed to deter a beneficiary from suing over his share by causing him to lose his share entirely if he does so.

The majority of states and the UPC have held no-contest clauses to be unenforceable against claimants as long as the claimant had **probable cause** to contest. If the claim is spurious, then the clause is enforceable. Unif. Probate Code §§ 2-517; 3-905. A minority of states give the no-contest provision full effect, regardless of whether probable cause to challenge existed. Indiana and Florida do not enforce no contest clauses at all.

I. TORTIOUS INTERFERENCE WITH AN EXPECTANCY

1. In General

Section 774B of the Restatement (Second) of Torts recognizes the tort of intentional interference with a gift or inheritance. A plaintiff bringing a cause of action for tortious interference with an expectancy must establish: (i) the existence of an expected gift or inheritance; (ii) intentional interference with that expectancy through tortious conduct, such as undue influence, fraud, or duress; (iii) causation; and (iv) damages. *See Schilling v. Herrera*, 952 So.2d 1231 (Fl. Ct. App. 2007) (holding that a party who would have contested a will but was prevented from doing so by another's fraud could bring a claim for tortious interference with an expectancy). The action is not a will contest. It does not challenge the validity or probate of the will, but instead seeks to recover damages from a third party for interference.

2. Longer Statute of Limitations than Will Contests

Will contests typically have a short statute of limitations. The statute of limitations on tortious interference with an expectancy, on the other hand, is longer, starting to run at the time the plaintiff discovered or should have discovered the undue influence, duress, or fraud.

3. No-Contest Clause May Not Apply

Since a suit for tortious interference is not a will contest, a no-contest clause in a will (*see* § VII.H, *supra*) may not apply to discourage such suit.

4. Requirement to Pursue Probate Remedies First

Most states that recognize the tort require a plaintiff to first pursue probate remedies, if they are adequate (and available – the statute of limitations on the probate remedy may have expired, for example). A failure to do so will result in barring a tortious interference suit. If a plaintiff brings a will contest and loses, she will generally be barred under *res judicata* from subsequently bringing a tort suit.

5. Punitive Damages Apply

Unlike in a will contest, in a suit for tortious interference with an expectancy, punitive damages may generally be recovered.

VIII. EXECUTION OF WILLS

A. WILL FORMALITIES

Traditionally, for a will to be admissible to probate, the testator must have met the formal execution requirements of the applicable jurisdiction's statute of wills (i.e., that jurisdiction's requirements for the execution of a proper will). Although a will is usually contemplated to dispose of property, it does not necessarily have to do so. The requirements may vary depending on whether the will is in a traditional (i.e., witnessed) form or in a holographic (i.e., handwritten) form. At a minimum, most jurisdictions require a signed writing that has been witnessed for traditional attested wills. While the statute of wills varies from jurisdiction to jurisdiction, the sections below will detail the traditional requirements for a valid attested will (in addition to testamentary capacity, which is discussed above at § VII.C).

At common law, **strict compliance** with the formal requirements of wills was required, as these were thought to serve important ritual, evidentiary, and protective functions. *See e.g., In re Groffman*, 2 All E.R. 108 (1969) (holding that even though court was confident testator intended document to be his will, will was invalid because testator did not acknowledge signature in presence of two witnesses at same time).

> **EXAM NOTE:** The validity of a will is one of the most frequently tested areas of the law of wills. Remember that a will requires a **writing** that the testator **signs** with present **testamentary intent** in the **joint presence** of two witnesses, that both witnesses **understand** the significance of the testator's act, and that the will has no legal effect until after the testator's death.

1. Writing Signed by the Testator

The entire will must be in writing and must be signed by the testator or by some other person in his presence and at his direction. Video wills have not been permitted, although a video of an execution ceremony may be admissible to prove due execution. Only one state, Nevada, permits an electronic will, meaning a computer file with a unique electronic signature. Nev. Rev. Stat. § 133.085.

a. Form of signature

While the writing must be signed, the testator's complete formal name is not required, as long as the signature indicates her desire to sign (e.g., even an "X" is acceptable). If the testator signs by a mark, some jurisdictions may require that the mark be made in the presence of a witness. Additionally, in most jurisdictions and under the UPC, the will may be signed by another provided that the "conscious presence" test is satisfied (i.e., the other person signs the testator's name, in the presence and at the express direction of the testator).

b. Location

Some states require the signature to be at the end of the will, whereas others (and the UPC) allow the signature on any part of the will. In these states, while a signature elsewhere will not invalidate the will, any language appearing after the signature will be held invalid.

c. Order of signature

Traditionally, the testator must have signed or acknowledged the will before the witnesses attest. The modern trend, though, is to allow a witness to sign before the testator, so long as all parties sign as part of a single or continuous transaction, meaning while all parties remain present in the room.

2. Witnesses

a. Signatures

The majority view is that a will must be signed in the joint presence of, and attested to by, two witnesses. There are jurisdictional differences as to the number of witnesses (e.g., some states require three). Also, the witnesses need not sign at the end of the will.

As noted above, will execution statutes commonly provide that another person may sign a testator's will if it is done at the testator's direction and in the testator's presence. Under the UPC, the witnesses, all of whom need not be present at the same time, must sign the will within a reasonable time after witnessing the testator sign or acknowledge the will. Unif. Probate Code § 2-502(a)(3).

Some courts have found that the testator's request that the two witnesses sign can be implied and does not have to be explicit. *See In re Estate of Graham*, 295 N.W.2d 414 (Iowa 1980).

b. Attestation clauses

An attestation clause in a will recites that the will was duly executed. An attestation clause is not required, but it can be helpful to prove due execution of the will in cases when the witness has no memory of signing or has a faulty memory. It gives rise to a **presumption of due execution** and the will can be admitted to probate even if the witnesses predecease the testator or cannot remember the events of execution.

c. Presence

The witnesses need not read the will, but they must be aware that the instrument is a will. In most jurisdictions, the testator must sign or acknowledge the will in the presence of the witnesses, and the witnesses must sign in the presence of the testator.

The UPC, however, does not require the witnesses to sign the will in either the presence of the testator or the presence of the other witnesses. Rather, each witness must sign only within a reasonable time of the original signature by the testator, at his direction, or while observing the testator's acknowledgment of the will. Unif. Probate Code § 2-502(a)(3).

There are two other approaches followed by some jurisdictions: the line-of-sight test and the conscious-presence test.

1) Line-of-sight test

The "line-of-sight" test, which is the traditional approach, requires the joint presence of the witnesses and the testator, who must observe or have the opportunity to observe each other sign the will. If the testator does not sign in the witnesses' presence, then that signature must be acknowledged.

For example, when a witness signs from his office, while the testator signs in his home, the attestation requirements are not satisfied because of the risk that fraud as to the authenticity of the document being signed or the identity of the witness or testator, known by voice only, could occur.

2) Conscious-presence test

The modern approach, known as the "conscious-presence" test, is broader than the line-of-sight test. The conscious-presence test requires only that the party observing the act, either testator or witness, be aware that the act is being performed.

This method is endorsed by the UPC only for situations in which the will is signed by another person on behalf of the testator. Unif. Probate Code § 2-502(a)(2).

When a testator acknowledges her signature to witnesses over the telephone, courts have held that this does not satisfy the "conscious-presence" requirement—the witness must either observe the testator signing the will or observe the testator's acknowledgment of her will. *See In re Estate of McGurrin*, 743 P.2d 994 (Idaho Ct. App. 1987).

d. Age and competency

Witnesses must be of sufficient mental capacity and maturity to comprehend the value of the act of witnessing a will. Competency is determined as of the **time of signing**; the subsequent incompetence of a testator or witness does not invalidate a will.

e. Interest of a witness

At common law, a witness with a direct pecuniary interest under a will was not competent to witness the will. The will was invalid, unless two disinterested witnesses also witnessed the will.

1) Purging statutes

a) Majority rule

Most states now use a purge theory and invalidate the portion of the will providing an excess to the interested witness. To determine the portion to be purged, you calculate the amount the interested witness would receive if the will were invalid (i.e., under the intestacy statute or prior will) and the amount the witness stands to receive under the will. If the amount to be received under the will is greater, then the excess interest is purged. A few states, such as Massachusetts, purge the witness of his entire devise. Mass. Gen. Laws c. 191, § 2.

b) Exceptions

If the interested witness is a third witness signing along with two other disinterested witnesses, his interest will not be purged. Similarly, if the interested witness would have taken had the will not been probated, most states allow him to take his full bequest.

A party who is adversely affected by a will can serve as a witness to the will because she will receive no beneficial distribution under the will. In *Estate of Morea*, 645 N.Y.S.2d 1022 (Sur. Ct. 1966) the court concluded that a decedent's son, who witnessed the decedent's will, had nothing to gain under the will because New York law provided that a party who was both a witness and a beneficiary was entitled to the lesser of an intestate share or the legacy under will. Thus the son constituted a disinterested witness and the decedent's will was, therefore, held valid.

c) UPC

The UPC, which previously followed the purge theory, has now abolished the interested witness doctrine, as have a large minority of the states. Unif. Probate Code § 2-505(b).

d) California

California law creates a rebuttable presumption that a bequest to a witness was procured by undue influence, duress, or fraud. Cal. Prob. Code § 6112.

3.   Testamentary Intent

a. Understand the nature of the act

The testator must execute the will with present testamentary intent. When the testator signs the instrument, he must understand that he is executing a will and must intend that it have testamentary effect.

b. Know and approve

Testamentary intent is a question of fact to be determined by an examination of the will and the surrounding circumstances. The words in the will are not automatically conclusive.

A will is ineffective if the testator intends it only as a joke or to accomplish some other purpose. The testator need not read the will or understand all of its technical provisions, but he must generally know and approve of its contents.

B.   CURATIVE DOCTRINES

1.   Curing Defects by Ad Hoc Exception

As explained above, traditionally any mistake in execution was grounds to invalidate the will. Most jurisdictions still follow this approach. Courts have struggled with the harshness of this result, however, and that has led to inconsistent treatment of similarly-situated parties. Thus, in *In re Pavlinko's Estate*, 148 A.2d 528 (Pa. 1959), a husband and wife mistakenly signed each other's wills. After both had died, the person who had been named the residuary legatee of both wills tried to probate the wife's intended will, which the husband had mistakenly signed, leaving all the property to the husband. The court followed the traditional strict approach with regard to defects in execution, concluding that a court may not rewrite a clear and unambiguous will even to implement the obvious intentions of the testator. Under very similar facts, the court in *In re Snide*, 418 N.E.2d 656 (N.Y. 1981), held that the will the husband signed could properly be admitted to probate, emphasizing that the wills were identical and the parties' intentions clear.

2. Substantial Compliance

One modern approach to curing an execution defect is the doctrine of substantial compliance. Under the doctrine, a court may deem a will that was defectively executed to be statutorily valid if the defective execution fulfills the purposes of the statutory formalities. *See e.g., In re Will of Ranney*, 124 N.J. 1 (N.J. 1991) (adopting rule that when witnesses, with intent to attest will, sign self-proving affidavit, but not will or attestation clause, clear and convincing evidence of intent may be produced to establish substantial compliance with wills statute).

3. Harmless Error Rule

A minority of jurisdictions and the UPC have adopted the harmless error approach (sometimes known as the "dispensing power"), under which a court can probate a will if there is clear and convincing evidence that the decedent intended the instrument to constitute his will. *See e.g, In re Estate of Hall*, 5 P.3d. 1134 (Mont. 2002) (holding that draft of joint will that had not been witnessed could be probated as valid will of testator where there was clear and convincing evidence that testator intended document to be his will).

C. NOTARIZED WILLS

Under the UPC, a will is valid if signed by two witnesses *or* by a notary or any other person authorized by law to take acknowledgments. Unif. Probate Code § 2-502(a)(3).

D. "SELF-PROVED WILL"

Under the UPC, a will that is executed with attesting witnesses may be made "self-proved" by the acknowledgment of the testator and affidavits of the witnesses before a court officer in substantial accordance with a prescribed form. The effect of executing a "self-proved will" is that it removes the necessity for testimony of the attesting witnesses in formal probate. Unif. Probate Code § 2-504. Moreover, in many jurisdictions the witnesses' signatures on an affidavit may be counted as signatures on the will if the witnesses failed to sign the actual will.

E. HOLOGRAPHIC WILLS

Holographic (i.e., handwritten) wills are recognized by the UPC (§ 2-502(b)) and in approximately one-half of the states.

1. Signed and Handwritten

A holographic will is one that is completely handwritten and signed by the testator. Unlike attested wills, a holographic will cannot be signed by another person on behalf of the testator. Jurisdictions differ on whether the entire will needs to be in the testator's handwriting. Some jurisdictions require a strict compliance approach under which any markings not in the testator's handwriting invalidate the will. Others, including the UPC, merely require that the material provisions of the will be written by hand. Unif. Probate Code § 2-502(b).

Holographic wills have been found on a variety of different materials, including clothing, napkins, wall paper, and furniture, and been admitted to probate.

Note: A holographic will **need not be witnessed**.

2. Dated

Some states require that a holographic will be dated. Other states, including those that have adopted the UPC, have no such requirement.

3. Testamentary Intent

It must be clear that the document was intended by the testator to be a will. *See e.g., Kimmel's Estate*, 123 A. 405 (Pa. 1924) (holding that testator's handwritten letter to children evidencing intent of conditional gift and intent to execute could serve as valid testamentary document). Intent can be presumed by the use of certain language (e.g., "I bequeath"), or by the testator's use of a printed form will.

The UPC expressly states that the testator's intent need not be found exclusively in the testator's handwriting, but it can be discerned from other written parts of the will or from extrinsic evidence. Unif. Probate Code § 2-502(c). *See Estate of Gonzalez*, 855 A.2d 1146 (Me. 2004) (holding that pre-printed portions of a form will could be considered part of a holographic will when a court finds testamentary intent to do so); *In re Estate of Kuralt*, 303 Mont. 335 (Mont. 2000) (holding that letter written by decedent, while on deathbed, evidencing intent that another "inherit" a specific bequest of property, was valid holographic codicil to decedent's formal will and could be probated). A jurisdiction requiring strict compliance, however, will require that the testator's intent be discernible by the handwritten parts of the will as opposed to pre-printed parts on a form will or extrinsic evidence.

4. Handwritten Changes

Interlineations after the will is complete are effective in most jurisdictions that recognize holographic wills.

F. NUNCUPATIVE WILLS

Nuncupative (oral) wills are generally valid only for the disposition of **personal property** in contemplation of immediate death and are invalid under the UPC and in most states. In jurisdictions where they are valid, nuncupative wills require at least two witnesses, can devise only a limited amount of personal property, and may require that the testator die within a prescribed period after making the oral will.

G. CODICILS

A codicil is a supplement to a will that alters, amends, or modifies the will, rather than replacing it. **A codicil must be executed with the same formalities as a will.**

A validly executed codicil republishes the will as of the date of the codicil and may even validate an invalid will if the codicil refers to the will with sufficient certainty to identify and incorporate it, or if the codicil is on the same paper as the invalid will. Courts look to the intent of the testator to determine whether to read the provisions of the will as having been republished as of the date of the codicil.

Note: A holographic codicil to an attested will and an attested codicil to a holographic will are valid.

IX. REVOCATION

A. ANY TIME PRIOR TO DEATH

A testator with testamentary capacity retains the ability to revoke his will at any time prior to his death, even if he has executed a valid contract not to revoke the will. In such a case, the revoked will must be denied probate, but the interested parties may bring an action for breach of contract against the estate of the decedent.

A will may be revoked wholly or partially in three ways: by **subsequent writings**, by **physical destruction of the will**, or by **operation of law**.

1. **Subsequent Instrument**

   A testator can expressly revoke a will by a subsequent writing, a later will, or a codicil. Under the UPC, a subsequent writing expressing the intent to revoke must qualify as a valid holographic or attested will. Unif. Probate Code § 2-507(a)(1). The revocation can be express or can be implied by the terms of the subsequent instrument.

   > **Note:** An oral revocation of a will is not valid.

   a. **Inconsistency**

      To the extent possible, the will and any codicils are read together. If there are inconsistencies, then the **later document controls** and revokes the prior inconsistencies. If a later will contains a residuary clause (e.g., "I leave all remaining assets of my estate to my brother"), then it **revokes** the first will by inconsistency. If a later will has an express revocation clause, then the first will is revoked.

      > **Note:** If a subsequent will does not revoke a prior will in its entirety by inconsistency, then it is merely a codicil.

      > **Example:** T executes a will that leaves his house to A, his watch to B, and his car to C. One year later, T executes a new document that says in its entirety, "I hereby leave my car to Y." Assuming that the subsequent document was executed consistent with the requisite statutory formalities, that subsequent document will be a codicil. A is still going to get the house, B is still going to get the watch, but now Y is going to get the car and not C. If, however, the subsequent document had said, "I hereby leave my car to Y and everything else to Z," then it would have actually revoked the prior will because it is entirely inconsistent with the prior will.

      > **EXAM NOTE:** On an exam, you must be able to distinguish a codicil to an existing will from a new will. If the subsequent document has a residuary clause, then it is likely a new will. If the subsequent document does not have a residuary clause but the first document does, then the subsequent document is likely a codicil.

2. **Destruction With Intent to Revoke**

   A will may be revoked by burning any portion thereof, or by canceling, tearing, obliterating, or destroying a material portion of the will with the intent to revoke it. Both the **act** and a simultaneous **intent to revoke** must be proven to yield a valid revocation.

   a. **Defacement of the language required**

      The majority rule is that an effective canceling of a will requires defacement of the language of the will (i.e., at least some of the language must be crossed out, including the signature). *See e.g., Thompson v. Royall*, 163 Va. 492 (Va. 1934) (holding that revocation by act not accomplished unless written words of instrument are mutilated or otherwise impaired). The UPC, however, rejects the majority rule and requires that the destructive act merely affect some part of the will. Unif. Probate Code § 2-507(a)(2). Some states require that the method of revocation be of a type specified by statute; any other non-specified method will be ineffective.

1) Presumption of revocation

If a will once known to exist cannot be found at the testator's death, or is found mutilated, then there is a rebuttable presumption of revocation. *See e.g., Harrison v. Bird*, 621 So.2d 972 (Ala. 1993). The presumption is inapplicable if a duplicate original is found. Extrinsic evidence is permitted to rebut the presumption.

Note: The attorney-client privilege does not apply to a lawyer's testimony concerning the contents of a will.

2) Only one copy destroyed

The prevailing view is that the effective revocation of the original or a duplicate original presumptively revokes all other copies of the will, but that destruction of an unexecuted copy does not.

b. Third party

A third party can revoke on behalf of the testator as long as the revocation is:

i) At the testator's **direction**;

ii) **Witnessed** by two persons; and

iii) In the testator's **presence.**

If a testator calls his attorney requesting that she tear up his will, then the revocation is not valid because it was not done in the testator's presence or proved by two witnesses.

Note: An attorney can be subject to liability for failing to advise his client regarding the proper revocation or execution of his will.

3. Operation of Law

a. Divorce

In most states, divorce revokes all will provisions in favor of the former spouse, unless it can be shown that the testator intended for the will to survive. Unif. Probate Code § 2-804. In some states, however, divorce revokes a will provision for the former spouse only if the divorce is accompanied by a property settlement agreement. If a divorced couple remarries before the testator dies, then the will provisions relating to the former spouse or domestic partner are revived.

Note: The UPC also applies the revocation by operation of law doctrine to will substitutes (i.e., non-probate property like life insurance, pension plans, and payable on death accounts). This is unlike the law of most states. Furthermore, the UPC takes a broader approach than many jurisdictions and revokes the provisions containing devises to the relatives of the ex-spouse. Unif. Probate Code § 2-804.

b. Separation

Separation without divorce *does not* affect the rights of the spouse or domestic partner unless a complete property settlement is in place.

4. Partial Revocation

The majority of jurisdictions and the UPC permit partial revocation to revoke a provision of a will. The majority of jurisdictions provide that if the revoked gift falls outside of the residuary, it is *not* given effect until re-execution (signed again) or republication (new document) of the will. The UPC, however, provides that partial revocation is permissible regardless of the effect, even if it increases a gift outside of the residuary clause. Unif. Probate Code § 2-507(d).

5. Alteration

A testator cannot increase a gift to a beneficiary by canceling words in his will, but he may be able to decrease the gift as long as the alteration is made to the existing language of the will rather than through the addition of new language.

6. Holographic Wills

A holographic will can be altered or revoked in whole or in part by holographic changes and without a new signature. States that allow holographic wills also allow their revocation by formal wills and vice versa. On the other hand, some state statutes require both the holographic will and any changes be signed. *See* Unif. Probate Code § 2-502 and § 2-502 (b).

If a subsequent holographic will disposes of part of an estate already disposed of in a typewritten will, then the typewritten will is revoked only to the extent that it is inconsistent with the later holographic will.

B. LOST WILLS

If the decedent had possession of her original will before her death, but the will is not found among her personal effects after death, jurisdictions are split as to whether a rebuttable presumption arises that the decedent destroyed the will with the intent to revoke it.

1. Duplicates and Copies

Duplicate originals are two copies of the same will executed in the same manner, each complying with the same formalities. A duplicate original may be admitted to probate.

A copy of a will, such as a photocopy, cannot itself be admitted to probate, although it may be used as proof of testamentary intent in the case of a lost or missing will.

2. Burden on the Proponent

If a will cannot be found, then the burden is on the proponent of the existence of a will to prove the will's existence by clear and convincing evidence. An attorney's copy of an original is sufficient, whereas testimony by an interested witness is not.

3. Absence of Intent to Destroy

If there is proof that a will has been destroyed, but there is no evidence that the testator intended to revoke the will, then the will can still be probated if there is clear and convincing evidence of the lack of intent to revoke and of the contents of the will.

C. REVOCATION OF CODICILS

Revocation of a will revokes all codicils thereto, whereas revocation of a codicil does not revoke a will, but rather revives it.

Example: In 2005, the testator executes a will. One year later, he adds a codicil. In 2011, he revokes the codicil with the intention of revoking the will as well. The testator dies in 2012. The 2005 will is offered for probate, and it will be admitted because the revocation of the codicil revives the underlying will.

D. REVIVAL

1. Republication

At common law, the revocation of a will or codicil that had revoked another will automatically revived the original will. Most states and the UPC no longer support automatic revival of the original will but instead require proof that the testator intended to revive the original. *See* Unif. Probate Code § 2-509. Extrinsic evidence is admissible only if the revocation was by physical act. A will may be re-executed if a testator, with testamentary formalities, acknowledges the will. The burden is on those opposing the revival to prove that the testator did not intend to revive the original terms of the first will.

> **Example:** Testator executes will A and then later executes will B (thereby revoking will A). Testator then destroys will B. Both wills have been revoked, and the revocation of will B revives will A only if will A still exists and Testator intended to revive it.

2. Dependent Relative Revocation (DRR)

Under certain circumstances, many jurisdictions employ the equitable doctrine of dependent relative revocation (DRR), which allows a court to disregard a testator's revocation that was based on a mistake of law or fact and would not have been made but for that mistake. The testator's last effective will, prior to the set-aside revocation, will once again control his estate. The doctrine of DRR can apply to partial revocations as well.

Typically, courts apply this doctrine only when there is a sufficiently close identity between the bequest that was revoked and the bequest that was expressed in the invalid subsequent will. Most courts apply the doctrine only if there is an alternative plan of disposition that fails or if the mistake is recited in the terms of the revoking instrument or is established by clear and convincing evidence. *See e.g., LaCroix v. Senecal*, 140 Conn. 311 (Conn. 1953) (holding that DRR applied to sustain bequest to testator's nephew when it was clear that testator's sole purpose in executing codicil that was invalid because of interested witness was to reaffirm gift to nephew).

> **Example:** T creates a second will and then writes on the first will, "I am revoking this will because I made a new will." T did not realize that the second will was not valid. The revocation of the first will is set aside, and the first will is given effect.

> **EXAM NOTE:** If you see an otherwise valid revocation based upon a mistake (whether of fact or law), begin your analysis by stating the DRR rule.

X. COMPONENTS OF A WILL

A. INTEGRATION OF WILLS

Through the doctrine of integration, a will consists of all pages that are present at the time of execution and that are intended to form part of the will, which can be shown either by physical connection of the pages or by the ongoing nature of the language of the will. Litigation often occurs when pages are not physically connected or there is evidence that a staple has been removed. Problems can be prevented by carefully fastening the pages before the testator signs and by having the testator sign or initial each numbered page of the will.

B. INCORPORATION BY REFERENCE

In most jurisdictions, a will may incorporate by reference another writing not executed with testamentary formalities, provided the other writing:

    i) **Existed** at the time the will was executed;

ii) Is **intended** to be incorporated; and

iii) Is **described in the will** with sufficient certainty so as to permit its identification.

Unif. Probate Code § 2-510; *see also, Clark v. Greenhalge*, 411 Mass. 410 (1991). The UPC waives the requirement that the document have been in existence at the time the will was executed if the document disposes only of testator's tangible **personal property.** The will, however, must expressly state the testator's intent. Unif. Probate Code § 2-513.

In *Johnson v. Johnson*, 279 P.2d 928 (Okla. 1955), an instrument offered for probate consisted of a single page with three typed paragraphs giving away property and at the bottom of the page, in the handwriting of the decedent, the statement, "To my brother James, I give ten dollars only. This will shall be complete unless hereafter altered, changed or rewritten" along with the decedent's signature. The court concluded that the handwritten statement at the bottom of the instrument constituted a valid holographic "codicil," which incorporated the typed portion of the instrument by reference, giving effect to the intent of the testator. A dissent asserted that there was nothing in the handwritten portion of the instrument that referred to the typewritten material and that incorporation by reference was not appropriate.

C.   REPUBLICATION BY CODICIL

Under the doctrine of republication by codicil, a will is treated as re-executed as of the date of the codicil. The doctrine is not applied automatically, but only when updating the will carries out the testator's intent.

> **Example:** In 2010, T executes a will in a state that has a statute requiring the purging of any gift to an attesting witness. The will devises all of T's property to A. A and B are the only witnesses to the will. In 2011, T executes a codicil devising his watch to C. C and D are the only witnesses to the codicil. In 2012, T executes a second codicil, devising $10,000 to C. D and E are the witnesses to the second codicil. Under the doctrine of republication by codicil, upon the execution of the second codicil with two disinterested witnesses, the will and the first codicil are deemed re-executed in 2012 and both A and C are not purged of their gifts.

D.   ACTS OF INDEPENDENT SIGNIFICANCE

1.   In General

A will may provide for the designation of a beneficiary or the amount of a disposition by reference to some unattested act or event occurring before or after the execution of the will or before or after the testator's death, if the act or event has some significance apart from the will. Unif. Probate Code § 2-512 ("Events of Independent Significance"). The act may be in relation to the identification of property or of beneficiaries.

> **EXAM NOTE:** When analyzing a testator's acts on an exam, look to the timing of the event. Recall that the doctrines of republication by codicil and incorporation by reference apply only to events that occurred in the past. For example, republication by codicil looks at a will executed before the codicil and incorporation by reference requires the document to be in existence before the execution of the will (unless the UPC exception applies). The acts of independent significance doctrine, however, is the only doctrine that applies to future acts or events.

2.   Independent Legal Significance

If the testator, the beneficiary, or some third person has some control over the act or event, it may still have independent legal significance if it is unlikely that the testator or other person would perform such act solely for testamentary reasons. The execution or revocation of a will of a third person is an act of independent significance.

> **Example:** A will might leave a certain gift to "the man who is my niece's spouse at the time of my death." The law does not presume that the niece would marry or divorce merely to complete the terms of the will.

XI. WILL CONTRACTS

Will contracts include contracts to make a will, contracts to revoke a will, and contracts to die intestate, all of which are controlled by contract law.

A. WRITING REQUIREMENT

Proof of contract can be established if:

i) The will states the material provisions of the contract;

ii) The terms are contained in a written contract; or

iii) Express reference is made in the will to the contract and extrinsic evidence proves the terms.

The UPC requires that the contract be in writing and be within the will to be enforced through probate. Unif. Probate Code § 2-514. Otherwise, the contract must be enforced through contract law.

B. CONSIDERATION

As with any other contract, consideration must be given for a will contract to be enforceable. Situations in which the beneficiary promises to care for the testator in exchange for a bequest provide sufficient consideration and make the contract enforceable.

C. ENFORCEABILITY AND REMEDY

To be enforceable in most states, a contract relative to making or not making a will must be in writing and signed by the party sought to be charged; otherwise, the plaintiff may recover only his consideration, including the fair market value of any services rendered. Whether the contract is breached will not generally be known until after the testator's death. Thus, there is no remedy for a breach while the testator is still alive.

D. RECIPROCAL PROVISIONS

1. Joint Wills

A joint will is a will signed by two or more persons that is intended to serve as the will of each. A joint will that is not reciprocal is merely the individual will of each of the persons signing the same document (and is treated as if there were several separate wills). A will that is both joint and reciprocal is executed by two or more persons, with reciprocal provisions, and shows on its face that the devises were made in consideration of the other.

2. Reciprocal Wills

Reciprocal wills are wills with identical or reciprocal provisions. Because reciprocal wills are separate, there is no contract between the parties to dispose of the property in a particular way, which means that either party can modify his will without knowledge of the other.

3. Contract Not to Revoke

In most jurisdictions, and under the UPC, the mutual execution of a joint or mutual will does not create a presumption of a contract not to revoke the will. Unif. Probate

Code § 2-514. However, if a contract not to revoke is proved and the second party attempts to make an inter vivos transfer not in accordance with the contract, or attempts to revoke her will after accepting the benefits under the first party's will, then a constructive trust may be imposed for the benefit of the original beneficiaries. In a joint will contract, on the death of one party, the transaction is said to become an irrevocable contract as to the survivor.

> **Example:** H and W wish to leave everything to each other with the balance to their children. H and W can either create two separate wills with reciprocal provisions (reciprocal wills), or they can create one joint will that includes reciprocal provisions stating that the property of each goes to the survivor, if any, otherwise to the children. A joint will labeled "joint and mutual," with other factors listed above, is likely to be deemed a contract not to revoke, whereas reciprocal wills are unlikely to be so deemed absent clear and convincing evidence to the contrary.

> **EXAM NOTE:** Generally, if a fact pattern includes a joint will, then the issue of a contract not to revoke is likely being tested.

XII. CONSTRUCTION

A. CLASSIFICATION SYSTEM

Traditionally, a "devise" refers to a gift of real property by will, and a "bequest" or "legacy" refers to a gift of personal property by will. Classifying gifts establishes the order of distribution and abatement if the estate's assets are insufficient to satisfy all of the gifts contained in the will. The judiciary often assigns classifications with reference to the intention of the testator when the will was written. The classes of gifts made under the will are distinguished by the type of item given.

1. Specific

A specific legacy, devise, or bequest is a gift of property that can be distinguished with reasonable accuracy from other property that is part of the testator's estate.

> **Example:** "My car to my dentist."

2. General

A general legacy is a gift of personal property that the testator intends to be satisfied from the general assets of his estate.

> **Example:** "$100,000 to John."

3. Demonstrative

A testator intends that a demonstrative legacy be paid from a particular source, but if that source is insufficient, then he directs that the legacy be satisfied out of the general assets of the estate.

> **Example:** "$100,000 to John from my X account, but if funds are not sufficient, then the rest paid out of general funds."

4. Residuary

A residual legacy is a legacy of the estate remaining when all claims against the estate and all specific, general, and demonstrative legacies have been satisfied.

> **Example:** "I give all the rest and residue of my property, wheresoever situated, whensoever acquired, and whether known to me or not, to John."

B. AMBIGUITIES AND MISTAKES

1. Plain Meaning Rule

The majority of jurisdictions have been reluctant to admit extrinsic evidence (i.e., evidence that is not contained in the text of the document, itself) regarding varying the terms of a will. The general approach has been that courts will not disturb the plain meaning of a will regardless of mistake, although they are apt to treat certain mistakes as ambiguities, some types of which could be resolved through extrinsic evidence.

Example: In *Mahoney v. Grainger*, 186 N.E. 86 (Mass. 1933), T told her attorney she wanted to leave the residue of her estate to her 25 first cousins, equally. T also said that her first cousins were her nearest relatives. In actuality, her maternal aunt was her nearest blood relative. Instead of naming each cousin in the will, the attorney drafted the will to leave the residue of T's estate to her "heirs at law," believing that the cousins would take as T's nearest blood relatives. After T's death, the aunt claimed the residue, as T's heir at law. The court, applying the plain meaning rule, found for the aunt, holding that the term "heirs at law," was not ambiguous.

a. Ambiguities

At common law, there was a distinction between patent and latent ambiguities: patent ambiguities appeared on the face of the will and were required to be resolved within the four corners of the instrument but without extrinsic evidence; latent ambiguities were not apparent from a reading of the will and were allowed to be resolved by extrinsic evidence.

b. Mistakes

Extrinsic evidence is admissible to show a mistake in the *execution* of a will, such as when the testator is unaware that she was signing a will. In a case of the wrong will being signed, courts are divided as to whether relief should be granted, although the modern trend is moving in the direction of granting relief.

At common law and under the approach taken by most states, no extrinsic evidence is allowed and no relief is granted, if the mistake involves the reasons behind the testator making the will or a particular gift. For example, if a testator would normally make a will leaving his estate to his two children, but, under the mistaken belief that one of his children has died, instead makes a will devising his entire estate to only the other child, the court would not allow evidence of the mistake and only the one child would take the estate. There is an exception to this rule if the testator was fraudulently induced or the mistaken inducement appears on the face of the will.

If a will is missing provisions, a court applying the traditional rules will not allow extrinsic evidence to show the omission was accidental and will not grant relief. The rationale is that the testator presumably knew of the will's contents when he signed it.

2. Modern Trend

a. Repudiation of plain meaning rule

In a trend against formalism, some courts have repudiated the common law plain meaning rule. Many states no longer distinguish between patent and latent ambiguities and allow both to be resolved by extrinsic evidence. If the ambiguity cannot be resolved, then the gift in question becomes part of the residue. Some states, while purporting to stick to the rule that no reformation of a will is allowed, have moved in ways that effectively permit reformation.

> **Example:** In *Arnheiter v. Arnheiter*, 125 A.2d 914 (N.J. Chancery 1956), T's will instructed her executor to sell her interest in "304 Harrison Avenue" and use the sale proceeds to establish trusts for her beneficiaries. At the time the will was executed and at the time of her death, however, T owned no such property. She did own a 50 percent interest in 317 Harrison Avenue. The court allowed extrinsic evidence to establish the erroneous description and then struck the number 304 from the will, allowing it to construe an ambiguity in the will to mean T's actual Harrison Avenue property.

b. Scrivener's error doctrine

Some jurisdictions have adopted the "scrivener's error doctrine," under which if there is clear and convincing of a scrivener's error's effect on a testator's intent, extrinsic evidence is permissible to establish and correct the error.

> **Example:** In *Erickson v. Erickson*, 716 A.2d 92 (Conn. 1998), two days before his marriage to W, T executed a will leaving the residue of his estate to her. Under Connecticut law, a marriage revokes a will made prior to the marriage unless the will expressly provides for the marriage. On T's death, his children from his first marriage sought to void the will and take a share of T's estate through intestacy. W sought to admit evidence that T's attorney mistakenly executed the will two days before the marriage without acknowledging the marriage in the will. The court applied the scrivener's error doctrine to hold that if there is clear and convincing of a scrivener's error and its effect on a testator's intent, extrinsic evidence is permissible to establish and correct the error.

c. Reformation

A few states have adopted the Restatement (Third) of Property's more liberal approach, which allows a court to openly reform a donative document based on clear and convincing evidence of (a) a mistake of law or fact or (b) the donor's intention. The UPC now provides, after amendment in 2008, that a "court may reform the terms of a governing instrument if it is proved by clear and convincing evidence that the transferor's intent and the terms of the governing instrument were affected by mistake of fact or law, whether in expression or inducement." Unif. Probate Code § 2-805.

C. ADEMPTION

1. Ademption by Extinction

The doctrine of ademption applies only to specific bequests. If the subject matter of a specific bequest is missing or destroyed (i.e., extinct), then the beneficiary takes nothing, not even the insurance proceeds or the equivalent in cash. This rule does not apply when the testator was incompetent, unless the will was executed prior to the incompetency.

a. Traditional approach—"identity theory"

The intent of the testator is not relevant in most states if the bequest is extinct. If the specifically-bequeathed item is not a part of the estate at the testator's death, then it is adeemed.

1) Substantial change

A substantial change in the nature of the subject matter of a bequest will operate as an ademption, but a merely nominal or formal change will not.

2) Ademption disfavored

Courts are inclined to avoid ademption by a variety of means, including the classification of a specific bequest as general or demonstrative, the classification of an inter vivos distribution as a mere change in form, and the creation of other exceptions to the doctrine.

b. "Modified intention" approach

Some jurisdictions apply a "modified intention" approach to ademption, generally following the identity approach discussed above, but exempting property that was transferred through an act that was involuntary to the testator or made without the testator's knowledge and consent. The beneficiary will get either the full value of the bequest, or whatever is left of the bequest less proceeds that were used to support the testator. See *In re Estate of Anton*, 731 N.W.2d 19 (IA 2007) (holding that identity rule adeeming bequests not specifically found in the estate would not be applied when specifically devised property was removed from testator's estate by act involuntary to testator).

c. UPC approach—"intent theory"

The UPC fully rejects the traditional identity approach to ademption, adopting an intent approach instead. Under the UPC, the testator's intent at the time he disposed of the subject matter of the bequest is examined. The UPC has essentially established a "mild presumption" against ademption and has created several doctrines to avoid it. The bequest to the beneficiary is adeemed if the facts and circumstances establish that the ademption was intended. The UPC permits a beneficiary of a specific extinct gift to inherit the property acquired by the testator as **replacement property** or, if the testator is owed money relating to the extinction, the **outstanding balance**. Unif. Probate Code § 2-606(a).

If neither the replacement property nor the outstanding balance doctrine applies, then the UPC provides that a beneficiary of a specific gift is entitled to money equivalent to the value of the specific property as of the date of disposition if ademption is inconsistent with the testator's:

i)   Intent; or

ii) Plan of distribution.

Example: X's will devises 123 Main St. to his son, Y. At the time of the will's execution, X owned the property, but he later sold the property and used the proceeds to buy bonds. X still owned the bonds at this death. Under the majority rule and common law, Y would not receive the bonds at death, as the specific devise of property was adeemed. Under the UPC, Y would receive the bonds under the replacement property exception.

EXAM NOTE: If an exam question does not specifically indicate the approach the jurisdiction takes with regard to ademption by extinction, be prepared to discuss both the traditional approach and the modern trend.

---

d. Beneficiary entitlement

If a gift is adéemed, then the beneficiary is entitled to:

i) Whatever is left of the specifically devised property;

ii) The balance of the purchase price owing from the purchaser of the property;

iii) Any amount of condemnation award for the taking of the property, to the extent unpaid upon death; or

iv) Property acquired from the foreclosure of a security interest on a specifically devised note.

2. Exoneration of Liens

Under the common-law doctrine of exoneration, the specific devisee of encumbered real property was entitled to have the mortgage on the property paid from the estate as a debt of the decedent, unless there was evidence of a contrary intent on the part of the testator. However, in many states, the specific devisee of encumbered property takes subject to the mortgage, notwithstanding the fact that the will contained a clause directing the executor to pay the decedent's debts. A specific devisee of encumbered property is not entitled to have the debt paid off by the residual estate unless the testator's intent to do so is clear in the will. Unif. Probate Code § 2-607. A testator can specifically require that a lien be exonerated, in which case the encumbered property will not abate to exonerate the lien unless specifically stated in the will.

Note: A general directive to pay debt is insufficient to direct the exoneration of liens.

3. Ademption by Satisfaction

A general, specific, or demonstrative devise may be satisfied in whole or in part by an inter vivos transfer to the devisee after the execution of the will, if it was the testator's intent to satisfy the devise by the transfer.

a. Intent controls

The testator's intent to adeem must exist before the legacy or bequest is rendered inoperative.

b. No presumption

The UPC presumes no ademption by satisfaction, absent an express writing, and it limits the sources of evidence of the testator's intent to adeem. Unif. Probate Code § 2-609.

4. Securities

a. Pre-death changes

At common law, the treatment of a gift of securities depended on whether it was a specific or general bequest. Many states hold that a stock dividend, like a cash dividend, is a property interest distinct from stock given by the specific bequest. A bequest of stock owned by a testator when the testator's will is signed excludes subsequently acquired shares of the same stock. A bequest of a certain number of shares of a security that were owned by the testator at the time the will was executed is deemed to include any additional shares of that security or of another security acquired by reason of a stock split, stock dividend, reinvestment, or merger initiated by the original security. However, the beneficiary is not entitled to any pre-death cash dividends or distributions. If the bequest is a generic gift (e.g., does not specify a number of shares), then the beneficiary does not take any additional shares.

Under the UPC, which rejects the common-law approach of classifying the type of bequest, a bequest of a security that was owned at the time the will was executed will include any additional shares of that security or of another security as long as the action was initiated by the corporate entity. A stock dividend is treated like a stock split instead of a cash dividend. Unif. Probate Code § 2-605.

b. Post-death changes

The classification of a gift controls the disposition of any income earned on the gift after the testator's death. Specific bequests carry with them all post-death income, such as interest, dividends, and rent. General bequests carry with them interest earned on the amount bequeathed beginning one year after the decedent's death, at a rate set by statute. Residual bequests are not interest-bearing.

D. LAPSE

1. Common-Law Rule

Under common law, if a beneficiary died before the testator, or before a point in time by which she was required to survive the testator under the will, then the gift failed and went to the residue unless the will provided for an alternate disposition. Absent a residuary clause, the gift passed through intestacy. A gift made by will to an individual who was deceased at the time the will was executed was treated as a lapsed gift.

2. Anti-Lapse Statute

Almost all states have enacted anti-lapse statutes providing for alternate disposition of lapsed bequests. Under the majority of the statutes, if the gift was made to a relation of the testator within a specific statutory degree, and the relation predeceased the testator but left issue, then the issue succeeds to the gift, unless the will expressly states the contrary. Most statutes require that the devisee who failed to survive was a grandparent, descendant of a grandparent, or a stepchild of the testator. Unif. Probate Code § 2-603. Most jurisdictions allow the statute to apply only to testamentary gifts. Under the UPC, however, the statute may also apply to non-probate transfers. Unif. Probate Code §§ 2-706; 2-707.

> **Example:** T's will provides, "I give $50,000 to my brother, B." B predeceases T. Under anti-lapse, B's issue would take the $50,000.

In *Ruotolo v. Tietjen*, 890 A.2d 166 (Conn. App. 2006), a testator devised one half of his property to his stepdaughter "if she survives me." The stepdaughter predeceased the testator and following the testator's death, the stepdaughter's daughter attempted to take her mother's share under an anti-lapse statute. The court concluded that words of survivorship in the testator's will did not constitute sufficient evidence of intent by the testator to prevent the application of the anti-lapse statute. Many states have reached the opposite conclusion adopting the view that if a testator specifically chose to include such words that shows intent to override the anti-lapse statute.

3. Class Gifts

At common law, a class gift is treated differently from a gift to an individual. A class gift is a gift to more than one individual that is intended to be taken as a group. There is an intrinsic right of survivorship among the members of the class. Whether a gift is to a class or just to multiple individuals with no right of survivorship is a question of the testator's intent. If the testator uses a generic class label, such as "to my nieces" in devising his property, that generally indicates a class gift. If the testator specifically names each beneficiary, that fact can suggest that the gift is not a class gift. Courts generally admit extrinsic evidence when the will is ambiguous as to the testator's intent. Many courts have held that when there is one gift in a will to multiple individuals that has an express right of survivorship in the will, the failure to include such an express right in another gift indicates that the testator did not intend for that gift to be a class gift. *See e.g., Dawson v. Yucus*, 239 N.E.2d 305 (Ill. App. 1968) (holding that when number of beneficiaries to a gift is certain and share each is to receive is certain and not dependent for amount on the number who shall survive, it is not a class gift but a gift to the specific individuals).

When a gift is to an entire class and one member of the class dies, only the surviving class members take. However, if an anti-lapse statute applies (because the predeceased class member was related to the testator), then the issue of the predeceased member also will take. The majority of states and UPC apply the anti-lapse statute first, before the determination of a class gift. Unif. Probate Code § 2-603.

The UPC extends anti-lapse to life insurance policies in which the beneficiary predeceases the policyholder. Unif. Probate Code § 2-706.

4. Residuary Rule and Future Interests

Under the UPC, if the residue is left to two or more persons and one dies, and if anti-lapse does not apply, then the remaining beneficiaries take in their proportionate shares. Unif. Probate Code § 2-604(b). This is contrary to the common law "no residue of a residue" rule, under which the testator's heirs succeeded to any lapsed portion of a residual bequest. *See Estate of Russell*, 444 P.2d 353 (Cal. 1968) (applying no residue of residue rule when testator attempted to leave half of residue to her dog).

Likewise, if a future interest is left to two or more persons and the gift to one of them lapses, then her share passes to the other future interest holders unless anti-lapse applies.

5. Void Gifts

Although there may appear to be no difference between a void gift and a lapsed gift, the law sometimes makes a distinction and treats them differently. A gift is void if, unbeknownst to the testator, the beneficiary is already deceased at the time the will is executed. As noted above, a lapsed gift occurs when the beneficiary predeceases the testator **after** the will has been executed. Most states allow anti-lapse statutes to apply to void gifts.

E. ABATEMENT (FIRST TO LAST)

1. Order

Gifts by will are abated (i.e., reduced) when the assets of the estate are insufficient to pay all debts and legacies. The testator may indicate his intended order of abatement, but if he fails to do so, the law prescribes an order. If not otherwise specified in the will, gifts are abated in the following order:

    i) Intestate property;

    ii) Residuary bequests;

    iii) General bequests; and

    iv) Specific bequests.

Unif. Probate Code § 3-902.

Demonstrative legacies are treated as specific legacies for abatement purposes to the extent that they can be satisfied, and otherwise as general legacies. Within each classification, abatement is pro rata.

2. Specific Bequests

A specific bequest may abate to satisfy a general legacy only if such intent was clearly indicated by the testator.

XIII. WILL SUBSTITUTES

A will substitute is a method of transferring a decedent's property outside of probate. Distribution of these non-probate assets does not involve a court proceeding; it is done in accordance with the terms of a contract, trust, or deed. Will substitutes come in many forms, the most popular of which are described below in this section of the outline.

A. REVOCABLE TRUSTS

For more detailed discussion of trusts, *see* § XV, *infra*.

1. In General

Virtually all jurisdictions permit a revocable inter vivos trust to serve as a valid will substitute. If a trustee holds legal title and a beneficiary holds equitable title, there is no need to transfer title upon the death of the creator. Inter vivos trust property is non-probate property. Under the traditional and majority rule, a trust that is silent as to its revocability is deemed revocable. If the trust states an express and particular method of revocation, only that method of revocation is permissible. If the trust is silent as to the method of revocation, any method of revocation is generally permissible, unless real property is involved, in which case only written revocation is permitted.

2. Settlor's Power and Control

There is a split among the jurisdictions as to how much power and control the settlor can retain and still have a valid inter vivos trust. Most courts permit a settlor to retain a lot of control over the trust. *See e.g., Farkas v. Williams*, 125 N.E.2d 600 (Ill. 1955) (holding that even when settlor of trust retains power to revoke and appoints self as trustee, if beneficiary obtains any interest in trust before settlor dies, trust is valid inter vivos trust).

3. Rights of Settlor's Creditors Following Settlor's Death

Under the common law, if a settlor retains a life estate in an inter vivos revocable trust, when the settlor dies, the life estate ends and there is nothing for the settlor's creditors to attach.

The modern trend, as reflected in the Uniform Trust Code, asserts that since the assets were available to the settlor during his lifetime, the creditors of the settlor should be allowed to reach those assets after the settlor's death. Thus, if a revocable inter vivos trust is not revoked and the settlor retained a life estate in the trust, after the settlor's death, the settlor's creditors can reach the assets in the trust if the settlor's probate estate is insufficient to pay off the creditors. *See State Street Bank & Trust Co. v. Reiser*, 389 N.E.2d 768 (Mass. App. 1979) (holding that given the extent to which the settlor had power over the assets in a revocable inter vivos trust during his lifetime, such assets should be available to creditors after settlor's death, after exhausting settlor's probate assets).

4. Beneficiary's Lack of Standing to Challenge Revocable Trust Amendments

A beneficiary of a revocable inter vivos trust has no standing to challenge amendments to the trust because her interest is contingent and unenforceable during the settlor's lifetime. *Linthicum v. Rudi*, 148 P.3d 746 (Nev. 2006).

B. POUR-OVER WILLS

A pour-over will includes a clause wherein some or all of the decedent's probate property is given to the trustee of the decedent's inter vivos trust.

Example: "I give the rest and residue of my estate to the trustee of my inter vivos trust, to hold and distribute pursuant to its terms."

A true pour-over clause must be validated. If the will states the terms of the trust, the clause is not a pour-over clause, but instead creates a testamentary trust, which requires probate supervision. If the will does not set forth the terms of the trust and they are set forth in a separate document, the clause is a pour-over clause and must be validated.

As the law developed with regard to pour-over wills, two theories were generally applied to validate the pour-over of assets into an inter vivos trust: acts of independent significance and incorporation by reference. Under the acts of independence significance doctrine, the "act" that is referenced in the will was the reference to the trust. If the trust is funded inter vivos and has property in it at the time of the settlor's death, the trust has its own independent significance. The doctrine, though, did not permit pour-over into an unfunded inter vivos trust. Under the doctrine of incorporation by reference, the will would incorporate the inter vivos trust instrument into it, giving it effect and allowing it to dictate who takes the settlor's probate property. However, the doctrine of incorporation by reference would not allow a trust instrument to be amended after the will is executed. In addition, the trust instrument incorporated by reference only created a testamentary trust at the death of the settlor, which meant that it became subject to probate supervision, contravening the whole purpose of using a trust.

Due to the uncertainty of these doctrines and some errors that embarrassed lawyers, lawyers and estate planners sought the enactment of legislation that permitted a will to pour over probate assets into an *unfunded* inter vivos trust. Originally, the Uniform Testamentary Additions to Trusts Act (UTATA), included within the UPC, validated the pour-over of probate assets into an inter vivos trust only if the original trust instrument was executed before or concurrently with the will. Subsequently, the UTATA/UPC was amended to allow the trust instrument to be executed or amended after the will. Unif. Probate Code § 2-511. In addition, no property need be put into the trust until the death of the settlor. The trust is then still treated as an inter vivos trust that is not subject to probate court supervision.

EXAM NOTE: In attempting to validate a pour-over clause, try to apply the UTATA/UPC approach, unless told that is inapplicable, If that will not work, try to validate with the incorporation by reference or acts of independent significance doctrines. If none of those options work, the clause is invalid and the gift under it fails.

C. PAYBABLE-ON-DEATH CONTRACTS

At common law, the only type of contracts with payable-on-death clauses that were exempt from the formalities required for wills were life insurance contracts. *See e.g., In re Estate of Atkinson*, 175 N.E. 2d 548 (Ohio Prob. Ct. 1961) (holding that use of words "payable on death" on bank account created invalid testamentary disposition). Under the modern approach, as reflected in the UPC, all contracts with payable-on-death clauses are exempt from wills formalities. Thus, a decedent may have a contract with a bank, employer, or some other individual or entity to distribute the property held under the contract at the decedent's death to a named beneficiary. *See e.g., Estate of Hillowitz*, 238 N.E.2d 723 (N.Y. 1968) (holding that a partnership agreement with clause that each partner's interest would pass to his spouse on the partner's death was valid and enforceable). To collect property held under a payable-on-death contract, the beneficiary must file a death certificate with the custodian holding the property.

1. **Life Insurance**

    A beneficiary of a life insurance policy takes by virtue of the insurance contract. The proceeds are not part of the decedent's estate, unless they are payable to the estate as beneficiary.

    In most jurisdictions, life insurance proceeds are payable to the beneficiary named in the beneficiary-designation form filed with the insurance company, even if the insured names a different beneficiary in a later-executed will. This rule is typically justified as a matter of contract: life insurance policies generally provide that policy proceeds will be paid only to a beneficiary named on an appropriate form filed with the insurance company; other possible methods of changing a beneficiary are thus viewed as being excluded by the insurance contract. *See, generally, Cook v. Equitable Life Assurance Society of the U.S.*, 428 N.E.2d 110 (Ind. 1981).

    However, some courts have rejected the majority rule on the grounds that the requirement that a beneficiary change be evidenced by a form filed with the insurance company is for the exclusive benefit of the company. These courts permit an insured to change a beneficiary designation by will if his insurance company does not object. *See, e.g., Burkett v. Mott*, 733 P.2d 673 (Ariz. 1986).

2. **Bank Accounts and Securities Registered in Beneficiary Form**

    Amounts on deposit in a bank account may be transferred at death by means of a joint account designation or any other multiple-party account designation. The surviving tenant or tenants have an absolute right to the account proceeds, unless extrinsic evidence is introduced that the decedent added the tenant or tenants for convenience purposes only. For example, giving the other co-tenant check-writing privileges is considered a convenience. In that case, some courts, including those following the UPC, set aside the joint tenancy in the bank accounts. Unif. Probate Code § 6-212 cmt. Other courts still affirm the joint tenancy, relying on the parol evidence rule to exclude evidence of the depositor's intentions.

    The owner of a security may register it in "beneficiary form" so that upon the death of the owner, the security is transferred to the designated beneficiary. Registration in beneficiary form does not limit the rights of a surviving spouse, domestic partner, or creditor.

3. **Totten Trusts**

    A Totten trust, similar to payable-on-death bank accounts, is a form of inter vivos trust whereby the depositor sets up an account and makes deposits "for the benefit of" the beneficiary. The depositor retains legal title, and the beneficiary has equitable title. As a general rule, Totten trusts are revocable and permit the depositor to withdraw money.

D. DEEDS

A deed is an effective non-probate transfer if it is delivered to the grantee prior to the grantor's death, even if the grantor retains a life estate in his own favor, as long as the delivery is unconditional. A deed is likewise effective if it is delivered to an escrow agent during the grantor's lifetime with instructions to turn it over to the grantee upon the grantor's death. Even if a deed fails for want of delivery, and is thus ineffective, it cannot be a will.

E. JOINT TENANCIES IN REAL PROPERTY

Most family homes are owned either by joint tenancy or tenancy by the entirety, both of which establish a right of survivorship in the co-owners. Upon the death of one of the tenants, the survivor owns the property in its entirety, with no need for probate. A joint tenancy in real property requires the agreement of all tenants to take the most important actions with respect to the property. A joint tenant cannot devise his share of the property by will. To do so, the joint tenant must sever the joint tenancy during his life and convert it into a tenancy in common. A creditor of a joint tenant must seize the joint tenant's interest during the joint tenant's life. If the creditor does not, the interest vanishes upon the joint tenant's death and there is nothing for the creditor to attach.

XIV. LIMITS ON TESTAMENTARY POWER TO TRANSFER

A. RIGHTS OF SURVIVING SPOUSE

1. In General

The law generally provides for two different types of protection for a surviving spouse of a decedent. In virtually all states, through a combination of state and federal law, a surviving spouse has certain rights for support for the rest of the surviving spouse's life. A surviving spouse is also entitled to a share of the marital property.

2. Spousal Support

The surviving spouse is entitled to the following means of support: social security, pension plans, homestead exemption, personal property, and family allowance. These rights apply even if the decedent spouse tries to defeat such rights.

a. Social Security

The surviving spouse would be entitled to a benefit based on the decedent spouse's benefits. Only a spouse can receive a worker's survivor benefits from Social Security. The benefits cannot be transferred to anyone else.

b. Pension plans

The Employee Retirement Income Security Act (ERISA) requires pension plans to give spouses survivorship rights. Unlike Social Security, a surviving spouse can waive her rights in the spouse's pension plan, but such waivers are subject to strict requirements.

c. Homestead exemption

Under homestead exemption statutes, which vary by state, a certain acreage or value of real property is exempt from creditors' claims, is inalienable during the life of the owners without consent, and passes upon death by statute, not by will. The amount of the homestead exemption differs by state, but the UPC, as amended in 2008, recommends a lump sum payment of $22,500. Any minor child or children of the decedent are entitled to the exemption amount in the absence of a surviving spouse.

d. Personal property set-aside

The surviving spouse is entitled to claim certain tangible personal property, even when the decedent has attempted to devise that property in his will. Some states have a statutory list of tangible personal property or a monetary limit to which the surviving spouse or, if none, any minor child or children of the decedent, are entitled.

e. Family allowance

The surviving spouse has a right to a family allowance during probate, the amount of which varies by jurisdiction. Some jurisdictions permit minor children also to receive a family allowance. Depending on the jurisdiction, the family allowance is either a set amount or one based on the marital standard of living.

3. Spouse's Right to a Share of the Marital Property

a. Separate property approach versus community property approach

Most states follow what is called the "separate property" approach to marital property. Eight states (Arizona, California, Idaho, Louisiana, Nevada, New Mexico, Texas, and Washington) follow what is called the "community property" approach. Alaska allows married couples to elect to treat their property as community property.

Under the separate property approach, whatever a worker earns is hers. If one spouse is the wage earner, while the other works at home, the wage-earning spouse will own all of the property acquired during the marriage other than gifts or inheritances from others or by the wage earner to the homemaker spouse. To protect the homemaker spouse (or a spouse who works at a lower paying job), the laws of almost all separate property states give the surviving spouse an "elective" or "forced" share in the estate of the decedent spouse.

Under the community property approach, the earnings of the spouses and the property acquired from such earnings are the property of both spouses, unless they both agree otherwise. Community property consists of the earnings and certain acquisitions of both spouses during the marriage. At the death of one spouse, one-half of the community property is already owned by the other, and only the decedent's half is subject to disposition by will. Quasi-community property is separate property that would have been community property had the parties been domiciled in a community-property state when acquired. Quasi-community property is treated like community property for distribution purposes.

b. Elective share

The application of the elective share, and the property to which it applies, varies depending on the jurisdiction. In common-law states, the elective share gives the surviving spouse a fraction (often one-third) of the decedent's estate if the surviving spouse elects to take the elective share rather than any gift contained in the will. The elective share applies to all property of the decedent, regardless of when it was acquired.

The elective share does not exist in community-property states. Instead, the surviving spouse is entitled to a forced share of one-half of the community property and quasi-community property. The spouse must elect to take this share in lieu of all other interests she may have under the testator's will and must file a notice of election within a specified time period. The elective share is personal to the surviving spouse.

1) Property subject to the elective share

Traditionally, and still in a number of states, the surviving spouse was entitled to a share of the decedent spouse's *probate* property only. As the use of non-probate transfers grew, courts struggled with ways to try to protect the surviving spouse. Some looked to whether the non-probate transfer was "illusory," meaning that the assets count as part of the decedent's assets to constitute the elective share. Some looked to whether the decedent spouse intended to defraud the surviving spouse by using the non-probate property transfer. To determine intent, some states applied a subjective test, while others applied an objective test. Other states looked to whether the decedent spouse had a present donative intent at the time the non-probate transfer was made. *See e.g., Sullivan v. Burkin*, 460 N.E.2d 572 (Mass. 1984) (establishing a prospective rule that if the settlor retains substantial rights and powers under an inter vivos trust instrument, the assets of the trust will be considered part of the estate for distribution to the heirs).

Many states, dissatisfied with the vague judicial standards described above, have enacted specific statutory criteria for determining what non-probate transfers are subject to the elective share. The UPC statutory approach is described below.

2) UPC "augmented estate"

The UPC introduced the concept of the augmented estate. Under the augmented estate, the probate estate is "augmented" with certain non – probate transfers. The current version of the UPC subjects property acquired before marriage, as well as that acquired during marriage, to the "marital-property" portion of the augmented estate to which the surviving spouse is entitled. The UPC augmented estate is broader than the share under a community-property state, as it includes property acquired before the marriage and property gifted to the spouse during the marriage.

a) Increasing share

Under the UPC, the surviving spouse may take an elective-share amount equal to 50% of the value of the marital-property portion of the augmented estate. The marital-property portion is calculated by applying to the augmented estate a schedule of percentages that increase as the length of the marriage increases (e.g., 6% for the first year, 30% at five years). Unif. Probate Code § 2-203(a).

b) Satisfying share

The elective share is satisfied first from property already received by the surviving spouse, then from the rest of the estate. Life estates granted to the surviving spouse are considered support and do not count in the valuation. Unif. Probate Code § 2-209.

3) Right to set aside transfers

In many states, the surviving spouse can set aside inter vivos transfers by the decedent made during the marriage without spousal consent if the decedent initiated the transfer within one year of his death, retained an interest in the property transferred, or received less than adequate consideration for the transfer.

4) Personal to the surviving spouse

In most states and under the UPC, the election is personal to the surviving spouse. Thus, if a husband dies and before the surviving wife exercises her election she dies, all of the husband's property passes to the husband's heirs rather than to the wife's heirs. Unif. Probate Code § 2-212(a).

5) Incompetent spouse

If the surviving spouse is incompetent, a guardian of the spouse can decide whether an election is in the spouse's best interests under the supervision of the probate court. A majority of jurisdictions hold that all of the surrounding facts and circumstances should be considered in making such a decision. *See e.g., In re Estate of Cross*, 664 N.E.2d 905 (Ohio 1996). Such a view allows the guardian to consider the preservation of the decedent's estate plan and whether the surviving spouse would have wanted to follow the decedent's wishes. A minority of jurisdictions hold that the guardian must elect to take the share if it is to the economic benefit of the surviving spouse, as calculated economically.

The UPC provides that if the elective share is exercised for an incompetent spouse, the portion of the elective share that exceeds the share the spouse would have taken under the will is to be placed in a custodial trust, with the surviving spouse having a life estate, and a remainder in the devisees under the will. Unif. Probate Code § 2-212.

6) Abandonment

In a minority of states, an elective share is not allowed for persons who abandoned or refused to support the decedent spouse.

7) Waiver

The right of the surviving spouse to take her elective or forced share can be **waived in writing** if the writing is signed after **fair disclosure** of its contents.

a) Scope

A spouse may waive in whole or in part, before or during the marriage, the right to receive any of the following from the estate of his spouse:

i)   Property that would pass by intestate succession or by testamentary disposition in a will executed before the waiver;

ii) Homestead, exempt property, or family allowances;

iii) The right to take the share of an omitted spouse; or

iv) The right to take against the testator's will.

b) Validity requirements

The terms of the waiver must be objectively fair and reasonable to both parties. The waiver must be voluntary and in writing and must be signed by the surviving spouse. It can be revoked or altered only by a subsequent writing signed by both parties, unless the waiver specifies other means of revocation. The surviving spouse must be represented by independent legal counsel at the time the waiver is signed. The surviving spouse must have had adequate knowledge of the property and financial obligations of the decedent at the time of the signing of the waiver. With regard to the standard for adequate knowledge, *see Reece v. Elliot*, 208 S.W.3d 419 (Tenn. Ct. App. 2006) (holding that adequate knowledge did not require husband to list value of company stock he owned when wife had independent counsel and could have asked questions about the value of the listed asset).

B. OMISSION

1. Omitted Spouse

a. In general

At common law, a premarital will was revoked upon marriage. In most states today, while a marriage after the execution of a will does not invalidate the will, a spouse who is not mentioned in a will is generally entitled to a special intestate share (generally one third) of the testator's estate if the marriage began after the execution of the will. When a spouse is omitted from a will, a rebuttable presumption is created that the omission was a mistake. In many states, the presumption cannot be rebutted unless the intent to omit the spouse is apparent from the language of the will or the spouse was provided for outside of the will.

b. UPC approach

Under the UPC, the share for the omitted spouse is required unless:

i) A valid **prenuptial agreement** exists,

ii) The spouse was **given property outside of the will** in lieu of a disposition in the testator's will; or

iii) The spouse was **specifically excluded** from the will.

Unif. Probate Code § 2-301.

The UPC expands the allowable evidence that can be used to prove that the spouse's omission from the will was intentional to include, in addition to the language of the will, any other evidence that the will was made in contemplation of the testator's marriage to the surviving spouse. Unif. Probate Code § 2-301.

Under the UPC, an omitted spouse has the right to receive no less than her intestate share of the deceased spouse's estate from that portion of the testator's estate that is not already devised to a child or descendant of the testator if:

i) The child is not a child of the surviving spouse; and

ii) The child was born before the testator married the surviving spouse.

2. Omitted Children

a. In general

A pretermitted child is a child that is born after a will was executed. Pretermitted heir statutes permit children of a testator under certain circumstances to claim a share of the estate even though they were omitted from the deceased testator's will. While the birth or adoption of a child after the execution of a will does not invalidate the will, such children are omitted from the will. If the testator then dies without revising the will, a presumption is created that the omission of the child was accidental.

Under the typical pretermitted heir statute, if the testator had no children at the time the will was written, then any after-born child or children will be entitled to their intestate share. If, however, the testator had children at the time the will was executed, then any after-born children (pretermitted children) are only entitled to get a share of the amount that was left to the earlier-born children named in the will.

Example: T writes a will leaving $75,000 to each of his two children A and B. After executing the will, T has another child C, who is not provided for in the will and T never amends his will. C is allowed to share in the bequests to A and B. The total bequest is $150,000. That means, instead of $75,000 per child, each child is only going to get$50,000.

b. Exceptions

In general, an omitted child statute will not apply if:

i) It appears that the omission of the child was **intentional**;

ii) The **testator had other children** at the time the will was executed and left substantially all of his estate to the other parent of the pretermitted child; or

iii) The testator **provided for the child outside of the will** (e.g., through a trust or through life insurance) and intended this to be in lieu of a provision in the will.

Pretermitted heir statutes generally fall under two types. Under the Missouri-type statute, it must appear from the will itself that the omission of the child or other heir was intentional. Extrinsic evidence of intent is not admissible. Under the Massachusetts-type statute, the child takes unless it appears that the omission was intentional and not occasioned by a mistake. Extrinsic evidence is admissible to show the presence or absence of intent to disinherit.

Mention of a child in only one of two instruments that are being read together or the republication of a will by codicil after the birth of a child will preclude that child from claiming as an omitted heir, although this rule is flexibly applied.

> **EXAM NOTE:** For both a pretermitted spouse and a pretermitted child statute, pay close attention to the possibility of republication by codicil. A minor modification to a will after a child is born might transform that pretermitted child into a child who was in existence at the time the will was executed. Therefore, it might result in disinheritance of that child.

c. UPC

1) Presumption

Unlike the UPC omitted-spouse doctrine, the UPC omitted-child doctrine does **not** expand the scope of evidence admissible to show the testator's intent to omit the child. However, extrinsic evidence is permitted to show the testator's lack of intent to omit the child, and ambiguities are resolved in the child's favor. The UPC does not permit the presumption to be overcome when a substantial portion of the estate is transferred to the other parent of the omitted child.

2) Omitted child's share

If the testator had no other children when the will was executed, then the child takes her intestate share. If the testator has at least one other child living at the time of the execution of the will, and the will devised property to at least one of those children, then the omitted child's share is taken from that portion of property already devised to the other child, and it must equal the share the other child receives.

While the UPC does not extend the protection of the omitted-child statute to children of whom the testator was unaware, it does extend omitted-child status to children whom the testator believed to be deceased. Unif. Probate Code § 2-302.

3) Adopted children

Unlike the rules in many states, the UPC rule applies to children adopted after the execution of the will.

XV. TRUSTS

A. INTRODUCTION TO TRUSTS

A trust is a fiduciary relationship wherein one or more trustees are called upon to manage, protect, and invest certain property and any income generated from such property for the benefit of one or more named beneficiaries.

To create a trust, the grantor must have intended to create the trust. A trust is valid as long as it has a trustee, an ascertainable beneficiary, and assets. Trust interests are alienable, devisable, and descendible unless the terms of a trust expressly or impliedly provide otherwise.

Trusts are classified according to the method by which they are created. There are three main types of trusts: express trusts, resulting trusts, and constructive trusts. An express trust is created by intention and gratuitously for the benefit of individual beneficiaries. There are private and charitable express trusts. Resulting and constructive trusts are remedial trusts, equitable remedies created by operation of law.

When a trust fails in some way or when there is an incomplete disposition of trust property, a court may create a resulting trust requiring the holder of the property to return it to the settlor or to the settlor's estate. When a testamentary trust fails, the residuary legatee succeeds to the property interest. The purpose of a resulting trust is to achieve the settlor's likely intent in attempting to create the trust. The primary aim of a resulting trust is the prevention of unjust enrichment. Courts use constructive trusts to prevent unjust enrichment if the settlor causes fraud, duress, undue influence, breach of duty, or detrimental reliance by a third party on a false representation. There must have been wrongful conduct in order to impose a constructive trust. A party with unclean hands will usually be estopped from arguing for the creation of a constructive trust.

B. OVERVIEW OF EXPRESS TRUSTS

1. Bifurcated Transfer

A trust involves a bifurcated transfer. The creator or settlor transfers property to a second party trustee to be managed for the benefit of a third party beneficiary. The trustee holds legal title and the beneficiary holds equitable title. No consideration is required.

2. Ongoing Transfers

A trust involves an ongoing series of transfers. Trust property is divided between income and principal, and the equitable interest is divided between the beneficiary holding the possessory estate and the beneficiary holding the future interest.

3. Revocable versus Irrevocable Trusts

a. Presumption

A revocable trust can be terminated by the settlor at any time. An irrevocable trust usually cannot be terminated. Unless otherwise stated in the instrument, a trust is presumed to be irrevocable. In some states, however, the presumption is that the trust is revocable.

b. Method of revocation

Absent language within the instrument prescribing the method of revocation, any action manifesting the settlor's intent to revoke will suffice. The revocation becomes effective when the action manifesting the intent occurs, rather than when the trustee or beneficiaries learn of the action.

4. Mandatory versus Discretionary Trusts

A mandatory trust requires the trustee to distribute all trust income. To protect the interests of the beneficiaries, a settlor may instead opt to create a discretionary trust, under which the trustee is given the power to distribute income at his discretion. The trustee does not abuse his discretion unless he acts dishonestly or in a way not contemplated by the trust creator.

5. Inter Vivos versus Testamentary Trusts

A trust that is created during the settlor's life is an inter vivos trust. An inter vivos trust may be created either by a declaration of trust, under which the settlor declares that she holds certain property in trust, or by a deed of trust, under which the settlor transfers certain property to another person as trustee. An inter vivos trust can be either revocable or irrevocable. Often inter vivos trusts are used to avoid the costs and delays of the probate process. Other perceived advantages of inter vivos trusts include lifetime asset management by a third party, privacy, and choice of law.

Testamentary trusts occur when the terms of the trust are contained in writing in a will or in a document incorporated by reference into a will. Testamentary trusts must comply with the applicable jurisdiction's Statute of Wills.

6. Rule Against Perpetuities

Because future interests are trust components, trusts are subject to the Rule Against Perpetuities, meaning that a trust may fail if all interests thereunder may not vest within the applicable period of perpetuities (usually a life in being plus 21 years).

Some jurisdictions take a "wait and see" approach to the application of the Rule, refraining from invalidating future interests until it is clear that they will not vest within the perpetuities period.

C. PARTIES TO AN EXPRESS TRUST

1. Settlor

The settlor, sometimes referred to as the grantor, is the creator of the trust. The settlor of a trust may also be a trustee and a beneficiary. If a trust is created by will, the settlor, obviously, cannot be a trustee.

2. Trustee

The trustee holds the legal interest or title to the trust property.

Note: The same individual cannot serve as sole trustee and sole beneficiary of a trust, because such an arrangement would result in a lack of enforcement power by the beneficiary against the trustee. If the trustee is the sole beneficiary, then title merges and the trust terminates.

a. Loss of a trustee

A trust will not fail if a trustee dies, becomes disabled, resigns, or refuses to accept the office. Once the appointment has been accepted, however, the trustee must obtain the court's permission to resign. Instead, the court will appoint a successor trustee, unless the settlor expressed an intent that the trust was to continue only as long as a particular trustee served.

If the settlor fails to designate a trustee, then the court will appoint one.

> **Example:** Settlor gives T $50,000 to invest, with income to A for life, remainder to B. T silently accepts the money. T's acceptance of the trust is presumed because he accepted the trust property. However, if T refuses to serve as a trustee, then the court will appoint a new trustee to comply with the settlor's intent that a trust be created.

b. Duties to perform

A trustee must be given specific duties to perform, or the trust will fail and legal and equitable title will merge in the beneficiary. The expressed intention of the settlor to create a trust along with the identification of trust property and beneficiaries is usually sufficient for the court to infer duties to be performed by the trustee.

> **Example:** A gives $1,000 to T as trustee for A's child, B, with the trust to terminate when B graduates from college. A does not outline any duties for T to perform. The court will infer the duty to accumulate income and to invest principal, to be paid to B when B graduates from college. The trust will not fail for lack of express duties.

c. Qualifications of a trustee

A named trustee must have the capacity to acquire and hold property for his own benefit and the capacity to administer the trust. Minors or insane persons will not qualify as trustees, as they can hold property but cannot administer it. Additionally, those eligible to serve as trustees may be limited by statute. A named trustee who fails to qualify will be replaced by the court, unless the trust names a successor trustee.

d. Removal of a trustee

Several grounds exist through which the court may remove a trustee. These include conflict of interest, old age, serious breach of trust, and habitual drunkenness, among others. However, if the settlor knew of the grounds for removal when she created the trust, then the court may allow the trustee to continue. The court's primary concern is ensuring the integrity and continuity of the trust. Beneficiaries may also be able to remove a trustee if the trust instrument specifically grants them this power of removal.

3. Beneficiary

The beneficiary holds equitable title to the property and therefore possesses the power to enforce the trust instrument. To be valid, a trust must name at least one beneficiary. Such beneficiary may be unborn at the time the trust is created, provided such beneficiary will be identifiable by the time he comes into enjoyment of the trust property. Notice is not required, but acceptance by the beneficiary is required. The beneficiary, however, has the option of renouncing his rights within a reasonable time.

Any individual or entity can be named as a trust beneficiary, provided the individual or entity is capable of taking and holding title to property. A named beneficiary is required to expressly or impliedly accept his interest for the trust to commence for his benefit.

XVI. CREATION OF A PRIVATE EXPRESS TRUST

An express trust is created as a result of the expressed intention of the owner of the property to create a trust relationship with respect to the property. A private express trust clearly states the intention of the settlor to transfer property to a trustee for the benefit of one or more ascertainable beneficiaries.

A. ELEMENTS OF A VALID PRIVATE EXPRESS TRUST

1. Intent

No special form is necessary to create a trust. The settlor must intend to make a gift in trust, though. The use of common trust terms (such as "in trust" or "trustee") will create a presumption of intent to create a trust, but these words are not required or even necessary. *See e.g., Lux v. Lux,* 288 A.2d 701 (R.I. 1972) (holding that will that provided that real property "be maintained" for benefit of testator's grandchildren and should not be sold until youngest grandchild reached age 21 indicated intent to create a trust). The settlor's intent may be manifested orally, in writing, or by conduct. Intent is only required to be expressed in writing when the Statute of Wills (i.e., the jurisdiction's requirements for the execution of a will) or the Statute of Frauds (UCC § 2-207) applies. To determine a settlor's intent, both in creating and administering a trust, the courts consider:

i) The specific terms and overall tenor of the words used;

ii) The definiteness or indefiniteness of the property involved;

iii) The ease or difficulty of ascertaining possible trust purposes and terms, and the specificity or vagueness of the possible beneficiaries and their interests;

iv) The interests or motives and the nature and degree of concerns that may be reasonably supposed to have influenced the transferor;

v) The financial situation, dependencies, and expectations of the parties;

vi) The transferor's prior conduct, statements, and relationships with respect to possible trust beneficiaries;

vii) The personal and any fiduciary relationships between the transferor and the transferee;

viii) Other dispositions the transferor is making or has made of his wealth; and

ix) Whether the result of construing the disposition as involving a trust or not would be such as a person in the situation of the transferor would be likely to desire.

Restatement (Third) of Trusts, § 13. The manifestation of intent must occur either prior to or simultaneously with the transfer of property. If the transfer does not take place immediately, then the intent should be manifested anew at the time of transfer. A promise to create a trust in the future is unenforceable unless the promise is supported by consideration sufficient for the formation of a contract.

> **EXAM NOTE:** The intent requirement for the creation of trusts is tested frequently. Whether a gift is given outright or in trust depends upon whether the beneficial interest vests with the **recipient** (outright gift) or a **third party** (gift in trust).

a. Ambiguous language

The intent to create a trust differs only slightly from the intent to make a gift. A determination must be made regarding whether a bifurcated transfer was intended and, if so, whether the intent was more than a mere hope or wish.

b. Precatory trusts

If a donor transfers property to a donee using language that expresses a hope or wish (rather than creating a legal obligation) that such property be used for the benefit of another, then the gift may be considered a precatory trust, which is not a trust at all, but merely a gift with a recommendation about how it should be used. The governing document must be construed in light of all the facts and circumstances. Determinations of intent can be very uncertain and result in litigation.

c. Failed gifts

When a donor has the intent to make an inter vivos gift, but the gift fails because it is never delivered (e.g., if the donor dies prior to delivery), the donee may attempt to save the failed gift by arguing that the donor intended to create a trust, appointing himself as trustee, and thus delivering the property. The Restatement (Third) of Trusts rejects the argument that a failed gift can be saved by a re-characterization of the donor's intent. *See also, Hebrew University Association v. Nye*, 169 A.2d 641 (Conn. 1961) (holding that a gift that is imperfect due to lack of delivery may not be turned into a trust in the absence of an express manifestation of intent). If a donee changes her position in reliance on the promised gift, such that it would be inequitable to not enforce the gift, a court of equity may compel the donor to complete the gift. The theory of enforcement would not be because the imperfect gift is being turned into an express trust, but instead to impose a constructive trust to prevent unjust enrichment.

2. Trust Property

A valid trust must contain some property that was owned by the settlor at the time the trust was created and was at that time transferred to the trust or to the trustee. Put differently, the trust must be "**funded**." Any property interest, including real property, personal property, money, intangibles, partial interests, or future interests (whether vested or contingent) will suffice, although a mere expectancy will not.

> **Example:** In *Uthank v. Rippstein*, 386 S.W.2d 134 (Tex. 1964), a few days before his death, C sent R a letter promising to give R $200 a month and stating that C's estate would be liable for the payments if C died. Upon C's death, R argued that this created a trust, while the executor of C's will argued that the promise was unenforceable. The court held that the promise was not a trust since there was no trust property and that the letter was merely a promise without consideration to make future gifts, which could not be enforced. Note that under modern statutes like the UPC, the letter might be given testamentary effect as a holographic will.

If a trust that is invalid for lack of assets is later funded, a trust arises if the settlor re-manifests the intention to create the trust. The exception is a "pour-over" gift, which is valid even if made before there is identifiable trust property.

a. Trust res

The requirement of identifiable trust property, or **res**, distinguishes a trust from a debt. A trust involves the duty of one party to deal with specific property for another, whereas a debt involves the obligation of one party to pay a sum of money, from any source, to another.

> **Note:** If the recipient of the funds is entitled to use them as if they are his own and to commingle them with his own monies, then the obligation to pay the funds to another is a debt, not a trust.

b. Segregation

Trust property must be identifiable and segregated. The property must be described with reasonable certainty.

c. Future profits

Most courts hold that future profits do not constitute adequate property for purposes of funding a trust. Some courts have held that future profits do constitute an adequate property interest for purposes of making an inter vivos gift. *See e.g., Speelman v. Pascal,* 178 N.E.2d 723 (N.Y. 1961) (holding that producer's gift to secretary of five percent of future profits of stage musical was effective as present transfer (gift) of his interest). Note that even though future profits are not adequate property to fund a trust, once such profits are actually earned, if the grantor still has an intent to hold them in trust, they then become sufficient to fund the trust, which will be created at that time.

3. Valid Trust Purpose

A trust can be created for any purpose, as long as it is not illegal, restricted by rule of law or statute, or contrary to public policy.

Trust provisions that restrain a first marriage have generally been held to violate public policy. However, a restraint on marriage might be upheld if the trustee's motive was merely to provide support for a beneficiary while the beneficiary is single. *See* Restatement (Third) of Trusts § 29 (2003).

In situations in which one of several trust terms is violative of public policy, any alternative terms provided by the settlor will be honored, and, if there are none, the term will be stricken from the trust, but the trust will not fail altogether unless the removal of the term proves fatal.

4. Ascertainable Beneficiaries

The beneficiaries of a private trust must be ascertainable (i.e., identifiable by name) so that the equitable interest can be transferred automatically by operation of law and directly benefit the person. The settlor may refer to acts of independent significance when identifying trust beneficiaries. If the names of the beneficiaries are not expressly stated in the trust document, the trust must state a method by which the court can objectively determine the beneficiaries. (Note that this rule is different for charitable trusts, which do not fail for lack of a definite beneficiary).

Example: In *Clark v. Campbell,* 133 A. 166 (N.H. 1926), decedent left her personal property to her trustees to dispose of to "such of my friends as they, my trustees, shall select." The court held that the term "friends" was too indefinite. The trust failed because the beneficiaries could not be adequately determined. Note that a few courts would treat the failed trust has automatically transformed into a power of appointment (*see* § XIX, *infra,* for discussion of powers of appointment).

Courts generally hold that terms such as children, issue, nephews, nieces, aunts, and uncles are objectively ascertainable.

a. Unborn children exception

Trusts for the benefit of unborn children will be upheld even though the beneficiaries are not yet ascertainable at the time the trust is created.

Example: S conveys property to T "in trust for A for life, remainder to A's children." The beneficiaries are sufficiently ascertainable even if A has no children

> at the time of the conveyance, because the identification of A's children will be possible at the time of A's death.

b. Class-gift exception

A trust to a reasonably definite class will be enforced. Even a trust that allows the trustee to select the beneficiaries from among the members of a class is acceptable, but traditionally, a trust to an entirely indefinite class will not be enforced as a private trust. Under the Uniform Trust Code (UTC), though, a trustee can select a beneficiary from an indefinite class, unless the trustee must distribute equally to all members of an indefinite class. *See* UTC § 402(c).

c. Charitable trusts exception

Only private trusts must have ascertainable beneficiaries. Because, by definition, charitable trusts exist for the good of the public at large, charitable trusts must not have individual ascertainable beneficiaries.

d. When beneficiary dies without settlor's knowledge prior to creation of trust

If a beneficiary has died without the settlor's knowledge prior to the creation of the trust, the trust will fail for lack of a beneficiary. In this case, a resulting trust in favor of the settlor or his successors is presumed.

5. Possible Writing Requirement

a. General rules

At common law and in most states, if a trust involves real property, the Statute of Frauds generally requires that the trust be in writing. Similarly, if the trust is a testamentary trust, the Statute of Wills generally requires the terms of the trust to be in writing. Otherwise, though, no writing is typically required to find a trust. Thus, a writing is not generally required to transfer personal property to a trust and may be proved by oral testimony. *See e.g., In re Estate of Fournier*, 902 A.2d 852 (Me. 2006) (holding that oral trust of personal property need not be in writing where clear and convincing evidence showed settlor's intent to create it). A few states, though, by statute do require all trusts to be in writing.

The trustee takes legal title upon the delivery of a deed or other document of title for real property, or upon the delivery of personal property.

b. Parol evidence

Generally, evidence outside of the written agreement is permitted to show the settlor's intent only if the written agreement is ambiguous on its face. A few states allow the introduction of parol evidence even if the writing is unambiguous.

An oral trust may be proved by oral testimony.

c. Testamentary trusts that do not meet a writing requirement

If a testamentary trust does not meet the requirements of the Statute of Wills, it may still be deemed a constructive trust or a resulting trust, depending on whether it is "secret" or "semi-secret."

1) "Secret" trust

A "secret" trust is not a testamentary trust. It looks like a testamentary gift, but it is created in reliance on the named beneficiary's promise to hold and administer the property for another. The intended beneficiary is permitted to present extrinsic evidence to prove the promise. If the promise is proven by clear and convincing evidence, then a constructive trust is imposed on the property for the intended beneficiary, so as to prevent the unjust enrichment of the "secret" trustee.

2) "Semi-secret" trust

A "semi-secret" trust is also not a testamentary trust. A semi-secret trust occurs when a gift is directed in a will to be held in trust, but the testator fails to name a beneficiary or specify the terms or purpose of the trust. In this situation, extrinsic evidence may not be presented, the gift fails, and a resulting trust is imposed on the property to be held in trust for the testator's heirs. *See e.g., Oliffe v. Wells*, 130 Mass. 221 (1881) (holding that semi-secret trust failed and imposing resulting trust to distribute property through intestacy).

3) Modern trend

The majority of courts still respect the common-law distinction between "secret" and "semi-secret" trusts. However, the modern trend and that adopted by the Restatement (Third) of Trusts, § 18, calls for the imposition of a constructive trust in favor of the intended beneficiaries (if known) in both "secret" and "semi-secret" trust situations.

XVII. RIGHT OF BENEFICIARIES AND CREDITORS TO DISTRIBUTION

It is the beneficiary's right to receive income or principal from the trust. Various devices have been developed to protect the trust property (and thus the beneficiary's interest) from creditors. Generally speaking, however, once trust property has been distributed to the beneficiary, any attempt to restrain the transferability of the beneficiary's interest will be invalid.

A. RIGHTS OF BENEFICIARIES

1. Mandatory Trust

A mandatory trust is the most restrictive type of trust. The trustee of a mandatory trust has no discretion regarding payments; instead, the trust document explains specifically and in detail how and when the trust property is to be distributed.

2. Discretionary Trust

If the trustee is given complete discretion regarding whether or not to apply payments of income or principal to the beneficiary, then a discretionary trust exists. This allows a settlor to postpone and delegate responsibility to the trustee over to whom to make distributions, in what amounts, and the timing of distributions.

a. Duties to beneficiary

In exercising his discretion, the trustee owes a fiduciary duty to the beneficiary and has a duty to inquire as to the beneficiary's needs. If the trustee fails to make an inquiry, he will be deemed to have breached his fiduciary duty to the beneficiary. *See e.g., Marsman v. Nasca*, 573 N.E.2d 1025 (Mass. App. 1991) (finding breach of duty to inquire into beneficiary's financial situation where beneficiary brought loss of employment to trustee's attention in effort to gain payment of principal and trustee responded by asking for explanation in writing and never followed up when no written explanation was forthcoming).

In deciding whether to make a payment, the trustee must act reasonably (an objective standard) and in good faith (a subjective standard). A settlor can change that standard by expressly stating in the trust instrument that the trustee will have absolute discretion. Even then, though, the trustee is generally still required to act in good faith. *See e.g.,* UTC § 814.

b. Consideration of other resources of beneficiary

Whether a trustee is required to consider a beneficiary's other sources of income in deciding whether to make a payment is a question of the settlor's intent. If that intent is unclear, most courts find a presumption that the settlor intended to provide for the beneficiary regardless of any other resources.

c. Exculpatory clauses

The beneficiary of a fully discretionary trust lacks standing to challenge the actions or inactions of the trustee unless there is a clear abuse of discretion. Discretionary trusts often include an exculpatory clause that protects the trustee against liability for breach of trust, absent willful negligence. Such clauses are generally upheld, but usually construed very narrowly. Under the UTC, if the trustee drafted the exculpatory clause or caused it to be drafted, it will be presumed invalid, unless the trustee proves it is fair under the circumstances and its existence and contents were adequately explained to the settlor. UTC § 1008(b).

d. Creditor rights

If the trustee exercises his discretion to pay, then the beneficiary's creditors have the same rights as the beneficiary, unless a spendthrift restriction exists (discussed *infra* at § XVII.B.3). If the discretion to pay is not exercised, then the beneficiary's interest cannot be reached by her creditors.

B. RIGHTS OF THE CREDITORS OF THE BENEFICIARY

1. Alienation

A beneficiary's equitable interest in trust property is freely alienable unless a statute or the trust instrument limits this right. Because a transferee cannot have a greater right than what was transferred to him, any transferee from a beneficiary, including a creditor, takes an interest identical to what was held by the beneficiary.

Unless otherwise provided by statute or under the trust instrument, a beneficiary's equitable interest is also subject to involuntary alienation. A beneficiary's creditors may reach trust principal or income only when such amounts become payable to the beneficiary or are subject to her demand.

2. Creditor Rights Regarding Discretionary Trusts

a. Pure discretionary trusts

In a pure discretionary trust, in which the trustee has absolute, sole, or uncontrolled discretion over the distributions to the beneficiary, a creditor has no recourse against the beneficiary's interest in the trust. The creditor cannot, by judicial order, compel the trustee to pay her. Since the beneficiary has no right to compel a distribution, neither does a creditor.

The creditor, may, however, be entitled to a court order requiring the trustee to pay the creditor before making any further distributions to the beneficiary. Thus, a creditor can deprive the beneficiary of any distributions, even if the creditor, herself, does not get paid.

b. Support trusts

A support trust directs the trustee to pay income or principal as necessary to support the trust beneficiary, based on need.

Creditors cannot reach the assets of a support trust, except to the extent that a provider of a necessity to the beneficiary can be paid directly by the trustee. In many jurisdictions, children and the spouse of the beneficiary may enforce claims for child support and alimony against a beneficiary's interest in a support trust.

c. Modern approaches

The UTC makes no distinction between discretionary and support trusts and provides that, subject to an exception for claims by children and spouses for support and alimony, a creditor of a beneficiary cannot require a discretionary distribution even if the beneficiary could compel one. UTC § 504. Section 60 of the Restatement (Third) of Trusts allows creditors to reach any distribution by the trust or that the trustee is required to make in the exercise of discretion.

3. Spendthrift Trust (Restraint on Alienation)

A spendthrift trust expressly restricts the beneficiary's power to voluntarily or involuntarily transfer his equitable interest. (Note that a trust restricting only involuntary transfers would be void as against public policy.) Spendthrift provisions are often inserted into trusts to protect beneficiaries from their own imprudence.

a. General rule

In general, spendthrift clauses are valid and enforceable, even with regard to remainder interests in trusts. *See e.g., Scheffel v. Krueger*, 782 A.2d 410 (N.H. 2001) (holding that tort judgment creditor of beneficiary of spendthrift trust was barred from reaching beneficiary's interest in trust).

The spendthrift restriction applies only as long as the property remains in the trust, and it is inapplicable after it has been paid out to the beneficiary. An attempted transfer by the beneficiary in violation of the spendthrift restriction is only effective in that it provides authorization for the trustee to pay funds directly into the hands of the attempted transferee.

b. Exceptions

A beneficiary's creditors usually cannot reach the beneficiary's trust interest in satisfaction of their claims if the governing instrument contains a spendthrift clause prohibiting a beneficiary's creditors from attaching the beneficiary's interest. Although generally valid, most states allow certain classes of creditors to reach a beneficiary's assets, notwithstanding the spendthrift clause.

In general exceptions to the validity of a spendthrift clause include:

  i) Children and spouses entitled to support;

  ii) Those creditors providing basic necessities to the beneficiary; and

  iii) Holders of federal or state tax liens.

b. Statutory limitations

A number of states have statutes that specifically limit the amount of the beneficiary's interest in the trust that can be protected against creditors' claims through a spendthrift clause.

Additionally, if a trust contains a spendthrift clause, then under federal law, the beneficiary's interest is not reachable in bankruptcy proceedings. Further, the federal ERISA law mandates that an employee's pension benefits cannot be reached by creditors.

c. Settlor as beneficiary

In general, courts will also not enforce spendthrift clauses if the settlor is both the settlor and the beneficiary, as this would provide an easy way for individuals to avoid their creditors. When the settlor of a trust is also a trust beneficiary, his creditors are entitled to the maximum amount that could be distributed from the trust to the settlor, even when withdrawals are discretionary or limited by a support standard. If it is unclear whether the settlor is also the beneficiary, the courts will examine who provided the consideration for the creation of the trust.

In recent years, a few states, including Delaware, have enacted statutes that authorize self-settled discretionary trusts. The trust must be irrevocable and the trust interest must be discretionary, and the trust must not have been created to defraud creditors.

XVIII. TRUST MODIFICATION AND TERMINATION

A. IN GENERAL

If the settlor creates a revocable trust, the settlor, by himself, can terminate or modify (by terminating and then creating a new trust with the modified terms) the trust. A revocable or irrevocable trust automatically terminates only when the trust purpose has been accomplished. An irrevocable trust can be modified or terminated if the settlor and all the beneficiaries consent. This is the case even if the trustee has an objection and even if the trust includes a spendthrift clause.

Subject to the *Claflin* doctrine, discussed below, a trust may terminate by consent of all the beneficiaries and the trustee, if the settlor is deceased or has no remaining interest in the trust. The trustee by herself cannot terminate a trust. If all of the beneficiaries wish to terminate, but the trustee objects, most courts allow the trustee to block the termination if she can show that termination would violate the settlor's intent.

1. Unfulfilled Material Purpose

Under the *Claflin* doctrine, a trustee can block a premature trust termination—even one to which all of the beneficiaries have consented—if the trust is shown to have an unfulfilled material purpose. Examples of a trust that intrinsically has an unfulfilled material purpose include discretionary trusts, support trusts, spendthrift trusts, and age-dependent trusts (those that direct the payment of principal to a beneficiary only after he attains a certain age).

Example: In *In re Estate of Brown*, 148 Vt. 94 (1987), the decedent's testamentary trust authorized the trustee to use income and principal to educate the decedent's nephew's children. Upon completion of that purpose, the trust property was to be used to care and maintain the nephew and his wife. When the educational purpose was fulfilled, all of the beneficiaries petitioned to terminate the trust. The trustee objected and the court agreed that even though the educational purpose had been fulfilled, the material purpose of care and maintenance of the nephew and his wife had not been fulfilled.

The most common example of a trust that has an unfulfilled material purpose is one in which the settlor provided for successive interests, in which case both the present and the future beneficiaries must agree in order for the trust to be terminated prematurely. Restatement (Third) of Trusts § 65(2).

Example: If a testator leaves property in trust "to A for life, remainder to B" and B dies before A, leaving his interest to A, A may terminate the trust because its purpose has been accomplished.

2. Revocation by Will

The traditional rule required a trust to expressly provide for its revocability by will. The UTC authorizes trust revocation by will unless the trust expressly provides for another method of revocation.

3. Revocation by Divorce

Traditionally, a spousal interest created by a trust, unlike one created by a will, was not revoked upon divorce. However, the trend now is to treat a spousal interest under a trust similarly to one under a will. *See,* Unif. Probate Code § 2-804.

4. Court Modification and Termination

A court may modify a trust if unanticipated events have caused its purposes to be frustrated by its terms. *See* UTC § 412; *In re Riddell* 157 P.3d 888 (Wa. 2007) (holding that court may use equitable deviation to modify trust when circumstances not anticipated by settlor occurred and modification would further primary purposes of trust and be consistent with law or policy). A court may prematurely terminate a trust if the trust's purpose has been achieved, or if it has become illegal, impracticable, or impossible.

A court may not alter the rights of beneficiaries due to changed circumstances, no matter how compelling, but may interpret certain changes as frustrating to the trust purposes in order to make such modifications. Extreme fluctuations in market conditions and substantial changes to the tax law have both been used to justify trust modifications.

B. SETTLOR'S INTENT

In most states, a settlor must expressly reserve the right to modify or terminate a trust to be granted such powers. In the absence of such a reservation, modification or termination can occur only with the consent of all beneficiaries and if the proposed change will not interfere with a primary purpose of the trust. Under the third Restatement, for a trust to be terminated, there must be a finding that the trust grantor intended the spendthrift provision to bar premature trust termination. *See* Restatement (Third) of Trusts § 65, cmt e (Tent. Draft No. 3).

Although it is possible for a court to modify or terminate a trust over the objections of the settlor, a modification or termination is much more likely to be granted if the settlor joins in the action, because the *Claflin* material-purpose test is satisfied under such circumstances.

C. TRUSTEE'S POWER TO TERMINATE

A trustee has no power to terminate a trust unless the trust instrument contains express termination provisions.

D. REMOVAL OF A TRUSTEE

Traditionally, if the settlor selected a particular trustee, the trustee cannot be removed, even if all the beneficiaries consent, unless the trustee is unfit to serve or has committed a serious breach of trust. While jurisdictions differ, generally, a trustee may be removed by the court under the following circumstances:

i) The trustee becomes incapable of performing his duties;

ii) The trustee materially breaches one or more of his duties;

iii) A conflict of interest arises;

iv) A serious conflict between the trustee and one or more beneficiaries, or between co-trustees, develops; or

v) The trust is persistently performing poorly as a result of the trustee's actions or inactions.

If any of the foregoing circumstances exist at the time the trustee is named and are known by the settlor, they will not necessarily suffice as grounds for removal.

Traditionally, a settlor did not have the right to petition for a trustee's removal. The modern trend, as reflected in UTC § 706, gives the settlor standing to petition for a trustee's removal.

XIX. POWERS OF APPOINTMENT

A power of appointment gives the person who holds the power the ability to distribute trust property. It allows the settlor to leave the responsibility to others in the future to deal with changing circumstances. Usually given to a beneficiary, a power of appointment enables the holder to direct a trustee to distribute some or all of the trust property without regard to the provisions of the trust.

The person who creates the power of appointment is the **donor** of the power. The person who holds the power is the **donee**. The donee of a power of appointment can direct the appointment of an interest of equal or lesser value to that specified in the power given to her. Thus, if a donee can appoint trust assets outright, she can also give, for example, a life estate to a permissible beneficiary. The persons for whom the power may be exercised are the **objects** of the power. When a power is exercised in favor of a person, that person becomes an **appointee**. If the donee fails to exercise the power, the persons who will receive the property are called **takers in default**. The property that is subject to the power is called the **appointive property**.

The power of appointment is personal to the donee, meaning the donee cannot transfer the power to anyone else. The power may be (i) testamentary (i.e., exercisable only by the donee's will) or (ii) presently exercisable (i.e., the donee may exercise the power during his lifetime).

If the power to appoint property in trust is created, it is usually given to one of the beneficiaries of the trust.

A. TYPES

There are two general categories of powers of appointment: **general** powers of appointment and **special** powers of appointment.

1. General Power of Appointment

A power of appointment in which there are no restrictions or conditions on the donee's exercise of the power is a general power of appointment. Thus, the donee may appoint himself, his estate, his creditors, or the creditors of his estate as a new owner. As such, if the donee exercises a general power, then the donee's creditors can reach the appointive property. The same holds true if the donee is also the donor of the power. Failure to exercise a general power of appointment causes the appointive property to revert back to the donor's estate. *See*, Unif. Probate Code § 2-608.

2. Special Power of Appointment

a. Exclusive

A special power of appointment is a more limited power than a general power of appointment in that it allows the donor to specify certain individuals or groups as the objects of the power, to the exclusion of others. This makes the power an exclusive special power of appointment. As such, the donor may decide to exclude the donee, the donee's creditors, the donee's estate, or the creditors of the donee's estate. In fact, a special power is presumed to be exclusive because it may favor some objects over others. In addition, the donor may make the donee's exercise of the power conditional on whatever factors, within legal bounds, the donor desires. Unlike with a general power, creditors are prevented from reaching the appointive property—even if the donee exercises the power—unless the transfer of property was intended to defraud the creditors.

b. Nonexclusive

A nonexclusive special power of appointment allows the donee to exercise the power to appoint among a class of individuals (e.g., grandchildren). It is nonexclusive because the donee cannot exclude a member of the class; he must appoint an equitable share to all appointees to prevent favoring one or two appointees over all others. When the donee fails to exercise the power, and when no gift in default of appointment is provided for in the will, the court will imply a gift to the objects of the special power and direct a distribution.

B. SCOPE OF AUTHORITY

1. Exercising Power

The donor's intent controls what is necessary to exercise a power of appointment. Any instrument, unless the donor directs otherwise, may be used to exercise a power of appointment. However, if the power is testamentary, then it may be exercised only by a will. Most jurisdictions hold that a residuary clause that does not make any reference to a power of appointment is insufficient to exercise any power of appointment held by the testator as donee. *See* Unif. Probate Code § 2-610. If there is a blanket power of appointment included within the residuary clause, then the courts will give effect to the power. A phrase such as, "including any power of which I may have a power of appointment" would constitute a blanket power of appointment.

A blanket exercise clause is effective to exercise powers unless the donor of the power of appointment specifically requires the donee to refer to the instrument creating the power when exercising the power. Most states allow a donee to exercise his power of appointment to create a trust for the benefit of the object of the power rather than transferring the property outright.

2. Contracting the Power

When a donee is given a testamentary power of appointment, a contract to make an appointment is invalid because it would defeat the donor's purpose of having the donee exercise the power of appointment at the donor's death. On the other hand, if a donee is given a presently exercisable power of appointment, then a contract to appoint would be valid.

3. Releasing a Power of Appointment

Although a contract to exercise a testamentary power is not enforceable, a similar result can sometimes be obtained by releasing the power of appointment.

4. Limitations on Exercise of Power

In almost all jurisdictions, the donee of a general power of appointment can appoint the property, as she desires, outright, in trust, or subject to a new power of appointment. The donee of a special power, however, has not traditionally been permitted to appoint in further trust and must appoint the property outright, absent express authority in the instrument creating the special power. The modern trend, however, allows the donee of a special power of appointment to appoint either in trust or subject to a new power of appointment so long as the donee and the objects of the new power are included in the original class of objects.

5. **Exclusive versus Non-exclusive Power**

If a special power is exclusive, the donee may appoint all the property to one or more members of the class of permissible appointees, excluding other objects. If the power is non-exclusive, the donee must appoint some amount to each object. It is unclear exactly how much, however. In some states, the amount appointed must be a reasonable amount. Whether a power is exclusive or non-exclusive is determined from the intent of the donor, as set forth in the governing instrument. The words "to any one or more" or "to such of" are usually held to mean an exclusive power. The words "to all and every one" or "to each and every one," are usually held to mean a non-exclusive power.

> **Example:** T leaves a fund to X in trust for Y for life, remainder as Y shall appoint by will to "each and every one" of Y's children. Y has three children, M, N, and O. The power is non-exclusive and therefore Y must give some amount to M, N, and O, if Y exercises the power. If the power had been exclusive, Y could appoint all of the property to one of his children.

6. **Fraud on a Special Power**

An appointment that is in favor of a person who is not an object of the power is invalid. Similarly, an appointment to an object to circumvent a limitation on a power is considered a "fraud on the power" and is void.

7. **Ineffective Exercise of a Power of Appointment**

If the donee intends to exercise a power of appointment, but the exercise is ineffective for some reason, it may be possible to carry out the donee's intent through the doctrines of allocation or capture.

a. **Allocation**

Allocation, sometimes called marshalling, can apply when appointive property and other property owned by the donee are inappropriately mixed in a common dispositive instrument (e.g., the donee's will). The blended property is allocated to the various interests in such a way as to increase the effectiveness of the disposition.

> **Example:** A holds a special testamentary power created by her father to appoint trust property among A's descendants. The trust property is worth $100,000 and A's own separate property is worth $350,000. A's will provides that she "gives all my property, including any property over which I have a power of appointment under my father's will, as follows: $100,000 to B, my daughter-in law; and all the rest to my daughter D. Since B is not an object of the special power, none of the trust property can be allocated to her. Under the doctrine of allocation, B would take $100,000 of A's own property and D would take the trust property, plus the $250,000 of A's property.

b. **Capture**

If the donee of a general power of appointment expresses the intent to exercise the power and blends the exercise with the distributive provisions of his own will, if any of the appointment gift fails, the donee is held to have appointed the failed gift to himself and the failed appointive property is distributed as part of the donee's general assets.

8. **Failure to Exercise a Power of Appointment**

Traditionally, if the donee fails to exercise a general power of appointment, the appointive property passes to the takers in default. If there is no such provision in the instrument creating the power, the property reverts to the donor or the donor's estate. If the donee of a special power of appointment fails to exercise it and there are no express takers in default under the instrument creating the power, if the class of objects is defined and limited, the court may imply that the donor intended that the appointive property be distributed equally among the members of the appointive class. *See Loring v. Marshall*, 484 N.E.2d 1315 (Mass. 1985). Otherwise the property reverts to the donor or the donor's estate.

XX. TRUST ADMINISTRATION AND THE TRUSTEE'S DUTIES

Before any duties are imposed, the trustee must accept the trusteeship. The trustee is then charged with safeguarding the trust property by purchasing insurance, earmarking assets, recording deeds, identifying and locating beneficiaries, and following the settlor's instructions. The trustee acts as a fiduciary, and, in most cases, his powers are not personal but rather attach to his office.

If there are two trustees, the majority of states require them to act with unanimity absent a contrary intent expressed in the trust agreement. However, if there are more than two trustees, most states require a majority only.

As a general proposition, a trustee's duties cannot be unilaterally enlarged by the settlor after the trustee has accepted his office. A well-drafted trust instrument will therefore include an **additions clause** if the settlor contemplates enlarging the trustee's responsibilities with additional trust assets. Even then, a trustee may be able to reject additions.

A. POWERS

1. **Within a Trust Document**

Common law grants no powers to the trustee outside of those authorized within the trust document itself.

a. **Judicial authorization**

The trustee can petition the court to obtain powers not expressly authorized in the trust.

b. **Modern trend**

The modern trend is for the court to grant the trustee all those powers necessary to act as a reasonably prudent person in managing the trust. There have been two different approaches. Some jurisdictions adopt a statute that sets forth a detailed list of powers it is presumed a trustee would need, allowing settlors to incorporate the statutory list by reference. Other jurisdictions grant the trustee a broad set of powers unless the settlor specifically provides that the trustee is not to have such powers.

2. **Power to Sell or Contract**

Unless otherwise provided in the trust instrument, a trustee generally has the implied power to contract, sell, lease, or transfer the trust property.

If the settlor specifies that the trustee may not sell certain property, then such property may not be sold without a valid court order permitting the sale, which order will be granted only if selling is necessary to save the trust.

3. Liability of Third Parties

A third party can potentially be held liable for his role in a breach of trust. Common law presumed that the purpose of a trust was to preserve the trust property, requiring those dealing with trustees to carefully inspect the trust property before dealing with the trustee. The modern trend presumes that the purpose of a trust is to hold and manage the trust property, and it provides greater protection to third parties.

a. Uniform Trustees' Powers Act (UTPA)

The UTPA obligates third parties to act in good faith and to give valuable consideration. Under the UTPA, third parties are protected as long as they act without actual knowledge that such action constitutes a breach of trust.

4. Other Common Trustee Powers

There are a variety of powers that the trust settlor may give to the trustee to carry out the trust's purpose.

a. Power to revoke

When the settlor names himself as trustee, the trust normally contains a power to revoke, which allows the settlor as trustee to revoke the trust in part or in its entirety.

b. Power to withdraw

Many trusts give the trustee the power to withdraw income, principal, or both from the trust to carry out the trust's purpose. The power to withdraw could also be conferred upon settlor, which would enable the settlor to withdraw assets from the trust without revoking it.

c. Power to modify

The settlor may include the power to modify to give the trustee the ability to change provisions of the trust to reflect the settlor's intent.

B. DUTY OF LOYALTY AND GOOD FAITH

A trustee is bound by a broad range of fiduciary duties designed to ensure that she acts solely in the best interests of the beneficiaries when investing property and otherwise managing the trust. The trustee has a duty to administer the trust in good faith, in accordance with its terms and purposes, and in the interest of the beneficiaries. Any beneficiary has standing against the trustee if his interests are violated, and he can choose either to set aside the transaction or to ratify the transaction and recover any profits therefrom.

Even if a trustee is granted complete discretion under the trust instrument, her actions are not immune from review if it can be shown that she failed to exercise judgment. When the trustee's decision is based exclusively on personal reasons unrelated to the settlor's goals, the trustee's decision may be overturned.

> **EXAM NOTE:** On an exam, determine whether the trustee acted reasonably (objective standard) *and* in good faith (subjective standard). Good faith alone is not enough.

1. Self-Dealing

When a trustee personally engages in a transaction involving the trust property, a conflict of interest arises between the trustee's duties to the beneficiaries and her own personal interest. A trustee breaches her duty of loyalty to the beneficiaries when she engages in self-dealing. *Hartman v. Hartle*, 95 N.J. Eq. 123 (1923). The following are generally prohibited transactions with trust property:

i) Buying or selling trust assets (even at fair market value);

ii) Selling property of one trust to another trust that the trustee manages;

iii) Borrowing from or making loans to the trust;

iv) Using trust assets to secure a personal loan;

v) Engaging in prohibited transactions with friends or relatives; or

vi) Otherwise acting for personal gain through the trustee position.

Example: Trustee sells stock from the trust to himself for fair market value. If the stock then goes up in value, the beneficiaries can trace and recover the stock for the benefit of the trust.

a. Irrebuttable presumption

When self-dealing is an issue, an irrebuttable presumption is created that the trustee breached the duty of loyalty.

Note: A trustee can employ herself as an attorney and can receive reasonable compensation, as long as the use of an attorney does not constitute a breach of trust.

b. No further inquiry

Once self-dealing is established, there need be no further inquiry into the trustee's reasonableness or good faith because self-dealing is a **per se breach of the duty of loyalty.**

c. Exceptions

Even when self-dealing is authorized by the settlor under the terms of the trust, by court order, or by all beneficiaries, the transaction must still be reasonable and fair for the trustee to avoid being liable for breach.

Courts tend to strictly interpret attempted exculpatory clauses relieving trustees from liability. Complete exculpatory clauses are void as contrary to public policy, and limited clauses are only honored if there is no finding of bad faith or unreasonableness.

1) Uniform Trusts Code (UTC)

Under the UTC, a trustee can avoid liability if he can prove that the transaction was objectively fair and reasonable, and not affected by a conflict of interest.

2) Statutory exceptions

Many states have enacted statutes permitting a bank trust department to deposit trust assets in its own banking department, and trustees are authorized to receive reasonable compensation for their services.

2. Conflicts of Interest

If an alleged conflict of interest arises that cannot be characterized as self-dealing, then the "no further inquiry" standard is inapplicable, and the transaction is assessed under the "reasonable and in good faith" standard. Thus, for example, in *In re Rothko*, 372 N.E.2d 291 (N.Y. 1977), a testator's will appointed three friends as executors of his estate, which was made up mostly of 800 valuable paintings. The executors entered into a contract with an art gallery to buy 100 of the paintings and sell the remainder on consignment. The testator's daughter brought an action, contending that the executors had violated their duty of loyalty by entering into a contract with a business in which they had an interest and selling the paintings for less than market value. The court, in analyzing the contract, found that one executor had a conflict of interest because he was a director and officer of the art gallery and the contract resulted in the executor getting paid more by the gallery and getting favorable treatment for his own art collection. The court also found that a second executor had a conflict of interest in that he was a struggling artist who was seeking to gain the gallery's favor so that it would buy and sell his own paintings. The court determined that the transaction was not fair and reasonable and did not meet the best interests of the beneficiaries.

The UTC provides that an investment in a corporation in which the trustee has an interest that might affect the trustee's best judgment is presumptively a breach of the duty of loyalty. The presumption of a breach can be rebutted by showing that the terms of the transaction were fair or that the transaction would have been made by an independent party. *See* Uniform Trust Code § 802(c).

Example: T is the trustee for trusts A, B, and C, and sells assets from trust A to trust B at fair market value. The assets increase in value after the sale. T had a conflict of interest as both the buyer and seller, but because T did not personally benefit, the presumption of self-dealing is not applicable. If T acted in good faith and did not reasonably anticipate a significant change in value, then T may not be liable for any lost profits by beneficiaries of trust A.

3. Legal Attacks on Trusts

Unless a challenge is well founded, the trustee must defend the trust against legal attacks.

4. Abuse of Discretion

Even if a trustee has complete discretion over a trust, she must still act in the best interests of the trust and its beneficiaries.

5. Co-trustees

Traditionally, if there is more than one trustee of a private trust, the trustees must act as a group and with unanimity, unless the trust instrument indicates otherwise. One of a group of trustees does not have the power to transfer or deal with the property alone. Since they must act jointly, a co-trustee is liable for the wrongful acts of a co-trustee to which she has consented or which by her negligence she enabled the co-trustee to do.

In many states and under UTC § 703(a), however, a majority of the trustees can act if there are three or more trustees. Even in the absence of unanimity, though, a co-trustee is still required to take reasonable steps to prevent a breach of trust by the other trustees, and must bring suit, if necessary to stop any improper action. Note that for a charitable trust, no unanimity is required. A majority can act for the charitable trust.

C. DUTY OF PRUDENCE

As a fiduciary, a trustee is required to invest the assets of a trust as a prudent person would in the management of his own affairs. *In re Estate of Janes*, 90 N.Y.2d 41 (N.Y. 1997). At common law, a trustee could not delegate any discretionary responsibilities because doing so would be assumed to be contrary to the settlor's intent. Under modern law, the trustee may delegate responsibilities if it would be unreasonable for the settlor to require the trustee to perform such tasks.

> **Note:** If a function goes to the heart of the trust or constitutes a critical function concerning the property, then the function is discretionary and is not delegable. Otherwise, the function is merely ministerial and can be delegated. These same rules apply when a trustee delegates to a co-trustee.

1. Duty to Oversee Decisions

A trustee can delegate the determination of management and investment strategies, and other duties as would be prudent under the circumstances, but must oversee the decision–making process. Otherwise, the trustee is responsible for actual losses, regardless of cause.

2. Trust Investments

At common law, trustees were limited to statutory lists of acceptable investments unless the trust instrument expressly authorized a deviation from the list. Only a few states continue to adhere to such lists.

a. Statutory legal lists

Statutory lists can be either permissive, which means the trustee may invest in securities that are not on the list, or mandatory, in which case the trustee must invest only in securities that are included on the list. In either case, the trustee must use reasonable care, caution, and skill. Additionally, the trustee must be expressly authorized to carry on the testator's business. Generally, unsecured loans and second mortgages are improper investments. Other investments such as stocks, bonds, government securities, and mutual funds are considered proper investments.

b. Model Prudent Man Investment Act (MPMIA)

The MPMIA, first adopted in 1940, is still followed in some states and permits any investment that a prudent man would make, barring only speculative investments.

c. Uniform Prudent Investor Act (UPIA)

The UPIA, adopted by the Restatement (Third) of Trusts and the Trustee Act of 2000, requires the trustee to act as a prudent investor would when investing his own property but puts less emphasis on the level of risk for each investment. The trustee must exercise reasonable care, caution, and skill when investing and managing trust assets unless the trustee has special skills or expertise, in which case he has a duty to utilize such assets.

Determinations of compliance under the UPIA are made with reference to the facts and circumstances as they existed at the time the action was made, and they do not utilize hindsight. In assessing whether a trustee has breached this duty, the UPIA requires consideration of numerous factors, including (i) the distribution requirements of the trust, (ii) general economic conditions, (iii) the role that the investment plays in relationship to the trust's overall investment portfolio, and (iv) the trust's need for liquidity, regularity of income, and preservation or appreciation of capital. Unif. Prudent Inv. Act § 2.

1) Duty to diversify assets

The trustee must adequately diversify the trust investments to spread the risk of loss. *See Wood v. U.S. Bank, N.A.*, 828 N.E. 2d 1072 (Ohio 2005) (holding that even if trust instrument allows trustee to retain assets that would not normally be suitable investments, the trustee still has a duty to diversify, unless there are special circumstances or trust instrument specifically states otherwise). Under the UPIA, investing in one mutual fund may be sufficient if the fund is sufficiently diversified.

a) Individual versus corporate trustees

A presumed greater expertise creates a higher standard for professional or corporate trustees than for individual trustees.

b) Duty not absolute

A trustee is justified in not diversifying if the administrative costs of doing so (including tax consequences or changes in controlling interest of a family-run business) would outweigh the benefits.

With respect to a revocable trust, a trustee's duties are owed exclusively to the settlor. When a trust is irrevocable, acting in accordance with a settlor's directives is inadequate to absolve a trustee from liability because the trustee's obligations are owed to trust beneficiaries. However, when there are no income beneficiaries other than the settlor, the settlor may be treated as the effective owner. *See* Uniform Prudent Investor Act § 3.

2) Duty to make property productive

The trustee must preserve trust property and work to make it productive, by pursuing all possible claims, deriving the maximum amount of income from investments, selling assets when appropriate, securing insurance, paying ordinary and necessary expenses, and acting within a reasonable period of time in all matters.

3) Commingling trust funds

The common-law approach required each trust fund to be separated from other trust funds and from the trustee's own funds. To decrease costs and increase diversity, the modern trend is to allow some commingling of trust funds and investment in mutual funds.

However, if a trustee commingles trust assets with his own property and some property is lost or destroyed, there is a presumption that the lost or destroyed property was the trustee's and that the remaining property belongs to the trust.

Additionally, if one part of the commingled assets increases in value and another part decreases in value, there is a presumption that the assets with increased value belong to the trust and that the assets with decreased value belong to the trustee.

4) Decision making

Part of being prudent is taking care to make informed decisions regarding the investment scheme and/or delegating such decision making to an expert.

d. Modern trend—portfolio approach

The UPIA assesses a trustee's investments based on the total performance of the trust, as opposed to looking at individual investments, so that a high-risk investment that would have been considered too risky under the common law can be offset by lower-risk investments.

The law has evolved away from the common-law statutory lists and toward the prudent investor standard and the modern trend portfolio theory. Diversification has become increasingly important, as has the trustee's duty to create a paper trail supporting the reasonableness of his actions. It is recognized that in today's market, there is a strong correlation between risk and reward, and it is undesirable for trustees to be limited to low-risk investments in the current climate. However, risk tolerance varies greatly depending upon the size and the purpose of the particular trust, both of which will be taken into account in evaluating the actions of the trustee.

e. Authorized investments

Exculpatory clauses that expressly authorize all investments do not protect a trustee who acts in bad faith or recklessly, but they do give trustees more room for minor lapses in judgment.

3. Duty to Be Impartial

A trustee has a duty to balance the often-conflicting interests of the present and future beneficiaries by investing the property so that it produces a reasonable income while preserving the principal for the remaindermen.

a. Duty to sell

Regardless of what the trust document says about the trustee's ability to retain trust assets, a trustee has a duty to sell trust property within a reasonable time if a failure to diversify would be inconsistent with the modern portfolio approach.

Any delay in disposing of under-performing or over-performing property creates a duty in the trustee to reallocate sale proceeds to those beneficiaries who were adversely affected by the delay.

> **EXAM NOTE:** If a fact pattern on an exam indicates that either (i) the trust principal is appreciating but not generating a reasonable stream of income, or (ii) the trust is producing a good amount of income but the principal is depreciating, then your analysis should center on the duty of impartiality. In these situations, the trustee may be favoring one class of beneficiaries over the other.

b. Allocating principal and income

Generally, life beneficiaries are entitled to the trust income, and remaindermen are entitled to the trust principal. The beneficiary of trust principal is not entitled to trust principal until termination of all preceding estates. The remainder beneficiary has no immediate right to the possession and enjoyment of any trust property. The remainder beneficiary must await the termination of the trust to receive any trust property. All assets received by a trustee must be allocated to either income or principal. The allocation must be balanced so as to treat present and future trust beneficiaries fairly, unless a different treatment is authorized by the trust instrument.

1) Traditional approach

The traditional approach assumed that any money generated by trust property was income, and that any money generated in connection with a conveyance of trust property was principal. The traditional approach serves as the starting point for the modern approach.

2) Modern approach

The Uniform Principal and Income Act (UPAIA), adopted in most states, focuses on total return to the trust portfolio, regardless of classifications of income or principal. Under the UPAIA, a trustee is empowered to re-characterize items and reallocate investment returns as he deems necessary to fulfill the trust purposes, as long as his allocations are reasonable and are in keeping with the trust instrument.

The trustee may not make adjustments under the UPAIA if he is also a trust beneficiary.

a) Factors to consider

The trustee must balance the following factors in determining how best to exercise such allocation:

i) The intent of the settlor and the language of the trust instrument;

ii) The nature, likely duration, and purpose of the trust;

iii) The identities and circumstances of the beneficiaries;

iv) The relative needs for regularity of income, preservation and appreciation of capital, and liquidity;

v) The net amount allocated to income under other sections of the Act and the increase and decrease in the value of principal assets;

vi) The anticipated effect of economic conditions on income and principal; and

vii) The anticipated tax consequences of the adjustment.

b) Unitrust

Under a unitrust, the distinction between income and principal is not relevant because the lifetime beneficiaries are entitled to a fixed annual share of the value of the trust principal.

c) Unproductive property rule

Under the traditional approach, if a trust asset produced little or no income upon the asset's sale, then an income beneficiary was entitled to some portion of the sale proceeds under the theory that such portion represented delayed income thereon. With the emphasis having shifted to the total return from the entire portfolio and away from individual investments, this rule is now seldom applied.

d) Distributions of stock

Under UPAIA § 6(a), a distribution of stock, whether classified as a dividend or as a split, is treated as a distribution of principal. This is also true under the Revised Uniform Principal and Income Act (RUPIA). The RUPIA gives a trustee a limited power to allocate the stock dividend between income and the principal when the distributing corporation made no distributions to shareholders except in the form of dividends paid in stock.

c. Allocation of receipts

Generally, except in cases in which the application of the UPAIA is justified, allocation rules follow traditional accounting rules.

1) Receipts from an entity

Cash money received from an entity is characterized as income unless the money is a capital gain for federal income tax purposes or is received following a partial or complete liquidation of the entity. All property other than cash money received from an entity (i.e., stock dividends) is characterized as principal.

2) Contract proceeds

Proceeds from life insurance policies or other contracts in which the trust or trustee is named as a beneficiary are allocated to principal unless the contract insures the trustee against loss, in which case the proceeds are allocated to income.

3) Deferred compensation plan proceeds

Receipts from a deferred compensation plan (e.g., a pension plan) are considered income if characterized as such by the payor and likewise are principal if so characterized. If the payor does not characterize the payment as income or principal, then 10% of the payment is income and the rest is principal.

4) Liquidating assets

A liquidating asset is one whose value diminishes over time because the asset is only expected to produce receipts over a limited period (e.g., patents or copyrights). Proceeds from liquidating assets are also allocated as 10% income and 90% principal.

5) Mineral rights

Oil, gas, mineral, and water rights payments are also allocated as 10% income and 90% principal.

d. Allocation of expenses

1) Expenses charged to income

Trust income will be charged with the following expenses:

    i) One-half of the regular compensation to the trustee and to those who provide investment, advisory, or custodial services to the trustee;

    ii) One-half of accounting costs, court costs, and the costs of other matters affecting trust interests;

    iii) Ordinary expenses in their entirety; and

    iv) Insurance premiums that cover the loss of a trust asset.

2) Expenses charged to principal

Trust principal will be charged with the following expenses:

    i) The remaining one-half of the regular compensation to the trustee and to those who provide services to the trustee;

    ii) The remaining one-half of accounting costs, court costs, and the costs of other matters affecting trust interests;

    iii) All payments on the principal of any trust debt;

    iv) All expenses of any proceeding that concerns an interest in principal;

v) Estate taxes; and

vi) All payments related to environmental matters.

D. INFORM AND ACCOUNT

1. Duty to Disclose

A trustee must disclose to the beneficiaries complete and accurate information about the nature and extent of the trust property, including allowing access to trust records and accounts. *See e.g., Fletcher v. Fletcher*, 480 S.E.2d 488 (Va. 1997). The trustee must also identify possible breaches of trust and promptly disclose such information to the beneficiaries.

a. Settlor's intent

The UTC requires the trustee to promptly provide a copy of the trust instrument upon request, unless otherwise provided by the settlor in the instrument.

b. Duty to notify

Unless disclosure would be severely detrimental to the beneficiaries, the trustee must notify the beneficiaries if he intends to sell a significant portion of the trust assets.

2. Duty to Account

A trustee must periodically account for actions taken on behalf of the trust so that his performance can be assessed against the terms of the trust. Trustees of testamentary trusts must account to the probate court. The UTC allows the settlor to waive the trustee's duty to report to the beneficiaries, or the beneficiaries can waive the receipt of reports.

Note: Waiver of the duty to report does not relieve a trustee from liability for misconduct that would have been disclosed by a report.

a. Constructive fraud

If an accounting includes **false factual statements** that could have been discovered to be false had the trustee properly investigated, then constructive fraud results.

E. OTHER DUTIES

1. Duty to Secure Possession

The trustee must secure possession of the property within a reasonable period of time. In the case of a testamentary trust, the trustee must monitor the executor's actions to ensure that the trust receives all of that to which it is entitled.

2. Duty to Maintain

In caring for real property, the trustee must take whatever steps an ordinary owner would take, including insuring, repairing, and otherwise maintaining the property.

3. Duty to Segregate

The trustee must separate his personal property (such as money and stocks) from trust assets to ensure that they cannot be switched if one outperforms the other. An exception to this duty to segregate applies when a trustee invests in bearer bonds.

Under common law, the trustee was strictly liable for damages to the trust property even if they were not caused by a breach of the duty to segregate. The modern trend holds the trustee liable only when the breach causes the damage to the trust property.

F. TRUSTEE'S LIABILITIES

1. Beneficiaries' Right of Enforcement

Lost profits, lost interests, and other losses resulting from a breach of trust are the responsibility of the trustee, and beneficiaries may sue the trustee and seek damages or removal of the trustee for breach. The trustee is also not allowed to offset losses resulting from the breach against any gains from another breach. However, if the beneficiaries joined the breach or consented to the trustee's actions, equity will prevent the beneficiaries from pursuing an action against the trustee. Note though that a beneficiary's failure to object to the breach does not rise to the level of consent.

2. Liabilities for Others' Acts

a. Co-trustee liability

Co-trustees are jointly liable, although the liability may be limited if only one trustee acts in bad faith or benefited personally from the breach.

A co-trustee may be liable for breach for:

i) Consenting to the action constituting the breach;

ii) Negligently failing to act to prevent the breach;

iii) Concealing the breach or failing to compel redress; or

iv) Improperly delegating authority to a co-trustee.

b. Liability for predecessor and successor trustees

If a trustee knew of his predecessor's breach and failed to address it or was negligent in delivering the property, then the trustee will be liable for his predecessor's breach. Successor trustees can maintain the same actions as the original trustees.

c. Trustee's liability for agents

A trustee is not liable for breaches committed by an agent unless the trustee:

i) Directs, permits, or acquiesces in the agent's act;

ii) Conceals the agent's act;

iii) Negligently fails to compel the agent to redress the wrong;

iv) Fails to exercise reasonable supervision over the agent;

v) Permits the agent to perform duties that the trustee was not entitled to delegate; or

vi) Fails to use reasonable care in the selection or retention of agents.

No clear-cut standard for the delegation of duties to agents exists, but it is clear that a trustee cannot delegate his duties in their entirety, but rather should limit the delegation to ministerial duties.

3. Third Parties

a. Trustee's liability to third parties

Unless otherwise specified in the trust instrument or in the governing contract, a trustee is personally liable on contracts entered into and for tortious acts committed while acting as trustee. If he acted within the scope of his duties, then he is entitled to indemnification from the trust.

b. Liability of third parties to a trust

When property is improperly transferred as a result of a breach of trust to a third party who is not a bona fide purchaser—one who takes for value and without notice of impropriety—the beneficiary or successor trustee may have that transaction set aside. If, on the other hand, the third party is a knowing participant in the breach, then he is liable as well for any losses suffered by the trust.

Because only the trustee is allowed to bring a cause of action against the third party, the beneficiary is limited to bringing a suit in equity against the trustee to compel the trustee to sue the third party. In a situation in which (i) the trustee is a participant in the breach, (ii) the third party is liable in tort or contract and the trustee fails to pursue a cause of action, or (iii) there is no successor trustee, then the beneficiary is given the option of directly suing the third party.

XXI. CHARITABLE TRUSTS

For a trust to be considered charitable, it must have a stated charitable purpose and it must exist for the benefit of the community at large or for a class of persons the membership in which varies. For public-policy reasons, charitable trusts are usually construed quite liberally by the courts.

Neither the settlor nor a potential beneficiary has standing to challenge a charitable trust. Only the state attorney general possesses such a right.

> **EXAM NOTE:** If a trust fails as a charitable trust, it still may be valid as a private express trust.

A. CHARITABLE PURPOSE

Purposes generally considered to be charitable include:

i) The relief of poverty;

ii) The advancement of education or religion;

iii) The promotion of good health;

iv) Governmental or municipal purposes; and

v) Other purposes benefiting the community at large or a particular segment of the community.

While a certain political party is not deemed to be a charitable beneficiary, those seeking to advance a political movement may be charitable beneficiaries. A determination as to whether or not a beneficiary is charitable involves an inquiry into the predominant purpose of the organization and the determination of whether or not the organization is aimed at making a profit.

The rules applying to charitable trusts are not applicable to those with both charitable and non-charitable purposes, unless two separate and distinct trust shares are capable of being administered, in which case the rules are applicable to the charitable share.

A charitable purpose can be found even if the settlor created the trust out of non-charitable motives.

1. Benevolent Trusts

A merely benevolent trust is not a charitable trust unless the acts called for therein fall under the acceptable charitable purposes listed above. Most courts no longer belabor the distinction between benevolent and charitable trusts.

2. Modern trend—validate as charitable

The modern trend is to characterize a trust as charitable if possible.

B. INDEFINITE BENEFICIARIES

The community at large, or a class comprising unidentifiable members, not a named individual or a narrow group of individuals, must be the beneficiary of a charitable trust. It is possible that a very small class could still qualify as a charitable beneficiary. Further, even though the direct beneficiary may be a private individual, a charitable trust may be found when the community at large is an **indirect** beneficiary of the trust; for example, when a trust is established to put a beneficiary through law school, but it stipulates that the beneficiary must spend a certain number of years of legal practice in the service of low-income clients.

C. RULE AGAINST PERPETUITIES

Charitable trusts are not subject to the Rule Against Perpetuities and may continue indefinitely. A trust can be created that calls for transfers of interest among charities, but it cannot direct the transfer of interest between a charitable beneficiary and a non-charitable beneficiary.

Example: A gift "to Sussex County Courts for as long as the premises is used as a courthouse, and if the premises shall ever cease to be so used, then to Sussex County United Way" is valid.

D. CY PRES DOCTRINE

In an effort to carry out the testator's intent, under the cy pres doctrine a court may modify a charitable trust to seek an alternative charitable purpose if the original charitable purpose becomes illegal, impracticable, or impossible to perform. *See e.g., In re Neher*, 279 N.Y. 370 (1939) (holding that when will gives real property for general charitable purpose, gift may be reformed by cy pres doctrine when compliance with particular purpose is impracticable). The court must determine the settlor's primary purpose and select a new purpose "as near as possible" to the original purpose.

Because the Rule Against Perpetuities is not applicable to charitable trusts, courts are called upon to apply cy pres often. The settlor's intent controls, so if it appears that the settlor would not have wished that an alternative charitable purpose be selected, the trust property may instead be subject to a resulting trust for the benefit of the settlor's estate.

> **EXAM NOTE:** If it is difficult to achieve the charitable trust purpose, apply the cy pres doctrine before applying a resulting trust.

1. Inefficiency Insufficient

Cy pres is not invoked merely upon the belief that the modified scheme would be a more desirable, more effective, or more efficient use of the trust property.

2. Uniform Trust Code (UTC) and Restatement (Third)

The UTC and the Restatement (Third) of Trusts both presume a general charitable purpose and authorize the application of cy pres even if the settlor's intent is not known.

E.   CONTRAST: HONORARY TRUSTS

An honorary trust is one that is not created for charitable purposes but has no private beneficiaries. The most common example is a trust for the care of a beloved pet. In the case of an honorary trust, the trustee is on her honor to administer the trust because there are no beneficiaries capable of enforcing its terms. Should the trustee fail to do so, a resulting trust may be imposed for the benefit of the settlor's estate.

A common problem that arises in the context of an honorary trust is the attempted application of the Rule Against Perpetuities. Such application is sometimes circumvented by using the trustee's life as the life in being, or by assuming that the trust will be exhausted before the perpetuities period has run.

F.   STANDING TO ENFORCE

The attorney general of the state of the trust's creation and members of the community who are more directly affected than the general community usually have standing to enforce the terms of the trust and the trustee's duties. Under UTC § 405, a settlor also has standing to enforce the trust, even if she has not expressly retained an interest. *See also Smithers v. St. Luke's-Roosevelt Hospital Center*, 723 N.Y.S.2d 426 (N.Y. App. Div. 2001) (holding that estate of donor of charitable gift had standing to sue to enforce terms of gift).